Cultural Change and Continuity

Essays in Honor of
James Bennett Griffin

STUDIES IN ARCHEOLOGY

Consulting Editor: Stuart Struever

Department of Anthropology
Northwestern University
Evanston, Illinois

Cultural Change and Continuity

Essays in Honor of James Bennett Griffin

Edited by
Charles E. Cleland

The Museum
Michigan State University
East Lansing, Michigan

ACADEMIC PRESS   New York San Francisco London

A Subsidiary of Harcourt Brace Jovanovich, Publishers

ACADEMIC PRESS, INC.
111 Fifth Avenue, New York, New York 10003

United Kingdom Edition published by
ACADEMIC PRESS, INC. (LONDON) LTD.
24/28 Oval Road, London NW1

Library of Congress Cataloging in Publication Data

Main entry under title:

Cultural change and continuity.

(Studies in archaeology)
Includes index.
CONTENTS: Quimby, G. I. and Cleland, C. E. James
Bennett Griffin, an appreciation.—Jones, V. H. Biography of James Bennett Griffin.—Considerations of variability in the archaeological record: Brose, D. S.
Locational analysis in the prehistory of northeast Ohio.
[etc.]
1. Indians—Antiquities—Addresses, essays, lectures.
2. America—Antiquities—Addresses, essays, lectures.
3. Griffin, James Bennett, Date I. Griffin,
James Bennett, Date II. Cleland, Charles
Edward.
E61.C93 970'.004'97 75–30465
ISBN 0–12–176050–2

To James Bennett Griffin
Professor of Anthropology
Chairman, Department of Anthropology
Director, Museum of Anthropology
University of Michigan

Contents

List of Contributors

Numbers in parentheses indicate the pages on which the authors' contributions begin.

Richard E. Blanton (223), Department of Anthropology, Hunter College, City University of New York, New York, New York

David S. Brose (3), Department of Anthropology, Case Western Reserve University, Cleveland, Ohio

Carl H. Chapman (121), Department of Anthropology, University of Missouri, Columbia, Missouri

Charles E. Cleland (xxi), The Museum, Michigan State University, East Lansing, Michigan

Kent V. Flannery (205), Museum of Anthropology, University of Michigan, Ann Arbor, Michigan

James E. Fitting (321), Commonwealth Associates, Inc., Jackson, Michigan

George C. Frison (147), Department of Anthropology, University of Wyoming, Laramie, Wyoming

Arthur J. Jelinek (19), Department of Anthropology, University of Arizona, Tucson, Arizona

Gregory A. Johnson (35), Hunter College, City University of New York, New York, New York

Volney H. Jones (xxxiv), Museum of Anthropology, University of Michigan, Ann Arbor, Michigan

Richard S. MacNeish (79), R. S. Peabody Foundation for Archaeology, Andover, Massachusetts

Joyce Marcus (205), Museum of Anthropology, University of Michigan, Ann Arbor, Michigan

Carol I. Mason (335), Department of Anthropology, University of Wisconsin—Fox Valley Center, Menasha, Wisconsin

Ronald J. Mason (349), Department of Anthropology, Lawrence University, Appleton, Wisconsin

Susanne J. Miller (293), Idaho State Museum, Pocatello, Idaho

W. W. Newcomb, Jr. (175), Texas Memorial Museum, University of Texas, Austin, Texas

Jeffrey R. Parsons (233), Museum of Anthropology, University of Michigan, Ann Arbor, Michigan

George I. Quimby (xxi), Burke Museum, University of Washington, Seattle, Washington

Martha Ann Rolingson (99), Arkansas Archeological Survey, University of Arkansas Museum, Fayetteville, Arkansas

Bruce D. Smith (275), Department of Anthropology, University of Georgia, Athens, Georgia

Albert C. Spaulding (59), Department of Anthropology, University of California, Santa Barbara, California

John D. Speth (35), Hunter College, City University of New York, New York, New York

Gary A. Wright (293), Department of Anthropology, State University of New York, Albany, New York

Richard A. Yarnell (265), Department of Anthropology, University of North Carolina, Chapel Hill, North Carolina

James B. Griffin visits the field headquarters of the Powers Phase Project, Naylor, Missouri, during the summer of 1975. Left to right: James J. Krakker, Nora Groce, Dennis Grega, James Griffin, Jerome Voss, Charles M. Hastings, Thomas K. Black, James E. Price, and Cynthia Bergstedt Price.

Preface

The word "retiring" is not one that people tend readily to associate with James Bennett Griffin! As a result, the approaching end of his long tenure as Director of the Museum of Anthropology, and the beginning of his new status as Professor Emeritus at the University of Michigan, came quite suddenly upon his friends, students, and colleagues. With the belated realization that Jimmy would be stepping down in July 1975, it was decided to honor him and his contribution to archaeology through two volumes of essays. This is the first; the other appears as "Papers for the Director: Essays in Honor of James Bennett Griffin" published in the *Anthropological Papers*, Museum of Anthropology, University of Michigan. These volumes will be sold in support of the James Bennett Griffin Fellowship Fund, which will be a permanent source of funding for worthy graduate students studying archaeology at the University of Michigan.

The organization of the volumes has been a problem from the start. Naturally, Academic Press would have preferred a collection of essays with a single areal or topical orientation. The committee decided, however, that as many individuals as possible should participate in the *festschrift* and that the best participation would be obtained by encouraging contributors to write on their own research interests rather than on assigned topics.

In June of 1974, an invitation to submit papers for the *festschrift* volumes was issued to over sixty of Jimmy's former students and a small number of colleagues with whom he shares research interests, with a very short deadline of 1 January 1975 for submission of papers. By this deadline, 35 papers were received—as well as many supporting letters from individuals who wanted to contribute papers but who could not do so on short notice because of other commitments. These letters and papers are an indication of the great enthusiasm with which this project was supported.

The contributed papers dealt with an almost unbelievable array of topics, from the classic civilizations of Mesoamerica to the Paleo-Indian hunters of the plains of Wyoming and from the habits of the bighorn sheep to glazes on Chinese ceramics. Although these volumes cannot be organized around an internally consistent theme, in a more abstract sense, Jimmy himself provides the organization. These are papers produced by scholars whom he encouraged to pursue their own interests and to carry these interests to all parts of the world. The breadth of these papers is a tribute to Jimmy's ability as a teacher and his willingness to help promote research opportunities for his students and colleagues.

The organization of this volume reflects not only Jimmy's own academic interests but his influence as a teacher and scholar. The first part, "Considerations of Variability in the Archaeological Record," presents chapters by Brose, Jelinek, Speth and Johnson, and Spaulding. In view of published statements that Griffin is not only antitheoretical but was also once "ironically" hailed as a master of statistical technique because he counted something, it would seem difficult to understand how Jimmy has influenced these authors. While it may be said that theory and methodology are not Jimmy's forte, I have never known him to oppose either. In fact, a large number of innovative methodological studies involving quantitative techniques have been done under his direction or with his support. Examples include his strong support for the development and refinement of the radiocarbon dating method, the spectrographic analysis of prehistoric copper, and, most recently, the use of neutron activation spectrometry for the analysis of obsidian, copper, and chert. Indeed, some of the leading exponents of the use of quantitative techniques, such as Spaulding, Speth and Johnson, Binford, and Whallon, have been either his students or his close colleagues at the University of Michigan.

Of the chapters presented in Part I, those by Spaulding and Speth and Johnson may be less interesting to Jimmy than to others who are more conversant with statistical procedure. I am sure he will read them and no doubt even appreciate the sophistication of these more elaborate means of "counting something"—for, as Spaulding notes, Griffin is a secret admirer of quantitative methods.

Part II, "Patterns of Culture History," offers a wide variety of papers. MacNeish revisits the Iroquois, Frison examines the Paleo-Indian occupation of the Big Horn Basin in Wyoming, Newcomb traces the development of Pecos River rock art, and both Rolingson and Chapman, perhaps with some temerity, present papers on the Mississippian—Jimmy's bailiwick. Without doubt, Jimmy's greatest contribution to American archaeology has been his insightful understanding of the change and continuity of prehistoric cultures. With his

great attention for scholarly detail and his incredible knowledge of the
published and unpublished data of the archaeology of the eastern
United States, James Griffin has become the master culture historian
of this area. One cannot help noticing his presence at scholarly
meetings, where he perches in the front row like a certain avian
raptor, pencil poised, eyebrows flickering, receiving the nervous
glances of the speaker. He prompts, amends, suggests, and challenges,
and, in so doing, provides the quality control for much of American
archaeology.

In the next part, "Patterns of Mesoamerican Urbanism," Flannery
and Marcus, Blanton, and Parsons discuss subjects geographically and
culturally distant from the region of his own professional specialization. It should be no secret, however, that Jimmy has had a long-stand-
ing fascination for Mesoamerican archaeology. Over the years, he has
been a frequent visitor to Mexico and, as a result, is conversant with
the archaeology of that area. As Director of the Museum, he has been
a strong supporter of the Mesoamerican and South American research
of his colleagues Kent Flannery and Jeff Parsons and has followed
with keen interest the work of his friends José Luis Lorenzo and
Scotty MacNeish in these same areas. Perhaps of more significance,
however, is the fact that a large number of Jimmy's former students,
including Parsons, Blanton, Webb, Hurt, and Wetherington, are
making major contributions to the Latin American archaeology.

Yarnell, Smith, and Wright and Miller present chapters in Part IV,
"Biotic Considerations in Prehistoric Adaptation." In these chapters,
we see a reflection of Jimmy's intense interest in the effects of the
natural and physical environment on the cultures of prehistoric man.
A good deal of his work in prehistoric adaptation took place during the
late 1950s and early 1960s. In part, this interest was a result of a series
of grand tours of the Great Lakes area with George Quimby in 1956
and 1957. Having visited Scandinavian prehistoric research facilities
in 1953–1954, he was impressed by the similarities between northern
Europe and the Upper Great Lakes region and the potential for
applying northern European ecological research techniques to this
area. As a result, he submitted a research proposal to the National
Science Foundation in 1960 to study the correlation of prehistoric
cultural complexes and Post-Pleistocene ecologies of the Upper Great
Lakes. Ultimately, many students were to earn Ph.D.s through this
grant, including those studying environmental problems directly as
well as those relying heavily on this type of data to reconstruct various
adaptative patterns of prehistoric peoples. In addition to these students, he stimulated research in paleoclimatology, geomorphology,
paleontology, paleobotany, and archaeozoology among his colleagues
in other departments of the university. H. R. Crane in physics through

his radiocarbon lab, Bill Benninghof in botany, Jack Hough and Bill Farrand in geology, Bill Burt in mammalogy, Henry Van der Schalie in malacology, and Claude Hibbard in paleontology at various times worked with Jimmy and his students on environmental problems. There can be little doubt that the results of this multidisciplinary research effort have had not only a substantial effect upon our understanding of the prehistory of the eastern United States but upon the nature and direction of subsequent research.

Part V, "Ethnohistory, Historic Archaeology, and Ethnicity," presents chapters by Fitting, Carol Mason, and Ron Mason. While Jimmy was never fond of historic archaeology, a number of his students have taken great interest in the archaeology of historic sites. He was, however, a pioneer in establishing the prehistoric ethnic identity of Indian groups through the combined use of ethnographic, linguistic, historic, and archaeological data. His studies of the relationship between the Oneota manifestation of Wisconsin and the Chiwere Sioux (Griffin 1937, 1960) and his attempts to examine the idea that Fort Ancient sites were occupied by the ancestors of the Shawnee (Griffin 1943) are examples. The papers presented here both extend and question the techniques of ethnohistory and will perhaps demonstrate for him the utility of historic site research.

Even given this ordering of the volume, the problem of finding a title remained. A request for suggestions from the contributors brought results but all sounded vaguely familiar—every combination of the words culture evolution–culture change–pattern–process–adaptation–theory and culture history. It seemed that all of the good overly inclusive titles had been used up in *festschrifts* for Radin, White, and Steward. Finally, Ted Guthe suggested a title from Jimmy's own classic work, "Cultural Change and Continuity in Eastern United States Archaeology" (Griffin 1946). Modified somewhat, this title seemed appropriate not only to describe the contents of this volume but also to identify Jimmy's major interests and contribution to archaeology.

Acknowledgments

In preparing this volume, credit is due to a large number of people who gave great portions of their time on short notice to bring this *festschrift* to fruition. First and foremost, very special thanks is due to Carol Burt (Dennie) Fitch, my editorial assistant at the Michigan State University Museum. It was she who did most of the real work on this volume, editing, copying, and mailing manuscripts, telephoning, and gently nagging me and contributors about numerous deadlines. It is quite accurate to say that this volume would not have been done on time nor done as well without her dedicated efforts. The review of manuscripts was the task of a committee composed of myself, Chuck Fairbanks, Marion White, and Ron Mason. Obviously, these people have been generous with their time, and their insightful comments have been helpful to both myself and the contributors. In addition to this review committee, a number of other individuals kindly consented to read and to comment on manuscripts. These include Bill Roosa, Bob Whallon, Martha Rolingson, Jeff Parsons, Rich Blanton, Jim Fitting, Dick Yarnell, Fred Matson, Bill Lovis, Dick Ford, Art Jelinek, Kent Flannery, Henry Wright, Dave Dwyer, Lee Minnerly, Chris Peebles, and Mike Webb.

I would like personally to thank George Quimby for joining with me in writing the appreciation. George's wit and memory for detail made working with him a real pleasure.

Special thanks is due to Volney Jones who came out of retirement to write Jimmy's biography. Unraveling a career as rich and varied as his was no small task; with the help of George W. Stueber, who purloined various photos and manuscripts from Jimmy's files, Volney was able to do a masterful job.

Finally, and as a personal note, I would like to observe that there is some poetic justice in the fact that the worst speller who ever wrote a dissertation under Jimmy's tutelage (his observation) also had the pleasure of editing his *festschrift.*

James Bennett Griffin: Appreciation and Reminiscences

George I. Quimby and Charles E. Cleland

The forty years between 1935 and the present were those in which American archaeology developed from antiquarianism into a scientific discipline. These are also the years during which James Griffin has been a major force in American archaeology. As a consequence, his academic history reflects and, to a great extent, parallels the development of American archaeology.

There have been two significant eras in this history. The first features the initial development of American archaeology with the appearance of a cadre of professional personnel, the development of systematic field techniques, and the expansion of the prehistoric data base. This era largely resulted from the massive influence of public-works archaeology during the 1930s. The great emphasis placed on scientific method and theory during, and subsequent to, the early 1960s characterizes the second era. The Midwest was the scene of the later development, since it was there that the great mass of public-works data, having been ordered by the development of radiocarbon dating during the 1950s, provided the opportunity for relatively broader and more sophisticated problem orientation. The Midwest also produced the post-World War II cultural evolutionary theorists who so strongly contributed to the philosophical underpinnings for the theories of this era. Only the addition of statistical rigor was needed to produce a new orientation to the investigation of the old problems, now called "new archaeology." Jimmy's influence during the first era is strong and unmistakable. He, probably more than any other individual, laid the groundwork for the changes of the 1960s and

1970s. If he didn't participate in the nurture of the new archaeology, its birth certainly took place on his doorstep.

As students at the University of Michigan, George Quimby was a witness to the events of the former era, while Chuck Cleland was in residence during phases of the latter. In writing these remembrances, we take a personal tone, giving our impressions of these periods and our evaluation of Jimmy's role in the developing discipline of archaeology.

I (George I. Quimby) first met James Bennett Griffin in the autumn of 1934 although I do not remember the details of our meeting. At that time, I was a student with newly acquired junior standing in the College of Literature, Science, and the Arts at the University of Michigan. I had just been accepted as a major in the Department of Anthropology and, unknowingly, was about to begin a lifetime association with anthropology, museums, and James B. Griffin.

Back in those halcyon days, the Anthropology Department, then situated in the Museum of Anthropology, consisted of two professors, about a dozen undergraduate majors, both juniors and seniors, and several graduate students, one of whom was James B. Griffin. Of the professors, Leslie A. White was chairman of the department and Carl E. Guthe was director of the museum. Class size ranged from about four or five students to thirty or slightly more. The small classes were taught in the Museum and the large classes in Angell Hall. With so few students and professors in the department and with most of the activities centered in the Museum, it was no wonder that students received a great amount of individual attention and that there was considerably scholarly and social interaction among students, faculty, and museum staff. Living and studying at that time in such a milieu was how I became a participant observer of the development of American archaeology from 1934 and of the place of James B. Griffin in that development.

The time was the middle of what now has come to be known as the Great Depression. In this period, at least 24% of the nation's labor force was unemployed, more than five thousand banks failed, and nine million savings accounts vanished. It was also a period of violence. There were gang wars over liquor distribution and other interesting matters, and wars between unions and industries; and, in the South, lynchings occurred at the rate of one every three weeks. In short, it was not the best of times, but, archaeologically speaking, neither was it the worst of times.

Out of the Depression was born the federal financing of public works projects to provide employment for thousands of unemployed men and women. And, of these public works, archaeological projects were ideal because they provided employment without in any way competing with existing industry or business. Great sums of money were spent on public archaeology. For instance, more than $1,500,000 was spent annually on archaeological projects in the southeastern United States alone.

Prior to 1934, there had been significant, but comparatively modest, growth in the archaeology of the eastern United States, which had been supported by programs in some of the museums and universities of the region. The Department of Anthropology at the University of Chicago, with Fay-Cooper Cole as chairman, had emerged as a leading center for graduate training in archaeology within the context of anthropology. And the basic anthropological training of James B. Griffin (hereinafter referred to as Jimmy) took place at the University of Chicago. Jimmy had received his degree of Master of Arts in anthropology in 1930 and had continued studies toward the doctorate there until the end of 1932. At the University of Chicago, Jimmy studied not only under Fay-Cooper Cole but also under such luminaries as Robert Redfield, Edward Sapir, Leslie Spier, and A. R. Radcliffe-Brown.

Meanwhile, at the University of Michigan, Carl E. Guthe had established the Ceramic Repository of the Museum of Anthropology in 1927. In the same year, Dr. Guthe became Chairman of the Committee on State Archaeological Surveys, Division of Anthropology and Psychology, National Research Council.

In January of 1933, James B. Griffin left the University of Chicago and became "Fellow in Aboriginal Ceramics in the Museum of Anthropology at the University of Michigan under the Auspices of the Committee on State Archaeological Surveys of the Division of Anthropology and Psychology of the National Research Council." He continued his graduate studies at Michigan and received his Ph.D. in 1936, the same year in which I received my B.A. But the period from 1934 to 1936 was the beginning of my association with Jimmy. We were in several classes together, I as a novice and he probably as an auditor since he had already received advanced graduate training at Chicago. I recall especially two courses, "The Mind of Primitive Man" and "The Evolution of Culture," taught by Leslie A. White. For me, the material and methods were all new and most interesting, but Jimmy, steeped in Cole, Sapir, Redfield, and Radcliffe-Brown frequently signaled his disbelief and/or disapproval in emphatic body language.

At about this time, I began working in the Museum. As part of my course work in museum methods from Dr. Guthe, I worked on small ethnographic collections of Northwest Coast, Eskimo, and Aleut materials housed in the Ethnobotanical Laboratory under the watchful eye of Curator Volney H. Jones. I also was cleaning the Museum's collection of trade silver ornaments using a dilute solution of formic acid. This was a somewhat dangerous procedure inasmuch as I was then addicted to chocolate-covered mints which I ate with one hand while dipping silver with the other. Moreover, the laboratory table at which I worked was beneath a window that faced across the street to the dormitory window of the residence of the student nurses who frequently neglected to pull down the window shades while changing their attire. In spite of the distractions, I never did dip the chocolate mints in the formic acid.

The next semester, as part of some special courses from Dr. Guthe, I worked in the Ceramic Repository under Jimmy. My introduction to ceramics consisted principally of washing potsherds in a laboratory sink beneath a large window that faced another window directly across the street in the women's ward of the university health service. Notwithstanding the distractions, I must have washed several tons of potsherds and reached the point where I could recognize Hopewellian sherds merely by feeling them. For all practical purposes, Jimmy became my teacher of archaeology, and most of the archaeology I learned at Michigan, I learned from him. It was he who suggested that I prepare for publication a paper on silver ornaments used in the fur trade; and, under his influence, I began a study of Hopewellian culture in Michigan and Indiana which eventually became the major part of my master's thesis.

In 1935, W. C. McKern, Carl E. Guthe, and Fay-Cooper Cole were the most important figures in North American archaeology. This is not to say that there were not any others, but the three of them interacting as they did exercised a tremendous influence. Guthe was the organizer *par excellence*, Fay-Cooper Cole was the great teacher, and McKern was father of Midwestern Taxonomic Method, which was expected to bring order out of chaos. And Jimmy, in the Ceramic Repository, was right in the middle of this sphere of interactions involving Cole, Guthe, and McKern.

The newly formed "Society for American Archaeology" became active in 1935 publishing its journal *American Antiquity*. Dr. Guthe was secretary–treasurer of the new society and W. C. McKern was the editor of its journal. At Michigan and other colleges and universities, students who were interested in archaeology were encouraged to join the Society for American Archaeology and to participate in the annual meetings of both the S.A.A. and the Central States Branch of the American Anthropological Association.

The meetings in those days were small. There were no parallel sessions, and everyone in attendance went to all of the sessions and heard every presentation on the program. This was not difficult to do. For instance, at the 1936 annual meeting, sixteen persons presented papers. In 1938, there were twenty-three papers delivered during the two days of the meeting. The total number of professional archaeologists and students, especially graduate students, was so small that it was possible for one person to be acquainted with all the others.

In spring and autumn, Jimmy also organized "study trips" in which he and graduate students visited famous sites and collections in various places. I remember a small brigade of cars from Ann Arbor visiting Hopewell sites in Ohio and Fort Ancient sites in Ohio and Indiana. On such trips, besides myself, there might be graduate students, James Ford, Albert Spaulding, Fred Matson, and museum personnel, such as Volney Jones and Georg Neumann. These trips were really intensive seminars with constant discussion and argument while traveling, eating, visiting sites and collections, and, of course, long bull sessions in the evening.

Under the guidance of Jimmy, the Ceramic Repository (and he as well) became a national center for the storage and retrieval of archaeological information, and Jimmy became a walking computer, analyzer, and advisor on the data and synthesis of North American archaeology. By 1938, large numbers of professionals, amateurs, and students funneled their data into the Ceramic Repository. Jimmy would discuss, argue, interpret, and question archaeological data with everyone. He has always acknowledged the help of graduate students and amateurs both orally and in print.

With the founding of the Southeastern Archaeological Conference at the Ceramic Repository in the spring of 1938, there came into being an organization of archaeologists primarily involved in the various federally supported projects which were operating on a vast scale. And from that time onward, Jimmy and the Ceramic Repository, already a kind of central nervous system for the archaeology east of the Rocky Mountains, became even more so.

The decade 1932–1941 inclusive was possibly the most eventful in the history of North American archaeology. The magnitude of the field work probably will never be matched again. More archaeological excavation was undertaken in those ten years than had been done since the beginning of the United States. And thousands of unemployed people were put to work on site excavations and in associated laboratories, financed for the most part by federal funds, and directed by professional archaeologists and advanced graduate students. Such a scale of archaeological endeavor not only made possible archaeological research and excavation on a scale previously undreamed of but also salvaged materials and information from important sites about to be destroyed by industrial and urban expansion or to be inundated behind dams built for flood control and production of electrical power. This decade witnessed the emergence of archaeological synthesis and interpretation from a condition bordering on chaos to a recognition of

Participants in the Southeastern Archaeological Conference at Ocmulgee National Monument, November 1939. Front row (left to right): Charles E. Snow, Charles G. Wilder, James B. Griffin, and James A. Ford. Second row, far left: George I. Quimby; toward right (with hand on head): John W. Bennett.

the broad outlines of the prehistory of North America. Although most of the information was not published, it was nevertheless generally known by all the younger professionals and graduate students. And every bit of the information was sent to Jimmy in the Ceramic Repository, transmitted by letter or word of mouth, or presented at the meetings of the Southeastern Archaeological Conference or the Society for American Archaeology with Jimmy in attendance. I can recall some of my own role in the system of relaying information to Jimmy and vice versa. I had spent the summer of 1939 in Hudson's Bay with George Stanley, and, in the autumn, I followed the migrating ducks to New Orleans where I joined James A. Ford in directing the federally financed Louisiana Archaeological Survey, working on various Louisiana sites representative of Tchefuncte, Marksville, Troyville, Coles Creek, Plaquemine, and Natchezan as well as processing collections from Arkansas and Mississippi.

Back in his headquarters in Ann Arbor, Jimmy was the "computer" into which flowed information from many different directions and sources. But, if Jimmy was the computer, he was also the programmer; and I hope to illustrate the process by which data were passed rapidly from centers to excavation to Jimmy and vice versa by excerpts from correspondence between us. I hasten to emphasize that

I was only one of many persons who had this kind of relationship with Jimmy.

November 6, 1939 (Griffin to Quimby):

I will be very interested in hearing more of this Tchefuncte culture, or should I say focus, when I see you at Macon. The evidence you have presented in your letter does not clearly indicate to me an earlier date than Marksville, but it certainly is a different cultural congeries. I heard that [James] Ford is going to state that Hopewell developed out of Marksville. I hope he does not.

November 1, 1940 (Griffin to Quimby):

How are we going to process the rest of the material obtained by the Central Mississippi Archaeological Survey if it can't be done in Louisiana. Can it be done by N.Y.A. help instead of W.P.A., at least when the W.P.A. inspectors are around. Or are you going to try to run the project according to rules now that [James] Ford is at Columbia.

It was my understanding that the pottery was to remain at Louisiana in storage whereas your letter states that the collections have been broken up—and are shortly to be shipped to Harvard and Ann Arbor. Whose room shall I use for this collection. [Leslie] Whites?

[Philip] Phillips was through here last night and this morning, and his speed reminded me of an overdose of Phillips M. M.

November 27, 1940 (Griffin to Quimby):

I don't know whether or not it will come as a surprise to you and Walter [Beecher] but evidently all of the decorated types which were boxed up to go to Harvard were shipped to Ann Arbor and Georg [Neumann] unpacked all the stuff, thinking that the whole shipment was the six skulls from the Caddo site that he was supposed to study. We will send Harvard's material to Harvard.

In spite of your assertions to the contrary it appears to me that you must be drinking more than ever.

February 14, 1941 (Griffin to Quimby):

Holmes [Ellis] delivered the Arkansas photographs satisfactorily and I was very glad to get them. I wish someone would tell your photographer which way is up. Your note that you still have some of the Arkansas pottery is illuminating, for we had noticed that all of the types were not represented. That is a considerable relief. We hope to be able to get down to see you some time during the next month or so.

April 22, 1941 (Quimby to Griffin):

We sure enjoyed your visit and are sorry that you couldn't stay longer. Fred [Kniffen] and Andrew [Albrecht] showed up at 3:30 A.M., but everyone had gone home by then. I am starting preliminary analyses on the Tchefuncte midden and will let you know how they come out.

May 28, 1941 (Quimby to Griffin):

What I formerly considered Chickachae Combed at the Bayou Goula site, I am now calling Bayou Goula Incised. It does not have the sand temper that Chickachae Combed has nor does it ever have the angular body design arrangement.—What Jesse [Jennings] was calling Choctaw Incised was sand tempered and much the same as [Henry] Collins' material from Chickachae. I talked about it to Jesse [Jennings] and he said he would follow the term Chickachae Combed for his sand tempered material and I would call the stuff here Bayou Goula Incised.

Am working on Troyville and am of the opinion that French Fork Incised is not a

Troyville type at all, but rather a Coles Creek type. Also the Troyville pipes when present, are straight based, clay platform pipes, whereas Marksville pipes are curved based.

The pottery from the enclosure wall at the Troyville site contained Coles Creek pottery types and therefore can not be older than Coles Creek.

The war looks rather serious and I don't know what our future here is. I certainly hope that nothing happens before I get my trait lists all in shape and the Tchefuncte report finished.

June 3, 1941 (Quimby to Griffin):

Just saw a swell tubular pipe from the Lafayette mounds, a Tchefuncte site that we are digging. This is the first example to have come from a mound site. Once again we have supported one of [James] Ford's unsupported statements of fact.

My statement about three-line Fatherland Incised pottery being in a majority in sites east of the Mississippi is an error. The division is north–south, three-line in northern sites. Just so happened that the first northern sites I played with were east of the river.

June 5, 1941 (Griffin to Quimby):

I was all ready to whip off a letter to you when your epistle arrived bringing the pictures and permission to shoot off my mouth "On the Relative Age of Marksville and Hopewell." I think a nice little paper can be prepared and I will send it down to you when I get a draft finished.

If the main stream of Natchez poured from Plaquemine did Caddo? Or is Plaquemine an eastern modification of middle period Caddo. Early Caddo we don't know very well but I have a hunch that some of the incised stuff from Texas and Oklahoma is early Caddo and its influence from Marksville is probably indirect.

June 9, 1941 (Quimby to Griffin):

By the way, Louisiana Pottery descriptions in the [Southeastern Archaeological Conference] newsletter which say limestone occasionally used as tempering are all wet. It is volcanic tuff. Tell Fred [Matson] that there are deposits in central Louisiana that are mined commercially.

In the summer of 1941, the federal financing for the Louisiana Archaeological Survey was terminated as the United States began to prepare for probable expansion of the war in Europe. Many of the men in the Survey's field crews were shifted to landscaping projects in the new military training camps then being constructed in Louisiana. The new and young English-speaking officers never understood why the French-speaking ex-archaeological field men dug everything in six-inch levels and five-foot squares which, by this time, was their tradition. Nor did the military ever know that the ex-archaeological field men were finding artifacts, bagging them by square and level, and bringing them to their old field supervisor in Marksville.

I moved northward to the shores of Lake Michigan and became Director of the Muskegon Museum. By the end of 1941, the United States was at war and, for the duration, very little archaeological field work was undertaken. However, those of us not engaged in military and other wartime pursuits continued working on reports and interpretations of data gathered previously, and Jimmy continued to be the focal point and data bank for many of us. From January to June of 1942, my correspondence with Jimmy was mostly about Hopewell in Michigan and Indiana.

> *June 16, 1942* (Griffin to Quimby):
> I had a letter from Jim [Ford] asking me to write a letter of recommendation for him to give to the Navy. He was in New York. I have finally finished my paper which I am calling "Culture Change and Continuity in Eastern United States Archaeology." It was 69 pages long, had a bibliography of about 175 titles and averaged 5 footnotes to a page. That will be a semester's work for someone looking up the references.

In the decade ending in 1941, the University of Chicago was the primary teaching center for archaeologists trained in the context of anthropology. And Jimmy received his training at Chicago. When he moved from Chicago to the University of Michigan, he was the agent for the diffusion of the Chicago cultural system of archaeology to Michigan. Jimmy was Fellow in Aboriginal North American Ceramics at the University of Michigan 1933–1936; Assistant Curator of Archaeology 1937–1942; Associate Curator of Archaeology 1942–1945; Curator and Professor of Anthropology 1945 to the present; and Director of the Museum of Anthropology 1946 to the present.

Between 1945 and 1950, there was a reorganization and expansion of the Department of Anthropology at the University of Michigan which coincided with a decline in archaeological activities at the University of Chicago. The Chicago decline was coeval with the retirement of Fay-Cooper Cole in 1947, and Jimmy, the old University of Chicago man, established at Michigan the kind of excellence in archaeological training that he had experienced years earlier at Chicago. By 1950, Michigan was granting doctorates in anthropology, and archaeologists were going to Michigan. By the later 1950s, Michigan had surpassed Chicago in the training of archaeologists.

In 1957, Jimmy was the Viking Medalist in Archaeology. As President of the Society for American Archaeology, at an elegant presentation ceremony in New York City, I had the pleasure of delivering the following citation:

> One of the most productive and influential archaeologists working in the American field, James B. Griffin early stimulated important studies through his analysis and systematization of the aboriginal ceramics of eastern North America. He has an unsurpassed knowledge of the form, range, and distribution of artifact styles in North America, and has been indefatigable in his examination of collections both in museums and in the hands of amateur archaeologists. Through his innumerable contacts with both amateur and professional archaeologists and by his teaching at the University of Michigan he has exercised a great influence in

The professional staff of the Museum and the Department of Anthropology (except for Leslie A. White, who probably took the picture), at a party in honor of Ralph Linton during a professional visit in July 1942. Front row (left to right): Estelle Titiev (Mrs. Mischa), Volney H. Jones, Carl E. Guthe, Mary White (Mrs. Leslie A.), Joyce H. Jones, (Mrs. Volney H.), and Kamer Aga-Oglu. Standing (left to right): Mischa Titiev, Grace Guthe (Mrs. Carl E.), Virginia Truttman (Guthe's secretary), Georg K. Neumann, Mary Haas, Ralph Linton, James B. Griffin, and Emerson F. Greenman.

promoting the aims of scientific archaeology and encouraging able students. Since the 1930s his syntheses of eastern United States prehistory have been invaluable. More recently his interest in coordinating the results of research on several continents show promise of fulfillment.

More than any other one person, Jimmy has been involved with the archaeology of North America, both the old "new archaeology" and the new "new archaeology." In the 1930s, Jimmy was the leader of the "young turks" who brought forth the old "new archaeology." In the 1960s, Jimmy was teaching and making possible the training of the new "young turks" who spread the gospel of the new "new archaeology."

As early as 1960, William Haag observed that "only a rare individual, such as Griffin, may be an American Athena." In my opinion, he is. He is also the only person I have ever known who was able to shake a well-built log cabin on the shore of Lake Nipigon simply by snoring. I carefully have omitted from this account my exciting adventures as a passenger in vehicles driven by Jimmy!

The post-sputnik push to develop American science was climbing toward its apogee when I (Charles Cleland) arrived at the University of Michigan to study archaeology in the fall of 1960. Universities across the country were busy constructing new buildings and developing new programs. This was an era of academic boom with seemingly limitless job opportunities and ample research funds. Jimmy Griffin was the boss at the Museum, and he too was riding the crest of his career.

My presence at the university was due directly to his recruitment of specialists to work on a large multidisciplinary National Science Foundation research grant designed to study the correlation between prehistoric cultures and the post-Pleistocene ecologies of the Upper Great Lakes. Jimmy carefully had prepared the proposal and had enlisted an interesting array of students and colleagues in other departments of the university to work closely and cooperatively on this project. As a fledgling paleozoologist, I joined Dick Yarnell, who was already analyzing botanical materials to reconstruct the changing ecological sequence since the retreat of glacial ice.

As a zoologist and a student new to both anthropology and archaeology, my socialization into the Museum research team and the Department of Anthropology was interesting. In most regards, the academic atmosphere was impersonal. When, upon my arrival, I inquired about which courses to take, I was advised to see Yarnell because "he has been around for awhile." Yarnell in turn passed on some circular advice reported to have originated with Spaulding: "Don't ever, unless absolutely necessary, cross North Washtenaw Avenue." North Washtenaw runs between the Museum and Angell Hall where the Department of Anthropology is located. I thus learned of the traditional rivalry between the Museum and the department. We Museum students always felt we were laboring under some implicit handicap in the courses of Leslie White, Marshall Sahlins, Elman Service, and Eric Wolf; but we also felt a certain *esprit de corps* and the equally good feeling of knowing that we were Griffin's students.

This is not to say that we students viewed Jimmy as a gentle teacher and protector. While personally warm and extremely supportive of his students, he was in many ways a distant and awesome figure. The reason for this was that he was (and is) a master of academic intimidation. He obviously respected those who would debate with him and respected even more those who could give him an argument, and few could. As students, we knew that we had to express our views forcefully, that when we did, we had better know what we were talking about, and also that it was next to impossible to make a good showing. Consequently, it gave us all a great deal of satisfaction when George Quimby made one of his numerous visits to Ann Arbor. We could be sure that both daily coffee breaks would be enlivened by a blistering argument between Jimmy and George. George could argue with Jimmy and he became the alter ego for a whole generation of Michigan students.

With Al Spaulding's departure from the University for the National Science Foundation in 1959, and Emerson Greenman's decision to reduce his field commitment to Great Lakes archaeology, Jimmy came to depend on Mark Papworth and Lew Binford, both of whom were advanced graduate students. Of particular importance was the execution of the NSF post-Pleistocene–cultural adaptation project for which Mark was given primary responsibility. While Jimmy was the principal investigator, Lew, and particularly Mark, were given almost free reign in developing and directing this project on a day-to-day basis. Jimmy's *modus operandi* was to give graduate students responsibility —to let them run the field projects and to learn from their own mistakes. There were mistakes, but, as a general method of education and research, this system worked well. With a dissertation at stake, the responsibility given was an investment in responsible research and the results got published.

Lew Binford was the idea man. He was innovative, challenging, and capable of working at a pace two notches beyond the ordinary mortal. He seemed to have had (and perhaps still does) a love–hate relationship with Jimmy. Mark Papworth was energetic to the point of a mania, a great wit, and a natural leader. He, above all others, enjoyed an almost father–son relationship with Jimmy. It was, in fact, rumored that Mark had once in good spirit called Dr. Griffin "skin head" to his face, a feat that made him a near-hero among the other students. Mark and Lew were, for a time, a great team.

Since Binford in his *An Archaeological Perspective* (1972) has given his version of the atmosphere at the Museum of Anthropology during this era, and Griffin (1976) has been compelled to correct certain of Binford's errors in fact, another perspective might be helpful. First, however, one must understand the means by which archaeologists were educated at the University of Michigan during the late 1950s and early 1960s.

Instruction was usually informal. If you wanted to learn about ceramics, you went to the Ceramic Repository and learned about ceramics. If you became interested in a particular theory or concept, you read and studied on your own, then formalized your position, and shared your ideas with fellow students. Students were required to take very few formal courses—we normally just "sat in" on classes without paying. Leslie White was a spellbinder, and I sat in on his course "The Evolution of Culture" three times. Livingstone, Meggitt, Wolf, Service, Jones, and especially Marshall Sahlins seemed to stimulate new and good ideas every lecture. Despite Yarnell's admonition, Angell Hall turned out to be an exciting place. At various times, I sat in on, or took for credit, archaeology courses from Jelinek, Anta White, and Griffin. During 1961, I often visited Binford's course on the "Archaeology of North America," which I found to be interesting and provocative but, in many ways, obtuse. Binfordian language was catching on—suddenly a good fishing hole became "a locus of the maximum availability of aquatic resources."

However, successful participation in Griffin's graduate seminar on the archaeology of the eastern United States was the key to informal accreditation. In most respects, Binford has described the scene very well but to some extent he errs, particularly in tone.

Jimmy had an extensive library in his office, a file of photos, and a huge collection of unpublished or rare reference material. All of this material was available to students, and he was always willing to spend time discussing it with those who were interested. In the course of Griffin's seminar, we students were occasionally inclined to discuss various Mississippian manifestations in terms of the development and structure of chiefdoms or to speculate on the similarities between Hopewellian trade and the exchange cycles of the western Pacific. Jimmy usually would remain calm and let the conversation drift back to more "concrete" content. He didn't discourage such discussion, but he didn't encourage it either. As a matter of fact, I have never known him to use his influence to squelch any type of intellectual activity. Like all of us, he had his own ideas about what constituted fruitful research, and he simply believed that firm control over data—places, dates, attributes, and types—was a necessary prerequisite to reasonable problem formulation. He was the inquisitor, and the seminar inquisitions took on an almost game-like quality with Jimmy—it was, however, a serious game at which he was a master.

Clearly, Jimmy's seminar tactics were not designed to humiliate people but to teach students something about scholarly research. The lesson to be learned had nothing to do with "talking potsherds"; the lesson was that a scholar must be thorough and critical. Most of us learned from Jimmy that both of these attributes were important.

Morning and afternoon coffee breaks were both staff meetings and informal classes. That is where Jimmy announced the latest professional news, coordinated Museum activities, and gave his opinions about the newest books. In this context, he frequently had occasion to dismember the work of his colleagues at other institutions. It took me some years to gain perspective on these "attacks" and to understand that they were not personal but professional. In playing his data game, Jimmy was as interested in the people who produced the data as he was in the data. The appearance of a new batch of radiocarbon dates was always an occasion. As we gathered around the coffee table, Roscoe Wilmeth, who was the lab clerk, would pass the newly calculated date list to Jimmy, who would announce the results: 1200 B.C. from a site on an Algoma beach ridge in Saginaw County—everyone smiled and nodded—just right! "A.D. 800 on the Smith site." Jimmy would look up for comment while we all averted our eyes as our minds were frantically trying to recall the location and content of the Smith site. Then, there would be a low chuckle from Jimmy as he read a date from one of Bill Ritchie's sites which seemed to him to support one of his frequent arguments with Ritchie. "Wait till Ritchie sees this!" he'd laugh, as he went on to relate the full circumstances and particulars of the argument. Bill Ritchie was not an enemy nor were the hundreds of other archaeologists who were fellow players at Jimmy's game. I am convinced that, in the fraternity of that era, people were as important as dates and potsherds, and I am not sure that the same is true today when theories seem to have become more important than people. To Jimmy's credit, he seemed able to treat everyone alike. He had as much time for a farmer who brought in a collection of arrowheads for identification as for a visiting scholar from Europe. When the Michigan crew went to meetings, he enjoyed making contacts for his students and talking to students from other universities about their sites, pots, and ideas.

Jimmy liked people he defined as gentlemen (with no reference to sex), and this was by far the most important criteria. Being smart, astutely argumentative, and punctual were other qualities he also admired and enjoyed in people. Jimmy could tolerate a degree of tardiness and even some occasional muddleheadedness, but he could not conscience ungentlemanly behavior.

Starting in the summer of 1960 and for the next several years, there was a great deal of ungentlemanly behavior around the Museum. Domestic problems drove a wedge between Papworth and Binford, and widespread strife began to affect the efforts of the entire research and educational process in the Museum. The coffee breaks became more and more intense and finally unbearable. Threats and pathetic lies abounded, self-ingratiating folk tales replaced good humored repartee, paranoia was rampant. This atmosphere spawned much of the mythology about the origin of "new archaeology" and what has been said of Jimmy's place in that history.

Some semblance of calm returned to the Museum with the departure of Papworth and Binford and the arrival of Art Jelinek as curator of Old World archaeology. As a matter of fact, Jimmy's interest focused for a time on Europe and northern Asia. In 1962, he became a member of the Executive Committee of the International Union of Prehistoric and Protohistoric Sciences and, during the year of 1963, received a Fulbright Fellowship to study in Copenhagen. During this visit, he lived and traveled for an extended period in the Soviet Union, examining Siberian collections pertaining to the origins of early man in the New World.

By 1964, the curatorship of Great Lakes archaeology had passed from Emerson Greenman to Richard Keslin and finally to one of Jimmy's own students, Jim Fitting. Fitting organized a very large and active Great Lakes research program in Michigan, which maintained the momentum achieved under the earlier paleoecology grant.

During the years of the late 1960s, there was a major change in the Museum staff. Between 1966 and 1969, Kent Flannery, Loring Brace, Jeff Parsons, Bob Whallon, Henry Wright, Ed Wilmsen, and Dick Ford were added to the staff. With the resignations of Jelinek in 1967 and Fitting in 1968, that left only Volney Jones, Kamer Aga-Oglu, and Griffin as the old guard. This new staff had a significant effect on the Museum's programs. First, the research emphasis shifted to the Near East and Mesoamerica and, secondly, the new staff had an intellectual orientation somewhat different from Jimmy's. Although this latter situation produced some consternation, it speaks to his talents as an administrator that he was able to maintain a workable equilibrium with this group of intellectually talented and aggressive young faculty.

During the late 1960s and early 1970s, the Department of Anthropology had, like so many other departments across the country, been torn apart by political and personal dissent. Faced with rebuilding, Jimmy was asked to assume the chairmanship in 1972. For the first time since the days of Guthe and the development of anthropology at the university, the department and the Museum of Anthropology were united under common leadership. In his usual style, Jimmy was a strong chairman, and he soon returned the department to a position of strength.

When, during this period, Moreau Maxwell sent a form letter to the "chairpersons" of the midwestern universities to make certain inquiries concerning a forthcoming Midwest Archaeological Conference, Jimmy replied as follows:

Professional staff of the Museum of Anthropology (fall 1974). Front (left to right): Kamer Aga-Oglu (retired), James B. Griffin, Volney H. Jones (retired), and C. Loring Brace. Back row (left to right): Karl L. Hutterer, Kent V. Flannery, Henry T. Wright, Christopher S. Peebles, Jeffrey R. Parsons, Robert E. Whallon, Jr., and Richard I. Ford.

Dear Max,
There *are* no Chairpersons in anthropology
at the University of Michigan.

JBG

At the University of Michigan, James Bennett Griffin was *the* Chairman and *the* Director. He has placed his mark on the university and on American archaeology. It is an indelible mark—a mark of quality. Those of us who were his students, his colleagues, and his friends salute him and wish him well.

James Bennett Griffin, Archaeologist

Volney H. Jones

During the last four decades, the name, personality, and accomplishments of James B. Griffin have made an indelible impression on the field of archaeology. His career spans almost precisely the period of development of North American archaeology from the "protoprofessional" era to what some refer to as "new archaeology." He has participated actively in many of the steps and innovations by which progress has been achieved, adding numerous significant contributions toward this development. In doing so, he has drawn quite freely upon the data of many disciplines that impinge upon archaeology. Thus, the development of his own career parallels closely that of the field, as delineated by historians of archaeology such as Willey and Sabloff (1974) for North America in general, and Guthe (1952), Griffin (1959), and Haag (1961) for the eastern United States.

To get Griffin into this world, we must go back to January 12, 1905, when he was born into the family of Charles Bennett Griffin and Maude Bostwick Griffin, then residents of Atchison, Kansas. His father's profession as a supplier of railroad equipment soon led the family to move to other railroad centers, first to Denver and then to the Chicago area. In this latter locality, they resided in Oak Park, which at that time was a quiet middle-class suburb of Chicago. He attended and was graduated from the public schools of Oak Park.

In the fall of 1923, he enrolled in the School of Business Administration at the University of Chicago. But after completing two years of study in that unit, he transferred into the program in General Social Science in which he received the degree of Bachelor of Philosophy in the spring of 1927. His first formal contact with anthropology came during this interval when he enrolled in classes under the tutelage of

James B. Griffin about the time he matriculated at the University of Chicago as a freshman (1923).

Fay-Cooper Cole, who was to exert a great influence not only on his professional career but also on him personally.

Following the receipt of his degree, Griffin was employed for over a year as a junior executive with the Standard Oil Company, but soon found that he and the business world were not compatible. In the fall of 1928, he again enrolled at the University of Chicago, this time to study anthropology in the Department of Sociology and Anthropology. He received the degree of Master of Arts in December 1930, presenting a thesis concerned with the burial practices of the Indians of the Eastern Woodlands area (Griffin 1930). His committee was distinguished, composed of Cole as chairman, Edward Sapir, and Robert Redfield. Following the receipt of that degree, he pursued studies toward the doctorate until January 1933 when he transferred to the University of Michigan.

During his years at the University of Chicago, Griffin continued to reside in Oak Park, commuting to the university by way of the suburb of Cicero (which at that time was Al Capone country). The skills in urban driving that he acquired through this practice have been a point of pride with him. He has been heard to remark that they held him in good stead in traffic in various cities and that he found he was able to compete on even terms with the notorious taxicab drivers of Mexico City.

During the years of Griffin's enrollment at the University of Chicago, anthropology was undergoing a period of rapid change and development. Fay-Cooper Cole had joined the staff in 1924 to become the anthropologist in a joint department of Sociology and Anthropology. The department was dominated by a group of distinguished sociologists including Ellsworth Faris, Robert E. Park, and Ernest W. Burgess. Cole was the replacement for Frederick Starr, who had just retired. By all accounts, Starr was a stimulating lecturer who presented a series of popular courses chiefly at undergraduate level, but he did not essay to develop either a strong concentration program or a research-oriented program. These things Cole undertook immediately and energetically.

Cole had joined the staff in 1924 as a "lecturer" but, by 1927, had become a full professor. In this latter year, the first doctorate in anthropology was conferred (this happens to have been to Leslie A. White, with whom Griffin later was to be associated at Michigan for almost forty years and who served on Griffin's doctoral committee). In 1929, a separate Department of Anthropology was established, with Cole as chairman. Edward Sapir had joined the staff in 1925, and Redfield in 1928. At about this time, both Paul Radin and Leslie Spier were visiting professors. In 1931, with the departure of Sapir, both A. R. Radcliffe-Brown and Harry Hoijer were added to the faculty. These were the professors under whom Griffin had the opportunity to study, but I believe that he would wish it placed on the record that he did not study under Radin.

Cole immediately instituted a program in field archaeology and made archaeological field experience an integral part of anthropological training. He seemed to feel that, whatever the interests and aspirations of his individual students, an immersion in dirt archaeology somehow was good for the soul. As a result of this experience, a large number of professional archaeologists were trained in field techniques.

During the summer of 1929, Griffin served as a member of a field party under the leadership of W. M. Krogman, which carried out surveys in Adams County, Illinois, and excavated the Parker Heights Mound near Quincy. Griffin (1934) issued a brief report on these

W. M. Krogman (foreground) demonstrates the excavation of a burial to students during excavation of Parker Heights Mound, Adams County, Illinois (1929). Left to right: Herlee G. Creel, William H. Gilbert, J. Gilbert McAllister, James B. Griffin, Henri S. Denninger, and Herbert Michael Sapir.

operations. During the summer of 1930, he worked under the direction of Cole and Thorne Deuel in the excavation of a large Hopewell mound on the Morton Farm near Lewiston, Fulton County, Illinois. The results of this excavation form a considerable portion of the landmark volume *Rediscovering Illinois* (Cole and Deuel 1937). This was Griffin's first experience with the Hopewell culture, which has remained one of his major interests.

In the summer of 1931, he was engaged to lead a field party sponsored by the Tioga Point Museum (Pennsylvania) in the excavation of Late Algonquian and historic Delaware sites in the Upper Susquehanna Valley, Bradford County, Pennsylvania. He published a brief note on this project (Griffin 1931). In 1933, he participated in an archaeological survey of Dearborn County, Indiana, led by Glenn A. Black for the Indiana Historical Society. In addition to his fieldwork, while still a student at Chicago, he engaged in one ethnological venture. He and Paul S. Martin compiled a bibliography for a book on Indian medicine men being prepared by William T. Corlett, and provided other technical assistance in the preparation of the volume (Corlett 1935).

Although courses in anthropology had been taught previously at some midwestern universities, the program instituted at Chicago by

Thorne Deuel, Henry C. Shetrone, and Fay-Cooper Cole (left to right) at Morton Farm, Fulton County, Illinois (1930).

Cole resulted in the first major graduate center in anthropology in the area and the first strong archaeological training center. At Chicago, this meteoric development took place around Griffin and may have conditioned him for the very active part he was to play in a similar explosive expansion of the anthropological program at the University of Michigan.

James B. Griffin (left) and Paul Weer (right) "survey" the Burkham Stone Mounds, Dearborn County, Indiana (June 1933).

Discussion at the Kincaid Mounds, Massac County, Illinois (about 1939). Front (left to right): Irvin Peithman, Fay-Cooper Cole, James B. Griffin, and Charles R. Keyes. Back (left to right): William M. Krogman, Richard Morgan, and Roger Willis.

The anthropological environment at the University of Chicago during Griffin's graduate study there was very lively and stimulating. Students responded to the growing program in considerable numbers, and many of them later made substantial contributions to professional anthropology. Among those with whom he was associated were: Wendell C. Bennett, J. O. Brew, Dorothy Cross, Fred Eggan, Harry Hoijer, W. M. Krogman, Paul S. Martin, Richard G. Morgan, Georg K. Neumann, Morris E. Opler, Cornelius Osgood, Froelich G. Rainey, and Frank M. Setzler. With several of these, he formed close and enduring friendships and, in some instances, strong loyalties. All became professional colleagues, the association with whom was to have a considerable influence on his career and life.

Griffin departed from the University of Chicago prior to completing the requirements for the doctorate to accept a research fellowship at the University of Michigan. January of 1933 marked the beginning of his connections with that university and his residence in Ann Arbor, which have persisted to the present. On February 14, 1936, he married Ruby Fletcher, formerly of Harrisburg, Illinois, and Racine, Wisconsin, who had been employed as a registered nurse at an Oak Park hospital. This marriage has been a highly compatible and enduring one. Additions to the family have been three sons, John Bennett born in 1938, David Moss born in 1942, and James Chapman in 1945. None have chosen to enter the field of professional anthropology.

In accepting his assignment at Michigan, Griffin thereby acquired the full title of "Fellow in Aboriginal Ceramics in the Museum of Anthropology at the University of Michigan under the Auspices of the Committee on State Archaeological Surveys of the Division of Anthropology and Psychology of the National Research Council." He managed to bear up very well under this cumbersome title. But to understand the implications of this title and the nature of the services expected under it, one must investigate the status of archaeology in the Midwest at about this time and, particularly, certain stirrings that were taking place.

Around 1920, archaeology in the Midwest was lagging somewhat, as compared, for instance, to programs in the Southwest, California, and the Northeast. Most activity in progress was sponsored by historical societies, local archaeological societies, or by unattached amateur archaeologists. Where archaeology did have its setting in academic institutions, it usually was in the hands of persons in disciplines other than anthropology. The aura of "the ancient moundbuilders" still lingered. Some from Eastern institutions recently had carried out excavations in the Midwest, such as Nels C. Nelson, Warren K. Moorehead, and C. C. Willoughby. Although some creditable work had been and was being done, many examples of poor techniques, looting of sites, and commercialization of artifacts and sites existed.

As a reflection of this situation, the National Research Council in 1920 established within its Division of Anthropology and Psychology a Committee on State Archaeological Surveys to focus on improvement of archaeology in the Midwest (Guthe 1930; 1952: 7–8). A. V. Kidder assumed the chairmanship of this committee in 1924, and, in 1927, he induced Carl E. Guthe to establish a Ceramic Repository at the University of Michigan. Thus was born the unit with which Griffin became associated. In 1927, Kidder relinquished the chairmanship which was accepted by Guthe, who retained it for the next ten years until the termination of the committee. Guthe's vigorous prosecution of the office of chairman and his dedication to the Ceramic Repository led to his recruiting Griffin to assist in bringing some order out of the confused status of archaeological ceramics in the Midwest.

The conduct of the chairmanship by Kidder and by Guthe reflect influence of their experience in the Pueblo (Anasazi) area of the Southwest. Their purpose was to transfer methods that had been successful in the Southwest to the solution of problems of the Midwest. In particular, they envisioned the utilization of pottery characteristics as an index to cultural entities and their relationships in time and space. Griffin became in effect a traveling agent of the committee, for in the three years that he held the fellowship, he traveled frequently to examine collections, visit sites, and to confer with professional and amateur archaeologists. He saw virtually every important collection within or pertaining to the area. In the preface of his volume on the Fort Ancient culture, Griffin (1943: vii–viii) refers to travel in twelve states, the District of Columbia, and Canada to examine collections pertaining to that culture. As Guthe became engrossed in other affairs, the operation of the repository was left largely to Griffin.

The data obtained were entered on cards, and these filed by site and state. The records include descriptions of sites, features, and diagnostic artifacts. Attention was given not only to pottery but to other artifacts and architectural features as well. Abundant photographic records were made, and, whenever possible, duplicate specimens were obtained for the repository. The collections and card files built up within the repository have had great value not only to the local staff but also to visiting archaeologists in giving a synoptic view of the archaeology of the area. These records still constitute a valuable resource, although, after forty years, they naturally have become somewhat shopworn. These collections and files were established in the Division of Archaeology of the Museum of Anthropology where they still remain.

The transfer of the chairmanship of the Committee on State Archaeological Surveys to Guthe in 1927 was logical for several reasons. In 1925, Guthe had been appointed acting director of the newly established Museum of Anthropology. Early in 1928, that museum moved into the new University Museums Building. Although Guthe soon had modern spacious quarters in a building that, for decades, was a showplace among museums, he was given precious little budget and inherited little in the way of technically trained staff. As the first chairman of the committee resident in the Midwest and with the facilities at hand, he was able to make the program of the committee a primary one. Depending chiefly on grants, he established several projects as aids to the development of archaeology.

The first of these facilities was the Ceramic Repository with which Griffin later became associated. An Ethnobotanical Laboratory came into existence in 1930 with Melvin R. Gilmore in charge and joined by Volney H. Jones in 1931. W. Vernon Kinietz in 1935 began his project in ethnohistory of the Great Lakes region. In the same year, Frederick R. Matson was added to establish a program in ceramic technology, which very closely resembled that carried out by Anna O. Shepard on the pottery of Pecos Pueblo, New Mexico, for A. V. Kidder. Also in

1935, Emerson F. Greenman was brought back to Michigan to institute a more vigorous program in archaeological field work.

Around the decade of the 1930s, the Museum of Anthropology was quite active in furthering ceramic studies. Shortly after the founding of the Ceramic Repository, Guthe (1928) published and circulated widely a paper outlining methods of pottery description. This was reprinted as a part of "Standards of Pottery Description" published by Benjamin March (1934), Curator of the Division of the Orient in the Museum. Although March's methods had been developed in his work with Oriental ceramics, they have served well for North American pottery. This work still is cited frequently and has been in such demand that it was reprinted in 1969. Between 1935 and 1942, Matson operated a well-equipped ceramic technology laboratory, just across the hall from Griffin's repository. He was investigating such things as properties and sources of clays, tempering materials, and firing temperatures. In 1938, Griffin and James A. Ford initiated and conducted a well-attended conference on pottery types of the Southeast, held at the Museum, in which they urged standardization of nomenclature, methods of description, and classification. This conference was sponsored by the Committee on State Archaeological Surveys, and the proceedings were issued by that organization. Following the untimely death of March in 1934 and the resignations of Matson and Guthe in 1942 and 1944 respectively, Griffin and the Ceramic Repository were the only local survivors of that era.

Approximately concurrent with Griffin's tenure of the fellowship, there were two developments that had a stimulating effect in shaping Eastern archaeology and in both of which he played a significant part. One was the formulation of the Midwestern Taxonomic Method, and the other was the enormous archaeological program pursued in connection with the Tennessee Valley Authority.

The Midwestern Taxonomic Method, which perhaps is better known as the "McKern Classification," was developed during conferences sponsored and reported on by the Committee on State Archaeological Surveys. The initial meeting was held in Chicago in December 1932, the roster of which (McKern 1939:301) shows that Griffin not only attended the meeting but that he was the only student present. He also participated in the "Indianapolis Conference" in 1935, at which the system was given its greatest impetus. In recounting the history of this system of cultural classification, Griffin (1943:331) lays claim, apparently with justification, to have been the first to report in print the testing of the system by applying it. This was in a preliminary report on the Fort Ancient culture (Griffin 1935). Although he assisted in the development of the classification and made use of it, he also has offered one of the more cogent critiques of it (Griffin 1943:327–341) and viewed it in retrospect after it served its major usefulness (Griffin 1959:384–385).

During the depression years and particularly in 1934 and 1935, a massive program of excavation was launched to serve the joint purposes of relief employment and salvage archaeology. One segment was connected with the dam-building work of the Tennessee Valley Authority. (A side effect of this was that employment and field experience were offered to a large number of young archaeologists.) The pottery from the Norris Basin, Tennessee, and the Wheeler Basin, Alabama, excavations was routed to the Ceramic Repository where Griffin studied it. These large consignments of pottery were from areas previously not well-known archaeologically. Griffin's extensive and detailed reports, therefore, considerably advanced the knowledge of ceramics of these areas (Griffin 1938, 1939). As we shall note later, the Norris Basin also furnished him material for his doctoral dissertation.

Although Griffin left the University of Chicago before completing the doctorate, he was well prepared in general anthropology after four years of graduate study there. While carrying out the duties of his fellowship at Michigan, he found time to continue his studies but found few suitable courses in anthropology. At that time, the Department of Anthropology was essentially a one-man affair, with offerings limited chiefly to undergraduate-oriented courses. His additional courses were taken mostly in cognate fields, such as geography, history, and geology, the content of which has served him well in his career in archaeology. Hence, the doctorate that he received in February 1936 was to a great degree an interdisciplinary one, although it was the first awarded under the aegis of the Department of Anthropology. The makeup of his committee reflects the interdisciplinary nature of the degree: Carl E. Guthe (archaeology), chairman, Leslie A. White (general anthropology), Arthur S. Aiton (American colonial history), Kenneth C. McMurray (North American geography), and Irving D. Scott (physiography).

Early in his career at Michigan, he had instituted a study of the then somewhat enigmatic Fort Ancient culture of the Middle Ohio Valley, with the consideration that this might be suitable as a dissertation topic. But as his investigation progressed, it became evident that the problem was too large, complex, and time consuming for that purpose. The analysis of this culture and the report (Griffin 1943) still stand as major contributions which were successful in placing this culture in perspective in its relationships to adjacent archaeological, ethnological, and historical entities.

The interpretation of the pottery from the Norris Basin presented a more manageable dissertation topic (Griffin 1936) which became an abbreviated version of the published report (Griffin 1938).

By about 1934, the Committee on State Archaeological Surveys had achieved most of its immediate goals, and consideration was being given to phasing it out, which eventually was done on 20 June 1937. However, Guthe and other Midwestern archaeologists had conceived the idea of a national archaeological society to continue and expand upon the former functions of the committee. Their planning resulted in the founding of the Society for American Archaeology late in 1934 (Unsigned 1935:141–143). Guthe became the secretary–treasurer of that organization and continued to hold the chairmanship of the committee in order to bring about a smooth transition. With the impending termination of the committee, provision needed to be made for the Ceramic Repository and for the Fellowship in North American Ceramics, which had been under the auspices of the committee. The repository has remained a permanent part of the Museum of Anthropology under the custody of the Curator of Archaeology.

The fellowship was terminated in 1936, and Griffin was given an appointment as Research Associate in the Museum of Anthropology. The following year, his title was revised to Assistant Curator of Archaeology, which he held from 1937–1942, and to Associate Curator of Archaeology, which he retained during 1942–1945. His promotion to Curator of Archaeology in 1945 will be considered later. Although his employment was in staff positions during these years, his duties remained essentially the same as they had been under the fellowship.

From the time of his assumption of the fellowship in 1933 and through his earlier staff years until 1941, Griffin's remuneration and expenses had been provided through a "Fund for Aboriginal North American Ceramics" which was administered by the Museum. The funding of this had been by an "anonymous donor" whose identity at first remained fairly well concealed but soon became well known. On at least two occasions, Griffin (1956:1479; 1971), to bestow credit where it was due, has revealed that his benefactor was Eli Lilly of Indianapolis. Beginning about 1930, Lilly had developed an interest in the archaeology and Indian tribes of Indiana and, in 1937, produced a sumptuous volume *Prehistoric Antiquities of Indiana* (Lilly 1937). He worked in close consultation with Cole and Guthe and, on several occasions, financed projects at both Chicago and Michigan.

Operating under the cover of the name and structure of the Indiana Historical Society, Lilly organized his own research team. In addition to Griffin, others receiving sustained support were Carl Voegelin (linguistics), Ermine W. Voegelin (ethnology), Glenn A. Black (archaeology), Paul Weer (history), and Georg K. Neumann (physical anthropology). Among others who were supported for less extended periods were Richard S. MacNeish, William A. Ritchie, Joffre L. Coe, Florence M. Hawley, Edmund S. Carpenter, and John Witthoft. These individuals were scattered among various institutions, working independently and with considerable freedom, but were brought together at least annually for a group conference. Griffin (1971) has provided a detailed account of the history, and the activities of this group, and the very considerable contributions that they made.

A central theme in these investigations was that of testing the historical validity of the Walum Olum, the tribal chronicle of the Delaware Indians. Griffin participated in discussions but made no direct contribution to the published volume concerning this (Walum Olum 1954). His reasons for some skepticism concerning the value of the chronicle as a historical source are well expressed in his review of it (Griffin 1955). Although the findings on the Walum Olum are inconclusive, a great deal of valuable research came from these investigations.

Griffin recalls with pleasure his working with the group, and he has retained a high regard and respect for Mr. Lilly, as well as gratitude for generous support in the critical early years of his career. A recognition of Griffin's contributions to the archaeology of Indiana was the invitation tendered to him to give the dedication address at the opening of the Glenn A. Black Laboratory of Archaeology on the campus of Indiana University. In the publication of this address, Griffin provides a detailed account of the history, activities, and research of the Lilly Group (Griffin 1971). At the dedication of the laboratory, held on April 21, 1971, the honorary degree of Doctor of Science was conferred upon Griffin by Indiana University.

During the decade of 1930–1940, a new generation of archaeologists was becoming firmly established in the region east of the Rocky Mountains, where previously there had been so few. These were primarily anthropologically trained persons who had received supervised training in archaeological methods. A very active program was being carried out in Nebraska by W. D. Strong, Earl H. Bell, and John L. Champe. Waldo R. Wedel was working in Nebraska and Kansas. Alex D. Krieger and Thomas N. Campbell were replacing the old guard in Texas. Henry B. Collins had begun work in Mississippi, James A. Ford in Louisiana, and Philip Phillips in the Lower Mississippi Valley. Irving Rouse was active in Florida, Joffre L. Coe in North Carolina, Arthur R. Kelly in Georgia, and David L. DeJarnette in Alabama. Frank M. Setzler had begun work in Ohio and Indiana but switched to the Southeast. Programs had been initiated in Tennessee by T.M.N. Lewis and Madeline Kneberg, William G. Haag in Kentucky, Richard G. Morgan in Ohio, and Glenn A. Black in Indiana. Illinois was receiving the attention of Thorne Deuel, and Minnesota that of Lloyd A. Wilford. Farther east were Dorothy Cross in New Jersey and

Pennsylvania, William A. Ritchie in New York, and Douglas S. Byers and Frederick Johnson in New England.

Undoubtedly I have failed to list others who should be included, but this is essentially the "gang" with which Griffin was associated and with whom he interacted at meetings, conferences, "bull sessions," and by visits, correspondence, exchange of reprints, and mutual review of publications. At that time, the fraternity of professional anthropologists constituted a relatively small circle, so that one could know most of them and meet them face to face on terms of friendship or, perhaps, enmity.

Although Griffin shared with other archaeologists an aversion to careless, inept, and destructive nonprofessional diggers and dealers, he encouraged and aided those who were doing constructive work. Among those with whom he kept in close touch were Paul F. Titterington of St. Louis, Missouri, Dan Morse of Peoria, Illinois, and John C. Birdsell of South Bend, Indiana. He retained a good relationship with a number of those working in Michigan, such as Wilbur M. Cunningham of Benton Harbor, and Fred Dustin of Saginaw. These relationships were mutually beneficial, particularly in getting some of the works of the amateurs into print.

Of the new generation of archaeologists who had come on the scene, each was busy in his own chosen area or areas, working out typology, stratigraphy, seriation, and relative chronology, but also looking beyond his own bailiwick to correlate with the results of others elsewhere and to devise broader sequences and relationships. Progress was exceedingly rapid with formulations and syntheses on state and regional levels emerging to construct a framework for Eastern archaeology. Of particular value were the descriptions and classifications of traits and of artifacts and the illustrations of these by the profusion of plates which were possible at that time. For instance, two volumes that were published by Griffin (1943) and Ritchie (1944) contain over 300 plates.

The unusual opportunity open to Griffin to travel widely in examining collections, conferring with archaeologists, and attending conferences permitted him to develop an unparalleled encyclopedic knowledge and panoramic view of Eastern archaeology. His earlier investigations had been chiefly in the Central Ohio Valley but soon were expanded to encompass the Illinois Valley, the Upper Mississippi, the southern Plains, the Iroquoian area, and eventually the entire region east of the Rocky Mountains. One particular step in the widening of his horizons was the participation jointly with Philip Phillips, representing Harvard University, and James A. Ford, then at Lousiana State University, in a survey of the archaeology of the Lower

Mississippi Valley. Two seasons in 1940 and 1941 were spent survey-ing portions of six states, in exploratory excavation of nine sites, and studying the correlations of sites with abandoned river channels and other surface features. This project was interrupted by World War II, and the final report did not appear until a decade later (Phillips, Ford, and Griffin 1951); even belatedly, this report has served as the major source on this previously little-known area. For instance, sections by Griffin, totaling about 140 pages, present descriptions of over 50 pottery types.

Some fifteen years of study of Eastern archaeology were distilled in Griffin's "Cultural Change and Continuity" (1946) paper to provide a broad appraisal of relationships and sequences. For the first time, detailed tables and maps were provided to illustrate locations and relationships. This tended to supersede earlier comprehensive outlines that had been published by Deuel (1935), Guthe (1940), and Ford and Willey (1941), as it is more detailed and encompasses a larger area, particularly to the west. It is, however, highly technical and can be comprehended only by persons exceedingly well versed in the ar-chaeology of the area. But this, in turn, was to be replaced by Griffin's later interpretive summaries (Griffin 1952, 1961, and 1967) which incorporated the added benefits of radiocarbon dating. The 1961 publication also covers not just the Eastern area, but all of North America north of Mexico for the edification of readers of the *Encyclo-paedia Brittanica*.

During World War II, the staff of the Museum became considerably depleted through leaves of absence and resignations. Kinietz and Matson, although technically given leave to enter war-related activi-ties, never returned to the Museum staff. Georg K. Neumann, who had been making studies of the physical anthropology collections since 1940 (under funds from Eli Lilly), left in 1943 to take a position at Indiana University. Jones was on war-related leave during 1943–1944. Griffin remained at the Museum and continued his research but engaged also in additional emergency activities. One of these was the teaching of courses in geography to military personnel stationed on campus. Another was "moonlighting" at the Argus Camera Company (Ann Arbor) grinding lenses for military equipment. In this latter job, he worked a shift from 6 to 11 P.M., which, with his required eight-hour day at the Museum, totaled thirteen hours with only a one-hour break between segments. The major staff loss, which came with little advance warning, was the resignation of Guthe to accept a position as director of the New York State Museum. This occurred in 1944, leaving open in the Museum of Anthropology the positions of Director and of Curator of Archaeology.

Guthe's departure was only one of a rapid series of events and developments that took place within the brief period of about 1944 through 1952, which were to bring drastic changes in anthropology at Michigan and in the career of Griffin. The first two were the appointment of Griffin as Curator of Archaeology in 1945 and his elevation to Director of the Museum of Anthropology in January of 1946. These are positions that he held until his retirement. Throughout his career, he cherished the curatorship as a direct link to the field of archaeology. He remained an archaeologist as well as an administrator. Apparently, the position of Director of the Museum offers a fair degree of permanence and security—in the half century from 1925 to 1975 the Museum has had only two directors.

In leaving, Guthe vacated not only the positions within the Museum, but also his lectureship in the Department of Anthropology, including the responsibility for teaching a course on the archaeology of North America. Almost simultaneously in 1944, and again with little advance warning, Mischa Titiev of the departmental staff was granted leave of absence to serve with the Office of Strategic Services in India, leaving his teaching schedule unfilled. As the recruiting of a substitute at that time was almost impossible, the department, in desperation, called upon Griffin and Jones for aid. Griffin took over Guthe's archaeology quite in stride, but, more remarkably, he also taught Titiev's survey course in the anthropology of Asia with little time for advance preparation. During the first year, these Museum staff members taught without the benefit of teaching titles, a violation of regulations, but when asked to continue teaching, they were granted the proper credentials. In 1945, Griffin became an associate professor in the department and, in 1949, was advanced to full professor. As routine as these actions may seem, they actually represented an exceedingly sharp break in tradition and established a very important precedent.

The primary architect of the Natural History Museum's establishment at the University of Michigan was the herpetologist, Alexander G. Ruthven, who held the directorship of the combined museums from 1913 to 1936. His philosophy of museums operation, as demonstrated in practice and as expressed in his volume "A Naturalist in a University Museum" (Ruthven 1931), leaned strongly toward the traditions of British museums. His expressed priorities were primarily the maintenance of collections and records, followed by research, exhibits, and teaching. Teaching was limited chiefly to advanced technical courses presented in an atmosphere of apprenticeship, with emphasis on museum methods and procedures. In 1922, Ruthven created the Museum of Anthropology and brought in Guthe as associate director of it. However, Ruthven was hardly settled in his sumptuous office in the new museums building when he was given the added chore of the presidency of the University of Michigan, a position he held from 1929 through 1951.

Guthe was a protégé and admirer of Ruthven and inured in the system. Actually, during the period of over twenty years in which he was associated with the museums, he was under quite direct supervision of Ruthven and was given only limited freedom to develop his own policies. During the period before Ruthven became president, Guthe held the title of Acting Director and Ruthven was, in effect, the director of the Museum of Anthropology. During the first seven years of his presidency, Ruthven retained the directorship of the museums and kept close check on them. In 1936, Guthe succeeded Ruthven as director of the composite museums (the Museum of Anthropology, Museum of Zoology, Museum of Paleontology, and University Herbarium), a position he held until his resignation from the university. Even in this period, Guthe held little power, for the separate museums continued to report directly to Ruthven, who maintained fairly close, although gradually waning, supervision over them.

There was a persistent and plausible rumor that Ruthven's intent was to hold open an option to return to the directorship after leaving the presidency. In any event, Griffin came along at the right time, for when he became director, Ruthven was within five years of retirement and had considerably relaxed his hold over the museums. With a fairly free hand in the directorship, and with his associate professorship, which allowed participation in affairs of the Department of Anthropology, Griffin was in a position to develop his own policies and program, a privilege never fully enjoyed by Guthe. These, it has turned out, have been in a direction away from museology as an end in itself toward the development of what has become essentially an archaeological institute rather than a "museum" in the more conventional sense.

Following Ruthven's death in 1971, the designation of the complex of natural history museums was changed from "The University Museums" to "The Alexander G. Ruthven Natural Science Museums."

Although Griffin and Jones did not teach lecture courses until 1944 and did not receive teaching titles until the next year, they and some other members of the Museum staff previously had done a considerable amount of surreptitious instruction. In the alignment of anthropology at the university, the department and the Museum always have been separate administrative and budgetary units. As the Museum itself cannot grant course credit nor offer degrees, teaching by the staff of the Museum can be accomplished only through affiliation with the department. Guthe was instrumental in achieving the beginning of a modest "Department" of Anthropology in 1928 by bringing Julian H. Steward to the campus as "Lecturer in Anthropology" in the College of Literature, Science, and the Arts. In his second and last year here, his title was revised to that of "Instructor." He was succeeded by Leslie A. White in 1930 as assistant professor, who taught for forty years at Ann Arbor.

Guthe was able to bring Steward and, later, White to the University only by transferring funds for a portion of their salaries from the budget of the Museum to the College. Also, in the earlier years from 1928 to about 1946, the Department was housed in the Museum, with office space and furniture provided by the Museum. The Department did not completely vacate this space and move entirely into its own quarters in Angell Hall until 1952, with White the last to move.

Guthe himself was given the title "Lecturer in Anthropology" in 1929, a title he held until he left the university. In addition to teaching a lecture course in North American archaeology, he also was certified to enroll and teach students in two other courses, "Museum Methods" and "Research and Special Work." Under these two titles, students could enroll for individual instruction and be assigned to anything agreed upon by the student and the instructor, such as washing pottery, reference work and readings, or writing a term paper. This allowed the students to work with the collections, to associate with the staff, and to become involved in ongoing research projects. Since Guthe was the only member of the Museum staff certified until 1945, students enrolled under his name, and he then delegated them to the various staff members or rotated them among projects in order to allow more varied experiences. Various staff members thus were able to do quite a lot of teaching in this anonymous fashion. Griffin was particularly active in the teaching, and, at one time at least, he convened four or five students into a veritable seminar in Eastern archaeology.

During these early years of 1930 to 1945, although the doctorate was granted only rarely and under special interdisciplinary circumstances, a number of persons who later were to make a contribution to professional archaeology received other degrees in anthropology and availed themselves of the resources of the Museum and of field experience with Museum staff members. Among these were George I. Quimby (B.A. 1936, M.A. 1937), Albert C. Spaulding (M.A. 1937), James A. Ford (M.A. 1938), and Alfred K. Guthe (B.A. 1941). Frederick R. Matson received a master's degree in anthropology in 1936, and a doctorate in 1939 in "ceramic archaeology," combining studies in anthropology, ceramic engineering, and mineralogy. Although the degrees received by Robert J. Braidwood (B.A. 1932, M.A. 1933) were granted in classical archaeology, several of his courses were in anthropology and a part of his work was pursued within the Museum facilities.

In his obituary of Ford in *American Antiquity*, Willey (1969) remarks on the deep impression on Ford of his study at Michigan and his association with Griffin while there, as well as the influence of his courses with White. Although Neumann and MacNeish, when they were visiting fellows, did not take formal courses, there was a learning experience by osmosis in their associations with the staff. MacNeish wrote (in Griffin 1971) that his association with Griffin was "the most important part of my entire academic training" which "definitely determined the direction of my career in archaeology."

During those early years, the "official" teaching staff was composed of just White, Guthe, and Mischa Titiev, who was added to the departmental staff in 1936. The considerations that brought about the appointment of Griffin and Jones to academic titles were primarily economic. Toward the end of the war and after its end, students were beginning to return in numbers, but the university budget was not keeping pace. A policy was adopted by the College of Literature, Science, and the Arts of utilizing salaried Museum staff members in teaching capacities to meet the growing demands. The receipt of academic titles by these Museum members not only gave them the opportunity to teach openly and to develop their own courses, but also the "magic" of these titles for the first time made them eligible for full membership in the academic community and for some very valuable academic privileges and benefits. This stop-gap measure, however, did set a precedent, and all members of the Museum curatorial staff added subsequently have immediately received teaching titles and faculty privileges.

The brief period between about 1943 and 1950 was one of exceedingly rapid development, if not complete transformation, in the program in anthropology at Michigan. White finally attained full professorship in 1943 and, in 1944, was appointed chairman of the department, after serving for many years more or less officially as "acting chairman." In 1945, the first formal departmental staff meetings were convened, with White, Titiev, Griffin, and Jones in attendance. For a brief time after Emerson F. Greenman of the Museum staff was given academic title in 1946, at departmental staff meetings, the Museum staff outnumbered that of the department and held the potential for out-voting them, but this possibility was never exercised. In these early departmental staff meetings, Griffin first came into the formal position of exerting influence on the teaching program in anthropology, and a prominent item of business at these meetings became that of strengthening the graduate program and looking forward to the offering of the doctorate.

In the next few years, accretions to the teaching staff were rapid. Albert C. Spaulding, who joined the Museum staff in 1947, immediately was given a teaching title. Richard K. Beardsley in 1947 and Frederick P. Thieme in 1949 joined the departmental staff. Horace N. Miner, holder of a doctorate in social anthropology, became a member of the Department of Sociology and was given joint title in anthropology, and his courses were cross-listed in anthropology. Kenneth L. Pike of the Linguistics Department also began to offer courses that were cross-listed and suitable for anthropologists. Both Miner and Pike attended staff meetings and assisted in the development of the graduate program. With this amplification and diversity achieved, candidates for the doctoral degree were accepted and encouraged.

William G. Haag gave the system something of a trial run, as he received a doctorate in a combined field of zoology and anthropology. Much of his study here was in anthropology, but the chairman of his committee was William H. Burt, Curator of Mammalogy in the Museum of Zoology. Haag prepared his dissertation on identification and interpretation of dog remains from archaelogical sites. Griffin was a member of the committee, his first participation on a doctoral committee. In 1951, almost simultaneously the first two doctorates in anthropology were conferred. One of these was to William H. Sears in Eastern archaeology, with Griffin as chairman, the other to Robert Anderson in Plains ethnography with White as chairman. Things have progressed from this meager beginning—in the next quarter century (to 1975) approximately one hundred doctorates have been granted in anthropology.

Beginning in 1934, the University of Chicago, under the direction of Cole, had carried out a massive seven-year archaeological program centered at the large Kincaid site situated along the Ohio River near its juncture with the Tennessee River (Cole 1951). This effort, which had been virtually completed, tapered off during the war and was not resumed afterward. Cole, who remained as almost the sole survivor of his earlier programs and of this particular project, was faced at this point with two sobering things. First of all, there was the mountain of notebooks and data from the Kincaid project that needed to be converted into a published final report. Secondly, he was to retire in 1947. Faced with these preoccupations, he did not reinstitute an active field program, and there was a slackening of action in Midwestern archaeology at Chicago. Precisely at this time, Michigan was accelerating its graduate program and welcoming doctoral candidates rather eagerly. Consequently, Michigan began to take up some of the slack and, through the next few years, became a primary training center in Eastern archaeology. There was even some migration of students from Chicago to Michigan. Griffin to a large degree replaced his former mentor as a magnet, and, during the next quarter of a century, served as chairman of approximately thirty-five doctoral committees in archaeology, a large portion of which involved specialization of the candidate in archaeology of the eastern United States. Many recipients of these degrees are professionally established in institutions within the area and have been a major force in furthering archaeology in the region.

The retirement of Cole had additional repercussions for Griffin. Fred Eggan and Griffin got together in 1946 to prepare a tentative outline of a volume to be published in honor of Cole, and the task of organizing and editing the book fell to Griffin. The resulting massive product *Archeology of Eastern United States* (Griffin 1952), which contains almost 400 pages and 200 illustrations, remains the most complete single source on this area. Chapters were contributed by 27 authors, all but one of which (Carl E. Guthe) were former students of Cole. The chapters cover the subareal and topical specializations of the authors. Griffin himself authored three chapters, one of which, "Culture Periods in Eastern United States Archeology," has remained particularly durable. An indication of the reception of the volume at the time is that it received a then unprecedented and since unequalled sixteen-page review in *American Antiquity* (Ford *et al.* 1953) with fourteen participating reviewers. Also, it may be speculated that the production of this volume provided a large increment of influence toward the inclusion of Griffin's biography in *Who's Who in America* (Marquis 1953). At least the timing is highly suggestive.

When Guthe left the University in 1944, Griffin inherited not only the titles and responsibilities of the directorship of the Museum and of the curatorship of the Division of Archaeology, but also a supervisory relationship with the staff of the three other divisions and their programs. Mrs. Kamer Aga-Oglu, Curator of the Division of the Orient, was pursuing a research program concerned chiefly with the study of Chinese trade ceramics from sites in the Philippines. Volney H. Jones, although titled Curator of the Division of Ethnology, also was operating the Ethnobotanical Laboratory. Emerson F. Greenman, Curator of the Division of the Great Lakes, had responsibility for prosecuting a field program in Michigan archaeology and the western Great Lakes area in general and for serving as a liason with amateur archaeologists and their organizations. These programs all were continued under these individuals for the next few decades until retirement of the curators.

Guthe himself had not engaged in field archaeology during his regime, for, as noted previously, his major concerns had been in administrative duties and promotional activities. The assignment that he gave Griffin also did not include excavation. Thus, from 1935, when he returned to the Museum, Greenman was the only archaeologist on the staff who was carrying out a program of field archaeology, and his

JAMES BENNETT GRIFFIN, ARCHAEOLOGIST

commitment was restricted geographically. On assuming the directorship, Griffin immediately took steps to enlarge the scope and range of
outdoor archaeology, beginning a trend that has continued to the
present. As of 1975, the Museum has six curators whose primary
responsibility is archaeology and who are engaged in programs on
several continents.

Albert C. Spaulding was added to the staff of the archaeology
division in 1947 and, at about this same time, Griffin became involved
in field archaeology. For the next fourteen years, they generally
worked together as a team in initiating and supervising surveys and
excavations. Their efforts were confined to the Eastern area, with the
exception of Spaulding's excavations in the Aleutian Islands (Spaulding 1962). Projects were carried out in Pennsylvania, Michigan, and
Illinois, and a five-year program was pursued in the Mississippi Valley
from the St. Louis area southward in Missouri, Illinois, Arkansas,
Mississippi, and Louisiana. Following Spaulding's resignation in 1961,
Griffin initiated two large projects himself, one at the Norton Mounds
at Grand Rapids, Michigan, and another over an eight-year period at
and around the Turner–Snodgrass sites in southern Missouri. An
exceedingly vigorous program also was carried out in Michigan by
James E. Fitting, who succeeded Greenman, with active field programs taking place particularly in 1964 to 1968 (Fitting 1970).

These surveys and excavations have had an important training
aspect, for, in all of them, students from the university and other
institutions have participated in large numbers. They have served not
only as "shovel hands," for more advanced students have been given
considerable responsibility in the supervision of sites or of some
topical aspect of the program. Not only was Greenman assisted by
students in all of his field projects, but he also operated a field school
from 1938 to 1953 under the joint sponsorship of the University
Summer Session and the Museum. This was located near Killarney,
Ontario, in connection with investigations of early beach-level sites in
that area. Griffin (1974:273) has presented an impressive list of
professional anthropologists who received a portion of their training
with Greenman. The policy of student participation has continued not
only in the program in North America, but also in projects instituted
on other continents. The data from the field and from follow-up
laboratory studies have constituted the basis for numerous doctoral
dissertations.

Michigan's archaeological program received great impetus in 1950
with the establishment of a radiocarbon laboratory on the campus.
The method of radiocarbon dating had been developed at the University of Chicago by Willard F. Libby and his associates, and the
machine there began to issue dates in 1949. The second radiocarbon

machine to come into operation was that built at Michigan by H. R. Crane of the Department of Physics. This originally was modeled on the Chicago machine, but, almost immediately, Crane began to make revisions. This machine operated in what was designated by the cumbersome name "University of Michigan Memorial–Phoenix Project Radiocarbon Laboratory." Operation began in 1950 and continued for the next twenty years before being shut down. During much of that time, two machines actually were in operation. Approximately 2500 dates were derived and issued in fifteen lists of dates published between 1956 and 1972. The first list was authored only by Crane (1956), but the other fourteen were coauthored by Crane and Griffin. The last (Crane and Griffin 1972) presents some history of the project and provides citations of some lists of dates.

Crane and his associates actually operated the machines, but a Radiocarbon Curatorial Committee was appointed to receive and record the materials and to establish priorities of routing to the machine. The members of the committee were selected from the various natural science units of the university, botany, geology, paleontology, natural resources, and archaeology. Griffin was appointed chairman of this committee, a position he held throughout the project. Receiving specimens, cataloguing and storing these materials, relaying them to the laboratory, and correspondence were carried out in the Museum of Anthropology under Griffin's supervision. The curatorial committee never operated in a formal manner, as it held no meetings. Instead, it functioned on the basis of personal negotiations between Griffin and the other members.

His position as chairman was highly advantageous for archaeology as it permitted considerable latitude and flexibility in selecting and routing specimens from critical sites, levels, sequences, and associations bearing upon late Pleistocene phenomena. During the first several years, the subsidy of the project was sufficient for operation, so no charge was made for dating; thus it was possible to actively solicit promising specimens. Later, when charges were imposed upon specimens from outside the university, local units as well as those from outside sources that had direct bearing on local research programs still received free service for their materials. Thus, the archaeological program at Michigan had a valuable adjunct, one that contributed enormously to the benefit of archaeology in general.

Griffin was closely involved with the archaeological applications of radiocarbon dating almost from the inception of the method. He was invited to participate in a symposium of archaeologists to appraise the first group of Chicago dates, to ascertain the degree to which they could be reconciled with conventional archaeological interpretations and relative chronology (Griffin 1951). This was at a time before the method was fully proven and when there was still some skepticism concerning it. The following year, Griffin (1952) collated all available radiocarbon dates bearing upon Eastern archaeology and applied them to determining the chronological limits of cultural periods, the first such attempt. By this time, he was able to include not only dates from Chicago but also some from both Michigan and Columbia University. Although, at that early time, he was able to assemble only forty-two pertinent dates, his chronological outline based upon them still holds up very well. He since has made extensive and consistent use of radiocarbon dates in his interpretations of archaeological sequences and the environmental relationships of cultures. Perhaps his most ambitious effort in this respect was his appraisal of the chronology of the Hopewellian culture and related manifestations (Griffin 1958).

A major accomplishment in Eastern archaeology during the decade of 1940–1950 was the providing of greater substance and clearer definition to the early preceramic cultures of the area. The Archaic began to assume more form and cohesion, and the presence of the still earlier Paleo-Indians became ever more definite. In succeeding decades, it has become evident that human occupation of the region has been of several thousand years duration, back to the time of waning glacial activity. This demonstrated presence of man at a time when natural conditions were considerably different from those of the present raised a whole new set of questions concerning the interrelationships of man and changing environments. Technical approaches involving several disciplines were mustered to attack these problems. One was pollen stratigraphy, reflecting post-glacial vegetational succession from which climatic conditions can be inferred. At about this same time, extensive refinements were being made in glacial geology involving interpretations of sea levels and lake levels, drainage systems, fossil beaches, clay varves, and glacially derived land forms. Progress also was rapid in paleontology, particularly concerning the times of extinctions of elements of the late Pleistocene fauna with which man was contemporaneous. Providentially, radiocarbon dating had come along at just the right time to provide a secure chronological framework of sufficiently long duration to encompass these phenomena and to enable comparisons to be made with parallel natural events around the world.

Working in cooperation with practitioners of these various sciences, Griffin developed a rather high level of sophistication in applications of these complex data to studies of correlations of culture and changing environments. He held membership and participated actively in the American Quarternary Association (serving as secretary) and in the less formal Friends of the Pleistocene. In the early 1950s, he collaborated with James H. Zumberge (glacial geology) and Pierre Dansereau (plant ecology) in establishing a very successful graduate-level seminar, the "Quaternary Seminar," which has continued to the present. He has utilized data from these various approaches in an array of publications illuminating paleoecology of the period of transition from the late Pleistocene into the early Recent. His most exhaustive and definitive paper on this subject seems to be his "Late Quaternary Prehistory in the Northeastern Woodlands" (Griffin 1965).

With the filling in of these earlier periods, a continuity of human occupation for at least a twelve thousand year period was established for the Eastern area. In many localities, the cultural record can be shown to have continued up to the present through the occurrence of European trade goods in sites. And further, by weighing such factors as typology, geography, history, and traditions, reasonable ethnohistorical assumptions can be made as to continuities from the aboriginal period into still extant language groups and tribes. Griffin began to cope with these problems early in his career during his research on the Fort Ancient culture. His interest continued and, through the years, he has made a number of reasoned proposals, particularly concerning the archaeological antecedents of several Siouan-speaking groups.

With this long continuity established and cultural entities and complexes falling into place within it, major emphasis could be transferred from problems of description and classification to those of the processes and dynamics that induced interactions and changes. Many concerns along these lines were foreshadowed in Griffin's formulation in 1952, in which he spoke in terms of environmental effects on culture, changing subsistence patterns, nature and size of social groups, village size and locations, population fluctuations, technology and functions of tools, trade routes, and external influences on the Eastern area (Griffin 1952:352–364). These interests in explanation reflected there have continued and expanded especially in the areas of settlement patterns (Griffin 1956) and reactions of culture to climatic changes (Griffin 1960, 1961, 1967).

A problem of long standing in Eastern archaeology has involved the frequent occurrence of artifacts of malleated native copper in sites over much of the area. Although researchers generally have assumed that the supply of copper came chiefly from the western Great Lakes area, there have been many questions as to the precise sources, the technology of extraction, and the time and means of dissemination. Griffin, working in conjunction with Roy W. Drier of Michigan Technological University and George I. Quimby, then of the Field Museum of Natural History, attacked this problem at the source. Griffin participated in expeditions to the Lake Superior region in 1953, 1956, 1957, and 1959. The major resulting publication (Griffin 1961) reports not only the results of their field work in locating pits and their study of technology involved, but also presents a valuable miscellany of data on native copper compiled from a variety of early and sometimes quite obscure sources.

The changing goals of archaeology were implemented in part by the amplification and refinement of techniques, but, conversely, also were instrumental in stimulating new methods and accessories for archaeology. The Wenner-Gren Foundation (then the "Viking Fund") sponsored a seminar in 1950 dealing with "The Excavation, Preservation, and Identification of Archaeological Data." Griffin served as chairman of this conference and compiled and edited a report of the proceedings (Griffin 1951). He also participated in and contributed to the proceedings of a conference sponsored by the National Research Council in 1956, which was concerned with enlisting and utilizing the aid of specialists of various disciplines in identifications of nonartifactual archaeological materials (Taylor 1957).

During the last fifteen years, Griffin has instituted in the Museum a number of projects researching the application of technical approaches to archaeological interpretation. These have involved several curators and many graduate students, but most have been initiated by Griffin himself, and all have received his encouragement and close scrutiny. Among these have been studies of the differentials of natural radioactivity of archaeological materials (Jelinek and Fitting 1965), the adaptation of electronic instruments to archaeological reconnaissance, the interpretation of archaeological pollens, methods and styles of lithic technology (Montet-White 1968), and the identification and interpretation of faunal remains from sites (Cleland 1966). These were added to the ethnobotanical laboratory and the radiocarbon laboratory.

Perhaps the most immediately productive of these studies has been the investigation of applications of neutron activation of trace elements to the solution of archaeological problems. Shortly after this technique became available, Griffin initiated a project in collaboration with Adon A. Gordus of the Department of Chemistry and Gary A. Wright, then a graduate student. Their major success was in tracing the geological sources of obsidian items found in sites far removed from natural sources of that material. Specimens from Hopewellian sites in the Midwest were shown to have had their origins in Yellowstone National Park (Griffin, Gordus, and Wright 1969). Their research was equally valuable in tracing the ancient trade routes by which obsidian moved through the Near East (Wright 1969).

Other questions of long standing in Eastern archaeology have been those relating to cultural interrelationships of that region with other culture areas of North America and of possible extra-American sources of migrations and diffusions which affected North America in general and the East in particular. Answers were slow to materialize. One obstacle to progress had been that of the regionalization of archaeologists and their lack of specific knowledge of areas other than their own. To enhance his knowledge, Griffin began a rather systematic program of "circumnavigation" of the Eastern United States by making extended visits first to Mexico, then to the Southwest, and later to northern Eurasia.

The perennial question of possible cultural relationships between the Eastern U. S. and Mexico had been revived and pointed up in a paper by Phillips (1940) and was given further currency by the elaborate materials suggestive of Mexican origin that were being derived from the Spiro Mound group in Oklahoma. A flurry of remarks and papers resulted from this stimulation. Griffin and Alex D. Krieger teamed up to make investigations of the Huastec area of northeastern Mexico and the Caddoan region of Texas, Oklahoma, and Arkansas. They were joined later in this by Richard S. MacNeish, who worked chiefly in Tamaulipas. Griffin and Krieger attended the Third Roundtable Conference, which was held in Mexico City in 1943, with a theme of relationships between Mexico and areas north of the border. In his report of this conference, Ekholm (1944:443) referred to the contribution of Griffin to these proceedings as being "especially valuable."

Griffin resided in Mexico from February to September 1946, visiting sites in central Mexico, studying museum collections, and conferring with local archaeologists. While there, he served on the faculty of the summer session of the University of Mexico. On his return to the states, he, along with Krieger and MacNeish, participated in the "First Symposium on the Caddoan Archaeological Area," which was held at the University of Oklahoma. Krieger's report (1947) on this conference reflects that interrelationships with Mexico constituted an important aspect and that the presence of Pedro Armillas, Wilfrido Du Solier, and Eduardo Noguera, three archaeologists from Mexico, aided materially in attacking this problem. Several papers resulted from these visits and contacts, among which may be mentioned MacNeish (1947), and Du Solier, Krieger, and Griffin (1947). Griffin's major paper on cultural connections between Mesoamerica and the Eastern United States appeared much later in the *Handbook of Middle American Indians* (Griffin 1967c).

He maintained a valuable relationship with archaeologists in Mexico and was instrumental in bringing Armillas to the University of Michigan in 1960–1961 as a visiting curator and professor. He became a member of the Sociedad Mexicana de Antropologia and of the Pan-American Institute of Geography and History, serving as president of the Committee of Anthropology of the latter in 1954–1958. In

1951, he also participated in a conference held in Jalapa, of which the main concern was the history and anthropology of the state of Vera Cruz.

He also turned his attention to the Southwest, spending the summer of 1952 traveling and studying the archaeology of Texas, New Mexico, Arizona, and Colorado. He also participated in an extended seminar on Southwestern archaeology, which was held in Santa Fe in 1955, and contributed to the proceedings, which were edited by Jennings (1956). Additional familiarity with the archaeology of the western United States was gained during visiting professorships at the University of California (Berkeley) in 1960 and at the University of Colorado in 1962. He has utilized data from these experiences in several papers in making correlations between Western and Eastern archaeological phenomena.

Griffin and his family spent a full year in Europe in 1953–1954 with Paris as the base of operations from which he traveled to several nations including England, Spain, Austria, and Denmark. This journey had been spurred by the growing need for someone with a close knowledge of eastern United States archaeology, and pottery in particular, to make an intensive study of materials from northeastern Eurasia and their contexts. For many years, it had been realized that similarities and analogies existed between the archaeological traditions of these widely separated areas, and particularly in their ceramics. As early as 1937, W. C. McKern had suggested the then very daring hypothesis that the pottery pattern of the eastern U. S. may have had an origin and history independent of other American pottery traditions, and that other considerations of culture and geography qualified the Woodland Pattern as an intrusion from northeast Asia, and thus an appropriate vehicle for conveying the pottery pattern and other elements (McKern 1937).

As archaeological investigations progressed in such places as the northern Plains, Alaska, and Siberia, the geographical gap began to narrow. One exceedingly important ceramic discovery was that excavated by J. H. Giddings at Cape Denbigh in northwestern Alaska. Samples of this large quantity of rather early pottery were submitted to Griffin for study, and, in his report, he noted quite specific stylistic and technical features linking it to both Asiatic and eastern United States traditions (Griffin 1953). This direct involvement in the question of Asiatic–American connections appears to have triggered his studies in Europe, and to have induced a continuing concern with this problem. He maintained his European contacts by attending the 5th Quaternary Congress in Spain in 1957 and served as a delegate to the International Union of Protohistoric and Prehistoric Science meetings in Germany in 1958. His most definitive analysis resulting from his travels, consultations, and studies along these lines was his "Some Prehistoric Connections between Siberia and America" (Griffin 1960).

His interest in the archaeology of Eurasia has continued, but instead of an interest in the specifics of cultural connections, his concerns have moved more in the direction of comparisons of Eurasia and America in such terms as influences of environmental factors, cultural processes, and regularities and convergences that might emerge. His contacts with Eurasia have been maintained directly and indirectly in a number of ways. In 1961, he attended as a delegate the 6th International Association for Quaternary Research in Warsaw, serving as the secretary for this congress. He also spent three months in the U.S.S.R. in 1961–1962 investigating the prehistory of Siberia and adjacent areas in conjunction with A. P. Okladnikov and other Soviet archaeologists. In 1963, he held a Fulbright Lectureship at the University of Copenhagen. Anta Montet-White, formerly a student of Francois Bordes at the University of Bordeaux, while happening to reside in Ann Arbor from about 1960 to 1965, was given facilities and support to apply European methods of lithic analysis to North American materials. Her doctoral dissertation on this subject, although submitted to the University of Bordeaux, was published here in our series (Montet-White 1968). Jean J. F. Perrot, now a member of the French Archaeological Delegation to Iran, in 1966, accepted an invitation to come to Michigan as a visiting professor and curator.

Concurrent with the earlier of those activities, Arthur J. Jelinek joined the staff as a curator in 1961 and embarked on a program of excavations in France, Turkey, and Israel during the years of about 1963–1966. On leaving the Museum, he took with him the large project for excavations of Tabun, Israel, which was conceived and planned here, but later carried out from the University of Arizona. Griffin also instituted and supervised excavations in Europe carried out by graduate students. Sarunas Milisauskas worked in Poland in 1967–1969, and H. Martin Wobst in Yugoslavia in 1970–1971, with Griffin making field inspections of their projects.

On July 1, 1975, Griffin was granted a one-year retirement furlough which carries no obligation of services to the University, and entails the relinquishment of his parlay of active positions as director of the museum, curator of archaeology, chairman of the department of anthropology, and professor of anthropology. Following this year of leave, he will reach full retirement and emeritus status. It has been noted earlier that, when he became director of the Museum just over twenty-nine years ago, there existed four curatorships in the Museum, including the one he held. Three of these curators (archaeology, ethnology, and Great Lakes anthropology) were involved in programs dealing strictly with North America, and only the Division of the

Orient was concerned with extra-American problems. During his directorship, the number of curatorships has more than doubled. All of the four curators who were serving in 1946 when he became director have retired (or, in Griffin's instance, given leave) since 1965. The general development of the University has permitted the establishment of several additional curatorships in recent years. It happens then that, with the beginning of the current fiscal year (1975–1976), all of the curators are persons who have joined the staff within the last decade. Concomitant with the enlargement of the staff, there has been achieved amplification and diversification of activities, leading to what may be referred to as an "internationalization" of the Museum program.

Robert Whallon, Jr., joined the staff in 1966 and, although he had worked earlier in Turkey, while here, he has specialized in European archaeology with excavations in France and Holland, and in the application of analytical techniques to archaeology. Since his staff appointment in 1967, Henry T. Wright has pursued a very active field program in the archaeology of Iran, Iraq, Turkey, Kenya, and Mexico and he at present is working in Madagascar. Karl L. Hutterer, who is in his first year as curator of the Division of the Orient, has had experience in both ethnology and archaeology, particularly in the Philippines, and at present is working in Australia.

Kent V. Flannery came to the University in 1966 with prior experience in Iraq and Iran, but his more recent excavations have been in Latin America. He has led expeditions almost annually to Oaxaca, but also has worked in Peru. Jeffrey R. Parsons, who also received his curatorship in 1966, has divided his fieldwork almost evenly between the Valley of Mexico and Peru with annual expeditions, and has done some survey work in Guatemala.

Work in both the ethnology and the archaeology of North America has been pursued by Richard I. Ford, who received his curatorship in 1969. He has been engaged almost annually in fieldwork in the Southwest, studying Pueblo ethnology in particular. Also, he is in charge of the field and laboratory program in the ethnobotany of North America. Christopher S. Peebles, who joined the curatorial staff in 1974, has done his fieldwork chiefly in the southeastern United States, with a brief stint in Holland, but now assumes also the responsibility for the program in the archaeology of the Great Lakes area, where he has begun fieldwork.

The adding of C. Loring Brace as curator of physical anthropology constitutes a long-delayed victory for Griffin. In the initial establishment of the Museum, provision was made for a division of physical anthropology, but, although collections existed, no formal appointment of a curator was made until that of Brace in 1967. Georg K.

Neumann while here as a visiting scientist did some work with the collections, but, although Griffin was insistent on filling the position, his success was delayed until 1967. The investigations by Brace have been in biological anthropology and especially evolution and osteology, which have carried him to such places as Africa, Australia, Taiwan, and various countries of southeast Asia.

All of the Museum curators hold teaching titles, participate in affairs of the department, and offer courses paralleling their research interests. Throughout the history of relationships between the Museum and the department, all of the courses offered in archaeology have been presented by staff members of the Museum; this practice still is in effect. Presently there are listed about ten lecture courses in archaeology and about a dozen graduate-level seminars, although all of these are not given annually. In addition to these formal classroom courses, considerable teaching is carried out elsewhere. The individualized instruction and experience in "museum methods" and "research and special problems" still draw a large number of students. Participation in expeditions and the follow-up laboratory work constitute an important area of instruction. The supervision of doctoral dissertation research also engages a significant portion of time of the curators.

The present staff and ongoing program constitute a monument to Griffin, since the staff was recruited largely through his influence and the program in research and instruction was developed under his close supervision. When he was placed on leave, these were inherited by Richard I. Ford, who assumed the position of director after serving a few years as associate director. Robert Whallon, Jr., has become associate director. His vacated chairmanship of the department has been filled by Roy A. Rappaport.

Throughout his formal teaching career, Griffin has presented two basic courses almost annually. One of these, "Archaeology of North America," was a lecture course at advanced undergraduate level. On the campus, this always has drawn well, and it was offered several times in the Extension Service program in various cities around the state, where many amateur archaeologists availed themselves of the opportunity to enroll. The other, "Seminar in Archaeology of the Eastern United States," had two prerequisites, graduate standing and permission of the instructor. These made it possible to hand-pick the enrollees and to make this essentially a preprofessional training course. From all accounts, the participants were deluged with visual materials illustrating the minutiae of typology and classification, as well as a detailed introduction to the personnel, history, and politics of the archaeology of the area. Many of the products of this seminar now are ensconced in positions in professional archaeology. In addition to these two courses, he often presented a seminar in the archaeology of the Southwest.

It has been noted earlier that, during his first twelve years on the campus, he was not permitted to teach openly and that he had reached the age of forty years before he received a teaching title. This becomes somewhat ironic when it is observed that his progress since that time has been rapid, that he has served from 1972 to 1975 as chairman of the department that barred him from teaching, and that there have been a number of recognitions of his teaching ability. He has been in demand as a lecturer and visiting professor, serving several universities which have been named already. In addition to those, Florida State University in 1970 and Louisiana State University in 1971 also may be mentioned. His honorary doctorate from Indiana University undoubtedly was in recognition of his teaching as well as his research record. It was highly gratifying to him to be honored by his own university by his selection as the Henry Russell Lecturer for the year 1972, since this lectureship and award are conferred annually on a senior faculty member and are recognized as "the highest honor which the university can bestow" on a member of its faculty.

In addition to his classroom teaching, Griffin has been an enthusiastic and prominent spokesman for archaeology wherever he has gone. Opportunities for the "propogation of the faith" have been in invited lectures, public lectures, conferences, and meetings of various societies. In his annual report of the director of the Museum for 1953–1954, he was able to state that, during his travels in Europe, he had "lectured on North American archaeology at universities and archaeological societies in five European capitals."

He has held memberships and has been a quite active participant in a large number of professional societies and conferences. The scope of these ranges from local, state, and regional, to national and international. In many of these, he has been elected "fellow," has held offices, served on executive committees or other committees, and in other capacities in which he has made his presence felt and in which he has been able to be influential in the guiding of policies and programs. Several of these societies and conferences have been mentioned already in various geographical and topical contexts, so data concerning them need not be repeated here.

While a graduate student, he was elected to Sigma Xi and Phi Sigma societies, serving as president of the local chapter of the latter. On the local university scene, he was elected to the Science Research Club (holding the office of secretary–treasurer) and to the Research Club. It was this latter organization that nominated him for the Henry Russell Lectureship. Among state organizations in which he has been active is the Michigan Academy of Science, Arts, and Letters. On a couple of occasions, he served as chairman of the Anthropology Section, and almost perennially was a member of the nominating committee of that section. Other Michigan organizations in which he has been active are the Michigan Archaeological Society (honorary life member), and the Council of Michigan Archaeology (the presidency of which he has held since 1966).

Among his societies of national scope are the American Anthropological Association (president of Central States Branch, 1948–1949; program chairman of the annual meeting held in New York in 1949), and the American Association for the Advancement of Science (vice-president of Section H in 1953–1954). He was elected a fellow in both of these. It has been mentioned earlier that he was a delegate to the meeting of the International Union of Prehistoric and Protohistoric Sciences in Berlin in 1958, but it also should be on the record that he has served on the Permanent Council of that organization since 1948 and on the Executive Committee during 1962–1967.

Participation by Griffin in various archaeological conferences has been referred to a number of times, but a few additional ones deserve mention. A conference of historic note was the First Conference on the Woodland Pattern, which was held in Chicago in 1941 and to which he was invited as "consultant on pottery." He has been rather regular in attendance of the annual conventions of the Plains Archaeological Conference and usually has presented a paper. He also has attended the Iroquois Conference, particularly in its early formative years, serving as chairman of the Archaeology Section in 1947, and always entered into the discussions and deliberations. From time to time, he has held membership in various state and regional archaeological societies and sometimes has published in issues of their journals.

The whereabouts of one James Bennett Griffin during the late evening of December 28, 1934, is no mystery. He was at the Hotel Roosevelt in Pittsburgh, Pennsylvania, attending the organizational meeting of the Society for American Archaeology. He placed his signature, along with those of thirty other persons, on the constitution that brought about the establishment of that organization (Unsigned 1935). If that society had a category of "charter member," which it does not, he would be qualified to hold that distinction. He has been a member throughout the history of the society, and, of all his memberships, this has claimed his greatest affinity and allegiance. He has been exceedingly active in its affairs and has held almost every office. He was an assistant editor of its journal *American Antiquity* from 1935 through 1946 and an associate editor from then until 1950, a member of the executive committee 1945–1946 and again 1950–1953, became first vice-president in 1945–1946, and president in 1951–1952. He also served on the planning committee in 1944–1945 and as secretary

1952–1954. He has attended practically every annual meeting of the society. It would be difficult to find a year, except when he was out of the country, in which he did not either present a paper, serve as chairman of a section or symposium, act as a discussant, or serve on a committee—or some combination of these. The recent index to *American Antiquity* lists forty-seven contributions by him to that journal, either alone or with co-authors (McCracken 1972:26).

The bibliography of Griffin, which appears in the *Anthropological Papers* volume, speaks for itself; little more needs to be said. It contains over 200 titles of items of varying nature and length: books, monographs, chapters within books, publications edited, articles, book reviews, notes and commentaries, and obituaries. This accomplishment is all the more remarkable when one considers the administrative and teaching load he has carried, and the generosity with which he has given of his time to staff, students, and visitors.

Throughout his directorship, he has shown great concern for the progress and success of the publishing program of the Museum. Prior to and during his early directorship, the Museum had issued only one series, *The Occasional Contributions*. Between 1932 and 1956, only sixteen numbers of this series had appeared, and none has been issued since. In recent years, there has been great acceleration of publication. The *Anthropological Papers* series, which was established in 1949, now in 1975 has reached number sixty, and all but thirteen of these monographs have been issued since 1960. Recently two additional series have been launched. The *Memoirs* are designed to accommodate longer monographs, and the title of the *Technical Reports* is self-explanatory. Seven of the former and three of the latter have been issued. This expansion of publication has served to provide greater opportunity for staff, advanced students, and associates of the Museum to reach print, and has placed the Museum in a very favorable position in library exchange.

In his "advertisement" statement, which appears on the inside of the front cover of these volumes, Griffin identifies himself only as director of the Museum, and he has claimed publicly no other relationship to these series. In actuality, however, he has functioned as both supervising editor and business manager, with only the technical editing and bookkeeping delegated to others. He has exerted a great effort in decisions as to acceptance and solicitation of items for publication, in building up the publication fund, and in promoting the series.

During the almost three decades of his directorship, Griffin has set an example to his staff in industriousness, availability, and productivity. In his earlier years at the Museum, the staff was expected to work a forty-three-hour week of five eight-hour days, and from 9 A.M. until noon on Saturday; this on a twelve-month basis. This requirement posed no problem to him, since actually he worked those hours and, in addition, innumerable evenings, "holidays," and weekends. Although such rigid hours were relaxed long ago, he continues to be among the first to arrive and the last to leave, and he still can be found working extra hours on weekends and holidays. His one-month annual "vacations" generally have been spent in travel in pursuit of archaeology. This routine has not been interrupted by sabbatical leaves, for the staff of the Museum has not been classified among those to which that privilege is extended. Any computation of the total sum of the hours he has worked during his forty-two years here would yield a figure of staggering proportions. He always has preferred to deal directly person to person, and toward this end has made himself readily accessible. He usually has worked with his door open, allowing easy freedom of approach by staff, students, and visitors. His example has been instrumental in establishing such an "open-door policy" within the Museum which generally has been followed by the curatorial staff.

In reviewing Griffin's career, it becomes apparent that a major aspect has been in his bringing to bear upon archaeology the data derived by other disciplines, and applying these to the development of archaeology as a synthesizing and explanatory field. The importance of such an approach has been emphasized by Grahame Clark in a recent volume (Clark 1968:17–18):

> Much of the fascination of archaeology indeed resides in its many-sidedness. One can safely say that there are few faculties, experiences, or fields of special knowledge that cannot contribute to or are not stimulated by its pursuit.

And further:

> The fruitful practice of archaeology involves to a unique degree an ability and a willingness to comprehend the aims, methods, and potentialities of fellow-workers in the most diverse branches of both humanistic and scientific study.

Whether or not Griffin's reactions to archaeology have been precisely those of Clark's word "fascination," it is evident that he found his chosen profession to be quite absorbing and rewarding. Beyond his family and vocation, he seemed to have required and to have developed few other sustained interests and diversions. Perhaps travel might be suggested in this connection, but whatever enjoyment he may have derived from that source was an extra bonus, for his journeys were primarily for purposes of archaeological investigations.

One major interest that has persisted since at least his high school days has been that of sports. He was a member of the Oak Park high school swimming team, and that interest carried on into his years at the University of Chicago, where he participated on the varsity team in several collegiate swimming meets. While resident in Oak Park, he participated in church league basketball, and, after his arrival in Ann Arbor, has shown himself to be a pretty fair softball pitcher, as has been demonstrated in his performances in intramural competition, and more especially in the impromptu games played on anthropology picnics. Although of late his participation has diminished, he remains an avid and well-informed sports fan, with a continuation of his loyalties to the Chicago Cubs baseball club and just about anything that Michigan may be doing in athletics. One occasion he will always remember is his attendance of a dual track meet between Michigan and Ohio State University in June 1934 when he saw the great Jesse Owens break three world records and tie another, this within the time span of a couple of hours.

In connection with his long career, he has accumulated and built up a number of valuable resources. A major one of these is his large and comprehensive personal library. In addition to the more conventional sets and series, there are files of reprints that are exceedingly valuable, and issues of sometimes obscure and ephemeral journals, as well as other rare items. His voluminous correspondence files, along with his photograph collection, offer a cross section of the history of Eastern archaeology. He has seen personally to the building up of a slide collection numbering nearly 15,000 slides. In addition are miscellaneous notebooks, card indexes, and the original files of the Ceramic Repository, which were referred to earlier. Augmenting these more tangible and concrete things are his remarkably detailed memory of the history of archaeology in which he has participated, the events, developments, personalities, motivations, and anecdotes which are involved in this largely unwritten history.

Griffin has received just about every recognition and honor to which one occupying his particular niche could aspire. Several of these have been mentioned previously. Another quite recent one has been his election in 1973 as a Special Honorary Fellow of the Asiatic Society of Bengal (Calcutta). Very gratifying was his election in 1968 to the National Academy of Sciences, for membership in that organization is "in recognition of distinguished and continuing achievement in original research." But his most cherished honor seems to have been the receipt of the Viking Fund Award and Medal which was conferred on him in 1957, because he was chosen by a panel of his peers within the Society for American Archaeology "in recognition of his outstanding work in archaeology." It seems particularly appropriate that one of his earlier "unofficial" students read the citation at the presentation of this award. George I. Quimby, as president of the Society for American Archaeology at the time, had this pleasant task. The full text of the citation is quoted in Quimby's section of the present volume.

Apparently Griffin has no present intention of resting on these very impressive laurels. Following the granting of his retirement furlough, he has been provided with space and facilities for himself, his library and files, and the other tools of his trade. He continues to work with no perceptible diminution of interest, motivation, and pace.

References

Clark, Grahame
    1968   *Archaeology and society.* (University Paperback, 3rd reprinting). London: Methuen.

Cleland, Charles E.
    1966   The prehistoric animal ecology and ethnozoology of the Upper Great Lakes Region. University of Michigan, Museum of Anthropology, *Anthropological Papers* no. 29.

Cole, Fay-Cooper, and Thorne Deuel
    1937   *Rediscovering Illinois: Archaeological explorations around Fulton County.* Chicago: University of Chicago Press.

Cole, Fay-Cooper, and others
    1951   *Kincaid, a prehistoric Illinois metropolis.* Chicago: University of Chicago Press.

Corlett, William T.
    1935   *The medicine-man of the American Indian and his cultural background.* Springfield and Baltimore: Charles C. Thomas.

Crane, H. R.
    1956   University of Michigan radiocarbon dates, I. *Science* **124**(3224):664–672.

Crane, H. R., and James B. Griffin
    1972   University of Michigan radiocarbon dates, XV. *Radiocarbon* **14**(1):195–222.

Deuel, Thorne
    1935   Basic cultures of the Mississippi Valley. *American Anthropologist* **37**(3):429–445.

Du Solier, Wilfrido, Alex D. Krieger, and James B. Griffin
    1947   The archaeological zone of Buena Vista, Huaxcama, San Luis Potosi, Mexico. *American Antiquity* **13**(1):15–32.

Ekholm, Gordon F.
    1944   The Third Roundtable Conference. *American Antiquity* **9**(4):440–444.

Fitting, James E.
    1970   *The archaeology of Michigan, a guide to the prehistory of the Great Lakes region.* Garden City, N.Y.: Natural History Press.

Ford, James A., and Gordon R. Willey
    1941   An interpretation of the prehistory of the eastern United States. *American Anthropologist* **43**(3):325–363.

Ford, James A., and others
    1953   Review of James B. Griffin (editor), *Archeology of eastern United States.* *American Antiquity* **19**(2):172–190.

Griffin, James B.
    1930   Mortuary customs in the western half of the Northeast Woodland area. Master's thesis, University of Chicago.

1931   The Athens excavations. Society for Pennsylvania Archaeology, *Bulletin*
       2(2):3.

1934   Archaeological remains in Adams County, Illinois. *Illinois State Academy of
       Science* **2**(2):97–99.

1935   An analysis of the Fort Ancient culture. Ceramic Repository for the Eastern
       United States, *Notes* no. 1. Ann Arbor, Mich.

1936   The cultural significance of the ceramic remains from the Norris Basin.
       Doctoral dissertation, University of Michigan.

1938   The ceramic remains from Norris Basin, Tennessee. In *An archaeological
       survey of the Norris Basin in eastern Tennessee*, edited by W. S. Webb. Bureau
       of American Ethnology, *Bulletin* 118. Pp. 253–358.

1939   Report on the ceramics of Wheeler Basin. In *An archaeological survey of
       Wheeler Basin on the Tennessee River in northern Alabama*, edited by W. S.
       Webb. Bureau of American Ethnology, *Bulletin* 122. Pp. 127–165.

1943   *The Fort Ancient Aspect, its cultural and chronological position in Mississippi
       Valley archaeology.* Ann Arbor: University of Michigan Press.

1946   Cultural change and continuity in eastern United States archaeology. In *Man
       in Northeastern North America*, edited by Frederick Johnson. Robert S.
       Peabody Foundation for Archaeology, *Papers* vol. 35. Pp. 37–95.

1951a Essays in archaeological methods, proceedings of a conference held under the
       auspices of the Viking Fund. University of Michigan, Museum of Anthropol-
       ogy, *Anthropological Papers* no. 8.

1951b Some Adena and Hopewell radiocarbon dates. In *Radiocarbon dating*, edited
       by Frederick Johnson. Society for American Archaeology, *Memoir* no. 8. Pp.
       26–29.

1952   *Archeology of eastern United States.* Chicago: University of Chicago Press.
       (editor and compiler)

1953   A preliminary statement on the pottery from Cape Denbigh, Alaska. In *Asia
       and North America, Transpacific Contacts*, assembled by M. W. Smith.
       Society for American Archaeology, *Memoir* no. 9. Pp. 40–42.

1955   Review of the Walam Olum or Red Score. Indiana Historical Society, *Indiana
       Magazine of History* **51**(1):59–65.

1956   The Museum of Anthropology. Item in *The University of Michigan, an
       encyclopedic survey*, Part 8, edited by W. A. Donnelly. Ann Arbor: University
       of Michigan Press. Pp. 1476–1481.

1956   Prehistoric settlement patterns in the northern Mississippi Valley and Upper
       Great Lakes. Item in *Prehistoric settlement patterns in the New World*, edited
       by G. R. Willey. *Viking Fund Publications in Anthropology* no. 23. Pp. 63–71.

1958   The chronological position of the Hopewellian Culture in the eastern United
       States. University of Michigan, Museum of Anthropology, *Anthropological
       Papers* no. 12.

1959   The pursuit of archeology in the United States. *American Anthropologist*
       61(3):379–389.

1960   Climatic change: A contributory cause of the growth and decline of northern
       Hopewellian Culture. *Wisconsin Archeologist* **41**(1):21–33.

1960   Some prehistoric connections between Siberia and America. *Science*
       131(3403):801–812.

1961   North America: Prehistory and archaeology. *Encyclopaedia Brittanica*. Vol.
       16:506–513. Chicago: Encyclopaedia Brittanica, Inc.

1961   Lake Superior copper and the Indians; miscellaneous studies of Great Lakes
       prehistory. University of Michigan, Museum of Anthropology, *Anthropologi-
       cal Papers* no. 17. (editor and contributor)

1961 Some correlations of climatic and cultural change in eastern North American prehistory. *New York Academy of Science Annals* **95**(1):710–717.

1965 Late Quaternary prehistory in the Northeastern Woodlands. In *The Quaternary of the United States*, edited by H. E. Wright & D. G. Frey. Princeton: Princeton University Press.

1967a Climatic change in American prehistory. Item in *Encyclopedia of Atmospheric Sciences and Astrogeology*. Encyclopedia of Earth Sciences Series, vol. 2, edited by R. W. Fairbridge. New York: Reinhold Publishing, Pp. 169–171.

1967b Eastern North American archaeology: A summary. *Science* **156**(3772):175–191.

1967c Mesoamerica and the eastern United States in prehistoric times. Section in *Handbook of Middle American Indians*. Vol. 4 (Archaeological Frontiers and External Connections). Austin: University of Texas Press. Pp. 111–131.

1971 A commentary on an unusual research program in anthropology. Section in *Dedication program, Glenn A. Black Laboratory of Archaeology, Indiana University* (April 21, 1971). Bloomington: Indiana University Publications. Pp. 9–26.

1974 Emerson F. Greenman, 1895–1973. *American Antiquity* **39**(2):271–273.

1969 Identification of sources of Hopewellian obsidian in the Middle West. *American Antiquity* **34**(1):1–14. (With Adon A. Gordus and Gary A. Wright)

Guthe, Carl E.
1928 A method of ceramic description. Michigan Academy of Science, Arts, and Letters, *Papers*, vol. 8 (1927), pp. 23–29.

1930 The Committee on State Archaeological Surveys of the Division of Anthropology and Psychology, National Research Council. International Congress of Americanists, Proceedings of the 23rd Congress (New York 1927), pp. 52–59.

1940 Sequences of culture in the Eastern United States. In *The Maya and their neighbors*, edited by C. L. Hay and others. New York: Appleton. Pp. 368–374.

1952 Twenty-five years of archeology in the eastern United States. In *Archeology of eastern United States*, edited by J. B. Griffin. Chicago: University of Chicago Press. Pp. 1–12.

Haag, William G.
1961 Twenty-five years of eastern archaeology. *American Antiquity* **27**(1):16–23.

Jelinek, Arthur J., and James E. Fitting (editors)
1965 Studies in the natural radioactivity of prehistoric materials. University of Michigan, Museum of Anthropology, *Anthropological Papers* no. 25.

Jennings, Jesse D. (editor)
1956 The American Southwest: A problem in cultural isolation. Society for American Archaeology, *Memoir* no. 11.

Krieger, Alex D.
1947 The first symposium on the Caddo archaeological area. *American Antiquity* **12**(3):198–207.

Lilly, Eli
1937 *Prehistoric antiquities of Indiana.* Indianapolis: Indiana Historical Society.

MacNeish, Richard S.
1947 A preliminary report on coastal Tamaulipas, Mexico. *American Antiquity* **13**(1):1–15.

A. N. Marquis Co.
1953 *Who's who in America.* Vol. 27, 1952–1953. Chicago: A. N. Marquis.

McCracken, Claudia H. (compiler)
1972 Index, vols. 1–30 (of American Antiquity). *American Antiquity* **37**(3), Part 2.

McKern, W. C.
 1937   An hypothesis for the Asiatic origin of the Woodland Culture pattern. *American Antiquity* 3(2):138–143.
 1939   The Midwestern taxonomic method as an aid to archaeological culture study. *American Antiquity* 4(4):301–313.

March, Benjamin, and Carl E. Guthe
 1934   Standards of pottery description. University of Michigan, Museum of Anthropology, *Occasional Contributions* no. 3.

Montet-White, Anta
 1968   The lithic industries of the Illinois Valley in the Early and Middle Woodland Period. University of Michigan, Museum of Anthropology, *Anthropological Papers* no. 35.

Phillips, Philip
 1940   Middle American influences on the archaeology of the southeastern United States. In *The Maya and their neighbors*, edited by C. L. Hay and others. New York: Appleton. Pp. 349–367.

Phillips, Philip, James A. Ford, and James B. Griffin
 1951   Archaeological survey in the lower Mississippi alluvial valley, 1940–1947. Peabody Museum of Archaeology and Ethnology, Harvard University, *Papers*, vol. 25.

Ritchie, William A.
 1944   The Pre-Iroquoian occupation of New York State. Rochester Museum of Arts and Sciences, *Memoir* no. 1.

Ruthven, Alexander G.
 1931   *A naturalist in a university museum*. Ann Arbor: privately printed.

Spaulding, Albert C.
 1962   Archaeological investigations on Agattu, Aleutian Islands. University of Michigan, Museum of Anthropology, *Anthropological Papers* no. 18.

Taylor, Walter W. (editor)
 1957   The identification of non-artifactual archaeological materials. National Academy of Sciences—National Research Council, Publication 565.

Unsigned
 1935   The Society for American Archaeology organization meeting. *American Antiquity* 1(2):141–146. (Although the authorship of this report is not indicated, I can attest that it was prepared by Carl E. Guthe from shorthand notes made at the meeting by Mrs. Dorothy L. Schulte, secretary to the chairman of the Committee on State Archaeological Surveys.)
 1958   James B. Griffin, 1957 Viking Fund Medalist in Archaeology (Chosen by the Society for American Archaeology). *American Antiquity* 23(4):419.

"Walam Olum"
 1954   *Walam Olum or Red Score; the migration legend of the Lenni Lenape or Delaware Indians: A new translation, interpreted by linguistic, historial, archaeological, ethnological, and physical anthropological studies.* Indianapolis: Indiana Historical Society.

Willey, Gordon R.
 1969   James Alfred Ford, 1911–1968. *American Antiquity* 34(1):62–71.

Willey, Gordon R., and Jeremy A. Sabloff
 1974   *A history of American archaeology*. San Francisco: W. H. Freeman.

Wright, Gary A.
 1969   Obsidian analysis and prehistoric Near Eastern trade. University of Michigan, Museum of Anthropology, *Anthropological Papers* no. 37.

I

Considerations of Variability in the Archaeological Record

1

Locational Analysis in the Prehistory of Northeast Ohio

David S. Brose

Introduction

In recent years, a number of methodological and theoretical developments in the fields of locational geography, quantitative ecology, and statistical geology (Parsons 1972) have been incorporated into the study of prehistoric settlement patterns specifically and of archaeology in general. This has led to an increasing awareness of the nature of the archaeological data from which such studies are generated, and the need to control the methods of survey and sampling (Binford 1964; Mueller 1974). In many cases, the increasingly sophisticated methodology appears to have become an end in itself rather than a means to understanding prehistoric culture. This chapter represents an attempt to utilize several of these quantitative techniques as a means to generate testable, but more or less qualitative, hypotheses in an anthropological framework.

Prior Research Models

After moving to Cleveland in 1968, my attention was drawn to the Whittlesey focus. Previous descriptions of this complex (Greenman

3

1935a, b, 1937, 1939; Morgan and Ellis 1943) had concentrated upon trait lists designed to distinguish ethnic identity or to establish taxonomic boundaries. Fitting's (1964) ceramic seriation of major sites provided some temporal depth, but relationships south to Fort Ancient (Griffin 1943), or along the lake shore, were confused.

With National Science Foundation support (GS-3062) from 1969 through 1971, I directed excavations at the South Park site (Brose 1973) and the Greenwood village complex on the Cuyahoga River, and conducted salvage and test excavations at several disturbed sites on the Black, Cuyahoga, Chagrin, Rocky, Grand, and Conneaut Rivers across northeast Ohio (Brose n.d. a, b). As a result of these efforts, several functional site types were distinguished within specified physiographic zones. The site size functions were characterized following the criteria outlined in Brose and Essenpreis (1973: 69–70) and Ritchie and Funk (1973).

Large sites, many with evidence of bottomland occupation, existed from 5 to 12 miles upstream from Lake Erie on promontories overlooking major river valleys. Interspersed between these, farther upstream and along the lower 5 miles of these rivers, were smaller sites with no evidence of alluvial plain utilization. Near the mouths and from 1 to 3 miles upstream along the Black, Rocky, Cuyahoga, Chagrin, and Conneaut were small villages on ridges and promontories with no evidence of bottomland occupation.

Testing indicated the upstream sites with alluvial plain occupation were agricultural villages. Many components from similarly located sites without alluvial plain utilization also appeared to be small agricultural villages. The small sites in both the lower and upper river areas represented specialized seasonal extractive sites, primarily hunting stations or hunting and butchering base camps. The components of those sites located along the lake plain which had been tested or excavated represented small agricultural villages, fishing villages of all sizes, or small seasonal camps used for either fishing and migratory waterfowl collection or (upstream) small seasonal hunting stations.

Radiocarbon dates for several stratified sites throughout the region confirmed a rough ceramic periodization. This led to a diachronic model of Whittlesey settlement–subsistence patterns (Brose 1973: 38–39) showing a trend toward larger, more focused agricultural sedentism similar to Iroquoian patterns farther east (Ritchie 1969). To test hypotheses of specific ecological site-function locations for sequent periods, and to avoid bias resulting from data derived from a limited number of potential site locations, a thorough regional survey was organized and implemented as a statistically valid sampling strategy (Binford 1964). Quite clearly, the traditional archaeological surveys (cf. Brose and Essenpreis 1973) could not utilize non-site areas to test predictive hypotheses derived from the model. Previous analyses suggested a model in which differing ecotones were selected for specific site locations at particular periods, but stressing such ecological permutations in a sampling strategy would introduce both circularity and interdependence into the testing of hypotheses (cf. Plog and Hill 1971). It was, therefore, felt that survey strategy should be designed to evaluate negative data, to test all potential ecological site catchment areas (Jarman, Vita-Finzi, and Higgs 1972; Higgs and Vita-Finzi 1972), and statistically to control all quantifiable data recovered. Furthermore, the research strategy should be sufficiently unbiased to provide a model for evaluating traditional survey results yet not be weighted toward extraneous considerations (for example, Mueller 1974). With the support of the National Science Foundation (GS-28905), the following research design was begun during the spring of 1971 and continued through the fall of 1972.

Survey Methodology

Following methods suggested by Haggett (1965, 1968), an unaligned random sampling scheme—stratified by topographic relief, dominant floral communities, ranked drainage systems, winter and summer climatic isoclines, soils, and surface geology—was employed to create a number of microenvironmental zones. The variables utilized are presented in Table 1.1. Sampling areas circumscribed about the points (located by Monte-Carlo methods within the microenvironmental zones) were circular and contained approximately 270 acres. The ecological areas isolated were normalized to deal with variations in size, relative occurrence, and orientation. All reference is to such standardized areas. In the portions of the 7-county area investigated, a total of more than 500 such microenvironmental areas were created by this method. On the basis of previous Late Woodland sites located in these areas, it was estimated that, for any stratum, a 15% areal coverage by surface collection would yield a sample of artifacts representing the population from which they are drawn, with accuracy limits of $\pm 10\%$ and confidence limits of .10. Each such area was tested by an unaligned, random sampling system, stratified to deal with inaccessible areas. Although this seemed to weaken rigid statistical validity of such intra-areal sampling, the introduced bias could be evaluated critically.

After these procedures were carried out, the location of the minimal number of excavation units required for recovering a sample of artifactual and ecological data from a given sample area was determined by an unaligned stratified sampling scheme in the absence of

Table 1.1 Ranked Variables Survey Indices: Northeast Ohio

A. *Topography*

1 Lake plain
2 Alluvial bottomland
3 Secondary floodplain
4 Steep river bluff
5 Well-drained plateau
6 Poorly dissected interfluvial plateau
7 Rolling uplands

B. *Floral community*[a]

1 Marsh and fen
2 Elm–ash swamp
3 Spagnum bog
4 Oak openings
5 Mixed oak forest
6 Mixed mesophytic forest
7 Beech–maple climax

C. *Surface geomorphology*[b]

1 Beach ridge: coarse poorly sorted sands and gravels, cross-bedded
2 Lake deposit: fine to coarse well-sorted sands
3 Alluvium: fine to medium sandy silts and silty clays
4 Sand-gravel outwash: coarse sands and gravels
5 Glacial morain: poorly sorted sands, clay, gravels, cobbles
6 Glacial outwash plains: poorly sorted sands, gravels or bedded silts, clays, sands, and gravels
7 Kame, kettle, esker: poorly sorted gravel, clay, and sands

D. *Weighted annual temperatures*[c]

1 48°–49° F.
2 49°–50° F.
3 50°–51° F.
4 51°–52° F.
5 52°–53° F.

E. *Weighted annual precipitation*[c]

1 <30″
2 >30″–31″
3 >31″–32″
4 >32″–33″
5 >33″–34″
6 >34″–35″
7 >35″–36″
8 >36″

---

[a] After Gordon (1966, 1969).
[b] After White (1969), Rau (1968), and Hall (n.d.).
[c] U.S. Department of Agriculture (1941).

6

previous information about that site. Based on the South Park and Greenwood complex excavations (Brose 1973, n.d. b) and the testing at Reeve and Fairport Harbor, it was estimated that the excavation of seven 5-by-5-ft. units at each site would yield representative artifact samples with an accuracy limit of $\pm 10\%$ (confidence interval = .05), structural and feature data with an accuracy limit of $\pm .20$ (confidence level = .10), and representative floral and faunal samples with an accuracy limit of $\pm .20$ (confidence level = .25). The controlled surface and excavation sampling of the nearly 450 square miles covered by the Lake Erie drainage on the Glaciated Plateau in Ohio required over 10,000 man hours to complete. The analysis of data recovered is, to some extent, still in progress, and several modifications of the original conceptions have occurred.

Regarding the survey index variables (Table 1.1): Forsythe (1970), Sampson (1930), and Sears (1925, 1926, 1941) have shown that floral communities are good predictors of temperature and precipitation gradients. They also are capable of explaining a considerable amount $[>70\% \ (p = .02)]$ of the variance of temperature, precipitation, and soil types. Leverett (1917), White (1969), Black, Goldthwaites, and Willman (1973), Rau (1968), Hall (n.d.), and others have shown that the strong, statistically significant correlation that exists between local soils, surface geology, and slope approaches tautological equivalence in some cases. For the purposes of this chapter, since principal component analyses suggest that the maximum eigen-values for site locations lie along the axes of topography and floral community (Greber and Brose n.d.), these were considered the major "independent" variables in the analysis of prehistoric site distributions.

However, local soil types could have been utilized to yield information of a different nature. While this was considered, it introduced great nonindependence among variables of topography, geomorphology, and vegetation, biasing subsequent analyses. Furthermore, I felt that analytical stress on soils represented an ethnocentric decision on the yet undemonstrated importance of agriculture in the prehistoric periods under investigation. The two major variables, floral community and topography, thus represented the diachronic result of interactions among variables of drainage, climate, soils, and slope as well as among variables of drainage, relief, and surface and subsurface geomorphology, respectively. Furthermore, these two sets of variables could be ordered objectively.

Survey Evaluation

To test the efficiency of this system of archaeological survey against more traditional methods, portions of Lake, Geauga, and Ashtabula

Counties, which lay within the Lake Erie Drainage, were chosen for intensive analyses. Within this test region, a number of previous archaeological surveys of various types had been performed. Colonel Charles Whittlesey had located some 22 sites in the course of transect surveying between 1851 and 1873 (Whittlesey 1851, 1871). Greenman (n.d.) had located 15 sites by correspondence and automobile reconnaissance during the summers of 1929 and 1930. Bertram Krause (1942) had recorded 28 sites between 1938 and 1942 from field inspection and informants. W. J. Mayer-Oakes (1955) had located 7 sites in the process of reservoir salvage and correspondence. From the summer of 1971 to fall of 1972, our statistically random, ecologically stratified sample survey (or RESS survey) tested an additional 203 sample areas within this portion of these counties, locating some 67 components, none of which had been reported previously. In addition, during the summer of 1971 and during the spring of 1972, William Johnson and James Ross directed survey crews with the assistance of Larry LaBounty and Richard Ahlstrom in an additional "traditional county survey" (TRAC survey), talking to landowners and rereading forgotten county history books. This TRAC survey located an additional 43 sites within the test region. In this controlled region, a total of 318 potential site areas were tested: Of these, 203 were located via an areally standardized random sample of all possible microenvironmental site catchment areas (Higgs and Vita-Finzi 1972). The remaining 115 sites were located according to a number of differing (and ethnocentrically biased) criteria.

Following the criteria of Great Lakes prehistoric site taxonomy suggested by Fitting (1969) and employed by Brose and Essenpreis (1973) and Ritchie and Funk (1973), all prehistoric sites located were characterized either as special-purpose, limited-duration camps or as semipermanent or year-round villages. The ceramic chronology described earlier (e.g. Brose 1973) was utilized along with traditional projectile-point styles (Converse 1964; Ritchie 1961) to create a periodization of Archaic through early Late Woodland and three subsequent Whittlesey phases. The latter portion of the sequence has obtained radiometric support as well. All sites were assigned to a functional and chronological set, although the undiagnostic material recovered occasionally resulted in forcing these round archaeological pegs into less than comfortable square taxonomic holes. The distribution of prehistoric sites located by the RESS survey and the TRAC survey is presented in terms of the major independent variables of topography and proximate floral community in Table 1.2.

From the data in Table 1.2, several considerations follow: χ^2 tests indicate no statistically significant differences between the populations sampled in terms of site location by topography or proximal

Table 1.2 Comparability of Random Ecologically Stratified Sample (RESS) and Traditional County (TRAC) Survey Methods for Northeast Ohio Test Region

A. Site types against survey methods[a]

Survey	Early camps	Villages	Whittlesey I camps	Whittlesey I villages	Whittlesey II camps	Whittlesey II villages	Whittlesey III camps	Whittlesey III villages	Total
RESS	20	6	11	3	12	5	8	2	67
TRAC	34	5	23	10	14	7	13	9	115
Total	54	11	34	13	26	12	21	11	182

B. Topography against survey methods[b]

Survey	Lake plain	Alluvial bottomland	Secondary flood plain	Steep river bluff	Well-drained plateau	Poorly dissected interfluvial plateau	Rolling uplands	Total
RESS	7	8	9	12	11	8	12	67
TRAC	29	12	13	23	19	7	12	115
Total	36	20	22	35	30	15	24	182

C. Floral community against survey methods[c]

Survey	Marsh and fen	Elm–Ash swamp	Bog	Oak openings	Mixed oak forest	Mixed mesophytic forest	Beech–maple climax	Total
RESS	9	13	8	13	10	8	6	67
TRAC	20	15	23	26	10	11	10	115
Total	29	28	31	39	20	19	16	182

[a] $X^2 = 5.58649$; $df = 7$; $s > .50$.
[b] $X^2 = 7.47046$; $df = 6$; $s > .25$.
[c] $X^2 = 4.7773$; $df = 6$; $s = .40$.

floral community. Variances for the two samples were computed and their ratios compared to an *F*-test (Table 1.3). The results (Table 1.3a) indicated that the hypothesis of no significant difference between the functional–temporal type of sites located by either survey method could be accepted at a .05 level and that their variances could be pooled (Feller 1968). This suggests some statistical justification for combining the data obtained by differing archaeological sampling methods at the level of preliminary analysis. However, even within the parameters of general functional and/or temporal site categories, TRAC survey methods tend to underrepresent certain categories (for example, Phase II Whittlesey campsites). The explanation for this is apparent when the variances of the survey methods are analyzed for parameters such as topography or proximal floral community (Table 1.3b–c): The populations from which the samples have been drawn can be considered to be different at a .01 level of probability when compared to an *F*-test. Thus, pooling variances is unacceptable and the data from the two methods cannot be combined: Sites with

Table 1.3 **Variance Ratios for Sites in Northeast Ohio Test Region**

A. *Site type*

RESS survey $\bar{x} = 8.735$
$s^2 = 34.55$

$df = 6/6$ $F = 2.78$

TRAC survey $\bar{x} = 14.375$
$s^2 = 93.125$

B. *Topography*

RESS survey $\bar{x} = 9.57$
$s^2 = 4.286$

$df = 7/7$ $F = 3.05$

TRAC survey $\bar{x} = 16.429$
$s^2 = 57.952$

C. *Floral community*

RESS survey $\bar{x} = 9.57$
$s^2 = 6.953$

$df = 7/7$ $F = 6.27$

TRAC survey $\bar{x} = 16.429$
$s^2 = 43.619$

Critical *F* values

df	.95	.99
6/6	4.28	8.47
7/7	3.79	6.99

locations that do not strongly correlate with easily accessible and traditionally "obvious" topographic and vegetational features might be seriously undersampled by traditional methods.

To some extent, the apparent homogeneity of sites located by these two differing survey methods (Table 1.2) is a factor of the ecological "noise" introduced by the presence of Archaic and earlier Woodland occupations whose associations with modern floral patterns (and, to some extent, topography) is probably random. To test this possibility, Table 1.4 presents the comparability of the two differing survey strategies only for those Whittlesey focus sites occupied after A.D. 1000 when precontact vegetation and modern topography are effective ecological considerations. Although these X^2 tests still suggest that the two survey strategies are not significantly different in their representation of temporal–functional site types (Table 1.4a), they clearly demonstrate that these differing survey strategies cannot be considered to be valid samples drawn from the same ecological universe. The data presented in Table 1.4b–c show that traditional survey methods overrepresent sites in topographic zones, such as lake shores or river bluffs, where archaeologists, both amateur and professional, tend to think of prehistoric occupations as having been concentrated. At the same time, floral communities presently underexploited by our agricultural technology, such as elm–ash swamps or thin mixed oak forests, have yielded too little prehistoric site data to traditional surveys, while dredging and canalization of fens and bogs have provided more than their proportional share.

Traditional survey methods, being demonstrably biased in regard to ecological parameters, must preclude the legitimate use of many statistical analyses of settlement–subsistence patterns (Brose 1975). In addition, the random ecologically stratified sampling (RESS) method allows negative evidence or the demonstrable absence of prehistoric occupation in a defined microenvironmental zone to be treated as true negative evidence—that is, as something other than missing data.

The data recovered by the RESS survey can be considered to be the results of a Bernouli experiment; that is, in any sampled area, sites are either present or absent. Therefore, if sample size is sufficient, the frequency of encountering sites in any given number of areas should follow a binomial expansion and should approximate the probability distribution for a normal, or Gaussian, random variable (Feller 1968). Since 67 archaeological sites were located in some 203 ecological sample areas, the probability of encountering a site with this method is approximately .32. For TRAC surveys, the estimate of total areas investigated to yield a sample of 115 prehistoric sites thus should approximate 348. A perusal of Greenman's (n.d.) and Krause's (1942) journal entries and of Johnson and LaBounty's field notes suggests

Table 1.4 Comparability of Random Ecologically Stratified Sample (RESS) and Traditional County (TRAC) Survey Methods for Whittlesey Sites in Northeast Ohio Test Region

A. Site type against survey method[a]

Survey	Whittlesey I camps	Whittlesey I villages	Whittlesey II camps	Whittlesey II villages	Whittlesey III camps	Whittlesey III villages	Total
RESS	11	3	12	5	8	2	41
TRAC	23	10	14	7	13	9	76
Total	34	13	26	12	21	11	117

B. Topography against survey methods[b]

Survey	Lake plain	Alluvial bottomland	Secondary flood plain	Steep river bluff	Well-drained plateau	Poorly dissected interfluvial plateau	Rolling uplands	Total
RESS	5	2	8	5	8	6	7	41
TRAC	19	7	5	20	12	6	7	76
Total	24	9	13	25	20	12	14	117

C. Floral community against survey methods[c]

Survey	Marsh and fen	Elm–ash swamp	Bog	Oak opening	Mixed oak forest	Mixed mesophytic forest	Beech–maple climax	Total
RESS	2	10	4	10	5	7	3	41
TRAC	13	10	17	16	5	7	12	76
Total	15	20	21	26	10	14	15	117

[a] $X^2 = 4.137$; $df = 5$; $s > .70$.
[b] $X^2 = 12.613$; $df = 6$; $s < .05$.
[c] $X^2 = 12.531$; $df = 6$; $s = .05$.

that this figure is a gross underestimate, indicating that among other advantages, the RESS method is more efficient.

Analysis of Survey Data

Having determined the value of RESS survey for yielding an unbiased sample of Whittlesey site locations within the test region, it seemed reasonable to utilize data generated by this survey strategy throughout the surveyed portions of the glaciated Allegheny Plateau within the Lake Erie Drainage in Ohio. Admittedly, ceramic periods were difficult to fix at the western boundaries of the area following the second phase. It also was clear that the nature of testing employed in this survey strategy could yield relatively little information concerning the within-site spatial arrangement of features, structures, activity areas, or artifact clusters. For such information, extensive contiguous area excavation is required (Binford 1964). This has been performed at few sites located by the RESS survey. To characterize the nature of such cultural phenomena, extrapolation from previously excavated sites will be included. The following descriptions of the ecological location of Whittlesey sites, however, will be based primarily upon the statistical analyses of data obtained from the RESS survey. As Greig-Smith has noted (1964: 54ff):

> One of the principal contributions that may be expected from the use of quantitative methods . . . is the more exact detection and description of distribution patterns. . . .
> Before discussing technique the . . . significance of departure from randomness must be examined.
> If the effect of all [environmental] factors on . . . [site location and function] are relatively small it will be a matter of chance which [site type occurs] . . . at any point and the resulting distribution . . . will be random. . . . If one or a few factors have a disproportionately great effect on performance or survival . . . then the distribution will tend to be determined by that factor or factors. . . . Most environmental factors do NOT have a random distribution. We may thus put forward the hypothesis that departure from randomness of distribution of . . . [site type] indicates that one or a few factors are determinate. [Reprinted by permission of Butterworths Publications, London.]

To determine such factors, a number of techniques of locational analysis were employed to describe prehistoric site distributions for the 153 components of all Whittlesey phases. One difficulty is that most techniques of locational analysis assume that points are located on an isotropic plain with no topographic irregularities so that random movement in any direction is equally probable (Greig-Smith 1964; Haggett 1965) or that, if irregularities exist, they can be weighted

(Hudson 1969; Von Thunnen 1826). The assumption of isotropy cannot be met with the data available from northeast Ohio, and no statistically justifiable way to compute the relative "costs" of varying methods of prehistoric communications technologies exists. Nonetheless, I have assumed that the ease of direct water communication between sites would reduce the "effective cost" of transportation by a factor of 2.5, a figure for which some ethnographic support might be offered (Blair 1911; Brose 1968, 1970b, c). For instance, the ethnohistoric accounts of Chippewa or Ottawa can be compared with the Illinois, who contrast in their more terrestrial communications. These comparisons suggest that groups of comparable size and similar sociotechnic level will move 2.5 times farther for similar resources (in this case, French goods) when utilizing aquatic transport. An analytical quadrant size was set with an area approximately equal to the drainage basin of the secondary stream segments within the survey region (for example, the West Branch of the Cuyahoga, or French Creek); the assumption was that, since such stream segments represent the minimal areal units within which all potential microenvironmental zones are present, they may serve as an estimate for a macrocatchment zone within which seasonal subsistence–settlement cycles for discrete social units occur (viz., Binford 1964; Munson, Parmalee, and Yarnell 1971; Roper 1974; Vita-Finzi and Higgs 1970).

After establishing these parameters for further locational analyses, a principal components analysis (Greber and Brose n.d.) was performed for each of the three sequent Whittlesey phases. Using all ecological variables within the model for all Whittlesey village site locations and for most Whittlesey campsites, variables of proximal floral community and topography were nearly independent, and capable of predicting over 80% of the variation in known site locations. Eigen-values seemed to differ significantly between these factors for differing time periods and for different functional site types, however. Breaking the sample universe into separate functional site types for each chronological phase, the actual site frequencies for all sampled areas in all floral communities and in all topographic zones were tested by sets of two-way analyses of variance (Van der Geer 1971). These distributions are presented in Tables 1.5 and 1.6. The analyses showed major differences in the significance of floral and topography as variables capable of explaining the presence of functional site types at distinct temporal periods. For example, analysis of Phase I Whittlesey campsite locations indicates that proximal floral community accounts for 57.3% of the variance and topography 42.7%, but, for Phase I Whittlesey villages, proximal floral community explains only 26.5% of the variance and topography 73.5%. For Phase III Whittlesey campsites, proximal floral community accounts for

Table 1.5 Whittlesey Site Locations in Northeast Ohio Survey by Proximal Floral Community

	Marsh and fen	Elm–ash swamp	Bog	Oak opening	Mixed oak forest	Mixed mesophytic forest	Beech–maple climax	Total
Phase I campsite	2	3	5	8	5	1	2	25
Phase I village	3	2	0	1	4	8	5	23
Phase II campsite	2	3	2	2	6	5	6	23
Phase II village	1	6	0	2	2	4	3	18
Phase III campsite	7	5	4	9	11	9	2	48
Phase III village	1	1	0	2	4	5	3	16
Whittlesey site totals	16	20	11	24	32	32	18	153
Total areas sampled	54	61	27	69	97	118	110	536

Table 1.6 Whittlesey Site Locations in Northeast Ohio Survey by Topography

	Lake plain	Alluvial bottomland	Secondary flood plain	Steep river bluff	Well-drained plateau	Poorly dissected interfluvial plateau	Rolling uplands	Total
Phase I campsite	7	2	3	3	4	4	2	25
Phase I village	5	6	6	4	1	1	0	23
Phase II campsite	8	3	1	2	5	3	1	23
Phase II village	3	2	7	3	2	0	1	18
Phase III campsite	14	3	3	5	5	8	10	48
Phase III village	2	0	0	11	2	0	1	16
Whittlesey site totals	39	16	20	28	19	16	15	153
Total areas sampled	61	76	70	39	92	67	131	536

39.5% of the variance, and yet, for village sites of the same period, proximal floral community accounts for 18.8% of the variance only.

Finally, the explanation for these variations was sought in further analyses of the archaeological data as a series of settlement–subsistence patterns, rather than as isolated events. For these analyses, the concepts of seasonal scheduling (Flannery 1968) were introduced to understand the relationships of villages and campsites as complementary subsets within the settlement–subsistence system. Even though it was reasonable to assume that specific site locations were selected to minimize subsistence procurement efforts, differing ecological catchment areas vary seasonally in the availability of subsistence resources. It was, therefore, essential to establish the seasonal extractive economic activities performed at each of the 153 Whittlesey components to identify relevant ecological parameters for observed site locations. Ethnobotanical and ethnozoological analyses were employed, but, owing to the nature of the sampling strategy, many smaller components did not yield statistically significant frequencies of paleoecological samples. Less confidence thus can be placed in the seasonal assignment of some of the interfluvial campsites than in other aspects of the analyses. Nonetheless, the data displayed sufficient reliability for the purposes of creating a model from which to derive testable hypotheses. Several of these tentative seasonal assignments have received support from subsequent field work.

Now that the nature and validity of the research strategy, the parameters of the sample, the criteria for establishing site function and seasonality, and a gross chronology have been established, we may move beyond the simple demonstration of patterning among these variables and interpret these distributions in terms of more complex and elusive, but more interesting, sociocultural interactions which underlie both "culture history" and/or "processual archaeology." To quote Greig-Smith (1964: 55),

> Since the study of the factors determining the distribution of . . . [prehistoric occupation] is a prime concern of [archaeology], any technique that can assist in their detection is clearly of value. At the same time it must be emphasized that the detection and analysis of non-random [site location patterns] is a starting point for further investigation of those factors responsible. The failure to realize this imperative may account for the apparently barren nature of some statistical work in [archaeology] today. [Reprinted by permission of Butterworths Publications, London.]

To create a sociocultural model accounting for the results of the statistical analyses of archaeological data, I utilized a number of techniques for describing the relationships of one site to another or of one area of a site to another. Among these are median estimation nearest-neighbor analyses (Washburn 1974), mean estimation near-est-neighbor analyses (Whallon 1974), cluster analyses (Matson and True 1974), and Poisson Series analyses (Brose 1974; Brose and Scarry n.d.; Wood 1971). These techniques, where applicable, have generally yielded similar suggestions of pattern distribution. In discussing the patterned distribution of modes or attributes within a single artifact class, I have utilized multiple regression analyses (Brose 1968, 1970b; Freeman and Brown 1962) as well as a modified version of Whallon's (1968) index of heterogeneity and a modified version of Cronin's (1962) analyses of design element associations. By incorporating these various techniques in analyses of the RESS survey data with structural data from nonsample components which received block area excavation, I can refine my earlier subjective model of normative site location for the Whittlesey focus of northeast Ohio and introduce processual explanations for some of the data observed. Details of these analyses are scattered throughout several papers (Brose 1973, n.d.; Brose, Wentzel, Bluestone, and Essenpreis n.d.; Brose and White n.d.; Pratt and Brose 1975, in press), and a synthetic description of my model for Whittlesey settlement–subsistence patterns is also available (Brose n.d. b). Although such regional studies are essential for the creation of testable comparative data, it seems to me that the study yields more than a justification for the recent interpretations of the late prehistoric Whittlesey focus of northeast Ohio. I hope that additional benefits are present and can be applied beyond the study region.

Conclusions

One method for sampling a relatively unknown archaeological area has been proposed and implemented. In addition to efficiency, the method conforms to the assumptions necessary to perform unbiased statistical analyses of site distributions. Some attempt to indicate the results of such analyses also has been made. A number of methods for evaluating the significance of areally clustered data also have been suggested and implemented in conjunction with this specific sampling program. The results of these and other statistical procedures applicable to data collected within the requisite framework have been incorporated into a model yielding testable hypotheses concerning the nature of late prehistoric occupation in northeast Ohio. While similar results have appeared in other geographical regions, the methods by which data were obtained often renders the conclusions suspect and some of the statistical analysis unjustified.

Having gone, perhaps uncautiously, from these archaeological facts into ethnographic theory, it is possible to retreat to the archaeological facts, where some of the predictive capability of the model becomes apparent. First, it is possible to characterize correctly many parameters of archaeological sites on the basis of fragmentary or preliminary data. In addition, it is possible to predict with some confidence where certain site types might be located and "field experiments" have been rather successful. More important, owing to the nature of variation always present in any system, we can, within a general systems framework, predict the existence and evaluate the cultural significance of apparent distributional anomalies. As Washburn (1974) has demonstrated in her analysis of Pueblo I–III settlement systems, even under conditions of significant demographic change, realignment subsystems of resource procurement may be somewhat out of phase. Thus, as Washburn notes (1974: 325) there is a lag in site location strategy relative to site densities. This is a clear example of what Clarke (1968) has referred to as the "trajectory" of a system. Several examples of normative "lag" in site location are present in the data from northeast Ohio: Early Whittlesey summer villages located on interfluvial plateaus or on the edge of dissected uplands at secondary–tertiary stream junctions, and always in beech–maple climax forests, indicate lag in site location strategy, clearly representing the normative pattern of the early Late Woodland in this region (Brose n.d. d; Brose and Scarry n.d.); that is, they reflect the previous trajectory of the system.

Of greater interest, however, is the ability of this research strategy to identify those sites whose nonnormative location indicates not "lag" but the existence of variations which are selected as normative in the following phases: Late Phase I village sites which are *not* associated with mixed mesophytic forest communities but, rather, occur in several vegetational zones at random but on secondary flood plains; Phase II summer villages located on river bluffs above, rather than adjacent to, agricultural activities on secondary flood plains. Perhaps it is premature in the absence of reliable demographic reconstructions, but it is worth noting that such anomalous sites seem to occur in what would be, by coeval normative strategies, marginal environments. Further, these sites often display greater population density than coeval sites that correspond to the predictive model. The investigation of these phenomena in terms of providing a processual model of cultural change is the current focus of the research in this area.

Form, Function, and Style in Lithic Analysis

Arthur J. Jelinek

The interpretation of the chipped-stone industries of prehistoric man has concerned archaeologists for well over a century in both the Old and New Worlds. The two major areas of interest in working with these materials, as for most artifactual remains, have been: *(1)* the ways in which they may be related to chronologically and spatially distinct cultural groups, and *(2)* the ways in which they reflect distinct tasks or particular kinds of treatment of resources. The purpose of this chapter is to consider these two aspects of interpretation of lithic materials—first, in the sense of the basic assumptions and variables involved, and second, in the context of recent studies and possible future directions for research.

The finished form of an artifact is assumed to embody two distinct kinds of properties: those that are dependent upon the task for which it was intended and those that reflect choices on the part of the fabricator of the artifact from among a variety of ways in which those qualities necessary for its function can be produced. Following Sackett (1973: 320), the former properties can be referred to as "functional" attributes or variables and the latter as "stylistic" attributes or variables. The ability to distinguish between these kinds

19

of properties is of primary concern in any study that attempts to treat artifacts as a part of a functioning cultural system or to relate the particular industries of two or more prehistoric cultures in a meaningful way beyond spatial–temporal distribution. We can address the problems of artifactual interpretation through studies of *either* functional or stylistic variability. In doing so, we are working toward the isolation of those variables that seem best explained in the light of one or the other of these aspects of manufacture. In a theoretical sense, every morphological variable must be considered to have an equal potential for either a functional or a stylistic interpretation, and can be examined from either of these points of view. In a practical sense, we can distinguish some variables that seem most relevant to functional interpretation; in other cases, when no apparent functional correlates are in evidence, we are led to assign the variability to stylistic factors. These interpretations are based largely on inference from limited ethnographic observation and experimental reconstruction. Many variables, of course, fall outside this limited range of controlled data and are difficult to interpret in either a functional or a stylistic framework. It is useful, then, to recognize that the functional versus the stylistic status of any particular attribute pertains to the kind of question the archaeologist is asking and not to a kind of status that can be assigned to that attribute or variable in a final sense. This is what Sackett is saying when he states that "a given tool type can assume the significance of only one of its modes (stylistic or functional) at a given time" (1973: 324). Thus, although it is meaningful to discuss the probable functional or stylistic significance of particular attributes within the contexts of a particular problem, it is futile to attempt to assign a functional or stylistic significance to an attribute which will be expected to hold true for every circumstance in which that attribute could appear.

Since different cultures may exploit different aspects of similar environments, we would expect that the attributes of their artifacts might differ with respect to both function and style in a comparison of assemblages from any two or more prehistoric cultures. In a general sense, however, we would expect smaller differences in the functional aspects of particular attributes between cultures with generally similar patterns of exploitation of similar resources, and smaller differences in both categories between cultures closely adjacent in time and/or space. Given full artifact recovery, we should ideally be able to re-create systems of exploitation and processing within a prehistoric culture through the use of functionally correlated attributes and, using stylistically correlated attributes, distinguish a probable degree of communication (or "cultural distance") between two or more cultures. Unfortunately, the archaeologist seldom recovers more than a small, highly selected portion of the material culture of a prehistoric population. With these limited materials, he is seldom able to validate his hypotheses about function and style. In no area of prehistoric research are these restrictions more painfully evident than in those cultures whose preserved material remains are largely confined to chipped stone tools and the debris resulting from their manufacture.

One major problem in the analysis and interpretation of materials from purely lithic sites lies in the nature of the collections themselves. We can recognize three different kinds of sites with respect to stone tool manufacture and use: those primarily devoted to manufacture, those showing only selected products of manufacture, and those including both evidence of manufacture and evidence of the use of tools. In each kind of site, the materials left by the aboriginal inhabitants are largely objects having no further value in the context in which they were produced. Thus, manufacturing sites yield quantities of exhausted and unsuitable partially worked cores, broken or misshapen flakes and preforms, and great quantities of debris resulting from the reduction of cores and/or preforms. In contrast, sites on which little or no manufacturing debris is present yield primarily exhausted or broken tools and larger flakes. The presence of exhausted and broken tools on sites, along with strong evidence of lithic manufacture, is generally taken to indicate a wider range of activities than a simple manufacturing station. The main point is, however, that most materials on lithic sites (barring the occasional accidental loss of a functioning artifact) probably represent what was no longer wanted by the inhabitants of the site when they left the locality. Therefore, the direct equation of collections made from such sites with functioning tool kits or the full range of lithic manufacture should be viewed with some suspicion.

Undoubtedly, there were reasons other than simple exhaustion or breakage for discarding stone artifacts. Certainly, access to raw materials must have been an important consideration in determining the degree to which an artifact was used before it was discarded or whether or not it was conserved ("curated" in Binford's [1973: 242] terminology) for subsequent use. This would imply that in areas of abundant local resources for chipped stone the discarded artifacts would not be so exhaustively used as in areas of rare or restricted resources. This effect can be seen by contrasting the Middle Paleolithic industries from the Levant, where relatively complete tools are common, with the Zagros (for example, Hazar Merd, Shanidar, and Bisitun) where steeply flaked small stubs of tools are frequent. Raw material in the latter area appears to be derived primarily from relatively rare pebbles in river gravels, whereas, in the Levant, flint is almost ubiquitous in nodular and tabular form in the widespread exposures of Cretaceous and Eocene limestone.

A particular situation in which restricted access to raw materials has been shown to affect the ways in which tools were used, resharpened, and modified in form before being discarded was described in an important study by Frison (1968) at the Piney Creek site in northern Wyoming. In his analysis, Frison was able to trace the modification, breakage, and remodification of particular tools through the sequential butchering and processing of a group of *Bison*, and was able to show that the final form of the remnants of a tool might be quite different from its original form, the two being separated in time by possibly no more than a few hours. I suggest that this phenomenon be called the "Frison effect," in which the tool kit ultimately abandoned at the site is the result of the modification of an original set of tools and may be quite different in form from the original set. This modification occurs through the use of these tools in a succession of tasks related to the processing of raw materials. Consideration of these several factors relating to tool use, modification, and discard well might leave us in some doubt as to whether or not we ever, in fact, are likely to recover a completely functioning tool kit short of a deliberate interment or catastrophically precipitated preservation. This illuminates the need for studies designed to relate discarded materials (including broken and exhausted tools, materials inconvenient for transport, resharpening flakes, and so forth) to the functioning tool kits from which they were derived, since what we compare from one context to another is precisely this discarded material.

The question of conservation of tools for use elsewhere is a particularly difficult problem. Even though Binford's (1973) analogies between the modern Machine Age Eskimo and the Middle Paleolithic of Western Europe might be considered somewhat tenuous, one might propose the generalization from them that the amount of energy expended in the procurement and manufacture of a tool is directly reflected in the tendency to conserve the tool. Thus, lithic materials possessing special qualities and derived from sources far removed from the site might be discarded only when exhausted, and their presence on most sites would be indicated only by fragments or small resharpening flakes.

One final caution regarding the nature of lithic collections and the functional–stylistic inferences that can be made from them concerns contextual documentation. Ignoring the obvious difficulties of material derived from arbitrary layers cross-cutting natural stratigraphy, and restricting our discussion to material with good context in natural stratigraphy, clearly the potential of different collections for functional or stylistic interpretation can vary widely. For instance, a collection from a rock shelter with good context in a geological layer 10 cm or more in thickness provides less evidence for the contemporaneity of the artifacts than will a thin single layer of artifacts from the living floor of an open site. It is becoming clear that the chief value of shelter and cave sites lies in their preservation of a stratigraphic succession of restricted cultural elements, whereas the value of *in situ* deposits in open sites (with few exceptions) is in the clear functional associations of elements of single or traditionally linked occupations.

In summary, although the nature of the tasks that were performed is the most obvious criterion that might be expected to influence the composition of lithic collections, such variables as the proximity of lithic resources and factors relating to the human populations, including the size and structure of the group involved and the length and/or periodicity of the occupations, are all likely to have been important in their effects on the nature of the artifacts and their distribution in the site. The recovery of information that is adequate for the control of these variables is a goal seldom achieved in archaeological research, and only by weighing the degree of control achieved can we begin to judge the reliability of the collections that we are comparing. The nature of the *samples* in a comparative study is of course critical to the validity of that study. Questions of the extent to which the total resources of any occupation in the site are reflected in the sample, the context of the sample within the physical variability of the site, and the extent of artifactual recovery (size and nature of material saved), are all pertinent in determining the degree to which the samples are comparable. While all this may seem so fundamental as not to bear repeating, it is clear from recent literature that these basic principles are occasionally ignored.

The final group of variables pertinent to a study of functional and stylistic patterns in lithic analysis are those dealing with the attributes of the artifacts themselves. First among these are the raw materials from which the artifacts are manufactured. When a choice of raw materials is involved, it may relate to either function or style. An example of the former can be seen in the Fauresmith industries of southern Africa where diabasic rocks were selected for the manufacture of cleavers, while handaxes and other tools were generally made of indurated shale (Clark 1959: 147). Although stylistically determined raw materials are difficult to demonstrate in an archaeological context, the documentation of such choices in contemporary societies (for example, Gould, Koster, and Sontz 1971: 162) suggests an importance in prehistoric cultures which has only rarely been recognized. Perhaps the selection for crystalline rocks in the Late Stone Age microlithic cultures of southern India (Allchin and Allchin 1968: 92) would be a good prehistoric example of stylistic preference.

An important underlying factor in the selection of raw material is
the ease and extent to which different kinds of stone can be worked by
the techniques available within the cultural tradition. To the extent
that these techniques are traditionally restricted, the selection of raw
materials may be said to be determined on stylistic grounds. However,
the general advantages of all highly homogeneous and brittle crypto-
crystalline rocks over more irregular and granular materials for most
knapping techniques may mask particular stylistic preferences in
material. Thus, the effectiveness with which particular techniques of
manufacture can be employed on a specific material, a factor set apart
from the way the properties of the raw material relate to the
functional employment of the tool or stylistic preference for particular
raw materials, may be an important element in determining the extent
to which particular raw materials are transported and conserved. In
addition, the size and shape of raw materials valued for their qualities
relating to manufacture may have a direct effect on the form of the
finished product. The distribution and utilization of obsidian in
western North America furnishes many examples pertinent to these
effects.

Within the restrictions imposed by the size and shape of the raw
materials, the form of the products of a chipped-stone industry is
determined by the application of particular techniques of flaking. The
basic variables determining the form of the flakes and the flake scars
are the kinds of force applied (direct percussion, indirect percussion,
pressure), the nature of the instrument used in applying the force
(hard surface, yielding surface, rigid, resilient, pointed, dull), the
support of the piece, and the strength and direction of the force
applied. Even though it has become customary in archaeological
literature to speak of such techniques as direct hard-hammer percussion, direct resilient hammer percussion ("wood billet technique" or
"technique of bifacial retouch"), indirect percussion ("punch technique"), and pressure flaking, it now appears, on the basis of extensive
experiments in the replication of lithic artifacts by François Bordes,
Donald Crabtree, Jacques Tixier, Bruce Bradley, Mark Newcomer, and
others, that the narrow technological restrictions implied by some of
these distinctions are unwarranted. In particular, typical "flakes of
bifacial retouch" (Bordes 1961: 6) may occasionally result from use of
a stone hammer, typical "punched" blades may be manufactured by
direct percussion, and the circular fractures normally associated with
stone hammers (Semenov 1970: 2) can in fact result from percussion
with an antler. Despite these exceptions, these general distinctions
may still serve a useful taxonomic purpose, since they reflect particular morphological features despite the circumstances of their specific
technological origins.

Within these basic patterns, finer distinctions can be made which are pertinent to functional and stylistic discrimination. Examples of functional differences in flaking might include steep backing to produce a blunt edge, whereas stylistic differences may perhaps be seen in such types of flaking as the collateral and oblique pressure retouch on several varieties of North American Paleo-Indian projectile points. In some instances, a highly distinctive form of retouch suggests a particular stylistic or functional intent, but the actual purpose cannot at present be determined either way. An example of this sort is provided by the step-flaked Quina retouch (Bordes 1961: 8) which characterizes some aspects of the Middle Paleolithic cultures of Europe and the Near East. While Bordes interprets this form of retouch as a characteristic style of a distinct Mousterian culture, the numerous angular fractures on the face of the retouched edges might also be interpreted as a deliberate attempt to achieve a rasp-like surface for shaping wood or roughening hides (were Quina Mousterians wearing suede?).

The classification of tool retouch may also be viewed from the perspective of the maker's intent to produce an object with distinct functional parts. These have been separated by Bordes (1969: 3) into three basic tool parts: "the active part, the part of prehension (or handle), and the intermediate part." The active part of an implement has been most commonly referred to as the "working edge" in other literature on lithic description, while the remaining two categories are seldom distinguished outside of discussions of hafted pieces. Bordes also distinguishes the deliberate retouch that forms or partially modifies the part of prehension from that which is used in shaping the rest of the tool (1969). The latter he refers to as "the retouch of shaping" and the former as "the retouch of accommodation." In addition, he distinguishes two other useful categories of retouch (1969: 4): retouch that "corresponds to the stages of fabrication," which includes retouch resulting from the deliberate shaping of a core for the subsequent removal of particular kinds of flakes (such as blades and Levallois flakes), as well as retouch on the sides of cores to avoid injury during the use of the core. Thus, in effect, there are also shaping and accommodation categories within this class of retouch, whose manifestations are restricted to cores and the external surfaces of flakes (that is, not found on core tools). The final category of retouch in Bordes' classification is the "retouch of utilization" which is formed during the use of an implement. In summary, Bordes distinguishes two major classes of *deliberate* retouch, one used in shaping a core and the other used for shaping implements, and one class of *fortuitous* retouch resulting from the way in which an implement is employed. Within each class of deliberate retouch, he distinguishes that which is essential for the production of the object from that which is done for the comfort or convenience of the manipulator of the object.

Within the basic structure of implements as just distinguished, the active part or working edge has been the focus of most attention and is the basis for most attempts at the classification of chipped stone tools. Distinctions between different kinds of implements have been made primarily on the basis of the lateral shape of the modified edges and their geometric relationships to flake landmarks and/or to each other. Other factors of importance have been the nature and position of the retouch on the modified edges. In addition, Bordes (1970) now would include a category of "a posteriori" tools in his implement classification for objects that were unmodified by deliberate retouch but show utilization retouch. With the possible exception of this last category, which has not yet been extensively employed in comparative analysis, these current lithic classifications are generally unsatisfactory for studies that call for a distinction between functional and stylistic aspects of artifacts (see Sackett 1973). The taxonomic units of these classifications appear to have been defined by a mixture of both functional and stylistic criteria, resulting in taxonomies that are inapplicable to either type of interpretation. In effect, all artifact variability in these classifications has been treated as though it had stylistic significance (regardless of the functional names applied to the types) to distinguish the time–space clusters in morphology that have been pertinent to those interests in historical reconstruction which have long dominated prehistoric archaeology.

The only morphological aspects of chipped stone tools for which direct functional relationships have been studied are confined to two basic categories, edge angle and edge wear. Bordes (1965) and Semenov (1970) have shown that the unmodified, relatively wide-angled, prismatic lateral edges of burins can be used in shaving and shaping bone, wood, and antler. Although there has been relatively little information published on the effectiveness of different edge angles of these tools for different tasks, Semenov (1970: 5) implies that such studies have been made. Of more general interest in lithic studies are the papers of Gould, Koster, and Sontz (1971) and Wilmsen (1968a, b, c, 1970) relating to the quantification of edge angles of scrapers.

These writers also place emphasis on the other major area of morphological evidence relating to function: the modification of the edge that results from use. This kind of modification is normally termed "edge wear" and is best known from the pioneering studies of Semenov (1964); it would fall within Bordes' retouch of utilization in a strict sense, although much of the evidence is microscopic in character and includes abrasion or grinding as well as chipping. Although the literature on edge wear is fairly extensive, the lack of agreement on particular correlations of the kinds of materials worked with the resulting patterns of wear suggest that more comprehensive and better-controlled studies, considering such factors as variability in the lithic as well as the subject materials, are necessary before the usefulness of these techniques for the diagnosis of particular functions can be assessed.

It may be useful, at this point, to summarize the variables discussed which affect the stylistic and functional interpretation of lithic industries. The evidence pertinent to these interpretations falls into two basic classes: that relating to the nature of the collections being studied and that relating to the properties of the artifacts in those collections. Comparability of collections based on similar recovery techniques (or sampling to simulate similar recovery), similar locational controls, and similar kinds of samples from within those loci is fundamental to meaningful analysis. The general composition of the industries in terms of evidence of manufacture as opposed to tool use is pertinent to assessing the functional comparability of collections. In addition, an understanding of most collections as largely composed of materials that were no longer wanted is essential to their interpretation. This implies removal of materials that were desirable and the possibility that the remaining tools are the last stages of a series of metamorphoses (the "Frison effect"). Preferences for raw material may be based on suitability for particular techniques or in more esoteric cultural values. The techniques of manufacture, which may be recognized in both finished tools and debitage, and their distribution in terms of raw materials and the taxonomic categories of artifacts may provide information relating to both functional and stylistic questions. An additional aspect of artifact analysis concerns the various functional portions of tools interpreted in terms of their preparation and utilization. I suggest that current lithic classifications are inadequate for resolving either functional or stylistic problems, since they combine both kinds of information in no regular fashion. The most useful attempts to separate functional categories of lithic artifacts have been confined to studies of variation in edge angles or the patterns of modification of edges resulting directly from use.

In an attempt to assess the present state of our knowledge regarding stylistic and functional interpretations in lithic analysis, I would like to consider briefly two recent studies, each of which is a pioneering effort, in which such distinctions were a central focus. The first is Wilmsen's study of tools from eight Paleo-Indian sites, originally reported in several articles (1968a, b, c) and later more fully published as a short monograph (1970). The second is the study of

Near Eastern Middle Paleolithic industries by Binford and Binford (1966, 1969).

Wilmsen's study attempted to examine systematically the functional aspects of a group of samples of Paleo-Indian artifacts through the use of standardized techniques of observation of continuous and discrete variables. The monograph has been the subject of a lengthy review (Fritz 1974) whose content I will not attempt to duplicate here; I shall restrict the discussion to one aspect of functional analysis. The major conclusions reached by Wilmsen regarding the interpretation of functions of the materials that he analyzed are centered on the edge angles and edge wear exhibited by the scrapers and other utilized pieces. "Stylistic variation in non-projectile specimens was not recognized and was not systematically sought. While such variation may be present in the collections, it is not readily apparent" (Wilmsen 1970: 11). The study showed that marked differences in the frequency of edge angles of the pieces examined occur in different sites and that there is no correlation between the absolute thickness of the flakes used as implements and the angles of the utilized edges. (There does, however, appear to be a possible correlation of steepness of edges and *relative* thickness with respect to length and width.) Apparently, no attempt was made to determine whether or not the different raw materials from these widely separated sites might have had physical properties that affected the edge angles of the finished implements. In general, Wilmsen's assumptions regarding the functions of the three modal groups of edge angles which result from the study sound reasonable and appear to be supported by some of the evidence of edge wear. He postulates that the 26°–35° group was used for cutting; that the 46°–55° group was used for skinning, hide scraping, heavy cutting, shredding, and blunting of tool backs; and that the steep angles of 66°–75°, which occur with greatest frequency on end scrapers, were used for wood and bone working and heavy shredding. These kinds of uses of edge angles are generally similar to those reported by Gould, Koster, and Sontz (1971) for ethnographically observed Western Desert Aborigines in Australia, although there only two modes of edge angles were distinguished. In fact, the rather limited data (Gould, Koster, and Sontz 1971: 151) suggest that three modes may be present even though the difference between the two steepest modes is not recognized by the aborigines using the tools. On the basis of the functional categories of artifacts that Wilmsen distinguishes in conjunction with the full industry, he postulates different kinds of activities for the sites in his sample and expands this into a discussion of different kinds of occupations in those sites.

Wilmsen recognizes that the samples in his study are biased by the degree to which the sites had been exploited by amateurs and the material dispersed but feels that their essential composition with regard to the variables with which he was concerned is not seriously distorted. The variety of topographic and environmental circumstances are exploited to some degree in the explanation of the variation in the artifacts but perhaps are too dissimilar for a good comparative study. Another, and perhaps more serious, criticism concerns the assumption that the edge angle that was measured is the angle relating to the major function of the tool. In particular, the illustration of his technique of measurement (1970: Figure 10) indicates that, in some circumstances, the major flat surface of retouch was used to determine the angle when the actual "bit" of the tool had quite a different angle (1970: Figure 10b). On steep scrapers, the angle of the bit often is determined by fairly minute flakes, less than 1 mm in depth, which form a more acute angle with respect to the flat interior flake surface than does the retouch above them. In Wilmsen's illustration, a different effect is evident, one in which the angle of the bit of the artifact, through short retouch or curvature, is markedly wider than the angle measured. The degree to which these discrepancies are pertinent to the function of the tools could only be determined by experiment with the particular kinds of lithic materials represented in his collections. Inasmuch as the chief distinctions between many of the sites are based on the presence of sharp-angled implements, one may reasonably question whether or not these distinctions would have been as obvious if the edge angle observations had been confined to the bits, and if the angles being measured did not in fact relate more to flake proportions than to function. To summarize, Wilmsen's study is an interesting first step in the investigation of the position of certain classes of lithic materials in hypothetical functioning cultural systems.

A most interesting and original study aimed at the discovery of functional patterns in artifact assemblages and one that holds an almost unique position in this regard is that of Binford and Binford (1966, 1969). As is frequently the case with pioneering research, this work probably will remain notable largely for the stimulating ideas that it put forward rather than for the particular results which seem vulnerable to serious criticism.

In this study, the authors applied multivariate analysis (factor analysis) to the frequency distributions of artifact types classified in the system proposed by Bordes (1961) in 16 collections of Middle Paleolithic artifacts from two sites in the Near East (Yabrud I, Rust's excavation; Shubbabiq, S. R. Binford's excavation) and one in north central France (Houppeville, Série Claire) to discover if groups of artifacts could be defined which varied in the same way in their frequencies and therefore could be assumed to be linked in a meaningful way. Five such clusters of artifact types (factors) were

distinguished and were compared in terms of their frequency in each
collection with Bordes' classification of that collection within his
system of four basic kinds of Mousterian culture. Although the stated
purpose of the study was "to produce an alternative set of testable
hypotheses as possible explanations for the observed variation and
alternation of Mousterian industries demonstrated by Bordes" (Binford and Binford 1966: 240), the results seem to have little to do with
an explanation of the variation observed in Mousterian cultures by
Bordes (for example, Bordes' four basic kinds of Mousterian) or with
the way in which they alternate through time. Instead, the major
contribution of the factor analysis of the Near Eastern Middle
Paleolithic assemblages was a demonstration that recurrent groups of
tool types (factors), presumably representing functional tool kits of
various kinds, are present in these assemblages in frequencies that do
not conform to the cultural classifications of the assemblages by
Bordes (Binford 1973: 228; Binford and Binford 1966: 292). Rather, the
factors cross-cut them in such a way that each assemblage includes
significant numbers of tools from two or more of the postulated tool
kits. Thus, considering the limited sample involved, the study did not
eliminate the possibility that, with sufficient additional samples, a full
range of tool kits would be found with each kind of Mousterian. If this
were the case, it would, of course, tend to confirm Bordes' assumption
that the different kinds of Mousterian assemblages represent independent cultural traditions distinguished by styles of manufacture of
artifacts. The results of the subsequent studies on Mousterian industries from France (Binford and Binford 1969: 84) will be interesting.

   The Binfords' study is weak in several crucial respects. Such
possibly functionally significant variables as Bordes' Quina retouch
were ignored in the study; utilized and unretouched flakes and blades
were included although there is no assurance that they were retained
in predictable ratios from Rust's excavation of Yabrud; the "layers" at
Yabrud may be geological and not cultural and may contain mixed
cultural deposits that "average out" to one of Bordes' cultural types;
at least some of the deposits at Shubbabiq were admittedly mixed; the
functional categories based on Bordes' type list which were used to
define different kinds of activities are open to question; and, finally,
since no data were presented with the study, it is not possible either to
confirm the results of the analysis or to carry out comparable studies
with any certainty of duplicating the methodology employed by the
Binfords. An extension of inferences based on this study to the
Mousterian of France is highly questionable, since although the Near
Eastern Middle Paleolithic industries do share most tool types with the
Mousterian of France, they are quite different in other important

morphological aspects. The single example of a French industry included in the study (Houppeville, Série Claire) does not closely resemble any of the Near Eastern collections in the distribution of the five factors.

Clearly, more sophisticated studies are now possible. If we assume that technology reflects man's direct contact with the environment, we must also assume that the cultural variables for which we are testing can be seen in proper perspective only when we can control the environmental circumstances. These controls would, ideally, include not only those resources being exploited through use of the lithic technology, but the variability of the raw materials used in lithic manufacture in terms of accessibility, physical properties, and suitability for the processes of manufacture and the use to which they were subjected. The need for close chronological controls in comparing samples through periods of environmental change and in testing for stylistic trends is axiomatic. The necessity of comparable samples of artifacts for comparative studies was stressed earlier. Other necessary controls in such studies call for uniform systems of observation and description of the morphology of the artifacts in terms of such variables as landmarks, forms of retouch, and edge contours. Good contributions have been made in this area by Bordes (1961), Brézillon (1968), Leach (1969), Movius, David, Bricker, and Clay (1968), Wilmsen (1970), and others, but, since no single satisfactory scheme yet exists which includes all basic aspects of lithic description, it is important for purposes of comparison and replication that future studies be explicit with regard to the terms and the methodology they employ.

In addition, the traditional archaeological view of artifact materials as representative of a fully functional cross section of the range of activities carried out during a site occupation must, barring evidence of catastrophic interruption, be modified to consider this material as largely trash in the view of the people who were responsible for its deposition (that is, this artifactual material is, to a degree, a negative impression of the functional system and its necessary tools). The stage at which a tool may be discarded is likely to be affected by the proximity, quantity, and quality of resources (environmental factors). The cultural values and processes influenced by these factors may be manifest in a particular sequence of tool metamorphosis or in the selective reuse of materials with special stylistic or functional qualities. In spatially restricted samples especially, the possibility is always present that the "tool kit" represented is in actuality only a segment of a sequence of metamorphosis of tool forms, indicative of only one stage in a sequence of processing and tool use. This points up the need for the recovery and study of fragmentary tools as well as resharpening flakes for a full interpretation of an industry.

Other tests that can be employed to illuminate the relationships of function and style in lithic manufacture and use include both experimental and archaeological analysis. Experimental techniques may show differences in the physical properties of different raw materials related to both the technology of manufacture and their advantages for various kinds of functional employment. Such experimental data could be applied to collections (with suitable controls for material access, size, and other pertinent variables) that had been analyzed for correlations of morphological attributes with raw materials to show whether these correlations are best explained on the basis of functional advantage or if stylistic preference is a more likely explanation. Morphological variables that are amenable to testing with these techniques and that need further analysis in both an experimental and artifactual context include variation in the size and shape of the retouched edge and the circumstances of use of particular kinds of retouch.

In addition, the effects of the utilization of lithic materials on other substances may yet reveal distinctive patterns of edge wear under suitably controlled conditions. Perhaps the best that can be hoped for is the identification of general sets or categories of resistant materials that produce particular effects during particular kinds of contact with the stone tools. Ultimately, perhaps, the inferences based on these experiments can be tested in the prehistoric record by isolating traces of particular amino acids or other chemical substances that penetrated the edges of the tools during use.

The extent of chipped-stone material in the archaeological record, frequently to the exclusion of all other evidence of cultural activity, should provide the incentive to employ these materials to the limits of their potential for the interpretation of the prehistoric record. It seems justifiable to say that we have only begun to understand the kinds of information that can be extracted from these artifacts and the ways in which this information relates to the thoughts and tasks of the prehistoric people who were responsible for their manufacture and use. In the light of the currently contrasting opinions on the potential of lithic analysis for cultural reconstruction and the ways in which specific phenomena within this body of data should be interpreted, especially in the spirit of the purpose of this presentation, it seems appropriate to close with a partial quotation relating to a youthful stage of development in another area of prehistory: "The present apparent discrepancies between archaeologists' interpretations . . . will gradually be resolved by improvements in technique . . . by more carefully controlled selection of the specimens, and by time which heals all wounds" (Griffin 1952: 370).

Acknowledgments

I would like to express my appreciation for the comments of F. Bordes, W. A. Longacre, J. R. Sackett, A. Sullivan, R. H. Thompson, and Eloise Jelinek on the manuscript of this article.

3

Problems in the Use of Correlation for the Investigation of Tool Kits and Activity Areas

John D. Speth   Gregory A. Johnson

Introduction

Definition of tool kits and spatially differentiated activity areas has become an increasingly common component of the investigation of Paleolithic societies. This information usually is sought through quantitative analysis of material recovered from "living floors" within one or more Paleolithic sites. Such analysis often is begun by calculation of all possible pairs of correlation coefficients among the various classes of artifacts, cultural features, and bone debris available from a given level or site. The resulting matrix of correlation coefficients then serves as input data for one of a series of more or less complex multivariate techniques intended to isolate tool kits.

In the present chapter, we will examine briefly two basic categories of problems that we feel may have some implications for interpretation of the results of such analysis. The first type of problem involves a variety of factors that may influence the magnitude and sign of the correlation coefficients. The second, and probably more important, category involves the ability of correlation to distinguish idealized spatial patterns produced in a variety of very different behavioral contexts.

Problems of Correlation When Data Are Expressed as Raw Frequency Counts

Several factors control or influence the magnitude and sign of the linear product-moment coefficient of correlation (Pearson's r) when the data are expressed as raw frequency counts. We are certainly not the first to comment on the properties and behavior of linear correlation when applied to archaeological data. In particular, we would like to emphasize our debt to George Cowgill (1968a, b, 1970) for his work in this area.

The assumptions that underlie the product-moment coefficient of correlation place certain restrictions on the data which may meaningfully be correlated. Hays (1973: 616–674), Guilford and Fruchter (1973: 94–95), and Carroll (1961) thoroughly discuss these limitations. A particularly important restriction is that the relationship between pairs of variables be linear (Guilford and Fruchter 1973: 95). The distributions of the variables also should be more or less symmetrical and unimodal, although they need not be normal (Carroll 1961: 349; Guilford and Fruchter 1973: 95).

The distribution of each variable and the cross plots of all pairs of variables should be inspected carefully prior to computation of the correlation coefficients. Archaeologists commonly omit this important preliminary step of data screening. Unscreened data often are correlated by computer without prior inspection of the distributions and cross plots, and the resulting matrix of correlation coefficients is then subjected to multivariate procedures. Correlation coefficients generated in this manner may not provide suitable measures of the patterning of artifact classes on a prehistoric site. A few examples will illustrate the problems which may arise when the product-moment coefficient of correlation is used for the identification of activity areas and tool kits.

Archaeologists frequently expect that classes of artifacts belonging to the same kit will be correlated positively, while tools belonging to different kits will be correlated negatively. The archaeologist often hopes to find different tool kits segregated in spatially discrete activity loci. An ideal case of spatial segregation of two classes of artifacts belonging to different tool kits is shown in Table 3.1. In this example, the spatial distributions of the two tool types are mutually exclusive (that is, when Xs are present, Ys are absent). As the archaeologist

Table 3.1 **Mutually Exclusive Distribution of Two Artifact Classes (*X* and *Y*) in 16 Grid Squares of an Archaeological Site (Perfect Spatial Segregation)**[a]

1 XXX	2 XXX	3 YYY	4 YYY
5 XXX	6 XXX	7 YYY	8 YYY
9 XXX	10 XXX	11 YYY	12 YYY
13 XXX	14 XXX	15 YYY	16 YYY

[a] Frequency of *X*s and *Y*s does not vary. Pearson's $r = -1.00$.

might expect, Pearson's r provides a perfect negative coefficient of correlation between X and Y ($r = -1.0$).

If we introduce, and then increment, variability in the frequency of items per grid square, while maintaining total spatial segregation, the magnitude of the negative correlation decreases sharply (Table 3.2; Figure 3.1). As the sum of the standard deviations of the two artifact

Table 3.2 **Mutually Exclusive Distribution of Two Artifact Classes
(*X* and *Y*) in 16 Grid Squares of an Archaeological Site (Perfect
Spatial Segregation)**[a]

1 XXXX XXXX	2 XXXX	3 YYYY	4 YYYY YYYY
5 XXXX XXX	6 XXX	7 YYY	8 YYYY YYY
9 XXXX XX	10 XX	11 YY	12 YYYY YY
13 XXXX X	14 X	15 Y	16 YYYY Y

[a] Frequency of *X*s and *Y*s varies. Pearson's $r = -0.66$.

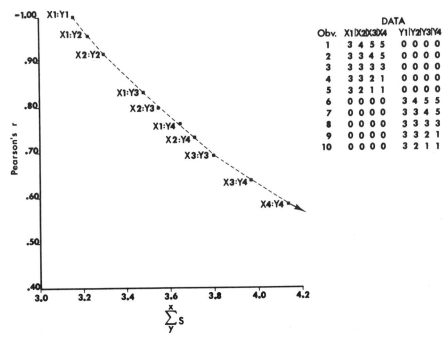

Figure 3.1 Complete spatial segregation of two artifact classes (X and Y): effect of increasing variability $\left(\sum\limits_{Y}^{X} s\right)$ on magnitude of Pearson's r.

classes increases, the magnitude of the coefficient decreases. The net effect of this phenomenon will be the increase of the number of weak negative coefficients in the final matrix of correlation coefficients. This conclusion is of particular interest to archaeologists. The identification of even the most clear-cut case of completely segregated tool kits through the use of correlation coefficients such as Pearson's r may be exceedingly difficult. Careful visual inspection of the data is essential before the correlation coefficients are computed and certainly before the matrix of coefficients is subjected to further analysis.

Another important problem that may lead to misleading correlation coefficients arises from the inclusion in the data of grid squares or stratigraphic levels in which both classes of artifacts are simultaneously absent (so-called "zero–zero cells"). The archaeologist is almost certain to encounter 0–0 cells (1) whenever certain classes of artifacts are generally rare; (2) around the perimeter of a site, where the density of material drops off rapidly; and (3) in the low-density zones between residential loci, discrete activity loci, areas of trash disposal, and so forth. The inclusion of 0–0 cells may alter drastically the magnitude of a correlation coefficient, and even may transform a statistically significant negative correlation into a significant positive value (Hesse 1971).

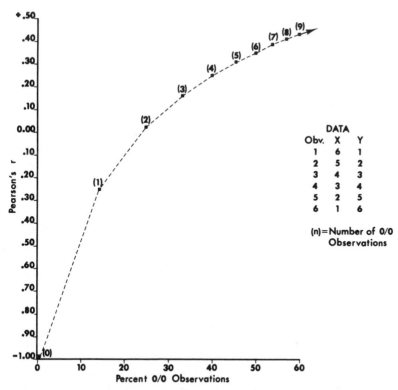

Figure 3.2   Effect of 0–0 observations on magnitude and sign of Pearson's *r*.

Figure 3.2 graphically illustrates the effect of 0–0 observations on the magnitude and sign of Pearson's *r*. The graph was generated by beginning with a perfect negative correlation between two artifact classes, X and Y (the original data are listed in the figure). A pair of 0–0 observations was added to the original data and a new coefficient computed. This process was then repeated several times. The graph clearly shows that negative correlations are very sensitive to the addition of 0–0 pairs. In this particular example, the addition of a single 0–0 pair reduced the coefficient from perfect negative to −0.25. The reason for the sensitivity of negative correlations to 0–0 observations can be visualized more readily by considering the cross plot of X and Y. A positive correlation that passes through, or near to, the origin of the cross plot will be unaffected, or even enhanced, by the addition of points at the origin. On the other hand, a negative correlation may be severely affected by the addition of points at the origin, especially if the sample size is small.

The number of 0–0 pairs included in the data depends on the manner in which the boundaries of the site or study area are defined (the sampling universe), on the number and size of grid units into which the site is partitioned (the sampling units), and on the number of items in each artifact class. Definition of the sampling universe and choice of appropriate sampling units pose a major theoretical and methodological problem for the archaeologist (Hesse 1971; Dacey 1974; Sokal and Sneath 1963). We are unable to offer a general solution to this critical problem. Our present purpose is to point out the nature and importance of the problem—the magnitude and sign of the product-moment correlation coefficient may be very highly related to the proportion of 0–0 observations. If 0–0 pairs are included in the original data, *(1)* significant negative correlations may be underrepresented or absent; *(2)* the number of low negative and positive values may be enhanced; and *(3)* already positive correlations may be inflated.

Many additional factors may influence the magnitude and sign of a correlation coefficient computed from raw frequency counts. Many tend to operate in the same direction, inflating the number of weak positives in the matrix. We will discuss briefly a few of the more important of these factors.

If the frequency distributions of two artifact classes are different in shape or if they are asymmetrical, the maximum possible range of the correlation coefficient will contract and may become substantially less than ± 1.0 (Carroll 1961; Ferguson 1941, 1959; Guilford and Fruchter 1973; Majone and Sanday 1971). For ease of presentation, we will illustrate contraction of the range of correlation with an example using the *phi* coefficient (ϕ). *Phi* is a special form of Pearson's *r* in which the data have been dichotomized into presence–absence, or 0 and 1. Carroll (1961) provides a more general method for determining the contraction of the range of Pearson's *r* when the data have not been dichotomized.

Suppose we have a site with 100 grid squares. If 50 of the squares contain both *X*s and *Y*s, and 50 contain neither, the correlation between *X*s and *Y*s is $+1.0$ (Table 3.3a). If 50 of the squares contain *X*s but no *Y*s, and the other 50 contain *Y*s but no *X*s, the correlation is -1.0 (Table 3.3b). In both examples, the marginal totals are evenly divided (50, 50) and add up to 100 (the total number of grid squares). Table 3.4(a and b) shows the same distributions as Table 3.3(a and b), but the numbers of grid squares containing *X*s and *Y*s have been changed into proportions of the 100 original squares. In Table 3.4(a and b), p_x is the proportion of grid squares containing *X*s; q_x is the proportion of squares not containing *X*s; p_{xy} is the proportion of squares containing both *X*s and *Y*s; and so forth. When $p_x = q_x = p_y = q_y$, the maximum possible range of the correlation coefficient is ± 1.0. If we now change the proportion of squares with

Table 3.3 Correlation (*phi*) between Two Artifact Classes (*X* and *Y*) Distributed in 100 Grid Squares of an Archaeological Site: (a) When 50 Squares Contain both *X*s and *Y*s and 50 Squares Contain Neither; (b) When 50 Squares Contain *X*s but No *Y*s and 50 Squares Contain *Y*s But No *X*s[a]

	X +	X −	Marginal totals			X +	X −	Marginal totals
Y +	50	0	50		Y +	0	50	50
Y −	0	50	50		Y −	50	0	50
Marginal totals	50	50	100		Marginal totals	50	50	100
		(a)					(b)	

[a] For (a), *phi* (ϕ) = +1.00; for (b), *phi* (ϕ) = −1.00.

*X*s to 0.33 and the proportion of squares with *Y*s to 0.33 (that is, $p_x = p_y \neq q_x = q_y$), we get a new 2 by 2 table, with marginals as shown in Table 3.5. There are many possible ways to fill in the table and still preserve the specified proportions of squares containing *X*s and of squares containing *Y*s (that is, $p_x = p_y = 0.33$).

Ferguson (1941) and Guilford and Fruchter (1973: 309–310) provide

Table 3.4 Correlation (*phi*) between Two Artifact Classes (*X* and *Y*) that Have the Same Spatial Distribution as in Table 3.3[a]

	X +	X −	Marginal totals			X +	X −	Marginal totals
Y +	(p_{xy}) 0.5	0.0	0.5 (p_y)		Y +	(p_{xy}) 0.0	0.5	0.5 (p_y)
Y −	0.0	(q_{xy}) 0.5	0.5 (q_y)		Y −	0.5	(q_{xy}) 0.0	0.5 (q_y)
Marginal totals	0.5 (p_x)	0.5 (q_x)	1.0		Marginal totals	0.5 (p_x)	0.5 (q_x)	1.0
		(a)					(b)	

[a] The number of squares containing *X*s and/or *Y*s is expressed as a proportion of the total number of squares. For (a), *phi* (ϕ) = +1.00; for (b), *phi* (ϕ) = −1.00.

Table 3.5 Marginal Totals When One-Third of the Grid Squares on an Archaeological Site Contain Xs and One-Third Contain Ys ($p_z = p_y \neq q_z = q_y$)[a]

		X		Marginal totals
		+	−	
Y	+	?	?	0.33 (p_y)
	−	?	?	0.67 (q_y)
Marginal totals		0.33 (p_x)	0.67 (q_x)	1.00

[a] Maximum possible positive correlation (phi) is +1.00; maximum possible negative correlation is −0.49.

the following formulas (Equations 1 and 2) for determining the maximum possible positive and negative correlation coefficients for a given set of marginals:

$$\phi_{max(+)} = + \sqrt{\left(\frac{p_j}{q_j}\right)\left(\frac{q_i}{p_i}\right)} \tag{1}$$

$$\phi_{max(-)} = - \sqrt{\frac{q_i}{p_i}} \sqrt{\frac{q_j}{p_j}} \tag{2}$$

In both formulas, p_i is defined as the largest marginal proportion in a given 2-by-2 table; p_i may thus represent p_x, p_y, q_x, or q_y in tables such as 3.4(a or b), depending upon the relative magnitudes of these values. The equivalences of the remaining factors in Equations 1 and 2 are determined by the definition of p_i. Thus, for example, if p_x is the largest marginal proportion, it becomes p_i in the formulas, and p_y becomes p_j. If, however, q_y is the largest marginal proportion, then q_y becomes p_i and q_x becomes p_j.

When $p_x = p_y \neq q_x = q_y$ (as in Table 3.5), the maximum possible positive correlation is +1.0; the maximum possible negative correlation, however, is no longer −1.0. In the example shown in Table 3.5, $\phi_{max(-)}$ is −0.49. A perfect negative correlation is possible only when $p_x = q_y$.

If we continue to change the marginals so that the proportions of squares with Xs is no longer the same as the proportion with Ys (that is, $p_x \neq p_y \neq q_x \neq q_y$), then neither $+1.0$ nor -1.0 is possible. Note the case shown in Table 3.6(a), in which the proportion of squares with Xs is 0.4 and the proportion with Ys is 0.8. The maximum positive correlation is $+0.408$ (Table 3.6b) and the maximum negative value is -0.613 (Table 3.6c).

These results illustrate two very important problems that should be recognized by archaeologists. First, if the proportion of grid squares containing Xs differs from the proportion containing Ys, the maximum possible range of the coefficient of correlation will no longer be ± 1.0. Second, the maximum positive and negative correlations are not distributed symmetrically around zero (Guilford 1965: 338). When p_j is less than q_j, the maximum positive coefficient will be restricted more than the maximum negative coefficient; when p_j is greater than q_j, the maximum negative will be restricted more than the maximum positive.

Two other factors, which may have a significant effect on the magnitude of the correlation coefficient, are *reliability* and *sampling error*. Cowgill (1970) has already discussed these in some detail, rightly emphasizing their importance in archaeological research.

Reliability is defined as the proportion of the total variance in a set of measurements which is true variance, as opposed to error variance (Beers 1957; Cowgill 1970; Guilford 1965; Walker and Lev 1953). Low reliability resulting from random error may lead to a reduction in the magnitude of the observed correlation coefficient, a phenomenon known as *attenuation*. Systematic error also affects reliability and may lead, in many situations, to an increase in the observed correlation. Archaeologists, with the notable exception of Cowgill (1970), have devoted very little attention to the nature and amount of error variance in their measurements.

There are numerous sources of systematic and random error that may be important to the archaeologist concerned with spatial analysis. We will list a few of the more obvious ones. Common sources of systematic error include: *(1)* using screens, which systematically eliminates artifacts smaller than the mesh size; *(2)* assigning artifacts that lie directly on the border between two grid squares to a particular square (such as the adjacent unit to the left); *(3)* fatigue or boredom on the part of the analyst, causing him to progressively shift his criteria of classification from morning to night or from day to day; *(4)* arbitrarily, but consistently, assigning an artifact to a particular class when it actually has characteristics that fit two classes (such as the Bordian practice of assigning composite tools to the category least abundant at the site [Bordes 1961: 11]).

Random error variance may be introduced into the data at virtually every stage in the analysis. A few common sources of random error

Table 3.6 **Maximum Possible Positive *phi* Coefficient (b) and Maximum Possible Negative *phi* Coefficient (c) That Can Be Obtained for the Marginal Totals Given in (a)** $(p_z \neq p_y \neq q_z \neq q_y)^a$

(a)

Y	X +	X −	Marginal totals
+	?	?	0.8 (p_y)
−	?	?	0.2 (q_y)
Marginal totals	0.4 (p_z)	0.6 (q_z)	1.0

(b)

Y	X +	X −	Marginal totals
+	0.2	0.6	0.8 (p_y)
−	0.2	0.0	0.2 (q_y)
Marginal totals	0.4 (p_z)	0.6 (q_z)	1.0

(c)

Y	X +	X −	Marginal totals
+	0.4	0.4	0.8 (p_y)
−	0.0	0.2	0.2 (q_y)
Marginal totals	0.4 (p_z)	0.6 (q_z)	1.0

[a] For (b), $\phi_{max(+)} = +0.408$; for (c), $\phi_{max(-)} = -0.613$.

include: *(1)* inadequate methods of artifact recovery; *(2)* inaccurate methods of measurement or counting; *(3)* inconsistencies in the classification procedure; or *(4)* mistakes in coding.

Several different methods are available in the psychological literature to estimate reliability and adjust for attenuation of an observed correlation, if the source of error variance consists exclusively of random error. We will describe one of these methods (see also Cowgill 1970). However, this method will be of relatively limited utility if a large component of the total error variance consists of systematic error.

The reliability of a set of measurements or counts (for instance, of the frequency of Xs in various grid squares or stratigraphic levels) is expressed by the coefficient of reliability r_{xx} (Equation 3):

$$r_{xx} = s_t^2/s_x^2 \qquad (3)$$

where s_t^2 is the true variance and s_x^2 is the observed variance (Walker and Lev 1953: 302). The reliability coefficient measures the intercorrelation among repeated observations or counts of the *same* variable. "If two measures [of a given variable] differ from each other only because of random errors of measurement, the correlation between the two is the ratio of the variance of true scores to the variance of observed scores" (Walker and Lev 1953: 298).

One major source of low reliability encountered in spatial analysis is the difficulty of assigning artifacts to particular typological categories. One possible way to estimate the reliability coefficient of a classification is to determine the number of Xs per grid square or stratigraphic level, wait for a period of time, and then repeat the classification. This procedure is comparable in many respects to the test–retest technique for estimating reliability, employed by psychologists (Guilford and Fruchter 1973: 408–409; Walker and Lev 1953: 309). The correlation between the frequency of Xs in the two classifications will serve as an estimate of the reliability coefficient of X (that is, r_{xx}). Systematic error sources may be encountered, using this procedure. The archaeologist may remember how he classified particular items the first time. This will reduce the error variance and artificially enhance the reliability. If the time interval between the two classifications is too great, the archaeologist may obtain additional information or alter the objectives of his typology, leading to inaccurate coefficients of reliability. The problems of estimating reliability have received considerable attention in other disciplines but have been largely ignored by archaeologists. Research into these problems is clearly warranted.

Once the reliability coefficient has been estimated for the counts on each of two artifact classes, X and Y, the attenuation of the observed correlation coefficient owing to low reliability can be determined by using Equation 4 (Cowgill 1970: 165; Ferguson 1959: 284; Walker and Lev 1953: 300):

$$r_{tt} = \frac{r_{xy}}{\sqrt{r_{xx}r_{yy}}} \tag{4}$$

where r_{xx} and r_{yy} are the reliability coefficients of X and Y, respectively; r_{xy} is the observed correlation between X and Y; and r_{tt} is the "true" correlation corrected for the effects of attenuation. The observed and "true" correlation will be the same only when the reliability of the two variables is perfect (that is, $r_{xx} = r_{yy} = 1.0$). Whenever the reliability of the measurements is less than unity, the observed correlation will be less than the "true" value. Attenuation will not change the sign of the correlation coefficient (Cowgill 1970: 165), but it certainly will increase the number of weak positive values in the correlation matrix.

Generally, the data being investigated by the archaeologist represent a sample of a much larger population or universe (Cowgill 1970). The coefficient of correlation in the sample is used as an estimate of the correlation in the population. Reliability affects the degree of agreement between the observed and "true" correlation *in the sample.* The "true" sample value, however, may still differ substantially from the population value because of *sampling error* (Cowgill 1970). Whenever a random sample is drawn from a larger population, there is a chance of selecting a sample in which two variables are correlated, although there actually may be no correlation between them in the population. The smaller the size of the sample chosen from such a population, the greater the probability of chance correlation. Convenient tables are available which permit the investigator to assess the probability that an observed correlation for a given sample size could have been obtained by random sampling error (see, for example, Arkin and Colton 1963: Table 22). Such tests of the significance of a correlation coefficient obviously are useful only if the sample has been obtained by a statistically valid sampling procedure. There appear, at present, to be no clear-cut guidelines to determine how many of the coefficients in a correlation matrix should be statistically significant (that is, having low probabilities of being a result of sampling error) to justify further multivariate manipulation.

The magnitude of the correlation coefficient may be affected by several other important factors. Pooling different populations or samples, for example, when each population or sample contains two uncorrelated artifact classes, may produce spurious correlation, if the means of the two variables in both populations are different (Guilford 1952: 32). Samples of Xs and Ys, drawn from two different populations, are illustrated in Table 3.7. The correlation coefficients in these samples are undefined because the frequencies of X and Y do not co-vary. The means of X and Y in the first sample differ from their respective means in the second sample. If the two samples in this example are pooled, the correlation between X and Y will increase to $+1.0$.

Pooling, therefore, may have a drastic effect on the magnitude and sign of the correlation coefficient. This problem is extremely important in archaeology. In Paleolithic research, for example, the majority of samples available for analysis probably are derived from pooled populations (that is, from pooled occupation horizons). Paleolithic caves provide an excellent illustration of this problem. Caves are bounded and, therefore, tend to confine repeated occupations to a relatively small area (Freeman 1973: 24). Solely for illustrative purposes, we have collected data on sedimentation rates during the Middle and Upper Paleolithic in three caves: *(1)* Abri Pataud in France; *(2)* Haua Fteah in Lybia; and *(3)* Shanidar Cave in Iraq. Abri Pataud had a sedimentation rate ranging from 100 cm to 182 cm per 1000 years (Movius 1972: 256–258). The rate at Haua Fteah ranged from 6 cm to 52 cm per 1000 years (McBurney 1967: 50); and, at Shanidar, the rate was approximately 30 cm per 1000 years (Solecki 1963: 187). For these three sites, the overall range is approximately 6 cm to 182 cm, with an average rate of about 74 cm per 1000 years. In terms of the sedimentation rates just mentioned, 1 cm of deposit may represent

Table 3.7   **Effect of Pooling on Magnitude of Correlation Coefficient**[a]

Sample from population 1		Sample from population 2		Pooled sample from populations 1 and 2	
X	Y	X	Y	X	Y
5	8	10	16	5	8
5	8	10	16	5	8
5	8	10	16	5	8
5	8	10	16	5	8
5	8	10	16	5	8
				10	16
$M_x = 5$	$M_y = 8$	$M_x = 10$	$M_y = 16$	10	16
				10	16
Pearson's r = undefined		Pearson's r = undefined		10	16
				10	16
				$M_x = 7.5$	$M_y = 12.0$
				Pearson's $r = +1.00$	

[a] M is the sample mean.

anywhere from 5 to 167 years, with an average of about 14 years. Assuming that our figures in any way correspond to reality and considering that a typical flake is about 1 cm thick, such a flake might lie on the floor of the cave for 5 to 167 years (or an average of about 14 years) before it is completely buried by natural depositional processes. Further, if the cave is occupied once per year during the annual round of a group of Paleolithic hunters and gatherers, many of our excavation samples probably will represent pooled occupations.

Although pooling of occupations poses a major problem, we feel that it is primarily a methodological issue which, in many cases, can be circumvented. For example, pooling may pose less of a problem in open-air sites, especially in comparatively small sites where occupations are not confined by fixed natural boundaries (Freeman 1973: 24) or in caves characterized by very rapid sedimentation rates.

Another important form of pooling occurs if the archaeological material on discrete living floors cannot be spatially partitioned, prior to correlation analysis, into natural provenience units (hut-floor deposit, pit fill, and so forth). We will discuss the difficulties presented by this form of spatial pooling in greater detail.

Another important factor that will influence the magnitude and sign of the correlation coefficient should be mentioned. Spurious positive correlation will be obtained when the sample sizes from different levels or sites are very different or when the samples represent different proportions of their respective assemblages (Cowgill 1968a, b). Archaeologists frequently convert their data to percentages to circumvent the problem of different sample sizes. We will attempt to show that the use of percentages is undesirable. Adjustment for density may be a more satisfactory procedure.

Problems of Correlation When Data Are Expressed as Percentages

Up to this point, we have been discussing several important problems of the correlation coefficient computed from data in the form of raw frequency counts. Many of these problems are applicable to correlation coefficients computed from data transformed to percentages. Certain difficulties, however, are unique to percentage data and warrant further discussion.

Transformation of data from raw counts (the "open array") to percentages (the "closed array") introduces constraint by forcing the variables, for each level or site, to range between 0% and 100% (Cowgill 1968a; Underwood 1969). The artificial limits imposed on variables by closure (conversion to percentages) make percentages very unsuitable for correlation analysis. Underwood (1969: 313) recommends various transformations that may be used to remove the constraints and to obtain variables that are distributed more normally.

Percentages that have not been transformed are unsuitable for correlation analysis for another important and interesting reason. Conversion to percentages can produce substantial spurious correlation in the closed array between variables uncorrelated in the original data set. Closure forces the variables for each level or site to add to a constant sum (100%). In addition, the sum of the covariances of each variable in the closed array is equal to its variance but negative in sign (Chayes 1960, 1971; Chayes and Kruskal 1966; Cowgill 1968a; Underwood 1969). Since the variance is always positive, at least one of the covariances associated with each variable must be negative. The sign of the covariance determines the sign of the correlation coefficient. Thus, each variable must be negatively correlated with at least one other variable. The variable of maximum variance will be negatively correlated with at least two variables. Chayes (1960: 4186) and Underwood (1969: 315) have shown that, if the standard deviation of one of the variables is greater than the sum of, for example, four other standard deviations, then the variable will be negatively correlated with $4 + 1$ (or 5) other variables. An example given by Chayes (1960: 4186) will help illustrate this phenomenon. If variables X_1, X_2, X_3, and X_4, in a 4-variable array, have respective standard deviations of 0.5, 1.4, 1.5, and 3.0, then the standard deviation of variable X_4, for example, is greater than the sum of two other standard deviations. By inspection, without regard to any "real" covariation among the variables, it can be concluded that X_4 will be negatively correlated with at least $2 + 1$ (or 3) other variables (that is, X_4 will be negatively correlated with X_1, X_2, and X_3). Thus, there will be a strong bias toward spurious negative correlations when there are substantial differences between the variances of the variables in a given data set. Spurious effects will be particularly important in arrays with small numbers of variables.

In a data set consisting of raw frequency counts, we can test the significance of an observed correlation coefficient against the null hypothesis that the true population correlation is zero. Conversion of the data to percentages generates spurious, especially negative, correlations. In a closed array, therefore, it is no longer reasonable to test significance against a null hypothesis of zero. Chayes (1971: 52–59) provides an alternative method of testing the significance of a correlation coefficient which corrects for the effects of closure.

Behavioral Patterning and Correlation

Many of the problems just discussed involve difficulties in obtaining a matrix of correlation relatively free of error and distortion. We have said very little, however, about the extent to which artifactual patterns resulting from different behavioral patterns can be distinguished through correlation analysis.

In the following discussion, we will describe briefly two distributional models in which artifacts are discarded in, or very close to, their locus of primary utilization and three distributional models in which artifacts are collected subsequent to use and disposed of elsewhere. We also will consider the case of mixed distributional models. Our purpose here is not to present a formal typology of distributional patterns occurring or expected on Paleolithic "living floors." We wish, rather, to consider the ability of correlation analysis to distinguish idealized spatial patterns produced in a variety of very different behavioral contexts. Throughout the following discussion, we will assume that the distributional data are expressed in the form of raw frequency counts.

The first model (dispersed activity areas) assumes that artifactual material is partitioned into spatially distinct units or loci, each corresponding to a single activity or group of related activities (for example, butchering, hide preparation, tool making, and so forth). Artifacts are assumed to have been discarded more or less where they were used. Archaeologists often expect that a well-preserved and properly excavated Paleolithic occupation horizon contains discrete activity areas which can be extracted by correlation analysis. Many archaeologists also assume that different classes of tools are more or less functionally specific. Given these assumptions, a correlation matrix would be expected to contain a large number of strong positive values among tools belonging to the same "tool kits," and a large number of strong negative values among tools in different "kits." However, we have previously demonstrated that the magnitude of negative correlations will decrease, in a situation of spatial segregation, as variability in the frequency of each tool class increases (Figure 3.1). Thus, even totally spatially segregated activity areas probably will yield a correlation matrix containing weak negatives and weak to strong positives. If attenuation, 0–0 observations, and related problems have not been resolved, weak negatives may disappear completely, and the number of weak positives may be enhanced substantially. In addition, if the fringes of the various activity loci overlap (departure from spatial segregation), the number and magnitude of positives may be enhanced even more.

The assumption that all or even most tool classes are functionally specific has not been tested adequately. Moreover, ethnographic descriptions of modern hunters and gatherers—for example, the Andaman Islanders and various groups of Australian aborigines—suggest that this assumption may be too simplistic in the case of Paleolithic flake tools. Such an assumption is certainly questionable for the Lower and Middle Paleolithic and perhaps for later periods as well. For example, we lack an adequate model to predict the circumstances under which flake tools were retouched (see White and Thomas 1972: 278; Wobst 1974). Ethnographic descriptions of the use of flaked stone tools suggest that a wide range of activities can be performed without using retouched pieces. The reasons for retouching a particular flake may not be related entirely or directly to the particular activity at hand (Wobst 1974). Distributional analyses commonly focus on the retouched category. This practice may prove to be a major built-in source of systematic error in Paleolithic research. Further investigation clearly is needed.

If many tool classes are not functionally specific, weak to strong positive correlations should predominate in the matrix. Their magnitude will depend in part on the reasons why certain flakes were retouched and others not, and in part on the extent to which the various activity loci overlap. Negative correlations probably will be weak or absent.

Obviously, however, activity areas need not be spatially dispersed. Among the Bushmen, for example, many activities are performed by family units in or adjacent to their respective huts (Yellen 1971). We will refer to this patterning as "agglomerated activity areas." This form of spatial distribution will yield a matrix dominated by positive values, their magnitude depending somewhat on the reasons why certain pieces were retouched, and also on the degree to which adjacent areas overlap. If a comparable range of material occurs in each area, negative correlations are not expected.

A third form of spatial distribution (agglomerated disposal areas) may result from the dumping or sweeping of discarded tools and other debris into a relatively compact area adjacent to residential loci, along the perimeter of the site or elsewhere. Reference to various methods of trash disposal and sweeping are scattered throughout the ethnographic literature. There are also a few possible examples of systematic trash disposal in the Paleolithic. De Lumley (1969: 202), for instance, provides evidence that the Lower Paleolithic hut in Lazaret Cave, southern France, was periodically swept clean. Areas within the

Magdalenian huts at the site of Pincevent also may have been swept (Leroi-Gourhan and Brézillon 1966). We are not aware, however, of any systematic discussion of trash disposal practices among modern hunters and gatherers or during the Paleolithic.

Agglomerated disposal probably will yield a correlation matrix very similar to that produced by agglomerated activity (that is, predominantly positive values). At first, the distinction between the two forms of distribution may seem trivial. Agglomerated activity areas among the Bushmen, for example, are in a sense also agglomerated disposal areas. There may be cases, however, such as in caves, in which debris was originally spatially dispersed by function or task group, rather than by family groups, but was subsequently agglomerated by sweeping. Agglomerated distributions need not correspond to families, task groups, or residence units.

A fourth type of spatial patterning may be termed "agglomerated storage areas." Items representing a wide range of activities may be stored together and subsequently abandoned in residence units (see Yellen 1971). In this case, the resulting correlation matrix may be very similar to that produced by agglomerated activity areas (that is, predominantly positives). Items representing a single function (seed-grinding tools, weapons, and so forth) may be stored together and subsequently abandoned (see Seligmann and Seligmann 1911: 86–87). The expected matrix in this case probably will resemble that produced by dispersed activity areas (negative values weak or absent; positive values weak to strong).

A fifth distributional form (scattered disposal areas) may result if debris, subsequent to use, is haphazardly tossed beyond the areas of intensive activity. This distribution actually subsumes at least two different patterns. If no sorting of the material occurs (for instance, by size), the correlation matrix should consist primarily of weak positives. If some degree of sorting does take place, the distribution may resemble dispersed activity areas. The patterning may form a series of concentric arcs around areas of primary activity. The matrix in this case may contain weak negatives in addition to positives.

The last distribution pattern we will consider consists of a mixture of two or more of the previously mentioned patterns. This model is perhaps the one most likely to be encountered on Paleolithic occupation horizons. Each distributional model entering into the mixture derives from a different behavioral context; as such, each represents a different subpopulation of the variability in the archaeological material. Therefore, mixture constitutes an important form of pooling that probably will lead to spurious effects in the correlation matrix. Spurious correlation will be most pronounced if the mean frequencies of the various tool classes in the mixed subpopulations differ substantially. In most cases, pooling probably will enhance the number of weak to strong positives.

The expected correlations for the various distributional models just discussed are summarized in Table 3.8. This summary is intended in no way to be all-inclusive. We are not dealing, for example, with geologic and other noncultural depositional factors. Table 3.8 and the previous discussion are presented strictly for heuristic purposes. Our results suggest, however, that all of these distributional patterns, regardless of their underlying behavioral origins, will yield relatively similar correlation matrices. These matrices probably will contain relatively few weak negative values (or none at all) and a predominance of weak to strong positives. If correlation is used to analyze spatial distributions, large numbers of strong negative values probably will be found only when the data are expressed as percentages. As we have indicated already, however, percentages are not suitable unless they are transformed to improve normality and to eliminate the spurious effects of closure. Large numbers of very strong positive values probably will be obtained most commonly if the data have been expressed as raw counts, without density correction, or when large numbers of 0–0 pairs have been included. Correction of these two factors may yield a matrix dominated by weak to intermediate positive

Table 3.8 Expected Correlations for Idealized Spatial Distributions When Data Are Expressed as Raw Frequency Counts[a]

Spatial distributions	Majority of tool classes are functionally specific	Majority of tool classes are not functionally specific
1. Dispersed activity areas	[b](+) weak to strong (−) weak	(+) weak to strong (−) not expected
2. Agglomerated activity areas	(+) strong (−) not expected	(+) weak to strong (−) not expected
3. Agglomerated disposal areas	(+) weak to strong (−) weak or not expected	(+) weak to strong (−) not expected
4. Agglomerated storage areas		
a. by residence	(+) weak to strong (−) not expected	
b. by function	(+) weak to strong (−) weak	
5. Scattered disposal areas		
a. unsorted	(+) weak (−) not expected	(+) weak (−) not expected
b. sorted	(+) weak to strong (−) weak	(+) weak to strong (−) not expected
6. Mixed spatial distributions	(+) weak to strong (−) weak or not expected	

[a] Spurious correlation effects are not included.

[b] (+) Expected positive correlations; (−) expected negative correlations.

values. If we now add additional spurious effects owing to sampling error, attenuation, pooling, and so forth, the correlation matrix may be so altered that the variability, reflecting different behavioral sources, may become totally masked.

Although our discussion to this point may seem rather discouraging, we can make several suggestions that may help us out of this dilemma. First, steps must be taken to eliminate spurious correlation in the matrix. Some sources of error will be easier to deal with than others. Raw frequency counts probably should be adjusted for density. Percentages, unless transformed, are unsuitable. Sampling error and reliability are more difficult to deal with, at present, because they are connected intimately with our methods of excavation and typological analysis. Systematic error sources are probably very common and difficult to eliminate. We probably can learn a great deal from psychologists who have invested a tremendous amount of energy to develop ways to assess and control reliability.

The inclusion of 0–0 observations in the data may produce serious spurious correlation in the matrix. Archaeologists generally lack criteria by which selectively to eliminate 0–0 pairs. One possible solution to this problem, therefore, may be to drop all 0–0 pairs. This procedure, however, will restrict the range of the variables and will enhance the number of weak positive values in the matrix. The problem posed by 0–0 observations should be of fundamental concern to archaeologists who are interested in spatial analysis. A suitable solution to this problem will necessitate a thorough investigation of the criteria by which archaeologists define the boundaries of their sampling universe and the number and size of their sampling units.

To minimize spurious effects in the correlation matrix, we offer the following tentative procedural guidelines. We assume, of course, that adequate samples have been obtained by a suitable method.

Step 1. Retain raw counts.

Step 2. Employ density correction where areas or volumes of provenience units vary.

Step 3. Correct for 0–0 observations, perhaps by their elimination. It may be necessary to eliminate variables with small sample sizes.

Step 4. Compile histograms of all variables prior to further analysis.

    A. If bimodal or multimodal distributions are observed:

        1. Bimodal or multimodal distributions should be dichotomized as close as possible to the median if it is assumed that the population from which the sample

was drawn has a unimodal distribution. If more than one distribution is dichotomized, the following correlation coefficients may be used (Guilford 1952: 33):

    a. Pearson's r between undichotomized variables;

    b. biserial r between variables when one is dichotomized and the other is not;

    c. tetrachoric r between variables when both are dichotomized.

  2. Bimodal or multimodal distributions should be dissected and a set of new variables created, if it is assumed that bi- or multimodality in the sample reflects pooling of distinct populations (such as primary activity areas and secondary trash disposal areas).

B. Transformation of the data may be required if one or more frequency distributions, including those resulting from dissection, are asymmetrical. A logarithmic or square root transformation may be appropriate in many cases (Dixon and Massey 1969: 322–325; Mueller 1949; Steel and Torrie 1960: 156–158).

Step 5. Compile all possible pairs of cross plots prior to further analysis to evaluate:

A. Presence of nonlinear relationships. Departure from linearity will require application of a suitable transformation to linearize the relationships.

B. Presence of spatial segregation not immediately evident from a computed correlation coefficient.

C. Possibility of spurious correlation resulting from presence of unusual "high-density" provenience units. Deletion or separate analysis of such provenience units may be required to prevent pooling of differential activity patterns (such as primary activity areas and secondary trash disposal areas).

Once the major sources of spurious correlation have been eliminated or minimized, multivariate procedures should produce groupings that reflect patterning in the archaeological material. These groupings, however, should not be interpreted automatically as entities, such as "tool kits." We have tried to show that many different behavioral contexts may generate very similar correlation matrices.

Multivariate groupings may represent covariation among items that were stored together, that were used at the same residential locus, or that, subsequent to use, ended up together in the same trash disposal area. Covariation among items in a trash deposit may reflect a mixture of several behavioral contexts. For example, items may occur together because they share a common factor, such as seasonality (all items were used in the fall) or proximity to an important resource (bones of aquatic birds and tools for processing reeds).

Whenever possible, multivariate analysis should be undertaken to test a series of explicit hypotheses formulated in advance, not as a procedure for "discovering" patterning. Techniques like factor analysis, for example, will generate groupings from a correlation matrix regardless of whether the variance in the matrix reflects real patterning in the archaeological material or spurious effects.

If natural provenience units, such as huts, pits, and hearths, can be identified on an occupation horizon, partitioning the archaeological material into reasonable subpopulations prior to analysis may be possible. This is common practice, for example, in the analysis of sedentary Neolithic settlements, where pit fill is handled separately from house-floor deposits. In order for multivariate groupings adequately to reflect underlying patterning in the data, the archaeological material should be divided, whenever possible, into its component subpopulations. Otherwise, the analysis may produce spurious groupings that merely reflect the effects of pooling. Psychologists, for example, would be very hesitant to factor analyze a correlation matrix derived from mixed populations (Guilford 1952).

Natural proveniences commonly are difficult to recognize on Paleolithic occupation horizons. Archaeological material from horizons of this type probably will consist of an undefined complex mixture of different behavioral subpopulations. Refined excavation and recovery techniques may help to provide a basis for partitioning the material. Many such techniques are available (three-dimensional plotting of all artifacts and debris; microstratigraphic analysis in conjunction with chemical, palynological, and sedimentological sampling; and so forth).

If the archaeological material on "living floors" cannot be separated adequately into discrete subpopulations on the basis of natural provenience units, the archaeologist may be able to increase the scale of units analyzed. Each discrete occupation horizon, at each of the various sites within the annual round of a group of prehistoric hunters and gatherers, may be treated as a natural provenience unit. This suggestion assumes, of course, that discrete "living floors" can be isolated. This is a difficult problem, but one which we feel may, in many cases, pose less of a problem than spatially partitioning material on a single floor. It may be possible, for example, to isolate reasonable approximations of discrete "living floors" (1) in caves that were occupied intermittently or in which the sedimentation rate was fairly rapid and (2) in open-air sites.

In situations in which "living floors" can be identified stratigraphically but not partitioned spatially, analysis can begin with a study of the intercorrelations among occupation horizons (Q-mode), instead of with the intercorrelations among classes of tools (R-mode). Rowlett and Pollnac (1971) and Tugby (1965) discuss Q-mode and R-mode analysis in archaeology.

If a sufficient number of discrete occupation horizons are included in the analysis and if there are sufficient differences among occupations in the number and types of activities represented, this approach may yield multivariate groupings that approximate the different "structural poses" (Binford 1972: 133; Gearing 1962) of the prehistoric group.

Once the Q-mode analysis has been completed, a variety of R-mode techniques may be employed to determine which groups of items are major contributors to each class of site. The minimal grouping of tool classes that can be identified in this manner probably will correspond to the assemblage obtained from the most functionally specific occupation horizon included in the analysis. In many cases, however, the multivariate groupings probably will be somewhat more inclusive, representing composites of activities strongly reflecting differences among sites in seasonality, group size, and duration of occupation.

Once minimal groupings of tool classes have been isolated, their spatial patterning can be investigated on individual "living floors," and hypotheses may be formulated concerning the organization of activities.

It should be apparent from the discussion in this chapter that the analysis of spatial patterning in archaeological material is an exceedingly complex problem. Multivariate analysis of correlational data must be undertaken with a clear appreciation of these problems to avoid erroneous interpretations of the analytical results. Clearly, multivariate groupings cannot be interpreted automatically as entities, such as "tool kits." Very similar groupings may be generated by a wide range of different behavioral patterns and by purely spurious sources. It is, therefore, incumbent upon the archaeologist to demonstrate that his results are culturally meaningful. Failure to do so may severely distort our understanding of the content and variety of "structural poses" in the annual round of Paleolithic hunters and gatherers.

Acknowledgments

We wish to thank H. Martin Wobst, Robert Whallon, Jr., and Bonnie Hole for their many helpful suggestions and criticisms of the manuscript. We assume full responsibility, however, for any errors or problems that remain in the final version of the chapter.

4

Multifactor Analysis of Association: An Application to Owasco Ceramics

Albert C. Spaulding

A fundamental problem of archaeology, with ramifications at all theoretical levels, is the description of culturally meaningful artifact assemblages. The goal of description is the economical presentation of the essential properties of the assemblage. We attempt to provide a description that is both simpler than the artifacts themselves and complete with respect to the properties and relationships of the assemblage judged to be culturally significant. In broad terms, one can distinguish three levels of procedures for attaining this objective.

The first is the traditional approach: It is based on careful observation of the collection and an impressionistic assignment of artifacts to polythetic or monothetic classes called "types" of artifacts. The observations in turn are based on an intuitive knowledge of human behavior supplemented by comparative and experimental study; more carefully stated, archaeologists are skilled in the recognition of behaviorally significant attributes of artifacts, and they observe the association of these attributes on artifacts. The traditional approach has, in general, produced good results: Some sense of the nature of assemblages is communicated, and the discriminated classes are useful in interassemblage comparison and ultimately in the study of cultural process. But the traditional approach has its defects. Broadly speaking, its results are somewhat too subjective because the high competence shown in attribute recognition and functional inference is not matched by a keen interest in the principles of classification and the statistical methods appropriate to the study of class relationships.

The second level of descriptive procedures results from an attempt to objectify the operations of the traditional approach. It is characterized by explicit description of the observed attribute combinations together with their frequencies in the group of artifacts under study. In the traditional approach, we customarily are informed that there are two classes of pots, large ones and small ones, and we are informed further that 20% of the large pots are red and that 30% have handles. We are not told how many of the large red pots have handles. In the second approach, we are given the number of pots in all possible combinations: large red with handles, large not red with handles, and so on; here, the description of the group of pots is complete with respect to the attributes recognized. The second approach continues with an analysis of attribute association by formal statistical methods, including consideration of sampling vagaries, and formal statistical methods are subsequently applied to problems of intrassemblage comparison, interassemblage comparison, and cultural process. Some 25 years of growth have given us a rich literature in the second mode, ranging from chi-square analysis of simple two-way contingency tables to the application of the elaborate multivariate techniques of numerical taxonomy, factor analysis, and multidimensional scaling, and the end is not in sight. I have followed this development with interest and admiration, but I have not been able to repress a certain sense of insecurity, a feeling that we are not quite solid at the base—that we are not solving the problem of describing assemblages in a clear, straightforward way. This insecurity was caused by the absence of an adequate statistical technique for analysis of multiple contingency tables.

We turn now to the third level of analytical complexity, or, if preferred, to a second stage in the second level. Quite recently, methods have been developed by mathematical statisticians that offer a systematic method of examining contingency tables with three or more variables which should be of great interest in connection with our fundamental problem. The structure of the analysis can be illustrated by a 2-by-2-by-2 contingency table—that is, a table setting out the interrelationships of three variables (or dimensions), each of which exhibits two discrete attributes. An example would be a collection of stone blades that exhibit or do not exhibit a prepared striking platform (Variable A), are made from obsidian or from some other kind of stone (Variable B), and are either crude or fine in workmanship (Variable C). The collection can be completely described by means of the eight cells of a 2-by-2-by-2 table:

	C1		C2	
	B1	B2	B1	B2
A1				
A2				

With each cell properly filled in with the observed number of specimens, we can test four kinds of hypotheses based entirely on the observed data, that is, with no prior hypotheses on relationships among the classes.

The first hypothesis is a familiar one, addressed to the question: Are these variables mutually independent? If the variables are in fact independent, the numbers in each cell should be predictable from the marginal totals for each attribute; for example, the number of $A1B1C1$ specimens should be simply the product of three proportions multiplied in turn by the total number of specimens. If we let N symbolize the total number of specimens, $A1++$ the total number of $A1$ specimens (the $A1$ marginal total), and so on, the formula for calculating the expected number of $A1B1C1$ specimens is $A1++/N \times B1++/N \times C1++/N \times N$. The eight expected numbers calculated in this way can be compared with the observed numbers by means of the chi-square distribution. The comparison requires, of course, both the chi-square value and the appropriate degrees of freedom (number of independent comparisons in the table). For our 2-by-2-by-2 table, there are four degrees of freedom. With these data, we can judge whether or not the difference between expected and observed values is large enough to suggest association of attributes rather than mere sampling vagaries.

The second kind of hypothesis and the appropriate analysis is less familiar. It comes in three variants. The question asked is: Is one of the variables independent with respect to the other two taken jointly? In the case of the A variable against the B and C variables taken jointly, a new table would be set up:

	B1C1	B1C2	B2C1	B2C2
A1				
A2				

Again, eight expected numbers would be calculated from the marginal totals for $A1$ and $A2$ and the four BC combinations and the chi-square value obtained by comparison with the observed numbers for each cell. In this table, there are three degrees of freedom.

The third hypothesis also has three variants. The question here is: Is the independence of two of the variables conditional on the level of the third variable? Here, the table for testing the independence of variables *A* and *B* conditional on the level of *C* (whether C1 or C2) is:

	C1			C2	
	B1	B2		B1	B2
A1			A1		
A2			A2		

Expected numbers are calculated from the observed totals of the combinations *A*1*C*1, *A*2*C*1, *B*1*C*1, *B*2*C*1, *A*1*C*2, *A*2*C*2, *B*1*C*2, and *B*2*C*2, and the *C*1 and *C*2 totals. There are two degrees of freedom for this table because we have, in effect, two 2-by-2 tables, each having one degree of freedom; the first 2-by-2 table investigates interaction between the *A* and *B* variables for the subclass of *C*1 specimens, the second for the subclass of *C*2 specimens.

The fourth hypothesis is less straightforward. In the first hypothesis, no combination totals are considered; there is no two-factor effect. In the second hypothesis, one two-factor effect (the *BC* combinations) is considered. In the third hypothesis, two two-factor effects (the *AC* and *BC* combinations) are considered. In the fourth hypothesis, all three two-factor effects are considered in calculating the eight expected numbers. The relationships cannot be exhibited in a table. Neither can a direct formula be written for calculating the expected numbers; instead, expected values must be computed by successive approximation, by iteration. When we have fitted all three two-factor effects in a 2-by-2-by-2 table, only one degree of freedom remains. I suppose the question addressed by this hypothesis is: Is any interaction evident when all three two-factor effects are considered?

The order in which these hypotheses were presented is not random. From the first through the fourth, each successive hypothesis added one new effect (or parameter) to its immediate predecessor, and the degrees of freedom correspondingly decreased steadily. If we had filled in some numbers and calculated a chi-square value under each hypothesis, we would have found that these values decreased steadily from the first hypothesis through the fourth hypothesis. This is inevitable because we use additional relationships of the observed numbers in calculating the expected numbers as we progress through the models; we are forcing the expected numbers to be more like the observed numbers. The hypotheses form a nested hierarchy; as we pass from the fourth through the third and second to the first, each hypothesis is a special case obtained by omitting one parameter from its predecessor. The hierarchy provides a systematic way of examining all possible kinds of interaction—the degrees of freedom are systematically exhausted. There is in fact a fifth hypothesis with zero degrees of freedom which adds to the fourth hypothesis the three-factor effect; the calculated expected numbers would simply reproduce the observed numbers. Finally, if likelihood ratio chi-squares are employed, the significance of the difference in goodness of fit between any two hypotheses can be obtained by subtracting the smaller from the larger chi-square value and similarly subtracting the smaller from the larger value for degrees of freedom. For example, suppose that the likelihood ratio chi-square value for the first hypothesis were 50.00 for four degrees of freedom, and for the second, 25.00 for three degrees of freedom. Then the significance of the difference in goodness of fit between the two hypotheses is estimated by 50.00 − 25.00 = a chi-square value of 25.00 for 4 − 3 = 1 degree of freedom, a highly significant difference.

If we think in terms of the logarithm of an expected number, we can introduce a new representation that makes the structure of the analysis clear. For a three-way table and the first hypothesis (Model 1 in the customary terminology), the logarithm of the expected number for some cell (log ex.$_{ijk}$) is $[1] + [A]_i + [B]_j + [C]_k$ where $[1]$ is the grand mean of the logarithms of the expected cell counts, $[1] + [A]_i$ is the mean of the logarithms of the expected counts for some particular attribute in Variable A, and so on. For the second hypothesis (Model 2), log ex.$_{ijk}$ is $[1] + [A]_i + [B]_j + [C]_k + [AB]_{ij}$, and the third, fourth, and fifth hypotheses successively add the remaining two two-factor effects and the three-factor effect. Omitting the subscripts and brackets, Table 4.1 represents the six loglinear hierarchies possible for a three-way table. I leave to your imagination the horrors of, say, a six-way table.

These matters badly need an illustration at this point, and I turn to a set of data very kindly provided by Robert Whallon, a deck of punch cards representing the rim sherds from the Owasco components at Canandaigua and Castle Creek, New York. We have worked with the data from Canandaigua. Each sherd is represented by a card describing its condition with respect to eight variables, and each variable is represented by from 2 to 10 attributes. The material has been studied by Ritchie and MacNeish and later by Whallon. For present purposes, I have worked with four variables: presence or absence of collar, shape of lip (5 recognized lip profiles), motif of lip decoration (7 motifs), and motif of neck decoration (13 motifs, including some combinations). The analysis is confined to three-way tables, that is, to sets of three variables, and I have analyzed three of the possible four combinations of four things taken three at a time. There are several reasons for this simplified analysis: *(1)* The variables used are those prominent in conventional typology, *(2)* I wished to avoid the hideous complexities of more elaborate tables for simplicity of exposition, *(3)* four-attribute combinations tend to produce very small observed numbers or "not observed" notations owing to absence of evidence for one or another variable, and *(4)* the simplified analysis suggests that we have the main story.

The first combination analyzed consisted of the variables presence or absence of collar, lip decorative motif, and lip profile, yielding a 2-by-7-by-5 table with 70 cells. A total of 262 sherds from Canandaigua were classifiable for these three variables. The result of the loglinear analysis is presented in Table 4.2.

This is a gratifyingly simple result. Model 1 shows that there is indeed association of some kind in the Canandaigua pottery so far as these three variables are concerned. Model 2, third variant ($+BC$), shows a probability of .11, indicating that the calculated expected numbers fit the observed numbers in a reasonable sort of way when sampling vagaries are allowed for. The significant *chi*-square of Model 1 is accounted for almost completely by association between the B and C variables, that is, by association between lip motif and the presence or absence of a collar on the vessel rim. Model 2, $+BC$ variant, removes this association because it considers B and C only in combination. More specifically, the 49 collared rims show more smoothed lips, and lips decorated with one horizontal line, than expected. The association is not strong, but it seems to be real. And, we can write a simple rule for combining these three variables: Take the observed proportions of the various collar and lip motif combinations and divide each set of the attributes of the third variable (lip profile) in these proportions for assignment to the BC combinations. The significant chi-square values for Models 2 and 3 in other hierarchies are a reflection of the BC association; informally, as the BC element moves to the right in the formulas heading the hierarchy columns, Models 2 and 3 become significant.

The second set of three variables analyzed for Canandaigua is lip profile, presence or absence of collar, and neck motif; this set is easily discussed. There is no significant association for Model 1 (chi-square is 116.93 with 112 degrees of freedom; more than 10% of the samples randomly drawn from a population with no association of attributes would exhibit a chi-square as large or larger). I conclude that there is no association of any form among these variables worthy of analysis. They are essentially independent on the evidence at hand (311 sherds).

The third set of three variables is lip decoration motif, presence or absence of collar, and neck decorative motif. The analysis produced some surprising results. These results coincided with the appearance of a revised and streamlined computing program. A painful hand check of the data indicates that there are serious strains on the entire concept owing to a number of zero margins and to a great many very low expected values, and the program fails to take these into account.

Table 4.1 **Six Hierarchies for a Three-Way Table**

Model 1	1+A+B+C	1+A+B+C	1+A+B+C	1+A+B+C	1+A+B+C
Model 2	+AB	+AB	+AC	+AC	+BC
Model 3	+AB+AC	+AB+BC	+AC+AB	+AC+BC	+BC+AC
Model 4	+AB+AC+BC	+AB+AC+BC	+AB+AC+BC	+AB+AC+BC	+AB+AC+BC

Table 4.2 **Likelihood Ratio *Chi*-Square Values for Six Hierarchies, Canandaigua: Lip Profile (A), Lip Motif (B), and Collar (C)**

	Hierarchy																	
Source of *chi*-square	+AB+AC+BC			+AB+BC+AC			+AC+AB+BC			+AC+BC+AB			+BC+AB+AC			+BC+AC+AB		
	x^2	df	p	x^2	df	p	x^2	df	p	x^2	df	p	x^2	df	p	x^2	df	p
Model 1	112.45	58	.000	112.45	58	.000	112.45	58	.000	112.45	58	.000	112.45	58	.000	112.45	58	.000
Difference	38.29	30	.14	38.29	30	.14	17.78	10	.06	17.78	10	.06	52.17	10	.000	52.17	10	.000
Model 2	74.16	28	.000	74.16	28	.000	94.67	48	.000	94.67	48	.000	60.28	48	.11	60.28	48	.11
Difference	17.78	8	.02	52.17	9	.000	38.29	28	.10	52.16	9	.000	38.29	29	.12	17.77	9	.04
Model 3	56.38	20	.000	21.99	19	.28	56.38	20	.000	42.51	39	.35	21.99	19	.28	42.51	39	.35
Difference	49.13	12	.000	14.74	11	.20	49.13	12	.000	35.26	31	.30	14.74	11	.20	35.26	31	.30
Model 4	7.25	8	.70	7.25	8	.70	7.25	8	.70	7.25	8	.70	7.25	8	.70	7.25	8	.70

The check further indicates that there may be complex reactions to combinations—that is, that understanding will come at the level of Models 2 and 3. The problem is complicated by a number of neck and lip motifs that are rare. In general, there are a few possibly real and certainly weak two-factor interactions among these three variables. The sample of rims at hand is too small for any clear interpretation.

I return to my original problem: What have we done to solve the fundamental problem of describing an assemblage? So far as the variables considered are concerned, we have made substantial progress. In the case of the first set, we showed that there is indeed association of attributes and that this association is simply a matter of association of lip decorative motif and presence or absence of a collar. For the second set, there is no interaction at any level; all we need for predicting the observed numbers reasonably well is the total number of sherds and the proportions of the attributes in each of the three variables. For the third set, we suspected the existence of some weak, but possibly real, interactions among the three variables, perhaps chiefly between the collar–no collar variable and combinations of lip and neck decorative motifs. The analysis was not pursued relentlessly, owing to technical difficulties. So far as our evidence goes, the Canandaigua potters were anything but fierce typologists, although they did exhibit some mild preferences for certain attribute combinations. It is interesting to compare this result with that of Whallon, an experienced analyst of Owasco pottery. He concluded that by "Spaulding's method," only two pottery types could be defined—collared and uncollared vessels. This is not far off my conclusion, although I might introduce some minor refinements. (Incidentally, I can now define Spaulding's method of 1953: It consists of calculating Model 1 and inspecting it for groups of positively associated attributes, perhaps with the aid of supplementary two-way calculations.)

I conclude with remarks on differing modes of analyzing collections. The loglinear method is directed to the question of what kinds and degrees of attribute association are exhibited by the collection under study. The same pottery was analyzed by Whallon with a somewhat different question in mind: In my terms, his problem was to divide the collection into a comparatively large number of classes in the most sensible way, and he employed a cascading (monothetic–divisive) technique for this purpose, choosing at each step the variable showing the strongest association within the subdivision at hand for the next subdivision. He argued, I believe essentially correctly, that this procedure coincides quite well with the implicit typological operations of traditional archaeology. He argued further that the classes produced were true types in the sense that they were reflective of space and time, a traditional justification in American archaeology. This latter argument can be shown to be off the mark: Association analysis is not relevant to the identification of artifact classes useful in frequency seriation. The utility of such classes derives from including as class-defining properties attributes and attribute combinations whose relative frequencies vary systematically in the group of components to be seriated. There is no method of analysis that can identify in advance in a component the classes that will be useful in some subsequent seriation. This kind of utility is identified by actual intercomponent comparison. This does not mean, however, that Whallon's method is wrong or useless; it does represent a rational approach toward "cleaving nature at the joints." But it is superseded, I believe, by the loglinear methods illustrated here. When one realizes that the tasks of defining classes for seriation and of looking for patterns of attribute association are both logically and practically distinguishable, the reason for this claim is apparent. Loglinear analysis provides and organizes all data relevant to detecting and describing patterns of association in a collection; the monothetic–divisive analysis provides only some of the data needed.

Some Technical Notes

1. The literature on hierarchies is growing so rapidly that I will not attempt to provide a formal list of references. My introduction to the concept was the article "The Analysis of Multidimensional Contingency Tables" by Stephen E. Fienberg (*Ecology* **51** [3], 1970: 419–433), called to my attention by Robert Vierra. More recent expositions include "Loglinear Models in Contingency Table Analysis" by Harry H. Ku and Solomon Kullback (*American Statistician* **28** [4], 1974: 115–122) and "Hierarchical Models for Significance Tests in Multivariate Contingency Tables: An Exegesis of Goodman's Recent Papers" by James A. Davis (In *Sociological Methodology, 1973–1974*, edited by H. L. Costner. Jossey-Bass, 1974). The Davis paper is a good introduction to some basic concepts for nonmathematical readers and provides a list of references to the important and highly technical work of L. A. Goodman in this field. Finally, we have an archaeological application and exposition of the method by Dwight W. Read in *American Antiquity* ("Some Comments on Typologies in Archaeology and an Outline of a Methodology," *American Antiquity* **39** [2, Part 1], 1974: 216–242). Read's paper appeared after we had completed much of the work on the Owasco pottery. I have no doubt that other applications will have appeared by the time this volume has been published.

2. The chi-square values appropriate to the loglinear hierarchies are not the familiar Pearsonian chi-square, in which the contribution of

each cell is calculated as the squared difference of the observed and expected values divided by the expected value. Fienberg and others recommended the likelihood ratio chi-square; for this chi-square, the cell contributions are calculated as twice the observed cell value multiplied by the natural logarithm of the observed value divided by the expected value.

Acknowledgments

I am grateful to Robert Whallon for providing the data treated here, and for his interest and stimulating comments. The particular work of his referred to is "A New Approach to Pottery Typology" (*American Antiquity, 37*, 1972: 13–33). Underlying this debt is still another, to my teacher and colleague, James B. Griffin; to him I owe most of my ideas and basic information on the archaeology of the eastern United States, as well as gratitude for encouragement in pursuing quantitative researches. A little-known fact is that Professor Griffin is a crypto-admirer of quantitative methods. Finally, I thank George Gregg and Ronald Jeffries of the Computer Center of the University of California, Santa Barbara, for their skillful and energetic assistance in accomplishing the formidable calculations.

References for Part I

Allchin, B., and R. Allchin
1968 *The Birth of Indian Civilization: India and Pakistan before 500 B.C.* Harmondsworth: Pelican.

Arkin, H., and R. R. Colton
1963 *Tables for Statisticians.* 2d ed. New York: Barnes and Noble.

Beers, Y.
1957 *Introduction to the Theory of Error.* 2d ed. Reading: Addison-Wesley.

Binford, L. R.
1964 Some Considerations of Archaeological Research Design. *American Antiquity* **29**:423–441.
1972 Contemporary Model Building: Paradigms and the Current State of Paleolithic Research. In *Models in Archaeology*, edited by David L. Clarke. London: Methuen. Pp. 109–166.
1973 Interassemblage Variability: The Mousterian and the "Functional" Argument. In *The Explanation of Culture Change*, edited by Collin Renfrew. London: Duckworth. Pp. 227–254.

Binford, L. R., and S. R. Binford
1966 A Preliminary Analysis of Functional Variability in the Mousterian of Levallois Facies. *American Anthropologist* **68**:238–295.

Binford, S. R., and L. R. Binford
1969 Stone Tools and Human Behavior. *Scientific American* **220**:70–72, 77–82, 84.

Blair, E.
1911– *Indian Tribes of the Upper Mississippi Valley and Great Lakes.* Vols. 1 and 2.
1912 Cleveland: C. Thomas.

Black, R., R. Goldthwaites, and H. B. Willman
1973 The Wisconsonian Stage. *Memoir 136 of the Geological Society of America.* New York.

Bordes, F.
1961 Typologie du Paléolithique Ancien et Moyen. *Publications de l'Institut de Préhistoire de l'Université de Bourdeaux, Memoire* No. 1. Bordeaux: Imprimeries Delmas.
1965 Utilisation Possible des Côtés des Burins. *Fundberichte aus Schwaben* **17**:3–4, Plate 30.
1969 Reflections on Typology and Techniques in the Paleolithic. *Arctic Anthropology* **6**:1–29.
1970 Réflexions sur l'Outil au Paléolithique. *Compte Rendu des Séances Mensuelles de la Société Préhistorique Française* **7**:199–202.

69

Brézillon, M. N.
1968   La Dénomination des Objets de Pierre Taillee. *Gallia Préhistoire* **4**(Supplé-ment). Paris.

Brose, D. S.
1968   The Archaeology of Summer Island: Changing Settlement Systems in the Northern Lake Michigan Area. Ph.D. dissertation, University of Michigan, Ann Arbor.
1970a Prehistoric Cultural Ecology and Social Organization in Northern Lake Michigan. *Case Western Reserve University Studies in Anthropology* No. 1. Cleveland, Ohio.
1970b Archaeology of Summer Island: Changing Settlement Systems in Northern Lake Michigan. *Anthropological Papers, University of Michigan, Museum of Anthropology* No. 41.
1973   A Preliminary Report on Recent Excavations at the South Park Site, Cuyahoga Co., Ohio. *Pennsylvania Archaeologist* **43**:25–43.
1974   The Poisson Series in Spatial Analysis of Archaeological Materials. Paper presented at the Ohio Academy of Science, Annual Meeting, Section H (Anthropology), Marietta.
1975   Review of "Aboriginal Settlement Patterns in the Northeast" by W. A. Ritchie and R. E. Funk. *Pennsylvania Archaeologist* **45**:56–57.
n.d.a The Whittlesey Occupations of N.E. Ohio. In *Late Prehistory of the Lake Erie Drainage Basin: A Symposium*, edited by David S. Brose. Scientific Papers of the Cleveland Museum of Natural History. In press.
n.d.b A Model of Whittlesey Settlement–Subsistence Systems in Northeastern Ohio, A.D. 1000–A.D. 1620: Cultural Inference from Statistical Archaeological Sampling. A Preliminary Report to the N.S.F. on Grant G.S.-28985, "Analysis of the Late Prehistoric Period in Northeast Ohio."
n.d.c The South Park Site: A Multicomponent Whittlesey Occupation in Cuyahoga County, Ohio. Scientific Papers of the Cleveland Museum of Natural History (new series). In press.
n.d.d Late Woodland Prehistoric Occupation at the Hale Farm, Summit Co., Ohio. *Bulletin of the Western Reserve Historical Society*. Cleveland.

Brose, D., and P. S. Essenpreis
1973   A Report on a Preliminary Archaeological Survey of Monroe County, Michigan. *Michigan Archaeologist* **19**:1–182.

Brose, D., and J. F. Scarry
n.d.   A Late Woodland Rockshelter at Boston I edges, Summit Co., Ohio. Manuscript on file at Case Western Reserve University, Department of Anthropology, Cleveland, Ohio.

Brose, D., G. Wentzel, H. Bluestone, and P. Essenpreis
n.d.   The Conneaut Fort Site: A Multicomponent Whittlesey Occupation in Ashtabula Co., Ohio. Manuscript on file at Case Western Reserve University, Department of Anthropology, Cleveland, Ohio.

Brose, D., and N. M. White
n.d.   Seventeen Prehistoric Sites in Northern Ohio. Manuscript on file at Case Western Reserve University, Department of Anthropology, Cleveland, Ohio.

Clark, J. D.
1959   *The Prehistory of Southern Africa*. Harmondsworth: Pelican.

Clarke, D.
1968   *Analytical Archaeology*. London: Methuen.

Carroll, J. B.
1961   The Nature of the Data, or How to Choose a Correlation Coefficient. *Psychometrika* **26**:347–372.

Chayes, F.
  1960   On Correlation between Variables of Constant Sum. *Journal of Geophysical Research* **65**:4185–4193.
  1971   *Ratio Correlation.* Chicago: University of Chicago Press.
Chayes, F., and W. Kruskal
  1966   An Approximate Statistical Test for Correlations between Proportions. *Journal of Geology* **74**:692–702.
Converse, R.
  1964   Ohio Stone Types. *Ohio Archaeologist* **13**:78–120.
Cowgill, G. L.
  1968a Counts, Ratios, and Percentages: Problems in Quantifying Archaeological Data. Unpublished manuscript on file at Brandeis University, Department of Anthropology. Waltham, Mass.
  1968b Archaeological Applications of Factor, Cluster, and Proximity Analysis. *American Antiquity* **33**:367–375.
  1970   Some Sampling and Reliability Problems in Archaeology. In *Archéologie et Calculateurs*, edited by Jean-Claude Gardin and Mario Borillo. Paris: Centre National de la Recherche Scientifique. Pp. 161–176.
Cronin, C.
  1962   An Analysis of Pottery Design Elements, Indicating Possible Relationships between Three Decorated Types. In Chapters in the Prehistory of Eastern Arizona. Vol. 53 of *Fieldiana: Anthropology*, edited by P. Martin. Chicago. Pp. 105–114.
Dacey, M. F.
  1974   The Random Pattern of Point Maps: Genesis and Hypothesis Evaluation. Unpublished manuscript on file at Northwestern University, Department of Geography. Evanston, Ill.
Davis, J. A.
  1974   Hierarchical Models for Significance Tests in Multivariate Contingency Tables: An Exegesis of Goodman's Recent Papers. In *Sociological Methodology, 1973–1974*, edited by H. L. Costner. San Francisco: Jossey-Bass.
Dixon, W. J., and F. J. Massey, Jr.
  1969   *Introduction to Statistical Analysis.* 3d ed. New York: McGraw-Hill.
De Lumley, H.
  1969   Une Cabane Acheuléenne dans la Grotte du Lazaret (Nice). *Mémoires de la Société Préhistorique Française* No. 7. Paris.
Feller, W.
  1968   *An Introduction to Probability Theory and Its Application.* Vol. 1. 3d ed. New York: Wiley and Sons.
Ferguson, G. A.
  1941   The Factorial Interpretation of Test Difficulty. *Psychometrika* **6**:323–329.
  1959   *Statistical Analysis in Psychology and Education.* New York: McGraw-Hill.
Fienberg, S. F.
  1970   The Analysis of Multidimensional Contingency Tables. *Ecology* **51**(3):419–433.
Fitting, J. E.
  1964   Ceramic Relationships of Four Late Woodland Sites in Northern Ohio. *Wisconsin Archeologist* **45**:160–175.
  1969   Settlement Analysis in the Great Lakes Region. *Southwest Journal of Anthropology* **25**:360–377.
Flannery, K. V.
  1968   Archaeological Systems Theory and Early Mesoamerica. In *Anthropological Archaeology in the Americas*, edited by B. Meggers. Washington, D.C.: Anthropological Society of Washington.

Forsythe, J. L.
  1970 A Geologist Looks at the Natural Vegetation Map of Ohio. *Ohio Journal of Science* **70:**180–191.

Freeman, L. G.
  1973 The Analysis of Some Occupation Floor Distributions from Earlier and Middle Paleolithic Sites in Spain. IXth International Congress of Anthropological and Ethnological Sciences, Paper No. 0285. Chicago.

Freeman, L. G., and J. A. Brown
  1962 Statistical Analysis of Carter Ranch Pottery. In Chapters in the Prehistory of Eastern Arizona II. Vol. 55 of *Fieldiana: Anthropology.* Chicago.

Frison, G. C.
  1968 A Functional Analysis of Certain Chipped Stone Tools. *American Antiquity* **33:**149–155.

Fritz, J. M.
  1974 Review of "Lithic Analysis and Cultural Inference: A Paleo-Indian Case." *American Antiquity* **39:**387–391.

Gearing, F.
  1962 Priest and Warriors. *Memoirs of the American Anthropological Association* No. 93. Washington, D.C.

Gordon, R. B.
  1966 Map of the Natural Vegetation of Ohio. Ohio Biological Survey, Columbus.
  1969 The Natural Vegetation of Ohio in Pioneer Days. *Bulletin of the Ohio Biological Survey* (n.s.) **3:**1–113.

Gould, R. A., D. A. Koster, and A. H. L. Sontz
  1971 The Lithic Assemblage of the Western Desert Aborigines of Australia. *American Antiquity* **36:**149–169.

Greber, N., and D. S. Brose
  n.d. Principal Component Analysis of the Ecological Factors Influencing the Location of Whittlesey Sites in Northeast Ohio. Manuscript on file at Case Western Reserve University, Department of Anthropology, Cleveland, Ohio.

Greenman, E. J.
  1935a Excavation of the Reeve Village Site, Lake Co., Ohio. *Ohio State Archaeological and Historical Quarterly* **44:**2–64.
  1935b Seven Prehistoric Sites in Northern Ohio. *Ohio State Archaeological and Historical Quarterly* **44:**202–237.
  1937 Two Prehistoric Villages near Cleveland, Ohio. *Ohio State Archaeological and Historical Quarterly* **46:**305–366.
  1939 The Wolf and Furton Sites, Macomb Co., Michigan. *University of Michigan, Museum of Anthropology, Occasional Contributions* No. 8.
  n.d. Field Notes of Survey and Excavation in Northern Ohio 1929–1930. On file at the Ohio Historical Society, Division of Archaeology, Columbus.

Greig-Smith, P.
  1964 *Quantitative Plant Ecology.* 2d ed. London: Butterworths.

Griffin, J. B.
  1943 *The Fort Ancient Aspect.* Ann Arbor: University of Michigan Press.
  1952 Radiocarbon Dates for the Eastern United States. In *Archeology of Eastern United States,* edited by James B. Griffin. Chicago: University of Chicago Press. Pp. 365–370.

Guilford, J. P.
  1952 When Not to Factor Analyze. *Psychological Bulletin* **49:**26–37.
  1965 *Fundamental Statistics in Psychology and Education.* 4h ed. New York: McGraw-Hill.

Guilford, J. P., and B. Fruchter
1973 *Fundamental Statistics in Psychology and Education.* 5h ed. New York: McGraw-Hill.

Haggett, P.
1965 *Locational Analyses in Human Geography.* New York: St. Martin's Press.
1968 Regional and Local Components in the Distribution of Forested Areas in Southeast Brazil: A Multivariate Approach. In *Spatial Analyses: A Reader in Statistical Geography,* edited by B. Berry and D. Marble. Englewood Cliffs, N.J.: Prentice Hall. Pp. 313–325.

Hall, J.
n.d. Field Notes on the Quaternary Geology and Modern Geomorphology, Soils, and Water Resources of Northeast Ohio. Manuscript on file, Case Western Reserve University, Department of Geology, Cleveland, Ohio.

Hays, W. L.
1973 *Statistics for the Social Sciences.* 2d ed. New York: Holt.

Hesse, A.
1971 Les Tarterets II, Site Paléolithique de Plein Air à Corbeil-Essonnes (Essonne), II: Comparaison par le Calcul des Distributions Horizontales des Vestiges Lithiques. *Gallia Préhistoire* **XIV**:41–46.

Higgs, E. S., and C. Vita-Finzi
1972 Prehistoric Economies: A Territorial Approach. In *Papers in Economic Prehistory,* edited by E. S. Higgs. Cambridge, Massachusetts: Cambridge University Press. Pp. 27–36.

Hudson, J. C.
1969 A Location Theory for Rural Settlement. *Annals of the Association of American Geographers* **59**:365–381.

Krause, B. S.
1942 Archaeological Survey of Ashtabula County, Ohio, 1941. Manuscript on file at Case Western Reserve University, Department of Anthropology, Cleveland, Ohio.

Ku, H. H., and S. Kullback
1974 Loglinear Models in Contingency Table Analysis. *American Statistician* **28**(4):115–122.

Leach, B. F.
1969 The Concept of Similarity in Prehistoric Studies. *Anthropology Department, University of Otago, Studies in Prehistoric Anthropology* **1**. Otago, New Zealand.

Leroi-Gourhan, A., and M. Brézillon
1966 L'Habitation Magdalénienne No. 1 de Pincevent près Montereau (Seine-et-Marne). *Gallia Préhistoire* **IX**:263–386.

Leverett, F. B.
1917 *Glacial Formations and Drainage Features of the Erie and Ohio Basins.* (Reprint of *1902 U.S. Geological Survey Monograph* No. 41.) Washington, D.C.: United States Government Printing Office.

Majone, G., and P. Sanday
1971 On the Numerical Classification of Nominal Data. In *Explorations in Mathematical Anthropology,* edited by Paul Kay. Cambridge, Massachusetts: M.I.T. Press. Pp. 226–241.

Matson, R. G., and D. L. True
1974 Site Relationships at Quebrada Tarapaca, Chile: A Comparison of Clustering and Scaling Techniques. *American Antiquity* **39**:51–74.

Mayer-Oakes, W. J.
  1955 Prehistory of the Upper Ohio Valley. *Annals of the Carnegie Museum* No. 34, Anthropological Series 2.

McBurney, C. B. M.
  1967 *The Haua Fteah (Cyrenaica).* Cambridge, England. Cambridge University Press.

Morgan, R. G., and H. H. Ellis
  1943 The Fairport Harbor Site. *Ohio State Archaeological and Historical Quarterly* **52:**1–62.

Movius, H. L., Jr.
  1972 Radiocarbon Dating of the Upper Paleolithic Sequence at the Abri Pataud, Les Eyzies (Dordogne). In *The Origin of Homo Sapiens,* edited by F. Bordes. Paris: UNESCO. Pp. 253–260.

Movius, H. L., Jr., N. C. David, H. M. Bricker, and R. B. Clay
  1968 The Analysis of Certain Major Classes of Upper Paleolithic Tools. *American School of Prehistoric Research Bulletin* No. 26. Cambridge, Massachusetts.

Mueller, C. G.
  1949 Numerical Transformations in the Analysis of Experimental Data. *Psychological Bulletin* **46:**198–223.

Mueller, J. W.
  1974 The Use of Sampling in Archaeological Survey. *Memoirs of the Society for American Archaeology* No. 28. *American Antiquity* **29**(2):Pt. 2.

Munson, P. J., P. W. Parmalee, and R. A. Yarnell
  1971 Subsistence Economy of Scovill: A Terminal Middle Woodland Village. *American Antiquity* **36:**410–431.

Parsons, J.
  1972 Settlement Patterns in Archaeology. *Annual Review of Archaeology* **3.** Palo Alto: Stanford University Press.

Plog, F., and J. N. Hill
  1971 Explaining Variability in the Distribution of Sites. In *The Distribution of Prehistoric Population Aggregates,* edited by G. Gummerman. Prescott, Arizona: Prescott College Press. Pp. 7–36.

Pratt, M. G., and D. Brose
  1975 C.W.R.U. Excavations at the Andrews School Site. *Ohio Archaeologist* **25:**26–31.
  n.d. Excavations at the Andrews School Site. *Ohio Archaeologist.* In press.

Rau, J. L.
  1968 The Evolution of the Cuyahoga River: Its Geomorphology and Environmental Geology. In *Cuyahoga River Watershed Symposium,* edited by D. Cooke. Kent, Ohio: Kent State University Press. Pp. 9–41.

Read, D. W.
  1974 Some Comments on Typologies in Archaeology and an Outline of Methodology. *American Antiquity* **39:**216–242.

Ritchie, W. A.
  1961 A Typology and Nomenclature for New York Projectile Points. *New York State Museum and Science Service Bulletin* No. 384.
  1969 The Archaeology of New York State. Rev. ed. New York: Natural History Press.

Ritchie, W. A., and R. E. Funk
  1973 Aboriginal Settlement Patterns in the Northeast. *New York State Museum and Science Service Memoir* No. 20. State Education Department, Rochester.

Roper, D. C.
   1974   The Distribution of Middle Woodland Sites within the Environment of the
          Lower Sangamon River, Illinois. *Illinois State Museum Reports of Investiga-
          tions* No. 30. Springfield.
Rowlett, R. M., and R. B. Pollnac
   1971   Multivariate Analysis of Marnian La Tène Cultural Groups. In *Mathe-
          matics in the Archaeological and Historical Sciences*, edited by F. R. Hodson,
          D. G. Kendall, and P. Tăutu. Edinburgh: Edinburgh University Press. Pp.
          46–58.
Sackett, J. R.
   1973   Style, Function and Artifact Variability in Palaeolithic Assemblages. In *The
          Explanation of Culture Change*, edited by C. Renfrew. London: Duckworth.
          Pp. 317–325.
Sampson, H. C.
   1930   Succession in the Swamp Formation in Northern Ohio. *Ohio Journal of
          Science* **30:**340–357.
Sears, P. B.
   1925   The Natural Vegetation of Ohio: A Map of the Virgin Forest. *Ohio Journal of
          Science* **25:**139–149.
   1926   The Natural Vegetation of Ohio: Plant Succession. *Ohio Journal of Science*
          26:213–231.
   1941   Postglacial Vegetation in the Erie–Ohio Area. *Ohio Journal of Science*
          41:225–234.
Seligmann, C. G., and B. Z. Seligmann
   1911   *The Veddas.* Cambridge, England: Cambridge University Press.
Semenov, S. A.
   1964   *Prehistoric Technology* (translated by M. W. Thompson). London: Cory,
          Adams, and MacKay.
   1970   The Forms and Functions of the Oldest Tools (A Reply to Professor F. Bordes).
          Quartar **21:**1–20.
Sokal, R. R., and P. H. A. Sneath
   1963   *Principles of Numerical Taxonomy.* San Francisco: W. H. Freeman.
Solecki, R. S.
   1963   Prehistory in Shanidar Valley, Northern Iraq. *Science* **139:**179–193.
Steel, R. G. D., and J. H. Torrie
   1960   *Principles and Procedures of Statistics.* New York: McGraw-Hill.
Tugby, D. J.
   1965   Archaeological Objectives and Statistical Methods: A Frontier in Archaeology.
          American Antiquity **31:**1–16.
Underwood, R.
   1969   The Classification of Constrained Data. *Systematic Zoology* **18:**312–317.
U.S. Department of Agriculture
   1941   Climates of the United States. *Yearbook of Agriculture.* Washington, D.C.:
          United States Government Printing Office. Pp. 701–747.
Van der Geer, J. P.
   1971   *Introduction to Multivariate Analysis for the Social Sciences.* San Francisco:
          W. H. Freeman.
Vita-Finzi, C., and E. S. Higgs
   1970   Site Catchment Analysis. *Proceedings of the Prehistoric Society* **36:**1–37.
Von Thunnen, J. H.
   1826   *Der Isolierte Staat in Beziehung auf Landwirtschaft und Nationalokonomie.*
          Pt. 1. Berlin.

Walker, H. M., and J. Lev
  1953   Statistical Inference. New York: Holt.
Washburn, D. K.
  1974   Nearest Neighbor Analyses of Pueblo I–III Settlement Patterns along the Rio
         Puerco in Eastern New Mexico. American Antiquity 39:315–335.
Whallon, R. W., Jr.
  1968   Investigations of Late Prehistoric Social Organization in New York State. In
         New Perspectives in Archeology, edited by S. R. and L. R. Binford. Chicago:
         Aldine Press. Pp. 223–244.
  1972   A New Approach to Pottery Typology. American Antiquity 37:13–33.
  1974   Spatial Analysis of Occupation Floors II: The Application of Nearest Neighbor
         Analysis. American Antiquity 39:16–34.
White, G. W.
  1969   Pleistocene Deposits of the Northwestern Allegheny Plateau, U.S.A. Quarterly
         Journal of the Geological Society of London 124:131–151.
White, J. P., and D. H. Thomas
  1972   What Mean These Stones? Ethno-taxonomic Models and Archaeological
         Interpretations in the New Guinea Highlands. In Models in Archaeology,
         edited by David L. Clarke. London: Methuen. Pp. 275–308.
Whittlesey, C. C.
  1851   Descriptions of Ancient Works in Ohio. Smithsonian Contributions to Knowl-
         edge 3: Article 7. Washington, D.C.
  1871   Ancient Earth Forts of the Cuyahoga Valley, Ohio. Western Reserve and
         Northern Ohio Historical Society Tracts No. 5. Cleveland: Fairbanks.
Wilmsen, E. N.
  1968a Paleo-Indian Site Utilization. In Anthropological Archaeology in the Ameri-
         cas, edited by B. J. Meggers. Washington, D.C.: Anthropological Society of
         Washington. Pp. 22–40.
  1968b Lithic Analysis in Paleoanthropology. Science 161:982–987.
  1968c Functional Analysis of Flaked Stone Artifacts. American Antiquity 33:156–
         161.
  1970   Lithic Analysis and Cultural Inference: A Paleo-Indian Case Study. Anthro-
         pological Papers of the University of Arizona 16.
Wobst, H. M.
  1974   The Archaeology of Band Society: Some Unanswered Questions. Memoirs of
         the Society for American Archaeology 29:v–xiii.
Wood, J. J.
  1971   Fitting Discrete Probability Distributions to Prehistoric Settlement Patterns.
         In The Distribution of Prehistoric Population Aggregates, edited by G.
         Gummerman. Prescott, Arizona: Prescott College Press. Pp. 68–83.
Yellen, J. E.
  1971   Ethnoarchaeology: Bushman Settlement Patterns. Unpublished manuscript
         on file at the Smithsonian Institution, Department of Anthropology, Washing-
         ton, D.C.

Patterns of
Culture History

The *In Situ* Iroquois Revisited and Rethought*

Richard S. MacNeish

Introductory Remarks

This paper, written for this *festschrift* for Dr. James B. Griffin, is to honor him at the time of his retirement, an event that I personally consider unwarranted and unfortunate. My chapter not only shows my appreciation for all he did for me when I was one of his students, but it also expresses appreciation for the intellectual stimulation I and many others of his colleagues have received from him over many years.

After a little arm twisting, I have chosen as the subject of this chapter Iroquois archaeology, because my brief endeavors in this field took place in that period when Jimmy gave me a fellowship at the University of Michigan and later hired me to excavate Iroquois prehistory (MacNeish 1952a). Although it is perhaps appropriate that

---

* During the spring of 1975, Scotty MacNeish suffered a serious illness which made it impossible for him to respond to the comments of reviewers. As a result, Marion White, a close observer of the Iroquois scene, was kind enough to revise Scotty's chapter. Prior to the publication of this volume, word was received that Marion died in Buffalo on October 31, 1975. The final version of this paper is, in part, a tribute to Marion White's contribution to the archaeology of the Iroquois.

I write on such a subject to honor and thank Jimmy, it really is but a token gesture. What I really should be doing to show my appreciation is writing my finest paper on a subject I know best, not one in a field to which I only briefly contributed, and left some 25 years ago.

However, enough of these excuses. What I shall attempt in this chapter is to discuss briefly my (and, in large part, Jimmy's) efforts in this field of archaeology, describe the data collection—both mine and others—and the development of my (and, in part, Jimmy's) *in situ* hypothesis of Iroquois development, and recent advances or confirmations of this "theory." After these brief discussions about information with which I once was familiar, I would like to delve into other matters of Iroquois archaeology that should logically follow the chronological investigations—contextual studies, then synthesis or cultural–historical integration, and finally, an attempt to analyze these specific data to formulate hypotheses about Iroquoian cultural changes that may have more general theoretical applications. This, perhaps, is an attempt to gaze into a future that is even more black and speculative than looking into the dark pàst.

Now, to briefly review how I became connected with Iroquois archaeology. . . . Although I had known Jimmy for a number of years in connection with Midwestern archaeology, while I was collecting data in Tamaulipas for my doctoral thesis for the University of Chicago, Jimmy, who was then also in Mexico, offered me a fellowship to come to the University of Michigan to work on his "Delaware Project" sponsored by Eli Lilly. Discussions with him in Mexico City near the end of June, after 10 months of a grueling field season, gradually defined what my duties would be on the Delaware Project (MacNeish 1958). Since Griffin and I had interests in ceramics (and I wanted to learn more from him on the subject), and because he knew I had worked on Iroquois sites during my usually unmentioned Colgate days 10 years before, and since the historic Delaware had pottery much like the Iroquois, it seemed logical that my part on the Delaware Project would be, for practically the first time, to undertake Iroquois ceramic typology. On a less formal basis, there also was Jimmy's general uneasiness about northeastern archaeology in the so-called "Mississippian period" (Griffin 1944). Further, he had rather definite ideas about culture and continuity in the eastern Woodlands that just did not mesh with the prevailing idea about Iroquois migrations into the Northeast (Griffin 1946). He wanted to explode this poorly documented speculation and felt that Scotty MacNeish was just the sort of little troublemaker to do the job. What is more, I agreed with him. So, in the fall of 1946, I folded up my tent and migrated to the Museum of Anthropology in Ann Arbor, fired with enthusiasm, to become, I hoped, a dynamic dynamiter.

Things were great. After a year of living (to quote de Terra) "in Tamaulipas at a slightly lower standard of living than the 10,000 year old Canyon Diablo cave dwellers," it was great to have a handsome Aboriginal fellowship plus adequate funds from a World War II compensation under Public Law 16 (all tax-free and with more take-home pay than I have now in my New England genteel poverty). But, more important than that, I had a desk in the Ceramic Repository (often pronounced "suppository" by my colleagues) full of potsherds from all over the eastern United States, and three great night-stalking colleagues of roughly my age—John Witthoft, Joffre Coe, and, later, Al Spaulding. Also, Leslie White and his deviationist evolutionary student anthropologists and Volney Jones were just down the hall, and all were a welcome relief from Chicago, whose social anthropologists had just sold archaeology down the river with the neat Machiavellian trick of making "Poppa" Cole take the blame for the end of an era never to be duplicated again. But even more important, in Jimmy's office, which was next to mine, books on Iroquois or related fields were piled up (for me to read); and, most of the time, when I went in to borrow one of the "master's" books, he and I became involved in an archaeological argument, usually loud and vociferous, that often lasted a couple of weeks and was far superior to any formal academic course I ever took.

Finally, by midwinter of 1947, I had read every available book or article on the Iroquois, seen every relevant potsherd in the "suppository," argued with all my colleagues and betters on the subject of everything Iroquois, contacted Bill Ritchie, the benevolent establishment despot of the Northeast, and had a long list of Iroquois collections in private, public, and illegitimate hands. My basic training (as a saboteur) was over, and now it was time to use some techniques and methods, to fix the fuse and mix the chemicals and do some data collection—that is, to see where and what I should blow up.

On the ideal level, the final objective was "an understanding of cultural dynamics" and this would be based upon a cultural–historical integration of Iroquois prehistory—my "cultural dynamics of the Iroquois" which would, in turn, be based on contextual and chronological descriptive studies, and, of course, the latter would be dependent upon data collection (MacNeish 1952a: 1). Let me say at the outset that the collected Iroquois data I was forced to use in my studies from 1946 to 1950, with the possible exception of Wintemberg's or Emerson's from Ontario, ranged, from the standpoint of archaeological field techniques and the recording of prehistoric information, from bad to worse, then horrible. Environmental or paleoecological studies were unknown. But, even with the fine analogous ethnographic material, real sophisticated contextual studies to describe ancient Iroquois

cultural systems were impossible. The collection of data for chronological studies was not any better, but I could use it by dint of
employing some not very well established assumptions about cultural
change and my "direct historic approach" through pottery types and
seriations—the tracing back of a tribal group's history by analysis of
pottery types from historic, documented sites and connecting them
with prehistoric sites, chronologically ordered, on the basis of seriated
or overlapping pottery types and ceramic trends" (MacNeish 1952a:
1). This, of course, on a practical level, meant the collecting or using of
two kinds of interconnected sets of information from both historic and
prehistoric sites.

Of course, basic to the whole study was the assumption that each
Iroquois tribe had distinguishable and distinctive ceramic complexes
with distinctive developments; and basic to the whole study was the
finding of adequate samples of collected sherds from well-documented
historic sites of each tribe. Fortunately, some attempts to identify sites
of specific historic tribes had been undertaken by a variety of people
with varying degrees of success (Beauchamp 1900; Fenton 1940).
Thus, when I started my investigations in the Iroquois area, I had a list
of the names of documented historic sites and, of course, later
acquired more, but the major problem was finding collections of actual
sherds from them. Here, Bill Ritchie, with knowledge of the Northeast,
was a great help, so, little by little, I did get to see and study many
collections from these historically documented sites. Unfortunately,
except for a few from Huronia and possibly the Seneca region, none
had been dug in a professional manner, and one could not really tell
whether or not they represented specific historic occupations. So,
inherent in my study was the assumption that each site was a discrete
single occupation. However, even more unfortunate than the archaeological field techniques was the quality and variability of the data.
Neutral–Wenro materials were extremely limited, and the documentation poor, and the identification of the Ripley site as Erie was open to
question. Tobacco Nation sites had yet to be identified, although two
Huron sites and some Seneca sites with fairly good documentation
had fair samples of sherds. Cayuga historic sites had mediocre
samples, but documentation was poor, while not only were collections
of related Susquehannock materials poorly documented but adequate
samples were not available. Documentation on Onondaga and Oneida
sites was bad, and samples from these sites worse. There were really
no materials that could definitely be identified as historic Saint
Lawrence Iroquois. Mohawk materials, thanks to some rather sincere
efforts by local amateurs, were somewhat better-documented but,
again, samples from the well-documented sites were poor.

As shall be seen in the discussions of each tribal group, collecting from documented sites has increased greatly in the last 25 years, and the excavation techniques have been improved. Yet, still, there are some bad gaps, and detailed site reports on specific historic sites are woefully inadequate. In light of the extremely poor data available to me at the time of my initial reconnaissance, it is surprising how little the basic tribal identifications of ceramic complexes has changed; but the situation is still far from perfect.

My second set of available data was, of course, the prehistoric Iroquois sites. Although they were more numerous than the historic materials, except for some from Ontario, they were just as badly excavated. In spite of this, preliminary analysis of the prehistoric Iroquois sherds showed some sort of continuity from the so-called "Iroquois" back into the early stages called "Owasco" and "Point Peninsula," so we still had to work with a third set of collected data. Here, the data used were mainly from Ritchie's excavations, and they were much more reliable (Ritchie and MacNeish 1949). Recent excavations by Ritchie and others have greatly augmented both these sets of data.

The techniques for building a chronology were also not the best. There was little or no stratigraphy of Iroquois or Owasco components, tree-ring dating (which I often recommend) had (and has) not been attempted, and the method of radiocarbon determinations were not yet known. The first two dating techniques are, for all intents and purposes, still not utilized in Iroquois archaeology, and the third, although now used, has not too great a reliability because most components are relatively recent and Carbon-14 errors are great. Ergo, then, as now, chronology was based upon trends of ceramic attributes or modes or mode clusters called "types" that could be connected with dated historic sites.

My mode clusters of Iroquois utilized the correlation of three kinds of ceramic attributes: those of form (125), decorative motif (241), and manner of decoration (5). The naive techniques I used for typology have been described elsewhere and certainly are not worthy of being reiterated here. Obviously, I was not using all the possible ceramic attributes nor were statistical formulae used to determine if the ones I used were, in fact, the most significant or sensitive to temporal change, that is, the best modes. Nevertheless, in the Iroquois and pre-Iroquois studies, about 500 motifs, 250 forms, and a dozen decorative techniques were utilized and these attributes clustered into about 100 types. These types were based on about 500 site collections examined with approximately a half-million sherds, but only about 60 of these components (12 from pre-Iroquoian) with about 20,000 (5000 being pre-Iroquoian) rim sherds were utilized in my study. Now, the samples of sites and sherds have greatly increased, and my types (peccadillos of one's youth) have gone forth and multiplied. More important, much more sophisticated analyses of sherd material (as well as pipes and other artifact materials) have taken place, some using computerized statistics. Whallon's restudies of Ritchie's and my Owasco types (Whallon 1972) and Tuck's analysis of Onondaga pottery (Tuck 1970) are fine examples of these procedures. Others exist and more should come that are, hopefully, even more statistically sophisticated.

In spite of an uncomfortable field life style under which I did the survey (somewhat like a lightly armed Iroquois night raider of every and any innocent available collector or collection of the settlers), the horrible way, archaeologically speaking, in which most of the data with which I had to work had been collected originally, the inadequacies of samples used in my study, and the naiveté of my ceramic analysis, I did just what Jimmy wanted me to do. We destroyed the migration myth of the Iroquois (foisted, as usual, on the archaeologists by individuals who were basically anthropologists and ethnologists), showed that there was culture and continuity in the Iroquois area and that it was not Mississippian, and built a new theoretical structure that nobody liked or wanted to see or accept—the *in situ* hypothesis of Iroquois prehistory (MacNeish 1952a). Since this is the most re-knowned and perhaps notorious contribution I made while working with and for Jimmy, I would like to repeat my hypothesis made in 1948 and printed in 1952.

A tentative historical reconstruction based on the archaeological data now available reveals the following situation.

1. The first culture that can possibly be connected with historic remains is Point Peninsula which, with little regional variation, was spread over southern and eastern Ontario and northwestern and central New York. This homogeneous widespread Point Peninsula culture may be considered to be proto-Iroquois.

2. Gradually four regional variants with an Owasco, or an Owascoid type of material culture developed from Point Peninsula. These developments may represent the first differentiations of the proto-Iroquois in the tribal and proto-tribal units. The easternmost regional variant (an Owasco culture represented by the Wickham, Castle Creek, and Bainbridge sites) is probably ancestral to the Mohawk, while the related north-central Owascoid variant (represented at the Pillar Point and the Calkins Farm sites) may be ancestral to the Onondaga–Oneida. In western New York the Levanna to Canandaigua Owasco sequence may have given rise to the material culture of the Cayuga and Seneca; while in the Ontario Peninsula area there is evidence that an Owasco variant (represented in the lowest levels of Middleport, Krieger, and Goessens

sites) is ancestral to the material cultural units of the Neutral–Erie and Huron.

3. There is a general tendency for these Owascoid variants to develop an Iroquoian type of material culture and to differ further in their material cultures. These further differentiations of the Iroquois general culture type represent the cultural assemblages of specific Iroquois tribes. Thus, the Mohawk continued their development from an Owasco base, while the Onondaga–Oneida did the same until almost historic times when they split into two tribal units. The Seneca and Cayuga (and possibly Susquehannah) seem to have separated from each other in late Owasco times just before their development of an Iroquoian type of material culture; the tribal differentiations in Ontario seem to have been later. The Huron and Neutral–Erie separated just after the Iroquois cultural type had developed in that area and the Neutral and Erie separated somewhat later. This general reconstruction has been labelled the "In Situ" theory of Iroquois pre-history.

This hypothetical reconstruction, although the one best fitting the meagre data available [in 1948], requires . . . considerably more [information] . . . in order that this hypothesis may be confirmed [MacNeish 1952a: 89].

The endeavors during the last 25 years have produced to a startling degree (except for Jimmy and me) considerably more information confirming this hypothesis. Even the original enemy of the hypothesis, Bill Ritchie, perhaps with a wince, now writes that "the validity of the *in situ* hypothesis of Iroquois origins thus seems to be established" (Ritchie and Funk 1973: 167). In the following pages, somewhat to illustrate how well it has or has not been validated, I would like to write briefly about the development of each of the tribes of the Iroquois as well as publish a map and chart (Figures 5.1 and 5.2) like the one in the original *Iroquois Pottery Types* volume which may be compared with the original ones of 1948 (MacNeish 1952a: Figures 22–23). However, let me hasten to add that, this time, the reader will be spared the dull pottery descriptions and the Queen's Printer's inadequate illustrations or editing. Instead, I will give my inadequate but, I hope, lively opinions based on some rather definite information rather than definite interpretations based on inadequate and dull data.

Sequences of Tribal Development

NEUTRAL–WENRO

In essence, my original hypothetical sequence still stands, but it has been modified, buttressed, and expanded backward in time to a considerable degree. In Ontario, the fine fieldwork of Noble, Wright, and others (Noble 1975a, c; Noble and Kenyon 1972; Stothers 1970; Wright 1966), following that of T. Lee (Lee 1950), has pushed the

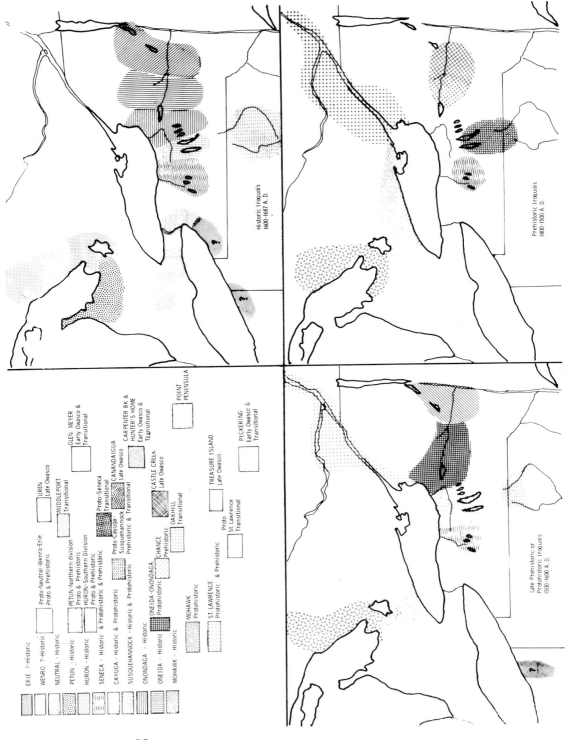

ERIE ? - Historic
WENRO ? - Historic
NEUTRAL - Historic
PETUN - Historic
HURON - Historic
SENECA - Historic & Protohistoric
CAYUGA - Historic & Protohistoric
SUSQUEHANNOCK - Historic & Protohistoric
ONONDAGA - Historic
ONEIDA - Historic
MOHAWK - Historic

Proto-Neutral-Wenro-Erie
Proto & Prehistoric

UREN
Late Owasco

MIDDLEPORT
Transitional

PETUN-Northern division
Proto & Prehistoric

HURON-Southern Division
Proto & Prehistoric

Proto-Seneca
Transitional

Proto-Cayuga-
Susquehannock
Prehistoric & Transitional

CANANDAIGUA
Late Owasco

CARPENTER BK &
HUNTER'S HOME
Early Owasco &
Transitional

GLEN MEYER
Early Owasco &
Transitional

POINT
PENINSULA

ONEIDA-ONONDAGA
Protohistoric

CHANCE
Prehistoric

OAKHILL
Transitional

MOHAWK
Protohistoric

ST. LAWRENCE
Protohistoric & Prehistoric

Proto
St. Lawrence
Transitional

TREASURE ISLAND
Late Owasco

PICKERING
Early Owasco &
Transitional

CASTLE CREEK
Late Owasco

Historic Iroquois
1600-1687 A. D.

Prehistoric Iroquois
1400-1500 A. D.

Late Prehistoric or
Protohistoric Iroquois
1500-1600 A. D.

86

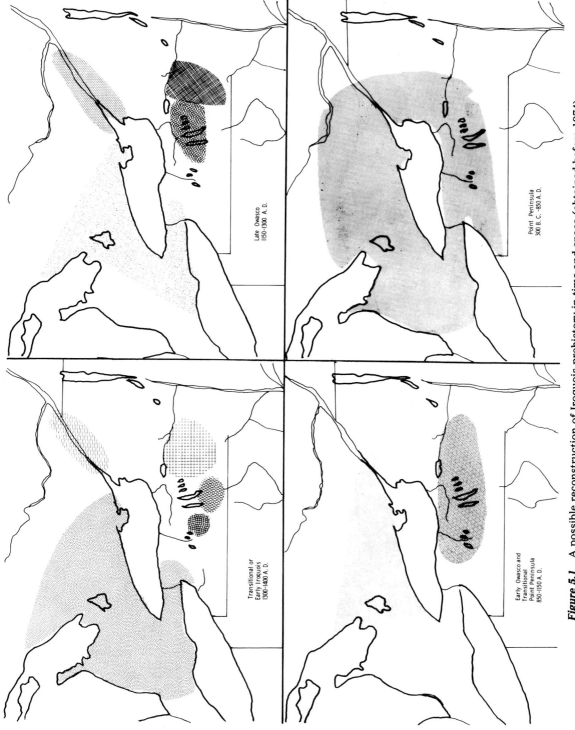

Late Owasco
1150–1300 A. D.

Point Peninsula
300 B. C. –850 A. D.

Transitional or
Early Iroquois
1300–1400 A. D.

Early Owasco and
Transitional
Point Peninsula
850–1150 A. D.

Figure 5.1 A possible reconstruction of Iroquois prehistory in time and space (obtained before 1974).

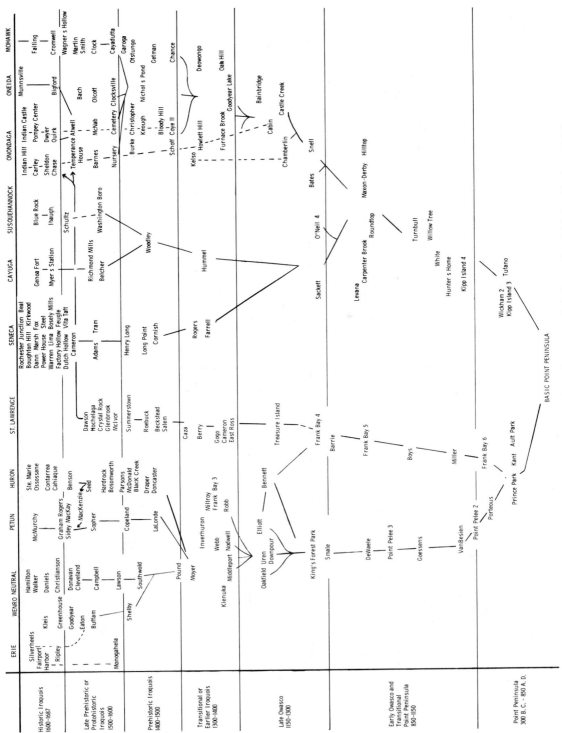

Figure 5.2 The development of the Iroquois, based on ceramic information (obtained before 1974).

origins of the western branch of the Iroquois (that is, the Huron, Tobacco, Neutral–Wenro, and Erie) to a "homogeneous widespread Point Peninsula culture" that "may be considered to be proto-Iroquois" which dates to about A.D. 500 or 600 (MacNeish 1952a: Figure 22, lowest right). Their new evidence indicates that these Point Peninsula people[1] used some domesticates, had sedentary village life, and were of the lenepid physical type of the Iroquois. These analyzed raw data based on numerous carefully excavated sites (as yet unpublished) seem to show that this developed into something they called the "Glen Meyer branch," roughly from A.D. 800 to 1150, with agriculture or horticulture, large palisaded villages, and burial practices like the late ossuaries. This stage, although I could not document it, is extremely similar to what I called "an Owasco variant (represented in the lowest levels of Middleport, Krieger, and Goessens sites)" that was "ancestral to the material units of the Neutral–Erie and Huron" and, I might add, the Wenro and Tobacco (MacNeish 1952a).

The next stage I saw developing was Uren (Wintemberg 1928), followed by Middleport (Wintemberg 1948); but, in light of new data, the situation seems to have been somewhat more complex. Wright would see Uren as "created by the Pickering branch conquest and absorption of the Glen Meyer branch in southwestern Ontario" (Wright 1966), while others would interpret it as exactly the opposite. Regardless of exactly what it was, Middleport seems to be the result of some sort of fusion of Glen Meyer and Pickering, but, nevertheless, there is *in situ* continuity from Point Peninsula to an Owascoid form, then to early Ontario Iroquois in the western part of the Iroquois area. Further, Uren and Middleport sites cover much of southern Ontario, and there are similarities in western New York at sites such as Oakfield and Kienuka (White 1961).

The Middleport horizon still is seen as the base from which the Huron–Petun development became differentiated from that of the Neutral. Noble's fuller data shows a direct development from Pound to Southwold to Lawson (Wintemberg 1939) into Donovan, Sealey, and Walker, the latter three being historic Neutral sites (Noble 1975a, b). Accumulating archaeological evidence and the reexamination of ethnohistorical and cartographic sources suggest that the term "Neutral" was applied to a group of allied tribes. The tribes included in the term

---

[1] Most Ontario archaeologists now recognize a contemporary and historically distinct culture known as "Princess Point." Its distribution lies south and west of that of Point Peninsula, stretching from Lake Erie north and from Toronto and the Niagara River west across Ontario. The Princess Point culture developed into Glen Meyer in the Ontario Peninsula, whereas Point Peninsula developed into Pickering to the east. Details can be found in Wright (1972) and in papers by Noble and Stothers.

probably varied from time to time and at least eight seem geographically distinct. One, the Wenro, may be represented by a village
movement that crossed to the east of the Niagara River during
Middleport times and that may have terminated in the Early Historic
Shelby site (White 1972a).

Of all the studies of Iroquois pottery, this one of the western area
has the clearest and greatest body of evidence to prove the validity of
the *in situ* "hypothesis," or should I now say "theory" or "generalization?" The exact development is extremely similar to the poorly
documented interpretation I gave in 1948 and printed in 1952.

ERIE

The picture on the Erie never was very clear, as White pointed out,
in large part because of poor documentation in early historic reports
as to just exactly where the Erie were located, and because the Erie
were sadly eliminated early in historic times (White 1961).

In the general Erie area, there are three or four sets of historic
materials—one set is from the area immediately south of Buffalo
(Niagara Frontier Erie), the second is from the Silverheels site
(Harrington 1922) in the Cattaraugus Creek Valley, and the third
and/or fourth is from Ripley, New York (Parker 1907), and from the
28th Street site in Erie, Pennsylvania. Several village movements must
be involved, but only the prehistoric–historic Niagara Frontier Erie
and the prehistoric Chautauqua culture movements have been studied
recently.

The Niagara Frontier Erie (White 1961, 1967, 1972a, b) were
composed of a pair of contemporary villages from about A.D. 1540–
1640. The eastern member of the pair can be traced to a guess date of
A.D. 1175 for the Ganshaw site. The conclusion is strong that the
Niagara Frontier Erie had an *in situ* development back to an as yet
undefined Owasco–Princess-Point–Point-Peninsula-like ancestor.

The Chautauqua culture (Schock 1972, 1974) refers to a maximum
of 15 prehistoric Iroquois sites in Chautauqua and Cattaraugus
Counties. At least four village movements can be recognized, and
suggest a long occupation of the area by ancestors of the Chautauqua
culture.

West of Erie, Pennsylvania, are the prehistoric sites of the Whittlesey focus currently being studied by Brose (1972), who does not
now regard them as Erie.

If the Niagara Frontier Erie, Ripley, and Silverheels sites are, in fact,
Erie sites, then the development came out of a Middleport base like the
Ontario Iroquois which underwent some Monongahela Woodland
influence (Guthe 1958). This would be similar to interpretations I

originally gave. If, however, the late aspects of the Whittlesey focus were Erie, then there was a whole separate development that has yet to be described adequately. Work on the Erie in the last 25 years has done little to clarify the picture. In fact, it has further confused it.

HURON–PETUN

Endeavors among the Huron–Tobacco (Petun) groups in the last quarter century fortunately have led to greater clarity rather than confusion. My original simplistic picture of Huron and Tobacco separating from Neutral on the Middleport horizon still stands, but endeavors by Norm Emerson, his students, and others have greatly augmented this *in situ* development.

First, the base for the Huron development, Uren and Middleport, has been found all over southern Ontario, including Huronia and not just southernmost Ontario (Wright 1960), so no gradual northward movement of the Huron–Petun need have occurred; rather, there was a real *in situ* development.

From this broad base, Wright (1966) sees a development of two general divisions of the Huron–Petun, a southern one and a north-ern (Lalonde) one (Ridley 1952a, b). Both developments are well-documented by many sites, with the prehistoric sequence of the southern division being Doncaster, Downsview, Draper, Black Creek, McDonald, Parsons, Hardrock, Seed, and Benson, and with the northern development including Lalonde, Copeland, Frank Bay II, Bosomworth, Woodbridge, Aurora, Sidey-Mackay (Wittemberg 1946), and Graham Rogers. At about historic times, these two divisions fuse with the southern one, becoming basically the Huron to the north and represented by the Frank Bay I, Shebishikong, Warminster, Orr Lake, and other components, while the Petun who ended up south and west of Huronia occupied the MacMurchy site, and this development was basically a development from the earlier northern division.

SENECA

Generally, the picture of the Seneca evolution has not greatly changed since my original speculations which were based on some rather good, well-documented historic sites, and a limited number of prehistoric sites, perhaps like Sackett, that perhaps came out of some sort of western Owasco along with Cayuga and Susquehannock.

Endeavors by Wray and Schoff, using historic materials, have much improved the historic part of the sequence (Wray and Schoff 1953). Adams and Tram were placed in the 1550–1575 period; Cameron in the 1575–1600s; Dutch Hollow, Factory Hollow, Feugle, and Vita-Taft in the 1590–1625 period; Warren, Lima, and Bosely Mills in the 1615–1645 period; Power House and Steele in the 1630–1660s; Dann and March, and possibly the Fox site, in the 1650–1675 period; and the final stage, 1670–1687, would include Rochester Junction (Sonnontuan), Boughton Hill (Ganagora), Kirkwood (Keinthe), and Beal (Gandougarae). Wray (1973) connects this historic sequence to the prehistoric Richmond Mills and Belcher sites which I regarded as Cayuga.

C. F. Hayes's recent work (Hayes 1962, 1963a) on the Fletcher (Can 28-3), Wheeler (Can 12-3), and Andrews sites (Can 5-3) may fill some of the gaps in the prehistoric period, and his Rogers site (Hayes 1963b) may be connected with the Sackett, Levanna, and Carpenter Brook (late to early) Owasco development which Ritchie has suggested may connect with a Point Peninsula development from Wickham to Kipp Island 4 and Hunter's Home (Ritchie and Funk 1973). If and when those speculations are based on archaeological facts, there may be further proof of an *in situ* development of yet another Iroquois tribe.

CAYUGA

My original proposed sequence of Cayuga out of a more poorly documented Hummel-like (Guthe 1955) assemblage, which, in turn, may have come out of the western Owasco–Point Peninsula sequence just mentioned, still is all we have in print on this group. My interpretations of the Iroquois part of the sequence, based on poorly collected samples and links with earlier horizons, were very speculative. I keep hearing rumors of people working on Cayuga materials but have seen nothing in print on a well-executed program. Until such appears, the Cayuga sequence remains one of the more poorly documented ones.[2]

SUSQUEHANNOCK

Reputedly, the Susquehannock sequence closely parallels that of the Cayuga and, evidently, sites linking Susquehannock clear back to Point Peninsula have been dug (Witthoft 1959). If this is true, I cannot find site reports or analyses of materials to document such a conclusion. The only pertinent reports I was able to obtain concern historic Susquehannock sites, such as Blue Rock (Hesey and Witmer 1964), Ibaugh (Kinsey 1960; Witthoft and Kinsey 1959), Shultz, and the late prehistoric Washington Boro site. Until more data become available,

---

[2] Unpublished work by White (1973) is defining a local sequence east of Cayuga Lake, dating back to Oak Hill horizon times. Several other village movements to the north and to the west of Cayuga Lake probably went into Early Historic Cayuga, represented by the Genoa Fort site.

the quality of the Susquehannock sequence remains about like that for the Cayuga—speculative.

ONONDAGA

In my original report, the Onondaga sequence was as bad or worse than the two just mentioned, and I incorrectly believed the Onondaga (and Oneida) came out of a development in the St. Lawrence–northern Lake Ontario region. Now, thanks to the excellent research of James A. Tuck, Pendergast, and Trigger, this has changed, and Onondaga research has moved from last place to first place.

Although there is some evidence for connecting Tuck's Onondaga materials with the early Owasco material of O'Neill and Maxon-Derby, and these, in turn, with Hunter's Home-like materials of late Point Peninsula investigated by Ritchie, Funk (Ritchie and Funk 1973), and others, Tuck's sequence really begins with the Late Owasco Castle Creek phase at about A.D. 1200 (Tuck 1971). It is represented by two carefully excavated sites, Chamberlin and Cabin. The next stage is called the "Oak Hill phase," roughly from A.D. 1300 to 1400, with materials coming from the Kelso site that is interpreted as being linked to Chamberlin and Maxon-Derby, while the Furnace Brook and Howlett Hill materials seem to develop from the Cabin lineage. This step is followed by the Chance phase, A.D. 1400 to 1500, and the Cabin lineage is represented by the Schoff and Burke site materials. Another development represented by materials from the Coye II, Bloody Hill, Keough, and Christopher sites also started in this phase. The next phase Tuck called "Garoga" and, although I am a great admirer of the fine work Tuck has done, my opinion is that this is an unfortunate designation. His ceramics, as well as other traits from the Nursery, Baines, and Temperance House sites of the Cabin lineage and those from Cemetery, McNab, and Atwell of the Coye line, show many differences from those of the Mohawk Garoga site itself or the related Cayadutta, Clock, and Smith Mohawk sites. (Although Tuck is cautiously silent on the matter, I have interpreted this as indicating the period when the Onondaga became separate from the Mohawk.) During this period, the Onondaga materials first contained traits from the St. Lawrence development of the Roebuck level. The final phase of historic times (after A.D. 1600) is called "Onondaga" and is represented by even more components: Chase, Sheldon, Conley, Indian Hill, Jamesville Pen, and Valley Oaks are in the Cabin lineage, and Quirk, Dwyer, Pompey Center, Indian Castle, Weston, and Toyadasso are of the Coye line. Materials of this period seem rather different from those of the Oneida, perhaps indicating the time when they had become separated.

Tuck's fine work has completely blown up my interpretation of 25 years ago—thus making Tuck a compatible little troublemaker, too—but his data are certainly a solid confirmation of the hypothesis of *in situ* development of the Iroquois.

ONEIDA

Obviously, Tuck's reworking of the Onondaga materials means that my interpretations of the related Oneida materials must be redone. Although Pratt, Peterson, Gibson, and others have dug almost as many Oneida sites as Tuck has dug Onondaga, there are few reports and no detailed analysis of Oneida development available. Oneida pottery has been studied by Engelbrecht (1971, 1972, 1975), who has considered Onondaga–Oneida–Mohawk relations from ceramic patterning. His conclusion (1971: 53–56) is that there was probably an Onondaga–Oneida split at an early prehistoric level. Oneida ceramics show decreasing similarity to Onondaga and increasing similarity to Mohawk. The Oneida development includes a Chance phase typified by Nichols Pond, then goes into a Garoga-like stage as manifested at the Clocksville, Olcott (Pratt 1963), and Bach sites, with the Munnsville and Bigford site (Pratt 1961) being historic Oneida. Although the evidence is not all in, the *in situ* hypothesis seems to be again holding up.

MOHAWK

From many standpoints, the basic tenets of the *in situ* hypothesis were conceived in the Mohawk area. This was a result, in large part, of the hospitable cooperation that a host of local amateur archaeologists gave me when they generously allowed me to study their very relevant materials. Their good work (particularly that of Don Lenig) has continued since my original studies, ably assisted by the endeavors of Ritchie and Funk (Ritchie and Funk 1973). The earliest traces of this development (as well as Oneida and Onondaga) seem to start in Point Peninsula at the time of the occupation of the Tufano site, which, in turn, develops into something like that of Willow Tree and Turnbull (Ritchie 1969). Out of this base comes eastern early Owasco, as represented by the Hilltop and Snell sites, which, in turn becomes Castle Creek (Ritchie, Lenig, and Miller 1953). Materials from Oak Hill and Dewongo Island represent the transition into early Iroquois (Lenig 1965), which developed into the Chance horizon or phase with the materials from the Getman, Chance, and Otstungo sites (Ritchie 1952). Up until this time, the Onondaga, Oneida, and Mohawk developments closely parallel each other, but only Mohawk becomes a distinguishable entity in the Garoga horizon (as represented at the Cayadutta, Garoga, Clock, and Smith sites) with Martin, Wagoner's Hollow, Cromwell, and Failing being historic Mohawk sites (Lenig 1965). Although my original sequence was not too far-fetched, these materials certainly augment it greatly and certainly assist in further establishing the "validity of the *in situ* hypothesis of Iroquois origins."

ST. LAWRENCE IROQUOIS

This section is an obvious addition to the original format in *Iroquois Pottery Types*, but some of these materials did, in fact, appear in my section on Oneida and Onondaga.[3] Although I did not recognize the St. Lawrence Iroquois as a separate development in my original study, I will take credit for the conception of the idea because its recognition is largely a result of the efforts of Jim Pendergast, who is one of my intellectual offsprings and, of course, is a revolutionary troublemaker! This sequence seems to have ended sometime between A.D. 1535 and 1600 with the demise of the Laurentian or St. Lawrence. Although no well-documented site has been found or excavated, the materials from the Dawson site, Glenbrook, Crystal Rock (Pendergast 1962), and the so-called (or should I say miscalled) "Hochelaga site" seem to represent the material remains of the Iroquois group met by the earliest explorers (Pendergast and Trigger 1972). These Iroquois seem to have developed out of a group of sites dating between A.D. 1400 and 1535, which ceramic separation and Carbon-14 dates would align from early to late as follows: Salem, Beckstead, Roebuck, Summertown Station, and McIver (Pendergast 1965; Wintemberg 1936). Ancestral to these seem to be five sites heavily influenced by Middleport remains. These are: Gogo, Cameron, East Ross, Berry, and Cazathat, which existed from roughly A.D. 1300 to 1400 (Pendergast 1966). The beginning of this *in situ* sequence seems to be a stage characterized by sites like Ault Park and Treasure Island, Brophy, and perhaps Lanorie. Exactly what this developed from is at present difficult to determine, but Pendergast suggests it comes out of a "Pickering–Mixed Canandaigua Owasco people"; however, it well could be a direct evolution from the Pickering branch (Pendergast n.d.). If it is the latter, then we could trace its ancestry through Barrie, Boys, and Miller, well into Point Peninsula times (Wright 1966). Be that as it may, this was a St. Lawrence *in situ* development.

---

[3] Other sites that were included as Onondaga–Oneida are located in Jefferson County, New York, and are considered a separate prehistoric development. Work in process by Earl Sidler of SUNY at Buffalo shows village movements traceable to the Calkins site of Owasco times.

Additional Questions for Consideration

All in all, the *in situ* theory of Iroquois origins, even if slightly modified over a quarter of a century, seems validated. The chronological framework of Iroquois prehistory is now quite complete, even though there are some gaps and a specific lack of an accurate dating system such as dendrochronology. However, I feel that great strides have been made, many sites have been better-excavated, and data better-collected, than ever before. These accomplishments, of course, are not ends but only means to further objectives, such as contextual studies, cultural–historical integrations, and generalizations or analyses about cultural change. Practically nothing of note had been achieved along these particular lines in my Iroquois days or before, but how have things progressed in the last 25 years?

I am afraid I must conclude, "not very well," in terms of contextual studies. Environmental, ecological, and other sophisticated study in Iroquoia, using the interdisciplinary approach, seems rarely to have been attempted or completed.[4] I wonder why? Did the diversity of environments and/or microenvironments never play a role in the various Iroquois cultural developments? What about complete studies of the subsistence systems through this long evolution from Point Peninsula to historic Iroquois bands? When I review the record and peruse the published materials, I am pleased to note that many reports contain a paragraph here and there variously entitled "Food Remains," "Faunal and Vertebrate Remains," "Foods and Their Storage," "Shell Hunting and Fishing Gear," "Vegetal Remains," and so on. Yet, I am less than pleased when I read assorted conclusions—for example, on subsistence—and find that these conclusions are actually based on ethnographic analogy rather than on concrete evidence from soil studies, pollen analysis, or pit studies using flotation techniques. Or, to take another example, rarely is horticulture distinguished from agriculture. Further, in related food-preparation discussions, where are the studies including activity areas, faunal analysis connected with butchering techniques, and/or Seiminov-like studies of the nicks and scratches on tools that were used to prepare food? Similar criticisms could be made of this unconnected, fragmented approach, unstrung rather than threaded through with testable hypotheses, when I read of endeavors in the realm of technological subsystems. Why, for instance, can I not find a comprehensive Iroquois or even pre-Iroquois

---

[4] A notable exception to this is the work of the geographer Conrad Heidenreich (*et al.* 1969; Heidenreich 1971; Heidenreich and Konrad 1973; Heidenreich and Navratil 1973). His analyses have examined physical geography, population, settlement, subsistence, and trading among the Huron.

study that presents an in-depth analysis of the chipping debitage to determine flint-knapping practices?

Population and settlement pattern studies have just begun in many of the Iroquois regions (Tuck 1971; Ritchie and Funk 1973), although Norm Emerson had collected fine data in this field even in my day. This is very encouraging and a start in the right direction, but what about using the sophisticated locational analysis techniques of the geographers in future endeavors? Some extremely good studies of skeletal populations have been attempted by Jim Anderson and others. Should not this type of data be used more in conjunction with the settlement pattern and population studies?

Perhaps the most encouraging turn in Iroquois studies has been the increasing interest in contextual studies on reconstructions of phenomena related to the evolution of ancient social systems or subsystems. Although, of course, Emerson, Ritchie, and Wittemberg long ago made steps in this direction, this interest in social behavior and institutions with the "New Archaeology" now in vogue has intensified. I hope it will continue and eventually yield some concrete results. But, even now, some studies have been done in this area. Bill Noble's doctoral dissertation, "Development of Iroquois Social Organization," particularly his section on burial patterns that shows the development of the ossuary practice and the institutionalization of the Feast of the Dead ceremonies in the western Iroquois area, is a good start (Noble 1968). But this study and others, using maskettes, pipes, house types, settlement patterns, burials, and other data, are being brought to bear upon development from matrilineages to clans to tribal councils to confederacies. Other data are being used to test hypotheses about the development of Iroquois warfare, associational, and ceremonial patterns (Engelbrecht 1971, 1972, 1974; Whallon 1968). Obviously, all this ferment and interest means Iroquois studies are beginning to advance in the right direction, and perhaps future excavation tactics and methodological strategies will be oriented to attacking well-defined contextual problems rather than to interpret data that happened to be found in terms of contextual conclusions. Then, perhaps, by the time I write my next "Iroquois Revisited" paper, we shall have some cultural–historical integrations for the area with the development of ancient cultural systems in both time and space.

If so, we can move on to the nitty-gritty of archaeology, anthropology, or, for that matter, social science. This will mean analysis of how and why one cultural system of the Iroquois development changed into another, or why others did not. We would then be asking the question: Why did changes in the Iroquois development occur? Some of these questions are being asked even now by Whallon (1968), Tuck (1970), Noble (1968) and others. Why did lineages develop into clans?

Why did a warfare pattern start? Why did the Point Peninsula develop into Owasco or it into Iroquois? Did the increasing populations of Hunter's Home of late or transitional Point Peninsula times cause them to take on agriculture and an Owasco way of life? Or, was it the increasing agriculture in Ontario (specifically the use of corn horticulture in Ontario, starting in Point Peninsula times in the Princess Point phase) that brought about sedentary village life and caused the development of Owasco cultural system with the much larger population of Glen Meyer or both? Do increasing conflicts and increasing populations cause Owasco matrilocal extended families to become Iroquois matrilineages? Does the increasing agriculture in the hands of women in Owasco lead to male feuding and the rise of the Iroquois pattern? Was European contact, and the rise of the fur trade with its guns, the reason for the Iroquois confederacies? Or, did the Owasco war pattern, with increasing population and economic competition, lead to tribal councils that in turn became confederacies? Thus, even now, there are some highly speculative hypotheses concerning the reasons for the Iroquois development. Future endeavors with fuller cultural–historical integrations should further test such speculative hypotheses and, as well, test new ones. If this occurs—and, hopefully, it will—then perhaps one day we will be able to form explanatory hypotheses about why Iroquois culture changed. Perhaps, then, these hypotheses, that is, statements of the conditions that brought about certain cultural events, may be tested by analysis and comparisons with other similar cultural developments (Nagel's corresponding happenings), such as among the Creek, Polynesia, the chiefdoms of South America, and so on, to change our hypotheses into multilinear generalizations about cultural change. Then, archaeology really would be fulfilling its ultimate goal and be a science of past human behavior and activities.

Besides, Jimmy and I, though we might bitch and moan, would feel satisfied that our troublemaking endeavors leading to the *in situ* theory had gotten a good thing going. . . .

The Bartholomew Phase: A Plaquemine Adaptation in the Mississippi Valley

Martha Ann Rolingson

Mississippian culture of the central Mississippi Valley, Plaquemine culture of the lower Mississippi Valley, and the related, but distinctive, Caddoan culture in the Red River Basin have long been recognized as parallel major cultural developments (Griffin 1952, 1967: 189–190; Willey 1966: 292–297). Archaeological investigation in each of these regions has emphasized exploration and description of individual sites and development of local culture history. The regional development and spread of each of these cultures and the nature of contacts among them are as yet poorly understood, partly because of the lack of investigation in the intervening areas. It will not be possible, however, to describe or understand the interaction of Mississippian, Plaquemine, and Caddoan cultures until specific situations in the intervening regions are analyzed in detail, such as has been done at the Winterville site (Brain 1970) and in the upper Tensas Basin (Hally 1966, 1972).

Recent research in southern Arkansas has produced information bearing on the nature and extent of Plaquemine culture beyond its previously defined range in the lower Mississippi Valley. The predominant culture in the upper Boeuf Basin during the Mississippi period was Plaquemine, in contrast to previous assumptions that it was Caddoan (Davis 1961; Phillips 1970: 861). The Bartholomew phase is, however, an intrusion along the western margin of the upper Boeuf Basin on the Bayou Bartholomew meander belt ridge. There is no indication of a local development of Plaquemine culture, since preceding Coles Creek sites are rare and scattered. Furthermore, the Bartholomew phase does not appear to have continued for a long time period, for late Mississippi period sites are also rare.

This chapter presents an analysis of the Bartholomew phase settlement pattern and utilization of the Bayou Bartholomew meander belt ridge. At the present stage of research, it is possible to partially reconstruct the prehistoric environment of the upper Boeuf Basin for the past 1000 years. The settlement pattern analysis provides information of two types (Trigger 1968)—the distribution of communities over the landscape and specialized functions of sites in a dispersed community pattern of the society. This analysis of the Bartholomew phase is one segment of a long-term project begun in 1969.

Prior to the formation of the Arkansas Archeological Survey in 1967, there have been only scattered and brief archaeological investigations, mostly in the vicinity of the lower Arkansas River and Bayou Macon (Thomas 1894; Moore 1908, 1909, 1911; Lemley and Dickinson 1937; Phillips, Ford, and Griffin 1951). The only investigator along Bayou Bartholomew was Clarence B. Moore (1909), although Ford and Redfield recorded a number of sites in the vicinity during a survey for Dalton sites in 1961 (Redfield n.d.).

Despite the lack of research, southeastern Arkansas and Bayou Bartholomew have been placed within the Caddoan area framework because of the discoveries of Moore (1908, 1909) in sites at the mouth of Bayou Bartholomew and on the lower Arkansas River. Excavations at the Keno and Glendora sites in Louisiana (Moore 1909: 27–80, 120–151) revealed late Caddoan ceramics associated with historic artifacts in aboriginal graves. This, as well as the fact that, in 1699, the Washita Caddo occupied a village in the vicinity of present-day Columbia, Louisiana, resulted in the identification of southeastern Arkansas as Caddoan territory (Davis 1961; S. Williams 1964). Caddoan ceramics at the Douglas and Greer sites on the Arkansas River (Moore 1908: 524–556) linked the cultures of the Arkansas and Ouachita River regions. The First Caddoan Conference, held in 1947, set the northern boundary of the Caddoan area at the Arkansas River, and the eastern boundary at Bayou Macon. However, the Fifth Caddoan Conference, in 1958, shifted the eastern boundary westward to Bayou Bartholomew (Davis 1961: 83, Fig. 2). The Keno, Glendora, Douglas, and Greer sites also were grouped into a Glendora focus (Orr 1952: 251; Suhm and Krieger 1954: 221–224), considered to be the archaeological manifestation of the historic Kadohadacho. S. Williams (1964: 564) later suggested that only the Glendora and Keno sites be placed in the prehistoric Glendora phase, separate from the historic Natchitoches Caddo and the Kadohadacho Caddo, and separate from the Douglas and Greer sites. The investigations of James A. Ford (1961) at the Menard site and of Charles R. McGimsey III (1964) on the Quapaw treaty claims established the Douglas and Greer sites as Quapaw, removing them from the realm of the Caddo. The most recent culture history of the lower Mississippi Valley, by Phillips, specifically excludes the Ouachita River, Bayou Bartholomew, and the lower Arkansas River from inclusion in the lower Mississippi Valley cultures because of these Caddoan identifications (Phillips 1970: 861). At the same time, Phillips (1970: 861–955) identifies a few sites with Mississippi Valley cultures because other investigators (Lemley and Dickinson 1937; Phillips, Ford, and Griffin 1951; Redfield n.d.; S. Williams 1966) have tended to align sites in southeastern Arkansas with Mississippi Valley cultures.

The Bartholomew Project

The Bayou Bartholomew Project initiated the systematic investigation of sites in southeastern Arkansas. There were five objectives of the project: *(1)* to establish a culture history in one portion of the Boeuf Basin to be used as an initial framework for the prehistory of the Mississippi alluvial plain of southeastern Arkansas; *(2)* to obtain some conception of the prehistoric environment of the Bayou Bartholomew locality; *(3)* to explore the prehistoric settlement patterns in order to formulate hypotheses concerning the adaptation to, and utilization of, the environment of the alluvial plain; *(4)* to establish the external relationships of the local area to neighboring regions having different patterns of cultural development; and *(5)* to evaluate the effects of modern agricultural practices on the archaeological resources in the alluvial plain (Rolingson n.d.).

The Bayou Bartholomew Project research began in the vicinity of Portland (Figure 6.1) with a group of sites reported to the University of Arkansas Museum by two amateur archaeologists. Since most of the land is in row-crop cultivation with the surface exposed, both small, unobtrusive sites and large, obvious ones may be located. Conditions appeared to be ideal for a comprehensive survey in which the relation of different types of sites to topographic features could be explored. During the spring and summer of 1969, a concentrated, walking site-location survey of fields on the Bayou Bartholomew meander belt ridge was conducted, followed by test excavations. The

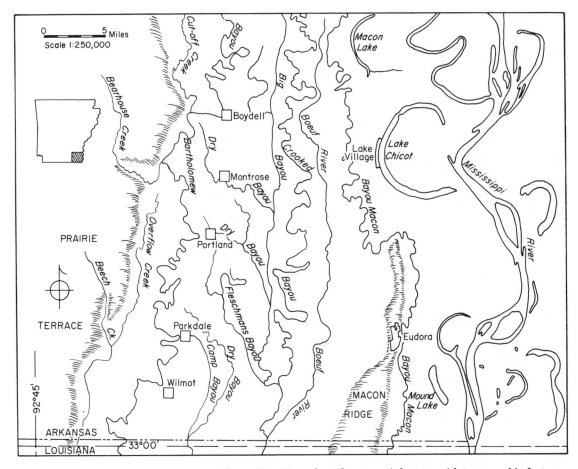

Figure 6.1 Map of southeastern Arkansas with topographic features.

backswamp west of the bayou was less comprehensively checked, but much of it is in woods or pasture because it is not good farm land for cotton or soybeans. The survey continued sporadically during the fall and winter and, in the spring, the concentrated site survey was renewed, followed by excavation during the summer. Sporadic site survey continued through 1972, but the main research emphasis has been on the analysis of the data.

The accomplishments of the comprehensive survey were to cover thoroughly the Bartholomew meander belt ridge, between Wilmot on the south and Boydell on the north (Figure 6.1), a lineal distance of 21 miles with a 4-mile width; to spot-check the paralleling backswamp west of the bayou ridge; to cover the backslope drained by Dry Bayou east of Portland, a lineal distance of 5 miles; and to test or excavate five sites. All the backswamp east of the bayou was not searched—especially Dry Bayou near Montrose, and Camp, Dry, and Fleschmans Bayous south and east of Parkdale and Wilmot.

Nearly 100 sites were investigated during the fieldwork. Surface collections were as complete as possible. All items on the surface were collected, crop row by crop row. Most of the sites are relatively small and the amount of material not abundant, so it was possible to make complete collections—in fact, in many situations, it was necessary in order to obtain an adequate sample. Since fieldwork was not concentrated in a limited field season, the sites could be revisited under differing conditions. As a consequence, the surface collections do, in general, reflect the sites' characteristics.

The excavated sites were in three different topographic situations with Bayou Bartholomew bank–oxbow lake, backslope, and backswamp environments represented. Three of the excavated sites had stratified deposits on the basis of which the relative temporal position of two of the seven phases defined in the project were established. Four different kinds of sites were excavated: camp, household, hamlet, and ceremonial center.

The area included within the comprehensive survey is, in a sense, arbitrary because the meander belt ridge and adjacent areas were deliberately chosen while the entire Boeuf Basin was not systematically sampled. Nevertheless, other site information accumulated during the past few years, along with a survey to assess the impact of agricultural practices on site destruction (Ford and Rolingson 1972), indicates that the Bartholomew ridge is culturally distinct for at least 3000 years. This is a locality in the sense that it "might be occupied by a single community or local group" (Willey and Phillips 1958: 18) during any period of occupation.

Several lines of evidence were used to establish the phase sequence and to identify site components. Since potsherds are the most abundant artifacts present, the decorated sherds are used to establish parallels with the lower Mississippi Valley (Phillips 1970) and the Caddoan area (Suhm and Jelks 1962) ceramic sequences. Evidence from both the small, single-component sites and the stratified deposits at the excavated sites made it possible to identify six distinct ceramic complexes. The relative temporal position of these complexes, however, is based primarily on type comparison with the sequence of ceramic types established elsewhere in the lower Mississippi Valley (Phillips 1970). A preceramic period of occupation is recognized on the basis of distribution of nonceramic sites and projectile-point types. Settlement pattern data are sufficient to recognize changes in settlement pattern at different periods of time. The seven phase definitions, then, are based on settlement pattern, ceramic complex, and tool complex. The environment in 1840 can be partially reconstructed from documentary evidence and, as a general pattern, seems to be valid for the past 1000 years.

Environment of the Bartholomew Locality

The early river travelers who visited Arkansas territory considered the country south of the Arkansas River and west of the Mississippi River to be a vast, horrid swamp. The first settlement was established in 1795 by Don Carlos de Villemont, Spanish commandant at Arkansas Post from 1793 to 1803, on a grant of land on the Mississippi River at Chicot Island (Ferguson and Atkinson 1966: 33) upriver from present-day Lake Village (Figure 6.1). This community was still the only settlement south of the Arkansas River in 1820, in contrast to a growing line of settlements and farms on the north bank, visited by Nuttall (Thwaites 1905: 296). The first few communities and plantations were established on the natural levee of the Mississippi River during the late 1820s and early 1830s. Timothy Flint (1833: 280) described the land of the Arkansas River toward the south as:

> only a narrow belt along the river is above the overflow; and even through this belt the river has torn great numbers of *crevasses,* through which, in high floods, its waters escape into the swamps. Directly beyond these belts are gum trees and other vegetation denoting swampy soil. Beyond these are vast cypress swamps; and in all its course, from the bluffs [Little Rock] to the mouth [of the Arkansas River], like Red river, it has its net-work chequering of bayous and lakes.

The Boeuf Basin is a unit of the Arkansas alluvial fan (Fisk 1944; Phillips, Ford, and Griffin 1951: 15–19) bounded on the west by the Prairie Terrace from Pine Bluff, Arkansas, to the Bastrop Hills in Louisiana. The eastern boundary is marked by the Mississippi River from the mouth of the Arkansas River to the north end of Macon ridge and southward along the western edge of the ridge to Sicily Island. The basin is connected with the Ouachita lowland through the Bayou Bartholomew gap and merges with it at its southern end (Fisk 1944: 30). The Prairie Terrace is a relict alluvial plain of the Arkansas and Ouachita Rivers and now has a 50-ft. escarpment above the Boeuf Basin (Saucier 1974: 6).

The Arkansas alluvial fan in southeastern Arkansas is only 20 to 30 miles wide from the Mississippi River meander belt to the Prairie Terrace escarpment (Figure 6.1). Aggradation and degradation always have been by the Arkansas River system which parallels the Mississippi River to join with the Ouachita River and finally the Red River in east central Louisiana. The lowest point of this basin is along the

Boeuf River channel, while the two highest points are Macon ridge and the Bartholomew meander belt ridge. At the Arkansas–Louisiana state line, the elevation of the Mississippi River is 112 ft.; Macon ridge, 130 ft.; Boeuf River, 85 ft.; Bartholomew ridge, 112 ft.; Bayou Bartholomew, 85 ft.; and the Ouachita River, 63 ft., m.s.l.

A tentative outline of the geologic history of the Arkansas alluvial fan has been constructed by Roger T. Saucier (1967, 1968, 1974; Saucier and Fleetwood 1970). The Prairie Terrace formation, largely relict backswamp and meander belt deposits, has evidence of slow valley aggradation over a long period, approximately 80,000 to 100,000 years ago (Saucier 1974: 16, Figure 3). Macon ridge is a glacial outwash or valley train deposit laid down by sediment-choked, braided streams of the Arkansas River formed during the waning stages of the early Wisconsin, ca. 35,000 to 40,000 years ago, that resulted in the introduction of large volumes of glacial outwash (Saucier 1974: 8, 18). Beginning with the waxing late Wisconsin glaciation, ca. 25,000 years ago, the Arkansas River was confined to the area west of Macon ridge in depositing its load of glacial outwash (Saucier 1974: 18).

The Arkansas River probably changed from a braided to meandering regime around 12,000 years ago, although there is as yet no direct evidence for this hypothesis. About this time, the river began forming what is now the oldest discernible meander belt, No. 1, southeast of Little Rock. Meander belt No. 2, in the area of the present Bayou Macon channel north of Macon ridge, was active around 10,000 to 8000 years ago. Meander belt No. 3, in the area of the present Boeuf River, was active around 8000 to 6100 years ago. Meander belt No. 4, in the area of Choctaw and Amos Bayous in Desha County, was active around 6100 to 5000 years ago. The No. 5 meander belt formed west of Macon ridge in the area of present-day Crooked Bayou and Bayou Bonne Idee. The latter segment was abandoned as a result of diversion through a gap in the Prairie Terrace into the Ouachita River Valley. Meander belt No. 6, in the present Bayou Bartholomew channel, was active from approximately 3000 to 1000 years ago, whereas abandonment of this channel into the present Arkansas River channel may have occurred as recently as 1000 years ago (Saucier and Fleetwood 1970: 883–884; Saucier 1974: 21, 23, Figure 3).

Bayou Bartholomew flows in an entrenched meander belt from Pine Bluff to Monroe, along the base of the Prairie Terrace on the western edge of the Boeuf Basin. The Bartholomew meander belt ridge is composed of point bar deposits and sandy natural levees and is approximately 4 miles wide. The channel is lined with oxbow lakes and abandoned channels in various stages of filling, ranging from open lakes to those that are almost completely filled. The elevation of the meander belt ridge grades from 130 ft. at Boydell to 112 ft. at Wilmot. The distance from the base of the terrace to the bayou varies, with a maximum distance of 5 miles. The surface of this backswamp is 10 ft. lower than the crest of the meander belt ridge, and the backswamp drainage system is in Overflow Creek, paralleling the bayou, along the base of the terrace. The backslope drainage east of Bayou Bartholomew consists of a number of shallow streams originating on the ridge and emptying into Big Bayou at a distance of 4 to 8 miles east of Bayou Bartholomew. This backswamp surface is 10 to 15 ft. lower than the crest of the bayou meander belt ridge. Big Bayou empties into the Boeuf River 1 mile north of the Arkansas–Louisiana state line.

The importance of elevation is illustrated vividly by the massive inundation of the 1927 flood, when the Arkansas River levee broke in three places during April. Portland on the Bayou Bartholomew meander ridge and Eudora on Macon ridge were the only communities not flooded, while the water rose in Boydell, Montrose, Parkdale, and Wilmot for only a brief period (*Arkansas Gazette* 1927a, b).

Records of flood conditions are sporadic until 1926, when a gauging station was established at Wilmot with the gauge at an elevation of 85 ft., allowing a rise of 25 ft. of water before reaching the bankfull stage (Patterson 1971: B-186). Records over a period of 43 years document that in only 7 of those years has the water risen over the bank, the highest being 1.3 ft. above flood stage in 1932. This flood-stage record is not typical of past conditions, however, since the recorded floods in the Bartholomew watershed have been the result of local runoff (except the 1927 flood) and have been limited by the fact that high water diverted into the Boeuf and Tensas Basins. Prior to 1921, the Boeuf Basin was subject to flooding from the Mississippi River overflows that diverted through the Cypress Creek gap in the Mississippi River levee near Rohwer, Arkansas (U.S. Army Corps of Engineers 1966: 25). Nevertheless, earlier floods of southeast Arkansas did not flood the Bartholomew meander ridge in 1922, 1912, 1882, or 1874 (Frankenfield 1923: 12–13; Moore 1909: 111). While modern conditions of inundation cannot be considered completely reliable in constructing an image of prehistoric conditions, the documentation does indicate that the Bayou Bartholomew meander belt was sufficiently high for settlements on it to be relatively free of the threat of floods. Flood water along the Boeuf River would have to reach 25 ft. in order to rise to the 110–115-ft. contour on the Bartholomew meander ridge.

Once the settlers penetrated into the country of the Bartholomew, the potential of the meander belt ridge was recognized. Thomas Mather, one of the land surveyors in southeastern Arkansas in 1824, reported (Carter 1953: 710–712):

The country in which I have been operating embraces a front on the Missisipi of 60 miles including the mouth of Arkansas and Point Chicot: most of the land on the margin of the river between these points, in consequence of the overflow, is valuable alone on account of the timber: when this is destroyed, the land will not be salable, and almost intirely useless without the expensive operation of leveeing. . . . The Surveys should be extended from the river west . . . to embrace a beautiful tract of country on Bayou Bartelemi (or Bartholomew). This stream heads in the Quapaw country in the neighbourhood of the Arkansas and runs a course parralell with the Missisippi about 12 miles distant to its Junction with the Washita [Ouachita] about 25 miles above the post. There is a considerable quantity of good cotton lands on this stream, conected with the fine lands on the Arkansas in the Quapaw country, but cut off from the Missisippi by the overflow.

Extensive clearing has taken place since Mather's report. The bottom land hardwoods were a major source of income during the nineteenth century. The meander belt ridge is good land for cotton, and, within recent years, much of the ridge and the adjacent lower land have been cleared to grow soybeans as well. Today only remnants of the earlier vegetation patterns can be found in the stream channels and oxbow lakes.

The earliest documents listing vegetation of the Bartholomew area are the United States Government Land Office surveys. The east and south lines of the townships were surveyed in the 1820s and the interior section lines in the late 1830s. Most of the plot maps were completed and submitted by 1843. Preliminary analysis of the survey notes indicates a sweetgum–oak–hickory forest, the specific forest composition varying with the amount of water present. Twenty-eight tree types are identified by common name but the species of most of these can be inferred by the species identification and distribution in *Trees of Arkansas* (Moore 1960). Most of the Bartholomew area is a ridge bottom forest (Braun 1950: 295) merging to a hardwood bottom forest (Braun 1950: 293) at the lower elevations. The floodplain oak–hickory forest as described by Shelford (1963: 102) is also similar to the Bartholomew situation.

The Bartholomew locality encompasses portions of 15 townships. A sample of 6 townships (17 and 18 south, and ranges 3, 4, and 5 west) provides a cross section of the locality in the vicinity of the present-day communities of Portland and Parkdale. This cross section extends from the upper edge of the Prairie Terrace across Overflow Swamp, the Bartholomew ridge, and east across the backswamp to Big Bayou. Within the sample area, 442 trees were noted in the bottom land, including 24 species. These species and the percentage of the sample for each are listed in Table 6.1, along with the distribution in Arkansas, as identified by Moore (1960). Worthy of note are the

Table 6.1 **Species Composition of Sweetgum–Oak–Hickory Forest in the Bayou Bartholomew Locality, 1840**[a]

Common name	Percent- age	Species	Distribution in Arkansas[b]
Sweetgum	15	*Liquidambar styraciflua*	extremely common through south and east
White oak	10	*Quercus alba*	does not grow in Arkansas River overflow except on higher, better drained terraces
Pin oak	10	*Quercus palustris*	chiefly on overflow soils of larger rivers
Shellbark hickory	10	*Carya laciniosa*	on floodplains of larger streams
Ash	8	*Fraxinus*	*F. pennsylvanica, caroliniana,* and *tomentosa* occur in wet overflow land
Slippery elm	7	*Ulmus rubra*	adaptable to various conditions
Spanish and red oak	6	*Quercus falcata*	in first bottoms on best loamy soils and on well-drained terraces
Overcup oak	5	*Quercus lyrata*	in wetter overflow areas
Black oak	5	*Quercus velutina*	grows in wide variety of soils, especially in drier ones
Hackberry	5	*Celtis laevigata*	wide variety of habitats
Pecan	5	*Carya illinoensis*	grows well in overflow
Maple	4	*Acer saccharinum*	likely to be encountered in flood plain of all streams
Cypress	3	*Taxodium distichum*	stream valleys, bayous, lake margins
Tupelo–blackgum	2	*Nyssa aquatica*	common in bayous and overflow land of southeastern half of state
Hornbeam	1	*Carpinus caroliniana*	in south in stream valleys

[a] Less than 1% are catalpa, dogwood, honey locust, mulberry, burr oak, post oak, persimmon, sassafras, and sycamore.

[b] From Dwight Moore, *Trees of Arkansas* (1960).

species favoring dry or well-drained situations, such as white oak, red or Spanish oak, black oak, dogwood, and sassafras. The undergrowth in the forest is primarily cane, briers, and vines, although palmetto and briers are noted on the poorer, wetter soils. Cypress–tupelogum swamp forest is limited to the channels of the streams and to the oxbows and abandoned channels of Bayou Bartholomew.

In contrast, the adjacent edge of the Prairie Terrace is a black-oak–pine–post-oak forest. Among the 70 trees noted in the sample township survey, 6 species are represented, with percentages ranging from black oak, 37%; pine, 28%; post oak, 18%; hickory, 8%; white oak, 6%; to blackjack oak, 3%.

Patterns of spring inundation and vegetation at the 1830–1840 dateline should be applicable to the entire period following the change in the Arkansas River from meander belt No. 6 (Bayou Bartholomew) to the modern channel. Saucier (1974) estimates that this change took place approximately 1000 years ago. It is likely that the environment was considerably different when the Arkansas River occupied the Bartholomew channel, between 1000 and 3000 years ago. The 1830s environment includes at least five microenvironments within 10 miles of any site in the Bartholomew locality. Largest of these is the sweetgum–oak–hickory forest of the meander ridge and backslope. It can be divided into the higher, sandy loam cane ridge, which would have been excellent farm land, and the oak–hickory forest on the backslope, where farming would be more hazardous but where nuts and deer would be plentiful. Second and third are the water resources of Bayou Bartholomew and the lakes in the oxbows and abandoned channels. The backswamps on each side of the ridge are a wetlands forest, while a pine–oak forest is present on the Prairie Terrace.

A topic for future investigation is the effect on the environment of the shift of the Arkansas River from the Bartholomew channel to the present channel. Saucier's (1974: 23) estimate that the channel change took place approximately 1000 years ago places it perhaps 300 years prior to the Bartholomew phase. The effect on the environment of a change from a major river to an abandoned river channel containing a stream fed primarily by local drainage should be studied. The question is whether or not it had a calamitous effect on the environment, which then gradually improved as local hydrographic conditions stabilized. Access to the Bartholomew locality also may have been affected by the change in the river channel, reducing communication with the north and especially the developing Mississippian cultures in the St. Francis Basin to the northeast. Overland travel to the south would continue to be possible on the relatively high Bartholomew ridge or on the easily accessible Prairie Terrace. Water routes of travel also would be possible, especially south on the lower Bartholomew and Ouachita Rivers or on the Boeuf River to the southeast.

Another possible factor in the occupation of the Bartholomew locality is the effect of a change in climate. A climatic optimum occurred about A.D. 1000 to 1200 with worldwide effects (Lamb 1966: 94–102; LaMarche 1974: 1048) characterized by a warm moist climate, followed by a warm dry climate at about A.D. 1200. If the warm dry climate had a local effect of reduced rainfall, then the alluvial valley may have been drier than it is today, making the environment more attractive, especially for a locality that was already marginal to seasonal inundations. The optimum was followed by a little ice age, around A.D. 1430 to 1850, with a colder climate than is present today.

This shift to a colder climate might be a factor in the apparent drop in population following the Bartholomew phase.

The Bartholomew Phase Settlement Pattern

Emphasis in the analysis of the settlement pattern is on the correlation of sites with the microenvironments and the differences among settlements. The types of sites present are small ceremonial centers, hamlets, individual houses, and camps. The small ceremonial centers have one rectangular flat-topped mound and a midden area of up to 2 acres. They differ from the hamlets in the presence of a mound. The hamlets range in size from .5 to 2.0 acres, as linear concentrations along high ridges of land. They would appear to have contained no more than 8 to 10 houses at any one time. The household or individual house sites are small, dense concentrations of midden no more than .25 acre in size. They generally appear as distinct circles of midden-stained soil less than 30 m in diameter. The campsites have much the same appearance as the household sites, but differences are evident with excavation.

Site location is clearly correlated with elevation (Figure 6.2). Only two sites, the camps, are located at an elevation of less than 110 ft., while two additional sites are at an elevation only slightly lower than 115 ft. Above the 115-ft. elevation, 47 sites are located. Other sites may be buried in the backswamp deposits, but the difference between the land above the 110–115-ft. contours and that below would seem to be critical for most periods of inundation. Since the low-water level of the Boeuf River is 25 ft. below this contour, the higher elevations have considerably less threat during spring inundations.

Sites are primarily located on the Bartholomew ridge (60%, or 31 of 51 sites) or along the streams draining the backslope of the ridge into Big Bayou (39%, or 18 of 51 sites), although two sites have been found in the backswamp. Sites on the backslope are located close to the edges of the streams. Sites on the Bartholomew ridge, however, are not as closely associated with the bayou. Ceremonial centers are on the bank of the bayou, two of them within 1 mile of an oxbow lake. Six of the hamlets are on the edge of the bayou, all within 1 mile of an oxbow lake, but four of the hamlets are on oxbows away from the bayou. Households are also predominantly on the edge of the bayou within 1 mile of an oxbow lake. The preferred location, apparently, was within easy walking distance of both the bayou and a lake, and with access to four of the microenvironments and their varied resources. No sites are on the edge of the Prairie Terrace, or at least it has not been possible to find them. Although the land is covered with thick woods and undergrowth, some search for sites has been made. It

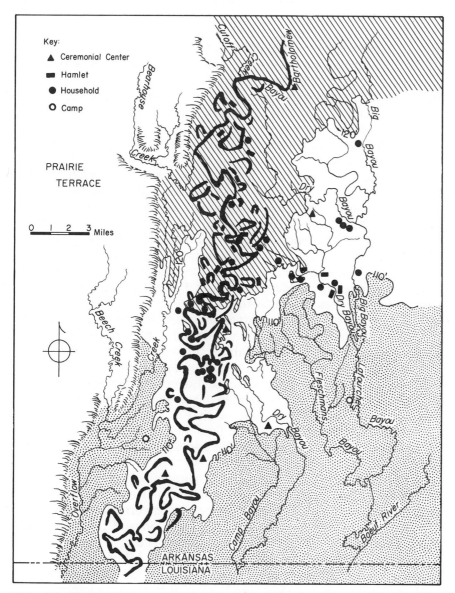

Figure 6.2 The Bartholomew locality with Bartholomew phase sites shown in relation to topography.

111

would appear that the bottom-land resources were more important than locations never threatened by inundation. Mississippi period sites have not yet been found along the Boeuf River, either. This river is the most poorly investigated in southeastern Arkansas, but the sites so far recorded are Archaic period sites.

The distribution of different types of sites indicates a dispersed community pattern like that reported for the Natchez and Quapaw at the end of the eighteenth century. St. Cosme noted that cabins were often a quarter of a league apart (Swanton 1911: 46) rather than in compact clusters. There is some clustering of sites, but not enough to define individual communities. Neither is there enough information to define time spans for sites or for the Bartholomew phase. Only two of the ceremonial centers have neighboring, possibly supportive, sites. They are situated so that 20 to 25 hamlet and household sites are within 5 miles. The other ceremonial centers do not have this clustering pattern, one center having only two other sites within 5 miles and a second center only five sites within 5 miles. All of the hamlets are at least 1 mile apart from each other. Four of the 14 hamlets have two household sites within 1 mile of them. There is one cluster of three household sites within 1 mile and another cluster of five household sites within 1 mile.

The six small ceremonial centers are characterized by a hamlet with a single, rectangular, flat-topped mound. The distribution of site midden is indicated by dark-stained soil scattered along the highest ridge of land near the mound. Sites encompass up to 2 acres of ground without specific orientation to the mound, nor is a plaza evident. Three of the ceremonial centers located on the bayou have the mound situated at the edge of the bank so that it appears to be much taller from the bayou than from the land side. Those mounds still in existence are from 4 to 5 m in height and are roughly rectangular with flat tops.

Minor testing of the best-preserved ceremonial center, the Henderson site (3 As 100), was conducted in 1970. The Henderson mound is at present 4 m high with a base 40 m square. The original dimensions of the mound may have been different, as the sides of the mound have eroded and the field is in cultivation up to the edge of the mound. The upper surface is irregular, with the west side 1 m higher than the east side. There are, however, several gravestones still standing at the east end, the earliest dating 1849. The bank of Bayou Bartholomew is 30 m south of the mound, and artifacts are scarce in the intervening open area. Burials reportedly were exposed along the bank of the bayou southwest of the mound when a road was constructed. A second mound, roughly 50 cm high, is reported to have been located 200 ft. west–northwest of the larger mound, but was leveled several years ago, with bones and artifacts being exposed at that time. Surface material extends for 60 m east and 100 m west of the mound. It has been in cultivation for over 100 years, and most of the subsurface features probably have been destroyed by the intensive cultivation. Test units were placed at the edge of the mound to determine the nature of the fill. The occupation apparently does not predate the mound construction, since no midden deposit was found beneath the mound, nor was midden a common component of the mound fill. Recovered from the mound were partial vessels which could be reconstructed, suggesting that they were refuse deposited from a structure on top of the mound, or were placed intentionally in the mound fill, rather than collected as generalized midden. No separate construction stages were exposed by the test excavation.

The 14 hamlets are characterized by midden-stained soil and a surface concentration of artifacts over an area ranging in size from .5 to 2.0 acres. The midden deposit is generally linear, on a ridge paralleling the bayou or oxbow lake. As with the ceremonial centers, most of these sites have been cultivated over a long period of time and have been badly damaged. Two of these sites have been tested, Wilson Brake (3 As 85) and Ellis Pugh (3 Ch 20). At both sites, the Bartholomew component was limited to the upper, disturbed levels. Both sites were stratified, however, with Middle Woodland components present in the lower, undisturbed zones. The Ellis Pugh site still has evidence of features. These are localized spots with darker-stained soil and heavier concentrations of artifacts and refuse, suggesting individual house locations. Two slight rises once may have been house mounds. Through past years, burials have been dug and plowed up from the area immediately north of the midden deposit. Nothing can be collected now from the surface of the burial area. Nothing about these sites suggests long occupations or large communities, since the midden deposits are shallow and are not heavily concentrated with refuse.

The homesteads or individual house sites are distinct with small, circular concentrations of artifacts and refuse in an area generally less than 30 m in diameter. Of the 29 house sites, 15 are located on the bank of Bayou Bartholomew within 1 mile of an oxbow lake. They occur individually, as dispersed clusters of individual houses and as clusters with hamlets. One of these, the MacArthur site (3 Ch 49), has been excavated. This site was dug at the request of the landowner, who had exposed two burials during the 1970 spring discing. The land had been cleared and in cultivation only 4 years, and the only surface indication was a dark patch of soil and a few potsherds. The features were largely undisturbed although distinct house floors could not be defined. The occupation area was strictly limited to an area 8 m in diameter, with the outer limit clearly defined. The midden was concentrated in a 10-cm zone, below the plow line. Postmolds were exposed at the base of the plow zone but the few years of cultivation had disturbed the floors of the structures. Two circular structures were defined, both 5.0 to 5.5 m in diameter, with small posts set 1.0 to 1.5 m apart. No daub was present, suggesting the structures were a light pole framework with cane-mat walls. The two structures were overlapping, so that only one household occupied the site at one time. Apparently, one structure burned and a second one was built at the same spot. Midden pits and concentrations were present within the walls of the structures. Also, there were extended, supine burials of two adult males and one adult female and four flexed burials of infants, all in separate graves, within the structures and apparently immediately below the floor. Fish and deer bone were contained within the midden pits and concentrations, and the site may have been used as a hunting and/or fishing camp. However, it is more likely a farmstead, with the diet of the occupants supplemented by wild foods.

The two campsites are similar in appearance to the household sites but are located in the backswamps. The soils of the backswamps are an extremely compact clay, in contrast to the sandy loam soils in which all of the hamlet and household sites are situated. The campsites are distinguished by the heavy concentration of artifacts and refuse in an area less than 15 m in diameter. One of these camps, the Currie site (3 As 141), has been excavated. This site is located in the middle of Overflow Swamp, with no apparent source of moving water within 1 mile of the site. The midden contained an abundance of deer bone and mussel shell, indicating that the environmental situation was different when the site was occupied and that wild foods in the vicinity were being utilized. The site was excavated in 1970 and had been in cultivation only 4 years. It appeared as a low rise, 15 cm high and 12 m in diameter. The maximum thickness of the midden was 40 cm and the midden had accumulated as the backswamp soils aggraded.

The as yet unexplained problem with the interpretation of this site is that it had four clearly distinct components present, including the late Marksville period, Alligator Point phase; the Coles Creek period, DeYampert phase; the early Mississippi period, Bartholomew phase; and the late Mississippi period, Wilmot phase (Rolingson n.d.). There is some stratification, since the Wilmot phase ceramics were entirely within the plow zone and in the only defined midden pit, whereas the Alligator Point phase ceramics were lying at the base of the midden on the clay. Cultural materials were mixed in the midden between the clay and plow zone. What was the site locale like during the 1500-year span that would make this such a desirable settlement location for four different groups of people at markedly different periods of time? A second campsite, the Currie site No. 1 (3 As 103), is located three-fourths of a mile to the north. Although the campsite has been disturbed by a drainage ditch and road, the surface collection indicates a late Mississippi Wilmot phase occupation. The Currie site does, however, demonstrate that swamp resources were being utilized during the Bartholomew phase. That this site was a farmstead is doubtful, since the clay soils of the backswamp are poor farmland and the ground is wet much of the year.

The Artifact Assemblage

The artifacts present on all of the Bartholomew phase sites are a consistent assemblage. The ceramic complex is limited to a few types. The paste of both the plain and decorated wares is similar to Baytown Plain except that bone tempering occurs as a minor percentage within the site samples. Bone tempering is generally present in 3% to 5% of a site sample, although in some samples, it is as high as 10%. Shell tempering is present but less common than bone tempering. This scarcity of shell as a tempering agent contrasts markedly to the succeeding Wilmot phase ceramic complex, where shell is the predominant tempering agent.

The predominant vessel forms are (1) unrestricted hemispherical bowl with shallow side walls either vertical or flaring, (2) a deep unrestricted bowl with vertical walls or barrel shape, and (3) a deep vessel with recurved rim, that is, a subglobular vessel with a slight constriction at the neck and a flaring rim. Less common are carinated bowls and shallow bowls or plates with slightly thickened rim set off by an incised line. Apparently, the bottle form is absent.

Decorative motifs are placed on the upper third of the vessel wall, the most common motif being a band of line-filled triangles with a variety of pattern arrangements. The decoration resembles both Manchac Incised (Quimby 1951: 111–113) and Barton Incised (Phillips, Ford, and Griffin 1951: 114–119) including punctations on the body of some vessels. This pottery is distinctive enough to warrant a new variety name (using the type–variety system of Phillips 1970), Mazique Incised, *var. Parkdale* (Rolingson n.d.). Other types with this filled-triangle motif are Plaquemine Brushed (Quimby 1951: 109–111) and Avoyelles Punctated, *var. Dupree* (Quimby 1951: 122–123; Phillips 1970: 43). Evansville Punctated is a common type, generally a body decoration with a plain rim. A variant of this, Evansville Punctated, *var. Beech Creek* (Rolingson n.d.), has the punctations arranged in alternating linear patterns, somewhat resembling Sinner Linear Punctated (Suhm and Jelks 1962: 143). Hollyknowe Ridge Pinched (Phillips

1970: 88–90), present in minor amounts, is another of the linear arrangements done by pinching ridges. Another decorative motif of parallel lines below the rim includes either a band of closely spaced lines similar to Hardy Incised (Quimby 1951: 113–114), here called Coles Creek Incised, *var. Kimball*, or a group of only two or three horizontal lines on the rim, here called Coles Creek Incised, *var. Big Bayou* (Rolingson, n.d.). Also present are Harrison Bayou Incised (Quimby 1951: 115–117), L'Eau Noire Incised (Quimby 1951: 117–118) with simple, rectilinear designs on vessel rims, and Winterville Incised, *var. Winterville*, and Winterville Incised, *var. Blum* (Phillips 1970: 172–174).

The ceramics are primarily utilitarian, and not much care was taken in shaping the vessel or in executing the design. However, some partially reconstructed vessels from the Henderson site exhibit considerable care in vessel construction, with highly polished surfaces and decorative motifs carefully arranged and implemented.

Other baked-clay artifacts are rare. A single effigy human head originally attached to a figurine or vessel rim was found at the Henderson site, and a large blocky right-angle pipe was collected from the Ellis Pugh site. Bone tools include turtle carapace cups, deer-ulna awls, and splinter bone awls. Stone tools are not common; most are made from small river pebbles with only occasional use of novaculite. The Ashley point is a small, bulbous stemmed projectile point (Rolingson 1971). Cutting and scraping tools are bifacially flaked pebbles roughly trianguloid in form. Small polished celts, generally triangular in form, are present at some sites. These stone tools are diagnostic of the Bartholomew and Wilmot phases and are distinct from the tools of the earlier phases in the Bartholomew locality.

That there was a ceremonial aspect in the culture can be inferred from the presence of mounds, but there is an outstanding lack of evidence for the accumulation of status goods by any members of the society. Some status distinctions within the society are indicated by the quality of the ceramics and the presence of a human effigy head at the ceremonial center, the Henderson site. This contrasts with the lack of distinctive artifacts that can be identified as status goods at the other types of sites. Of course, because of the poor preservation conditions, one cannot consider the problems of status differentiation in burials and probably will never be able to do so.

Cultural–Historical Placement of the Bartholomew Phase

The Bartholomew phase is sharply differentiated from both earlier and later phases in the Bartholomew locality. The scarcity of Coles

Creek ceramics suggests that the locality may have been used only sporadically between A.D. 700 and 1000. Three sites with Coles Creek ceramics are the basis for the DeYampert phase. These are widely scattered, located on Dry Bayou, Bayou Bartholomew, and in Overflow Swamp, and appear to be small camps with perhaps one small hamlet. None of the ceremonial centers have Coles Creek ceramics. The DeYampert phase contrasts markedly with the abundance of Coles Creek sites along the Ouachita River, where there are major mound centers and numerous small hamlets and farmsteads.

Components in the Bartholomew locality that may confidently be assigned to the succeeding Wilmot phase in the late Mississippi period are much less common than Bartholomew phase components. Nine components are identified, including three camps, three households, two hamlets, and one ceremonial center. Ceramics are predominantly shell-tempered and the types present have a decorative emphasis on curvilinear motifs, whether incised, trailed, punctated, or pinched. They are Winterville Incised, var. *Pugh* (Rolingson, n.d.), Parkin Punctated, var. *Transylvania* (Phillips 1970: 152), and Pouncey Ridge Pinched, var. *Currie* (Rolingson, n.d.). The curvilinear motif of the vessel body often is accompanied by outlining punctations and horizontal incised lines on the rim. Winterville Incised, var. *Winterville,* and Winterville Incised, var. *Blum,* are common types that cannot be considered diagnostic of the Wilmot phase because they are also present as minor types in the Bartholomew phase. Vessel forms include the globular body and constricted neck of the Mississippian jar and the shallow bowl.

To pinpoint a source of origin for the Bartholomew phase is at present a rather speculative activity because of the lack of research along the Ouachita River. The Bartholomew ceramic complex is in many ways similar to that of the Routh phase in the upper Tensas Basin dated at A.D. 1200 to 1350 (Hally 1966, 1972). To a lesser extent, it resembles the ceramics of the Fitzhugh phase dated A.D. 1350 to 1650. Settlement patterns differ between the Routh–Fitzhugh and Bartholomew phases, but the site-location surveys were organized with different objectives and techniques and, as a result, the data are not strictly comparable. Nevertheless, the population groupings of the Bartholomew phase are smaller in the Bartholomew locality than in the upper Tensas Basin and large ceremonial centers are not present. The ceramic complex of the Wilmot phase also indicates relationships to the Transylvania phase in the upper Tensas Basin, where Winterville Incised is the common ceramic type. Transylvania phase has been dated A.D. 1500 to 1650, coeval with the late Fitzhugh occupation in that basin.

The ceramic complex of the Bartholomew phase also resembles the ceramic complex of the Plaquemine culture in the Catahoula Basin and along the Ouachita River (Gregory 1969; personal communication) although the latter region is poorly documented. In the Catahoula Basin, there are also comparable settlement-pattern data, with sites located on the natural levees along bayous connecting Larto and Catahoula Lakes. Gregory (1969) hypothesized that these preferred locations relate to good farmland on the cane ridges despite periodic overflow. These locations also provided easy access to the swamp resources of the lakes. The only sites found on the Quaternary bluffs are small scattered camps, a situation similar to the Bartholomew phase lack of use of the Prairie Terrace.

Recent site survey in the proposed Felsenthal National Wildlife Refuge on the Ouachita and Saline Rivers in Arkansas (Lischka 1973; Rolingson 1972) has located a number of large sites with multiple components, indicating a Coles Creek–Plaquemine continuum with only minor Caddoan occupation. Coles Creek and Plaquemine occupations are also present at the Pawpaw site (3 Ou 22) on the Ouachita River below Camden (Weber 1973). The Pawpaw site Plaquemine occupation is estimated to date between A.D. 1000 and 1350, based on two radiocarbon samples.

The discovery of a Plaquemine occupation in the Ouachita River Valley raises the interesting point made by John R. Swanton (1939: 52–54, 1952: 215) that De Soto encountered Tunican-speaking peoples at the town of Tanico and possibly Natchezan-speaking peoples at Utiangue in the Ouachita Mountains in 1541. By the beginning of the eighteenth century, when more Frenchmen were in the area, the most often mentioned tribe in northeastern Louisiana were the Taensa, but Tunica and the related Koroa were also present (Swanton 1952: 193, 209). Possibly, the strong continuum of Coles Creek–Plaquemine–Taensa–Tunica occupation in the Tensas Basin was present in the middle Ouachita Basin as well. The prehistoric Caddo sites and the Caddo encountered by the early explorers on the middle and lower Ouachita River may represent a down-river movement out of the Ouachita Mountains near the end of the prehistoric period.

Summary and Conclusions

Specialized site functions are present in the settlement pattern of the Bartholomew phase. In addition to hamlets, there are small ceremonial centers, house sites that are probably farmsteads, and swamp camps. Although sites occur in clusters, the chronological control is not sufficient to identify possible communities. Nevertheless, occupants of the specialized sites probably were united into larger communities with sociopolitical and religious ties, and the ethnographic parallel of the dispersed communities of the eighteenth-century Natchez or Quapaw is pertinent. Specialized site functions of sites cannot be identified from the artifacts. The Bartholomew assemblage is simple in the range of artifacts present and in the decorative motifs of the ceramics, which are limited to a few basic patterns. There was little attention to skillful production, and only a few of the artifacts suggest status differentiation. Most tools probably were made of bone, wood, and cane and, therefore, have not survived.

The distribution of settlements indicates a preference for site locations on relatively high points of land, in proximity to Bayou Bartholomew and oxbow lakes or to the backslope streams, with easy access to all microenvironments within the bottom lands. The Bartholomew locality is an island within the alluvial plain of the Arkansas River, in the sense that the Bartholomew meander belt ridge is a long, narrow area not threatened by inundation except during the highest spring floods. This favorable situation is evident in the composition of the ridge bottom sweetgum–oak–hickory forest which includes species that grow in well-drained terraces. This ridge could have been readily utilized for farming. Although a preliminary description of the prehistoric hydrography and flora from nineteenth-century documents has been compiled, there is much more to do in reconstructing the total environment. It is doubtful that detailed information on the resources actually utilized will ever be obtained, since preservation conditions are poor and sites are being damaged or destroyed by modern agricultural practices. It can be hypothesized, however, that the subsistence pattern was based on corn–beans horticulture supplemented by wild resources including deer, various nuts, and other bottom-land flora.

The information gathered within the Bartholomew locality and from surrounding regions suggests that the Bartholomew phase is an intrusion of Plaquemine peoples into the upper Boeuf Basin, out of either the Tensas Basin or the Ouachita River Valley, dating approximately A.D. 1200 to 1400. A specific point of origin cannot yet be identified, and considerably more research is needed in the Ouachita River Valley before the regional pattern can be described.

7

Internal Settlement Designs of Two Mississippian Tradition Ceremonial Centers in Southeastern Missouri*

Carl H. Chapman

Introduction

The large Mississippian tradition ceremonial centers of southeastern Missouri are among the most outstanding prehistoric monuments in the south central United States. They hold information pertaining to social and political organizations and the lifeways of the people who lived in them. Their potential for archaeological interpretations of settlement systems, internal settlement designs, and social, political, and ceremonial organization and activities is unparalleled in the central Mississippi alluvial valley. Unfortunately, their large size, the lack of sufficient funds for extensive long-term excavations, and their private rather than public ownership have prevented their archaeological investigation until the last decade.

Archaeological investigations touching on the large townsites have

* The basic data for this chapter have been obtained through research projects under the direction of the writer since 1967. These were cooperative agreements between the Missouri State Park Board and the University of Missouri at Columbia and National Endowment for the Humanities Research Grants RO-5567-6 and RO-7728-73-198.

been primarily surveys (Adams and Walker 1942; Griffin and Spaulding 1952; Healan 1972; Houck 1908; Lewis 1972, 1973; Marshall 1965; Phillips, Ford, and Griffin 1951; Potter 1880; Thomas 1894; S. Williams 1954; and J. Williams 1964, 1967, 1968, 1972). There has been much indiscriminate digging for artifacts, little of which has been reported (Beckwith 1911; Putnam 1875). The most extensive investigation, which revealed a modicum of internal arrangement of one of the centers, was that of the Matthews site in 1941–1942 by Walker and Adams (1946).

The two sites chosen for this study have recently received the most attention in the area. They are Towosahgy (Beckwith's Fort), Mississippi County, Missouri, and the Lilbourn Mound Cemetery, New Madrid County, Missouri, only 20 miles apart (Figure 7.1). The

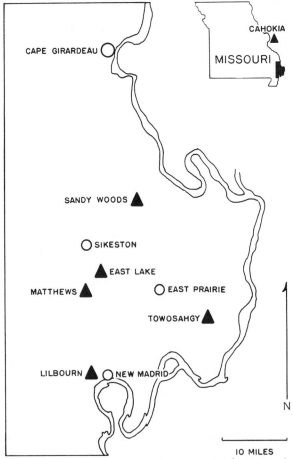

Figure 7.1 Location of Mississippian tradition ceremonial centers in southeastern Missouri mentioned in the text.

selection of the two sites was only partly based on their potential for providing comparable information. Towosahgy was publicly owned and had been under limited investigation for several years; a significant portion of Lilbourn was threatened with destruction by the construction of a new school, and intensive investigations were conducted there in advance of the destruction.

The purpose of the project, which was begun in 1970, was to investigate and compare the two fortified townsites. Usual archaeological procedures were applied to obtain information on the probable contemporaneity, village plans, internal organization, demography, and interaction of the villages. Another goal was to investigate the relationships of the village sites to the broader prehistoric community and to the occupation and exploitation of the resources of the region. Data on the lifeways of the people who inhabited the villages were gathered for additional knowledge about the sociopolitical organization of the past societies and for public understanding of the cultural heritage from the past in the central United States (Evans 1970, 1971).

Basic to the research goals was the assumption that the two fortified towns were expressions of the same cultural tradition and would reflect the parameters of closely related or similar cultural systems. Both sites had large ceremonial mounds and an open space (courtyard or plaza), dwellings, and other structures within the surrounding fortifications. Therefore, they were assumed to be ceremonial centers and perhaps redistribution centers for nearby extractive sites, hamlets, and villages, and possibly market exchange centers as well (Porter 1969: 158–162).

The scope of this chapter will be limited to testing the contrastive hypotheses of whether the internal designs of the two towns were based on similar culturally prescribed plans, perhaps the adaptation of a formal plan to the local topography (S. Williams 1954: 259–260), or were the result of haphazard growth, as Reed (1969: 40) has suggested. Information on the internal settlement designs of each site will be provided by cartographic data, surface collections of materials, and excavations. If formal planning existed, it should be reflected by the relationships of mounds to each other and to other features within the stockaded areas, including plazas, domiciles, and other structures. That the placement and distribution of structures used as dwellings and for special purposes had an integral relationship to mounds, the plaza area, the stockade, or specific parts of the town will be investigated. The possibility that class differentiation (social status) can be interpreted through analysis of the structure size and the presence or absence of special artifacts in the structures also will be explored. The location of burials and burial groups in relation to structures, the age of individuals associated with structures and burial groups, and the objects associated with the burials have been examined for possible indications of social differentiation or status. The time that the two fortified towns were occupied is indicated by radiocarbon dates. Correlations of dates have been noted as possible times when interaction between the towns could have occurred.

To provide background information on the collection of data from the two Mississippian tradition townsites, a brief history of their recent investigation follows. In 1966, the Missouri State Park Board purchased the Beckwith's Fort site and made a cooperative agreement with the University of Missouri at Columbia to conduct a program of archaeological research and interpretation which would be for the public benefit. The name of the site was changed to "Towosahgy" (derived from the Osage Indian word meaning "old town") to separate it from historic fort sites in public ownership elsewhere in the state.

Although excavations began at Towosahgy in 1967 and have continued each summer to date, they have been limited in scope, owing to lack of sufficient funds. Testing on the top of the largest mound (Figure 7.2, Mound 2) and a smaller mound (Figure 7.2, Mound 5) demonstrated that structures had been built on top of them.

The major excavations at Towosahgy have been in the southeast corner of the site to obtain information on fortification walls and associated structures. The center of the site also was tested to determine if a courtyard or plaza was located there. Such a feature had been postulated on the basis of the arrangement of the mounds and an aerial photograph that revealed a concentric circle of dots, potentially a woodhenge similar to those found at Cahokia by Wittry (1969).

The Lilbourn site had been excavated by Swallow (Putnam 1875), who noted a structure and burials in the center of the largest mound. The site had been mapped (Figure 7.3) by C. Henrich in 1878 (Potter 1880), and it was mentioned in some of the surveys of southeast Missouri (S. Williams 1954; J. Williams 1964), although no extensive excavations were accomplished. In 1970, a significant portion of the eastern segment was threatened with destruction by the building of a new school by the New Madrid R1 School Board. At that time, the site was tested through the efforts of volunteer workers from the University of Missouri, the Missouri Archaeological Society, people in the community, and members of the school board. This work was designed to test the validity of the 1878 map and to verify the existence of subsurface archaeological features. The results indicated that the old map was reasonably accurate but that the major surface features and much of the latest occupational evidences had been badly disturbed by farming. For example, all of the mounds mapped in 1878 had been reduced in height; the fortification embankments, which

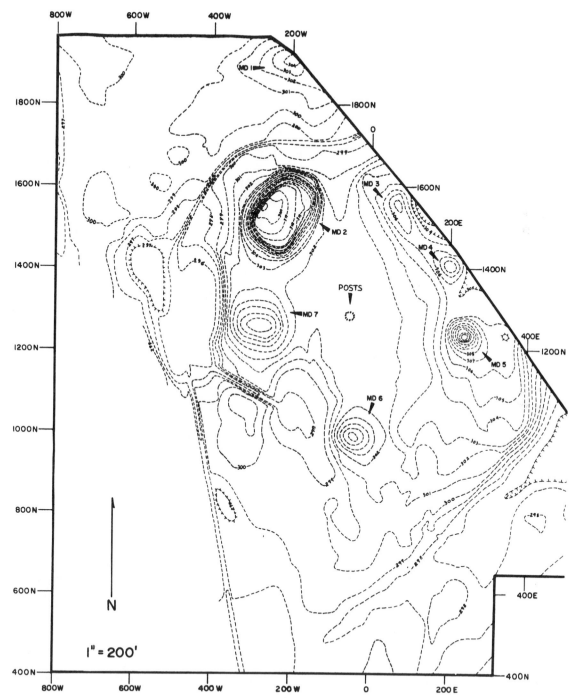

Figure 7.2 Topographic map of Towosahgy ceremonial center (courtesy Missouri State Park Board).

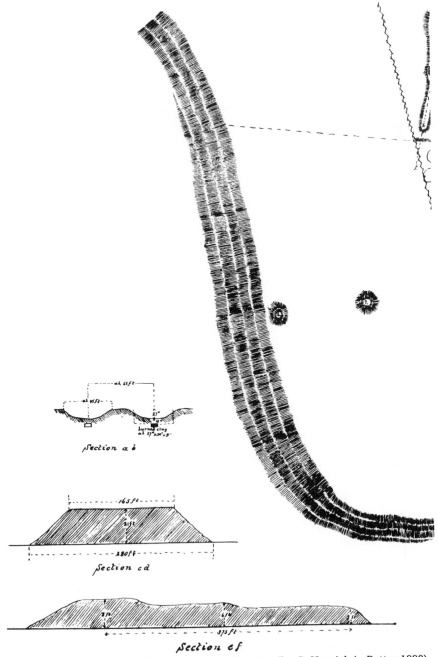

Plate D.

Settlement B.

Section a b

Section c d

Section e f

Figure 7.3 Map of the Lilbourn ceremonial center (by C. Henrich in Potter 1880).

126

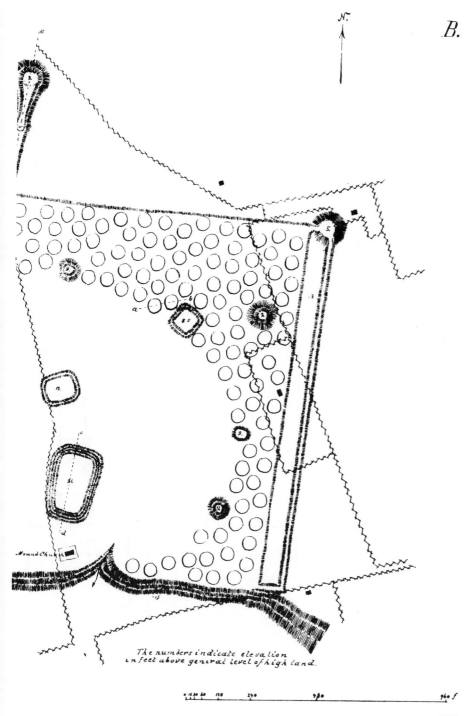

N.

B.

Mound Chu..

The numbers indicate elevation
in feet above general level of high land.

0 15 30 60   120   240   480   960 f

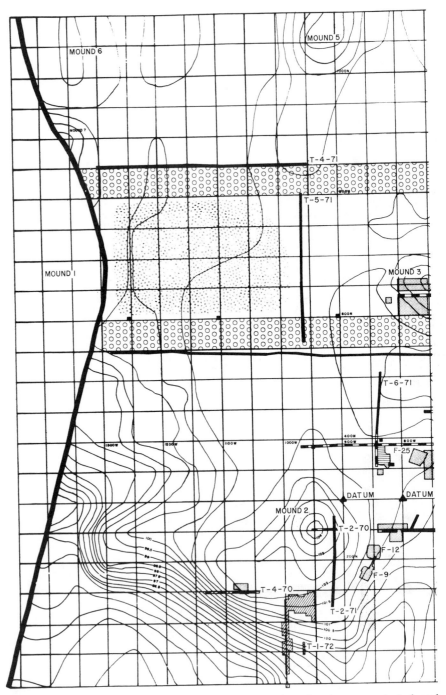

Figure 7.4 Map of the east part of the Lilbourn site, showing areas tested and excavated.

128

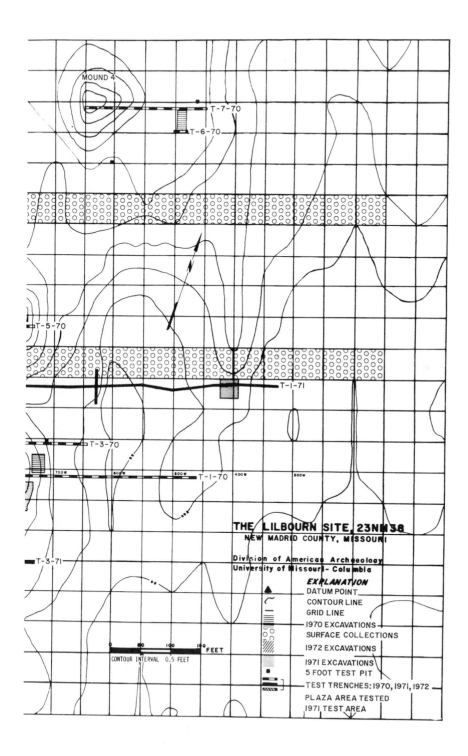

MOUND 4

T-7-70

T-6-70

T-5-70

T-1-71

T-3-70

700 W   600 W   500 W   T-1-70   400 W   300 W

THE LILBOURN SITE, 23NM38
NEW MADRID COUNTY, MISSOURI

Division of American Archaeology
University of Missouri - Columbia

T-3-71

EXPLANATION

▲ DATUM POINT
⌒ CONTOUR LINE
   GRID LINE
≡ 1970 EXCAVATIONS
∘∘∘ SURFACE COLLECTIONS
▨ 1972 EXCAVATIONS
   1971 EXCAVATIONS
■ 5 FOOT TEST PIT
   TEST TRENCHES: 1970, 1971, 1972
   PLAZA AREA TESTED
   1971 TEST AREA

0   50   100   150 FEET
CONTOUR INTERVAL 0.5 FEET

originally had been 3 to 5 ft. high, had been leveled; and all surface evidences of house pits had been eradicated.

Despite the damage to features on the site, the fact that an accurate map had been made while the major features of the site were still in existence pointed up its outstanding potential for the investigation of internal site design. Therefore, a concerted effort was made to recover data on the historical and anthropological aspects of the site prior to the imminent destruction of its eastern half.

A testing strategy was formulated to obtain information on the plan of the town. The area was so large that, to salvage the data in the limited time available, backhoe test trenches were run east–west and north–south across the section to be affected most by the construction of the school. Five-ft.² test pits, placed at intervals to secure detailed information, were excavated by hand, using 6-inch depth units, and 1-ft.² columns of soil were removed from each in 3-inch units and were water-screened to recover floral and faunal remains. Two 50-ft.-wide strips paralleling the test trenches were plowed east–west across the site so that controlled surface collections could be made more easily.

The preliminary investigations in 1970 proved to be very successful for planning future work, and the testing strategy was continued prior to the funding of excavations by the National Endowment for the Humanities in 1971. Two different areas of fortification constructions, three circumscribed cemetery areas, two structures toward the east edge, and structures on the south edge of the site were located. Excavations were conducted on structures in different parts of the site—sections of fortification walls, four burial groups, four mounds, and the plaza area (Figure 7.4).

A comparison of Lilbourn and Towosahgy was made by using early maps, recent contour maps, and aerial photographs. A relationship between mounds to both fortifications and courtyards (plazas) was noted as was the possible orientation of these features to bodies of water (Figure 7.5). Each site was surrounded by a stockade; each had a large trapezoidal platform mound, the longitudinal axis of which faced a low, relatively flat area that was postulated to have been a courtyard or plaza surrounded by several smaller mounds.

The shapes of the largest mounds at Lilbourn (Figures 7.3, 7.5), at Towosahgy (Figures 7.2, 7.5), and at the Sandy Woods settlement (Potter 1880: Plate Aa) were clearly trapezoidal. Although the map drawing of the largest mound in the East Lake site (Potter 1880: 15, Plate C, Settlement C) is not as clearly a trapezoid, the measurements at the base, "230' by 115' to 135'," indicate that it was. Some of the large mounds at other Mississippian ceremonial centers that have been reported as "rectangular" also may have been trapezoidal. The reason for the trapezoidal shape of the largest mounds is not clear but

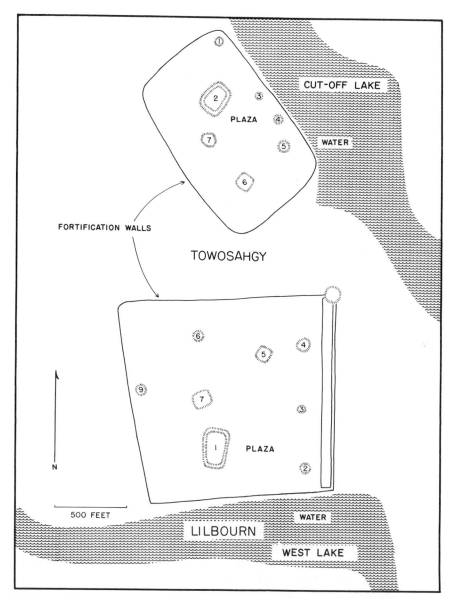

Figure 7.5 Sketch maps of Towosahgy and Lilbourn, showing internal relationships of mounds, plaza, and fortifications and external relationships to a body of water.

may be related to their use in assisting astronomical observations and calendrical computations (Baity 1973; Fowler 1969).

The relationship of the mounds to the nearest large water source may have been an important consideration: When the location of the largest mound in relation to the small mounds is studied, the plan of

Towosahgy is almost a mirror image of that of Lilbourn (Figures 7.2, 7.3, 75.). Stephen Williams (1954: 258), in discussing mound and plaza arrangement, noted that the main mound was usually on the side of the plaza away from the water. A relatively large lake to the south and southeast of both towns may have been a factor in the placement of mounds which were oriented to provide an unobstructed view across a body of water. This view could have been desirable for calendrical observations based on the relative position of the rising sun. In any case, the two fortified towns were planned, and a similar preconceived design was employed. The plan was adjusted to the terrain with special consideration possibly given to its orientation to the adjacent lake (Figure 7.5).

Evidence for a preconceived general plan for Mississippian tradition ceremonial centers has been given by Phillips, Ford, and Griffin (1951: 315–334) in their survey of the lower Mississippi Valley. They noted that, of 78 sites classed as small ceremonial centers, mounds in 37 of them clearly outline a plaza area that was generally oval in shape and 200 to 400 ft. long and half as wide. Furthermore, the largest mound tended to be at the west end of the plaza, usually at the west or northwest. The same general arrangement was found also in large ceremonial centers. They noted (Phillips, Ford, and Griffin 1951: 447) that "the majority of sites where the relation of the principal mound to the plaza can be determined show that this mound was placed on the west or northwest side of the plaza and the view across the plaza from it was toward the east or southeast, the general direction of the rising sun."

Town Plans of Lilbourn and Towosahgy

At Lilbourn, the designed and controlled surface and subsurface surveys verified the general location of the plaza area, the intensively occupied houses surrounding the plaza, and the fortification or stockade shown on the Henrich map (Figure 7.3). There was evidence that the area between the inner (earlier) stockade and the outer (later) held recessed areas filled with refuse.

At Towosahgy, a surface survey demonstrated that the area between the mounds, presumed to have been a plaza for ceremonial use, contained a limited number of Mississippian tradition artifacts. The distribution of daub in this survey indicated the locations of structures surrounding the plaza, and the presence in the area of finely made Mississippian tradition pottery may denote the location for houses of families with high social status (Healan 1972: Figures 8–9).

A map made prior to intensive cultivation (Thomas 1894: Figure 98) showed an area free of "house pits" southeast of the largest mound and near the approximate center of the site. Thomas (1894: 186–187) noted that there was "an open court adjoining one side of the great flat-topped mound. . . . [House sites or hut rings] almost literally cover the remainder of the area, the only open space of any considerable size being the 200 feet square just east of the large mound."

The credibility of Thomas's map of Towosahgy is questionable when compared with the Henrich maps of fortified centers in southeast Missouri (Potter 1880). A recent topographic map of the site (Figure 7.2) shows that Mounds 2, 3, 4, 5, 6, and 7 enclose a large rectangular area in the center of the site. To conceive of the entire area encompassed by the mounds as a plaza is difficult; nevertheless, the lack of recorded house depressions indicates that some part of the area was used as a plaza during the latest Mississippian occupation.

A recent aerial photograph of Towosahgy revealed a dotted concentric circular area with a maximum diameter of about 70 ft. just south of Mound 2. The circular shape of the feature suggests either a rotunda such as that illustrated by Bartram (Swanton 1928: 176–177) or a circle of poles similar to the woodhenge found at Cahokia, which was thought to have been used for calendrical observations (Wittry 1969: 43). Because both the rotunda and woodhenge are community structures found associated with plazas elsewhere, existence of either would indicate the use of the area as a plaza.

Test excavations in the supposed plaza area provided enough evidence to draw tentative conclusions concerning the area of concentric circles of dots on the aerial photograph. A small circle (less than 12 ft. in diameter) of large posts (1 ft. in diameter) was located (Figure 7.2). The circle of posts was smaller than had been anticipated; the large circle emcompassing it may yet be found when the area is further investigated. Cultural debris did not extend very deep, and the amount of midden was minimal in comparison to that near the stockade wall. The tentative interpretation is that a plaza or courtyard with accompanying public-use features was present in the area where it was originally thought to have been.

At Lilbourn, the surface and subsurface surveys of the space east of Mound 1 showed that this area was indeed the plaza (Figures 7.3, 7.4, 7.5). Neither domiciles nor the usual trash that accumulates in and around them were found. The structures there differed from the houses uncovered elsewhere on the site. They had not been constructed in pits, and contained very little refuse. Three had wall trenches on three sides only, basically a long trench with two short trenches placed at right angles to it. This suggests that they may have been arbors, ramadas, or beds (Howard 1968: Figures 23, 125; Swanton 1928: 181). These three-sided structures faced south and were on the south side of a long wall trench. The trench could be the remains of a wall constructed at the north edge of the plaza or could have divided the plaza into two sections. The same wall trench cut through another type of structure built much like the domicile at the south edge of the town but having inner wall trenches on both the north and south sides. Furthermore, this structure was not set in a previously prepared pit. Again, the lack of debris usually found in domiciles was interpreted as evidence that the structure was for ceremonial or public use. A similar structure with three inner wall-trench divisions was noted when the area was scraped during school construction.

Two rectangular pits, the bottoms filled with charcoal and the sides fired brick red, were located north of the structures in the area tentatively designated as the plaza. Between the structures and the rectangular pits were a number of very large postmolds (1 to 5 ft. in diameter) in semicircular arrangement. Their size and semicircular distribution suggest a form of woodhenge (Wittry 1969: 43).

The lack of significant amounts of cultural debris as well as the specialized structures and features noted in the area east of Mound 1 and southeast of Mound 7 (Figures 7.4, 7.5) seem to be supportive evidence that the area was a plaza or a space utilized for ceremonial or public functions. The wall trench that cut across structures in the area was perhaps a compound wall either separating two courtyards or screening a courtyard from view during a late phase of site occupation. It also could have been a wall of a street as described by Garcilasso (Swanton 1928: 174) and quoted later. Although the exact size and shape of the plaza area was not determined, it appeared to lie primarily due east of Mound 1, the largest (or temple) mound, the area free of house depressions on the Henrich map of 1878 (Figures 7.3, 7.5). The area proposed as a courtyard at Towosahgy also was placed in the same relationship to the largest mound (Figures 7.2, 7.5).

All structures investigated in detail at both Lilbourn and Towosahgy were close to stockade walls and far removed from the plaza area. They were potentially residences of low-status individuals, if early reports of southeast Indian sites are representative of their community organization. Swanton (1928: 174) quotes Garcilasso on the internal arrangement of Mississippi tradition towns at the time of the De Soto expedition, as follows:

> They choose a place where they bring a quantity of earth which they elevate into a kind of platform, two or three pikes high [a mound] the top of which is capable of containing ten or twelve or fifteen or twenty houses to lodge the cacique with his family and all his retinue [similar to Mound 1 at the Lilbourn site and Mound 2 at Towosahgy]. They then trace, at the bottom of this elevation, a square place [the plaza] conformable to the

extent of the village which they would make; and around this place the most important persons build their dwellings. The common people lodge in the same manner; and thus they all environ the house of their chief. In order to ascend to it [the mound] they draw in a straight line, streets from top to bottom each one fifteen or twenty feet wide, and unite them to each other with large posts, which enter very deep into the earth and which serve for walls to these streets. Then they make the stairs [ramp or stairway] with strong beams.

None of the domiciles excavated at Lilbourn were adjacent to or near the plaza area and thus could have been those of families of lower social status. The first house excavated was the nearest to the plaza (Feature 1-70) but was not adjacent to it. If the hypothesis that domiciles should provide evidence of status in proportion to their distance from the plaza is correct—that is, those nearest being larger and denoting high status, and those farthest, smaller and low status— this structure possibly could be significant. It was 17 by 18 ft. and had a floor area of 306 ft.² It was larger than one of the structures on the outer edges of the site (Feature 9-71), which was 13½ by 14 ft. and had a floor area of 189 ft.² The latter, located at the southeastern corner of the town, was the farthest from the plaza. Its construction was typical of most structures at the site (Figure 7.6).

Although the domicile (Feature 9-71) was the smallest of those uncovered in 1971, it contained items that might be considered indicative of high status. A fragment of a clay pipe with cross-in-circle (sacred fire) symbols incised upon it (Figure 7.7) was found near the original floor. The pipe and the decorative symbols usually are associated with the Southeastern Ceremonial complex (Howard 1968), and the pipe might be interpreted as a high-status object because few have been found, suggesting that only certain individuals or house- holds possessed them. Furthermore, a well-made discoidal of exotic stone cached in the west wall trench also might be considered a status object. The occurrence of these two items in Feature 9-71, if they do indicate high status of an individual or household, does not seem to support the hypothesis that small size and great distance from the plaza necessarily denote low status of the occupants.

Another structure, Feature 12-71, was to the north of and adjacent to Feature 9-71 and was approximately the same size. It was not excavated sufficiently to use the data for status interpretation. The third structure was Feature 25-71, which was in a direct line with Features 9-71 and 12-71, and was about the same distance from the fortification wall. Its size was 18 by 20 ft. or 360 ft.², thus making it larger than the other structures (Figure 7.8). Items in this structure that possibly would denote high social status were fragments of painted pottery vessels. These could represent a late period of

Figure 7.6 Photograph of domicile structure Feature 9-71, Lilbourn site.

Figure 7.7 Fragment of decorated clay pipe found near the original floor of domicile structure Feature 9-71, Lilbourn site.

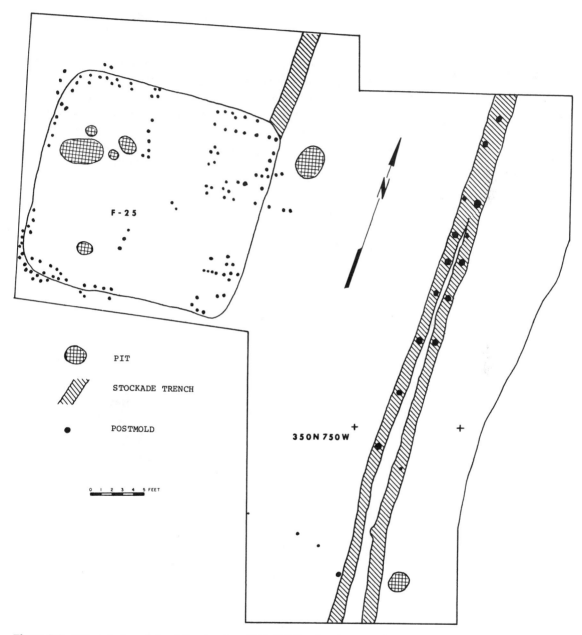

PIT

STOCKADE TRENCH

POSTMOLD

0 1 2 3 4 5 FEET

F-25

350N 750W

Figure 7.8 Ground plan of domicile structure F-25 (1971), showing its relationship to stockade walls, Lilbourn site.

occupation because they were above the original floor and because painted pottery is, in general, thought to be characteristic of the latest Mississippian tradition occupation in the southeastern Missouri area.

A complex of superimposed structures excavated in 1973 on the southern end of the Lilbourn site (Figure 7.9) contained possible high-status objects. They included a fragment of a pottery plate with a sun symbol design painted in red, fragments of a ground-stone bi-concave discoidal, and worked shell objects. Unfortunately, the size of the structure or which superimposed structures contained the objects could not be determined. The earliest structure was 8 by 11 ft.

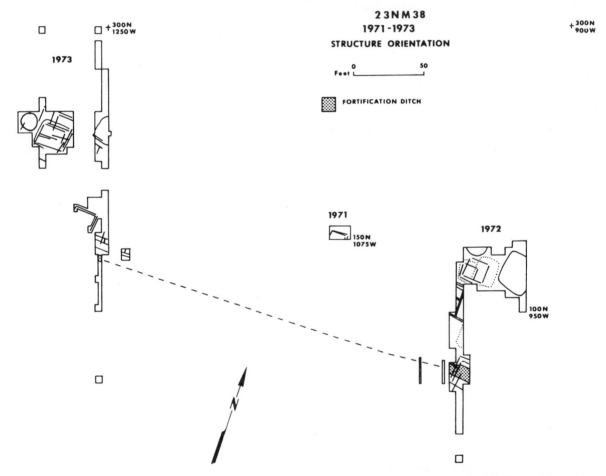

Figure 7.9 Distribution and orientation of structures and fortification evidence identified during 1972–1973 along the southern edge of the Lilbourn site.

with a floor area of only 93.5 ft.^{2}. The superimposed structures were larger, but the size of any one could not be determined. Again, there was no certain correlation of possible status objects and large house size.

The positioning of the structures (F-9, F-12, and F-25) in relation to the fortification wall, and their alignment with the wall and with each other along the eastern site edge (Figure 7.8), is evidence of town planning. The domiciliary structures may have been in an alignment similar to those described for the Snodgrass site (Price 1973: 81–90). Evidence for an internal town design also was derived from excavations along the southern edge of the Lilbourn site, where all structures were aligned in the same direction and in accord with the fortification ditch and wall along the southern edge of the town (Figure 7.9).

The evidence for planning through the orientation of houses and stockade walls was not clear at Towosahgy (Figure 7.10). Structures varied in their orientation, but the facts that they were superimposed and that there was more than one stockade wall denoted a time difference that may have been responsible for the differing orientations. One structure did align with the outermost stockade wall (Figure 7.10). At Towosahgy, no definite cemetery areas were defined.

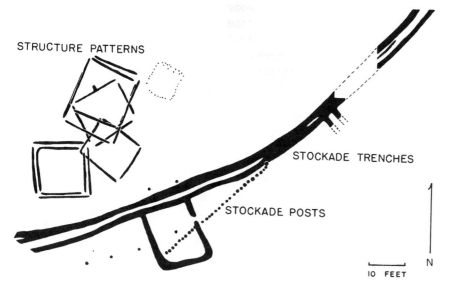

STRUCTURE PATTERNS

STOCKADE TRENCHES

STOCKADE POSTS

10 FEET

N

Figure 7.10 Distribution and orientation of structures and fortification evidence identified during 1970–1972 at the southeast edge of the Towosahgy site.

Burial Practices

Age, sex, membership in particular social units, relative status within the units, and personal achievement may be reflected in the treatment of the dead, but their cultural meaning must be interpreted in terms of the organization and complexity of the cultural systems in which they are found. Social distinctions in life often are expressed by location of interments within a site or by the burial of preserved status accouterments with them (cf. Binford 1962, 1971; Brown 1971a, b; Fowler 1969; Larson 1971; Peebles 1971; Saxe 1971).

Most burials at Lilbourn were in a supine position and were placed in specific cemeteries or under house floors. Four definite cemetery locations were discovered. In one instance, on the south edge of the site, several interments had been disturbed by the later digging of structure basins, the locus of domiciles by the town dwellers. This indicates that the cemetery perhaps had been forgotten. The cemetery was approximately 70 ft. north of the ditch associated with the fortification on the south edge of the site and may have had no connection with it. The burials in another cemetery in the southeastern corner of the site were located adjacent to and at right angles to a stockade or compound wall. Two other burial groups were adjacent to stockade walls and may have been correlated with them. These circumscribed cemeteries and their relationship to stockade walls demonstrate further evidence of town planning.

At Lilbourn, a special-status burial group was within what appeared to have been a structure that had burned and then had been cleaned of debris prior to the placement of the burials on the fire-hardened floor. The major group (Figure 7.11a) consisted of an adult male, three adult females, and isolated bones of other individuals. The adult male had a large chipped-stone mace on his chest (Figure 7.11b), and a polished bird bone point and a circular copper disk over the left side of his pelvis. In close association with him was a female who was an unusual pathological specimen. This skeleton displayed three of the classic signs of tertiary syphilis: "snail track" lesions of the frontal bone, destruction of the nasal bones and bony palate, and "saber shins" or anteriorly curved lower leg bones.

Below the burned floor were two burials, one of which was an infant with no grave offerings, and the other was a woman estimated to have been 60 or more years of age. The floor above the infant was fire-hardened, indicating that the burial had been made prior to the burning of the structure. The woman, however, had been intruded from above through the burned floor area. She may have been a shaman, judging from the artifacts buried with her (Figure 7.12). A

Figure 7.11 Special-status burial group at the Lilbourn site: (A) group in southwestern corner of special structure; (B) close-up of individual with mace, copper disk, and antler piece.

Figure 7.12 Possible shaman burial under floor of structure containing special-status burial group.

clay pipe, bone (sucking) tubes, sharp bone awls or lancets, a whetstone, small shaped fragments of pottery, and miscellaneous bones were adjacent to her left side. Two bone fishhooks were in the pelvic region and others were underneath the lumbar vertebrae.

The woman's skeleton showed evidence of crippling arthritis; furthermore, she had lived 15 to 20 years longer than the average member of the Lilbourn population, which might suggest that she had been provided for by others. Left to her own resources, she probably would not have had such an extended life span.

Age was an important factor in the treatment of the dead at the Lilbourn site. Adults and subadults were buried in groups in what appeared to be planned and circumscribed cemeteries. Infants usually were buried under the floors of structures rather than in cemeteries (Figure 7.6). This differential treatment has implications about concepts of the relationship of age groups within the community. Presumably, children less than 2 years of age, although an integral part of the family unit, were not as yet given the status of individuals within the larger social units of the community, which appear to have had separate cemetery areas.

The greatest death toll was among infants. The evidence indicated that an individual who reached the age of 2 years had a good chance of reaching adulthood. Of the 88 skeletons that have been studied from the Lilbourn site, 30 were less than 2 years old, 2 were 1½ to 2½ years old, 8 were juveniles, and 48 were adults.

At Towosahgy, nine burials were uncovered. None contained grave goods, none were in definite cemetery areas, and their poor state of preservation did not allow adequate age or sex determination. There were no infants, but two were probably adolescents. Burial mode was represented by extended supine and flexed or semiflexed positions, with the body placed on its side. None were under the floor of a structure. The data are insufficient to compare with that at the Lilbourn site.

The dating of features at the Lilbourn and Towosahgy sites indicates a long period of occupation at both (Figure 7.13). At Lilbourn, the date on the charred wood associated with a partially cremated burial overlying the innermost stockade wall was A.D. 1090 (N-1232, N-1233), whereas that in the burial group adjacent to the outermost stockade was A.D. 1355 (N-1493), a suggestion of at least two major periods of occupation for the Lilbourn site (Figure 7.14).

Conclusions

There is solid evidence from the Lilbourn site that the Mississippian tradition town established there prior to A.D. 1100 was planned and that the general design of the town continued at least until A.D. 1350. Although the data and the radiocarbon dates are not as clear for Towosahgy, it is probable that the internal design and the basic development of the ceremonial center was similar to that of Lilbourn. The occurrence at each townsite of a large, trapezoidal, flat-topped mound, east and south of which is a plaza surrounded by smaller mounds with a view across the plaza toward a body of water, must be more than coincidental. Consistent orientation of structures in relation to the cardinal directions and stockade walls at Lilbourn are further data supporting the hypothesis that the town was planned. Radiocarbon dates indicated that the design continued in effect for 200 years or more. The recurrence of circumscribed areas for cemeteries adjacent to stockade walls at different periods also supports the postulate of town planning over a long period.

No evidence has been obtained at Lilbourn to demonstrate a definite correlation between house size and social status, nor could the occurrence of objects possibly denoting status in small dwellings at the edge of the town be explained satisfactorily by ethnographic analogy. As no houses adjacent to the plaza have been excavated, it is still possible to test the proposition that houses closer to the plaza

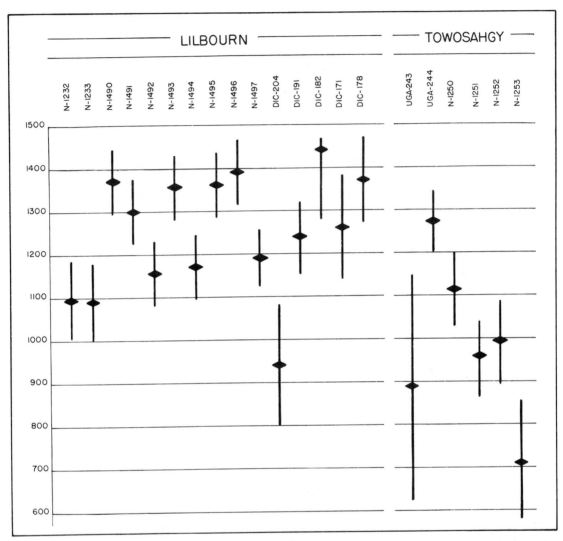

Figure 7.13 Radiocarbon dates from the Lilbourn and Towosahgy sites.

were larger and probably inhabited by families with high status. Special burial practices are considered to be evidence that the society was segmented and that certain individuals were accorded prestige and care beyond that of others. Social distinctions were based also on age, as was evidenced by the burial of most infants under house floors rather than in cemeteries.

Judging from the examples of Lilbourn and Towosahgy, the internal designs of Mississippian tradition towns appear to have been based on

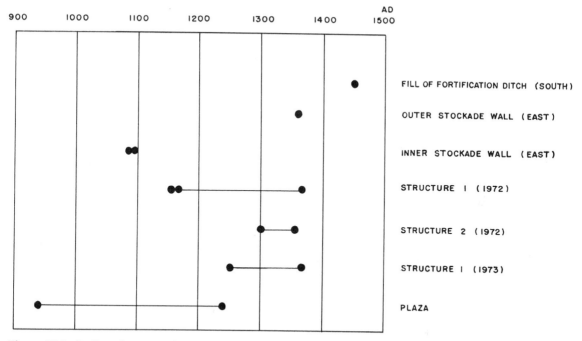

Figure 7.14 Radiocarbon year dates for features identified during 1971–1973 at the Lilbourn site.

preconceived plans that were adjusted to the topography and an adjacent body of water. The placement of the mounds around a plaza or plazas and the similar orientation of the longitudinal axis of the largest trapezoidal mound in each suggest such planning. The orientation of houses with stockade walls, the occurrence of selected and restricted cemetery areas, and radiocarbon dates at Lilbourn support the postulate that prescribed plans were used for the towns in the period A.D. 1100–1350. The data are not sufficient to assume the same for Towosahgy, but there are hints of similar planning. The derivation of the plans and how they were applied to each site is uncertain. It is logical to assume that they were based in part on astronomical observations and in part on the adaptation of a preconceived design to the terrain selected for the townsite. Sociocultural organization and segmentation of the society in various ways also may have been responsible for differences in internal town arrangements, such as canons for placement of houses and circumscribed cemeteries based on sociopolitical status.

More questions have been raised about Mississippian tradition town planning and internal design features than have been answered by the investigations at the Lilbourn and Towosahgy sites. Clearly, the only way they can be answered is by long-term investigations that involve all parts of these or similar townsites.

Acknowledgments

The Missouri Archaeological Society and its chapters, the Southeast Missouri Archaeological Society, Raytown Archaeological Society, University of Michigan Powers Phase Project personnel, and individuals too numerous to mention separately, participated in or supported the work involved in this study. Those supervising the investigations, other than the author, were Richard Annand, Phillip L. Born, John W. Cottier, David R. Evans, B. Miles Gilbert, Rolland E. Pangborn, Michael J. Reagan, Gerald R. Smith, and Michael D. Southard. Comments on the manuscript by John W. Cottier, David R. Evans, James E. Price, and Michael J. Reagan were especially helpful. Special thanks are due Eleanor F. Chapman for preparation of illustrations and John W. Cottier, David R. Evans, B. Miles Gilbert, and Michael D. Southard for the use of maps, charts, and other data from reports to the National Endowment for the Humanities in 1973 and 1974. The aid of all those concerned is gratefully acknowledged, for the work could not have been accomplished without it.

The Chronology of Paleo-Indian and Altithermal Cultures in the Big Horn Basin, Wyoming*

George C. Frison

Introduction

No student of northwestern Plains prehistory can ignore the fact that, for both the present and the past, there is no generalized description that fits the entire area. Changes in elevation, topography, rainfall, soil types, geological formations, flora, and fauna over short distances impart an ever-changing aspect to an area that always has had relatively meager resources to support human populations. The area is characterized by a variety of habitats, including mountain ranges with elevations over 13,000 ft., high mountain meadows, steep dissected mountain slopes, foothills, high- and low-altitude intermontane basins, open flat plains, rough badlands, active and stabilized sand dunes, mountain streams, major river valleys, minor uplifts, river breaks, buttes, and escarpments. Vegetative cover includes alpine plants above timberline, lodgepole pine, fir, and ponderosa pine forest at

* The writer wishes to acknowledge the support of the National Science Foundation (Grant No. SOC 7205578), the Wyoming Recreation Commission, and the University of Wyoming for their generous support of the Medicine Lodge Creek Project.

different elevations, open grassy parks at high elevations, sagebrush-covered slopes and flats, brush-covered slopes and river terraces, grassy turf and bunch grass plains, and low-lying saline flats and playa lake areas that support only greasewood and salt bushes. In the near and distant past, faunal resources have consisted of mountain sheep and deer in the rugged areas, and antelope and bison on the plains. There is no well-known documented record of elk until the late prehistoric period.

The ecological diversity of the northwestern Plains provided a variety of limited economic resources in comparison with the resources of the adjacent northern and central Plains and the Plateau. Proper economic exploitation, however, required a carefully planned routine of yearly activities, and, even then, food resources were never overly plentiful. As a result, human populations remained small and greatly dispersed until the historic period, when the horse made possible the exploitation of the bison herds.

The Big Horn Basin is a true intermontane basin located between the Absaroka and Owl Creek Mountains on the west, and the Big Horn and Pryor Mountains on the east (Figure 8.1). An enclave of the northwestern Plains, it is connected to them by a corridor running north–south. Only geographical position links the Big Horn Basin with the Plains. Its flora and fauna contrast sharply with the adjacent plains and plateaus, and the encircling mountains provide definite ecological barriers between them. The Big Horn Basin is about 90 miles long by 50 miles wide. The Wind River originates at Togwotee Pass between the Wind River and the Absaroka Mountains, flows southeast for about 100 miles, abruptly turns directly north through Wind River Canyon between the Big Horn and Owl Creek Mountains, and then enters the southern end of the Big Horn Basin. As it emerges from Wind River Canyon, it becomes the Big Horn River and continues north through the center of the Big Horn Basin. The river leaves the basin through Big Horn Canyon, a deep gorge between the Pryor and Big Horn Mountains.

The Big Horn Basin contains numerous ecological associations. The flood plain and terraces of the Big Horn River were covered with sagebrush and greasewood before artificial irrigation. Willow, buffalo berry, and wild rye thickets are common where moisture is sufficient, especially in and along old stream meanders. Cottonwoods line main streams and also grow along dry washes and around springs where sufficient moisture is present. The Big Horn River runs slowly at a gradient of about 6 ft. per mile through the Big Horn Basin. Several major internal drainages flow into the Big Horn, including the Shoshone, Greybull, and Nowood Rivers. The eastern part of the Big Horn Basin is extremely dry, with annual precipitation averages of as

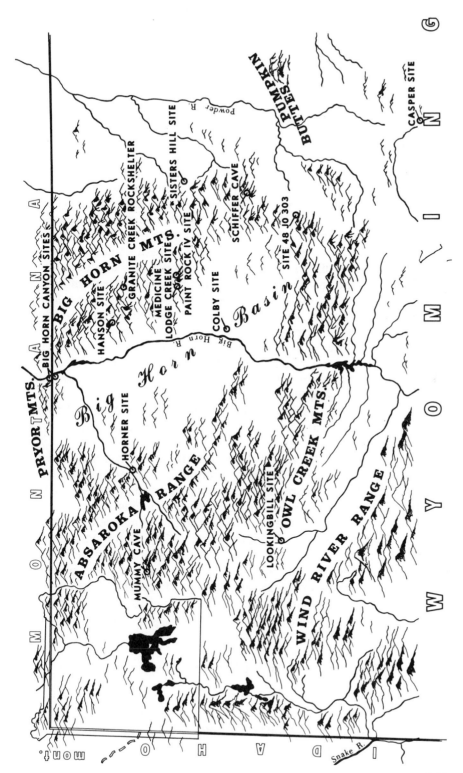

Figure 8.1 The Big Horn Basin and adjacent areas of northern Wyoming with locations of Paleo-Indian sites.

149

little as 7 inches at several recording stations below 4500 ft. At higher
elevations on the southern and western parts of the Big Horn Basin, in
areas more removed from the rain shadow of the Absaroka Mountains, precipitation increases. The mountain slopes receive more rain
as elevations increase, and the vegetational cover increases in proportion.

The entire Big Horn Basin is quite rugged, with the exception of
some river terraces or "benches" and alluvial fans where streams
emerge from the mountain slopes onto the basin floor. Several
geologic faults extend across the Big Horn Basin, exposing a variety of
strata. Remnants of tertiary sediments remain as isolated buttes away
from the mountains. "Gumbo" soils are a major feature of the interior
basin, resulting from extensive bentonite deposits that have eroded
and mixed with sediments. Sedimentary sandstones cap many softer
geological formations to form escarpments and buttes, and deeply
eroded sandstones compose many of the formations along interior
arroyos and streams. Older sandstones are exposed around the edge of
the basin, and these also are deeply eroded. The mountain slopes are
deeply dissected by both intermittent and permanent streams to form
a continuous sequence of deep, narrow canyons. A common feature of
the Big Horn Mountains are many areas of relatively flat or rolling
hills, at an elevation of 7500–8500 ft., usually covered with thick grass
and tall sagebrush. The Big Horn Mountains are typical "folded"
mountains and contrast sharply with the Absaroka Mountains, which
are largely volcanic.

This ecologically diverse, isolated intermontane basin has yielded
evidence of a long Paleo-Indian occupation. Paleo-Indians herein
include some of the commonly recognized cultural complexes, as well
as others that are as yet poorly defined and exist only as vague
projectile-point types that do not fit within the sequence described for
the Hell Gap site (Irwin-Williams *et al.* 1973). Later cultural complexes are as yet poorly defined and were present during the Altithermal period. These might better be considered as Early or Middle
Archaic period sites although the problem of the chronological order
of the post-Paleo-Indian cultural materials is yet to be resolved. Space
limitations do not permit discussions of the later Plains Archaic or
Middle Archaic period cultural groups.

Paleo-Indian Cultures of the Big Horn Basin

ARCHAEOLOGICAL INVESTIGATIONS

The first major Paleo-Indian site recognized in the Big Horn Basin
was the Horner site, the type site of the Cody complex. Discovered by
James Allen (for whom the James Allen site in the Laramie Basin was

named), it was excavated by Jepsen and the Smithsonian Institution. The Horner site is near Cody, Wyoming, and was part of a bison procurement operation. A brief report on the excavation was published (Jepsen 1953) but a definitive report has never appeared.

The Horner site is located on a high terrace near the confluence of Sage Creek and the Shoshone (Stinking Water) River a few miles east of the steep slopes of the Absaroka Mountains (Figure 8.1). The site is probably a processing area for which an actual kill area was never found. The actual procurement method includes several possibilities, such as arroyo trap, a stampede into an arroyo, or a stampede over a steep bank or bluff. The age structure of the bison remains suggest that the kill occurred in the fall. Several discrete procurement events probably are represented, although the time span over which the kills occurred may never be known. Regardless, the Horner site is a manifestation of the Paleo-Indian bison hunters in what, during later Altithermal and post-Altithermal times, was not prime buffalo country.

The next evidence for Paleo-Indian occupation of the basin was discovered during construction of the Yellowtail Dam near Hardin, Montana, which backs up the Big Horn River for several miles into Wyoming to form Big Horn Lake. Before flooding, rockshelters along the river on both sides of the Montana–Wyoming line were investigated for archaeological remains. This survey revealed a number of early cultural levels contemporaneous with, but typologically quite different from, known Paleo-Indian; no valid data for postulating connections or relationships between the two were found. At least two type names were coined to describe projectile-point types, both derived from local features. The first was "Pryor Stemmed" after nearby Pryor Mountain; the second was "Lovell Constricted" after the nearby town of Lovell, Wyoming. Other descriptive terms used were "Agate-Basin-like," "Scottsbluff-like," and "Alberta-like" to describe projectile points that were similar enough to those particular Paleo-Indian type forms to be compared favorably to them (Husted 1969). Big Horn Canyon sites provide evidence of human occupation in areas that did not support an open plains fauna at about the same time period as the Horner site (Cody complex) occupation.

At about the same time that the Big Horn Canyon investigations were under way, the Mummy Cave site along the North Fork of the Shoshone also was being investigated (Wedel, Husted, and Moss 1968). The deep levels appeared to be quite old, and a long record of occupation was found dating from before 7000 B.C. and continuing into the late prehistoric period. Of greatest interest to this study are early levels that are contemporaneous with, but apparently unrelated to, the Horner site. In addition, there is a long series of occupations that

spans the Altithermal period. Heretofore there had been few indications that the northwestern Plains were then occupied. Like the
Horner site, an adequate report of the Mummy Cave site excavations
has not yet appeared.

The flora of the Big Horn Mountains loses its alpine, high-country
aspect toward the southern terminus of the range. There, the eastern
slopes produce some evidence of an early cultural horizon in two
rockshelters. One of these, Site 48 JO 303, was dug by the Wyoming
Archeological Society and dates are around 6000 B.C. (Haynes,
Damon, and Grey 1966). The assemblage seems to be the same as the
Pryor Stemmed assemblages in Big Horn Canyon. A short distance
north of this rockshelter, Schiffer Cave produced similar materials and
dates (Frison 1973). Significantly, quantities of preserved seeds and
grinding tools were found in addition to a wide variety of animal
remains, indicating a hunting–gathering subsistence base. Dates for
the Pryor Stemmed complex range from about 5600 to 6400 B.C.

In 1971, deep test pits sunk at the Medicine Lodge Creek site (Figure
8.2) near Hyattville, Wyoming (at the base of the eastern slopes of the

Figure 8.2 The Medicine Lodge Creek site. Site extends for nearly 800 ft. along the
bluff indicated by the arrow.

Big Horn Mountains), yielded evidence of a long, uninterrupted sequence of Paleo-Indian occupations. The earliest date was about 7700 B.C. for a level that produced a projectile point similar to the Plainview type, and the latest date was about 6200 B.C. on a level that produced a large assemblage of materials of the now familiar Pryor Stemmed complex. Since the site covers a large area and the deposits are deep, a project was proposed and subsequently funded by the National Science Foundation (Grant No. SOC 7205578). Known as the Medicine Lodge Creek Project, its aims are to define the prehistoric occupations of the Big Horn Basin, using the Medicine Lodge Creek site as the key stratigraphic unit. Several other single- and multicomponent sites in the various environments from the floor of the Big Horn Basin to above timberline are also under investigation.

In the course of investigating sites peripheral to the Medicine Lodge Creek site, two fluted-point sites were found, one a mammoth kill (the Colby site) and the other a Folsom campsite (the Hanson site). These sites have not been fully investigated, but enough is known to provide preliminary statements on their position and their significance to the Paleo-Indian cultural sequence for the Big Horn Basin.

EVIDENCE FOR THE FLUTED-POINT CULTURES

The Colby site, a mammoth kill site, is located at the base of an old arroyo in badland country, at an elevation of 4280 ft., about 4 miles east of the Big Horn River near Worland, Wyoming. The present arroyo is the central one in a small dendritic drainage pattern eroded into a flat surface that drains about 40 acres. This arroyo begins about one-fourth of a mile from the kill site and parallels the old arroyo (which contains the mammoth bones) for several hundred feet. Reservoir construction removed much of the old arroyo downstream of the kill site. The present arroyo is shallow and narrow; the old arroyo was wide, with deep, perpendicular banks. Parts of six immature mammoths (Figure 8.3) and four fluted points (Figure 8.4) have been recovered to date. One flake tool of red chert, several flakes (red chert, grey chert, and quartzite) believed to be the result of tool use and sharpening, and the point of a quartzite chopper also have been recovered. No evidence indicates the past presence of a permanent water source. The procurement method is unknown, although the shape of the bottom and sides of the old arroyo suggests a possible trap. Bison, antelope, and jackrabbit have been identified in the faunal remains, although species of these have not been determined.

The Colby site establishes the presence of mammoth hunters in the Big Horn Basin. The radiocarbon date of 9240 B.C. ± 220 years (RL-392), taken from a sample of charred bone, is consistent with

Figure 8.3 Mammoth bones at the Colby site. Arrow indicates projectile point *in situ*.

Figure 8.4 Projectile points from the Colby site.

dates of other known mammoth kills in North America (Haynes 1970). However, the remains from the Colby site raise many questions. There is no association with permanent or intermittent water sources as there is with most mammoth kills. The projectile points differ slightly from the typical Clovis points recovered in known mammoth kills. In outline form, the corners are rounded, and deep basal indentations are present (Figure 8.4). The only definite statement that can be made about the site, until more excavation and analysis are completed, is that the distribution and marks on the mammoth bone indicate that cutting and dismemberment were underway. However, the assemblage does not contain as many processing tools as one would expect. Therefore, statements regarding procurement techniques and utilization of meat are only conjectural.

The Big Horn River Valley and its immediate environs may have supported a sizable mammoth herd under more abundant moisture conditions than at present. Soils in the area are generally devoid of pollens, but opal phytoliths from the Colby site have been recovered (McDonald 1974). These indicate the presence of taller panicoid grasses than are now present, a strong indication of better moisture conditions in the past. We know nothing of the mammoth's yearly activity cycles or when procurement would have occurred; hopefully, sufficient samples will be recovered eventually so that population studies can be developed that are comparable to those for bison (see Reher 1974) and antelope (Nimmo 1971). Other food sources exploited by man during this period are unknown, although the bison and antelope bone at the Colby site appears to have been butchered. Raw materials utilized in the manufacture of stone tools and projectile points indicate contact with the eastern part of the Big Horn Basin where sources of a distinctive red chert are located. To date, however, no indications have been found at the chert beds that demonstrate either surface collecting or quarrying of stone-flaking material, or other activities unquestionably diagnostic of the Clovis complex. Further insight into the Clovis occupation of the Big Horn Basin must await the collection and analysis of more data.

Folsom presence in the Big Horn Basin has been postulated for several years on the basis of scattered finds of Folsom projectile points. *In situ* evidence of a Folsom occupation was found in 1973 at the Hanson site, located a few miles from the base of the eastern slopes of the Big Horn Mountains at an elevation of 5100 ft. The site is in dissected foothill country along Davis Draw, a dry arroyo at the point at which it emerges from a narrow, steep-walled canyon. The site so far has produced classic Folsom projectile points, evidence of projectile-point manufacture, including channel flakes, a large amount of debitage, and several other stone tools (Figure 8.5). Radiocarbon

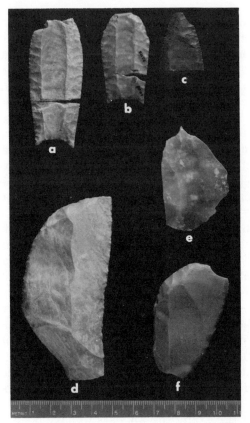

Figure 8.5 Projectile points (a–c) and tools (d–f) from the Hanson site.

analysis on a small charcoal sample yielded a date of 8750 ± 670 B.C. (RL-374).

Further investigation of the Hanson site is expected to provide some evidence of subsistence activities, since there are indications that bone and organic matter are preserved in the deeper levels of the site. Local sources of quartzite and chert were utilized, as was the red chert observed at the Colby site. Although Folsom occupation of the Big Horn Basin can now be definitely established, as is the case with the Clovis occupation, detailed knowledge of this occupation will come only with further investigations. A subject for further work is the occasional surface finds of Folsom points in the open, accessible areas at higher altitudes in the Big Horn Mountains. This suggests limited use of these areas, because today they can be reached only in late spring, summer, and early fall.

LATER PALEO-INDIAN EVIDENCE

As already mentioned, the Medicine Lodge Creek site has provided uninterrupted stratigraphic sequences of Paleo-Indian occupation (Figure 8.6a). No occupation level is extensive, however, suggesting it was never the scene of the occupation of more than a family group or two for a short period of time. The earliest radiocarbon date from the Medicine Lodge Creek site is 7750 ± 620 B.C. (RL-154) at a depth of 23 ft. below the original ground surface, a level that is at the top of the present water table. This level produced only a small amount of debitage and a single projectile point that is similar to Plainview

Figure 8.6 Stratigraphic sequences of Paleo-Indian age at the Medicine Lodge Creek site. Both columns are over 13 ft. high and cover a period from about 8000 B.C. to 6000 B.C. with at least 27 identifiable cultural levels.

Figure 8.7 Projectile points (b, d–f) and tools (a,c) from Paleo-Indian levels at the Medicine Lodge Creek site.

(Figure 8.7d). At least one other cultural level lies below the water table.

The stratigraphic unit immediately above the level from which the Plainview-like point was taken is as yet undated but has produced a rather distinctive projectile point that has a split expanding base, lateral restrictions of the blade edge toward the base, and a thick lenticular cross section (Figure 8.7e). Similar points have been found on the surface at many locations in the foothills and at higher elevations of the Big Horn Mountains, and long have been suspected to be quite old. Since neither floral nor faunal remains have been recovered from this level, little else can be said about this occupation.

In one part of the site, an extensive bone midden was recovered between 22.2 ft. and 23.3 ft. deep. A date on the bone is 7640 ± 180 B.C. (RL-393). A date from a level at still another part of the site is 7670 ± 260 B.C. (RL-153). On the basis of stratigraphic correlations, both levels very likely represent the same occupation as that represented by the split-based projectile point (Figure 8.7e), although exact stratigraphic correlation of the levels was not possible and diagnostic artifacts were not found in the two dated locations.

The bone midden contains a wide variety of mammal, reptile, bird, and fish remains (Table 8.1). Numerically, the midden contains mostly rodents and lagomorphs, along with a few carnivores, artiodactyles, birds, and an occasional reptile. The total weight of useable meat from a single deer, two mountain sheep, and a fetal bison is more than that of the entire assemblage of smaller animals. Signficantly, the bone midden provides evidence of a food-collecting pattern that utilized the entire spectrum of animal resources within the site area. Although no preserved plant remains were recovered at this level, some were found in higher levels—on this basis, it may be postulated that small groups had established a carefully scheduled hunting-and-gathering subsistence base by around 7500 B.C. Seasonal aspects of these food-procurement activities are as yet unclear, but there is some possibility that studies on the bushytailed woodrat *(Neotoma cinerea),* which were quite plentiful in the midden, may yield some evidence of their age at time of death. They are believed to have a regular breeding season and, knowing this and their age at the time of death, we may eventually establish the time of year at which they were killed (Walker 1975).

The next youngest date obtained from the Medicine Lodge Creek site is 7410 ± 380 B.C. (RL-150). This level produced a lanceolate projectile point (Figure 8.7f) that is similar to those from Level 4 (dated to 7280 ± 150 B.C.) of Mummy Cave (Wedel, Husted, and Moss 1968). The only other cultural material obtained from this occupational level at Medicine Lodge Creek consists of a few scattered chert flakes and unidentifiable fragments of small animal bones. At Mummy Cave, the cultural material was limited to a hearth area, and consisted of a single projectile point and two pieces of unidentified worked bone (Husted and Edgar n.d.: 74–75). Projectile points of this type occasionally are found on the surface, especially on exposed slopes of the Big Horn Mountains.

Nearly 5 ft. of continuous deposits in one excavation unit at the Medicine Lodge Creek site produced small pits from several cultural levels. Some pits appear to be fire pits, whereas others may be storage pits or possibly food-preparation features. They often appear to be at the center of a shallow, saucer-shaped depression (Figure 8.8, Figure 8.6b) and, in at least two instances, shallow postmolds suggest small wickiup-like structures built over the depressions. These pits may occur singly or may occur in multiple associations—as many as nine were found in close proximity. Those dug into a consolidated clay are sometimes lipped slightly, so that they are globular shaped, with the

Table 8.1 **Faunal List of the Bone Midden at the Medicine Lodge Creek Site**

Class, family, order	Minimum number of individuals
Class Mammalia	
Order Insectivora	
Family Soricidae	
Masked shrew (*Sorex cinereus*)	4+
Shrew (*Sorex* sp.)	1
Order Lagomorpha	
Family Ochotonidae	
Pika (*Ochotona princeps*)	2
Family Leporidae	
Cottontail (*Sylvilagus* sp. cf. *nutlllii* or *audobonii*)	11
Jackrabbit (*Lepus* sp. cf. *townsendii*)	5
Order Rodentia	
Family Sciuridae	
Marmot (*Marmota flaviventris*)	1
Richardson's ground squirrel (*Spermophilus* cf. *richardsonii*)	3
Red squirrel (*Tamiasciurus hudsonicus*)	1
Family Geomyidae	
Northern pocket gopher (*Thomomys talpoides*)	101
Family Cricetidae	
Deer mouse (*Peromyscus maniculatus*)	33
Bushy-tailed wood rat (*Neotoma cinerea*)	135
Red-backed vole (*Cleithrionomys gapperi*)	1
Heather vole (*Phenacomys intermedius*)	5
Meadow vole (*Microtus pennsylvanicus*)	2
Richardson's vole (*Microtus richardsoni*)	1
Montane vole (*Microtus montanus*)	134
Prairie vole (*Microtus ochrogaster*)	180
Muskrat (*Ondatra zibethicus*)	2
Family Erethizontidae	
Porcupine (*Erethizon dorsatum*)	1
Order Carnivora	
Family Mustelidae	
Ermine (*Mustela erminae*)	1
Long-tailed weasel (*Mustela frenata*)	2
Mustelid (*Mustela* sp.)	1
Order Artiodactyla	
Family Cervidae	
Deer (*Odocoileus* sp.)	1
Mule deer (*Odocoileus* cf. *hemionus*)	1
Family Bovidae	
Foetal bison (*Bison bison* subsp. cf. *B. b. antiquus*)	1
Mountain sheep (*Ovis canadensis*)	2
Class Osteichthyes	
Infraclass Teleostei	
Fish (genus and species indeterminate)	1

160

Table 8.1 Continued

Class, family, order	Minimum number of individuals
Class Reptilia	
Order Squamata	
Lizard (genus and species unidentified)	1
Order Ophidia (Serpentes)	
Family Colubridae	
Snake (genus and species unidentified)	1
Family Viperidae	
Rattlesnake (*Crotalus* sp.)	1
Class Aves	
Order Anseriformes	
Family Anatidae	
Mallard (cf. *Anas platyrhynchos*)	1
Duck (3–4 unidentified species)	5
Order Galliformes	
Family Tetraonidae	
Blue grouse (cf. *Dendragapus obscurus*)	2
Sage grouse (cf. *Centrocerus urophasianus*)	1
Grouse (1–2 unidentified species)	2
Order Strigiformes	
Family Strigidae	
Owl (genus and species unidentified)	1
Order Passeriformes	
Family Turdidae	
"Thrush" (genus and species unidentified)	1
Family Fringillidae	
"Finch" (genus and species unidentified)	1
"Junco" (genus and species unidentified)	1
Order unidentified	4+
Total of 40 species (33 genera, 15 orders, and 4 classes)	655

maximum circumference somewhat below the surface. These pits contain mostly clay, ash, and charcoal, with occasional stone flakes, bone, and charred seeds. Small mammals compose the majority of identifiable bone but remains of mountain sheep, deer, and, at one level, a grizzly bear, also have been identified. Several charred seeds have not yet been identified.

Projectile points from this 5-ft. sequence at Medicine Lodge Creek are lanceolate with parallel oblique flaking. The lower part of the unit tends to yield projectile points with relatively narrow concave bases (Figure 8.9a, b), but toward the top of the unit, the projectile points are relatively thick in cross section, with straight or slightly convex bases (Figure 8.9e–g). Projectile points of these types appear as surface finds

Figure 8.8 Excavated depression and hearth in profile at the Medicine Lodge Creek site. Same depression is indicated by the arrow in Figure 8.6b.

especially in the low foothills, slopes, and open rolling hill country at higher elevations of the Big Horn Mountains, in particular around springs. Several tools, including end scrapers, gravers (Figure 8.9h), retouched flakes, and a bone awl (Figure 8.9i), also were recovered. Dates include one of 6570 ± 230 B.C. (RL-388) for the bottom of the unit, and one of 6400 ± 285 B.C. for the top. The latter date is not regarded as satisfactory, owing to problems of obtaining sufficient charcoal; a dispersed sample composed of fine particles was run along with a small sample taken from a fire pit; and the data given are an average of the two (RL-384 and RL-384a).

All cultural levels in this sequence suggest small groups engaged in hunting and gathering. In addition to some charred seeds, some broken hammerstones and what may be very simple grinding tools are present, suggesting that the users may have been cracking the hulls of gathered seeds. Similar materials also appeared at several levels at Mummy Cave (Husted and Edgar n.d.: 78–96).

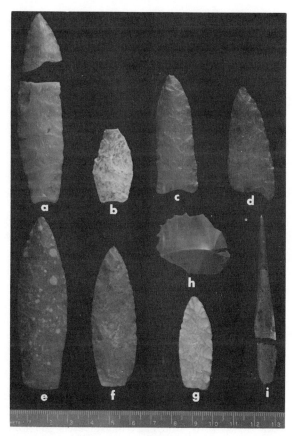

Figure 8.9 Projectile points (a–g), five-pointed graver (h), and bone awl (i) from Paleo-Indian levels at the Medicine Lodge Creek site.

Stratigraphically above this sequence, a subtle change in projectile-point type occurs, although there is no evidence of change in group size or subsistence activities. Husted (1969: 13) proposed a type designation of Lovell Constricted—and the points seem distinctive at first glance—but with larger samples beginning to appear in more sites, they do grade into other types with no real clustering. At the Medicine Lodge Creek site (Figure 8.10c), these points are associated with a radiocarbon date of 6370 ± 220 B.C. (RL-152). A projectile point of an altogether different type appeared at the same level also (Figure 8.9d). Lovell Constricted points are found regularly on the surface in the Big Horn Mountains (Figure 8.10d), as well as in rockshelter sites in Big Horn Canyon (Husted 1969), and they have been found at Mummy Cave (Husted and Edgar n.d.: 96). In both sites, they occurred in association with chipped stone and bone tools. Faunal remains at nearly all of the sites include small amounts of bighorn sheep and

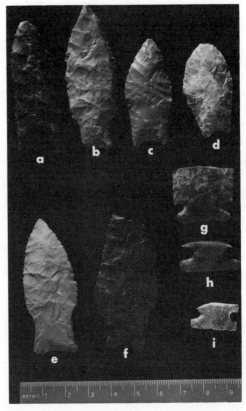

Figure 8.10 Projectile points (a–f) from Paleo-Indian levels and from Altithermal period levels (g–i) at the Medicine Lodge Creek site.

mule deer, and, in Big Horn Canyon, one bison was found in a rockshelter site. Grinding stones, presumably for processing seeds and other vegetable products, were found in the Big Horn Canyon rockshelter sites and at Medicine Lodge Creek. A radiocarbon date from Big Horn Canyon is 6320 ± 180 B.C. (Husted 1969: 82), and another radiocarbon date of 6020 ± 210 B.C. was obtained from Mummy Cave (Husted and Edgar n.d.: 53). The Big Horn Canyon and Medicine Lodge Creek dates are very close, but the Mummy Cave date is somewhat later.

Exploratory work in 1973 and 1974 at the Lookingbill site (Figure 8.1) yielded evidence of a further distribution of this cultural manifestation near the head of the Wind River, only a few miles west of the divide between the Big Horn Basin and the Wind River drainage. The Lovell Constricted point, or something very similar, was found in good stratigraphic sequence at the site although dates are not yet available.

Further investigations are expected to yield materials for radiocarbon dating. However, that this is a manifestation of the same as, or a complex very similar to, the Lovell Constricted is strengthened by its stratigraphic position below another cultural complex, similar to that at both Mummy Cave and Medicine Lodge Creek. The Lookingbill site (Frison n.d.) is at an elevation of 8400 ft., and preliminary analysis indicates that it is a seasonal high-altitude adaptation with an orientation toward mountain sheep and mule deer procurement. As might be expected, the site also is located by the only good local source of water. Judging from present evidence, this cultural manifestation was quite well-established over the mountains and foothills surrounding the Big Horn Basin, and its people were exploiting floral and faunal resources from timberline to the floor of the Big Horn Basin and surrounding river valleys and basins. They were familiar with seed-grinding tools, and it can be postulated that their subsistence base was augmented by plant foods that required a careful scheduling of movements in response to seasonal availability.

The best-known material from early cultural horizons in the Big Horn Mountain area, and so far restricted to that area, is the Bi-beveled projectile point complex, or the Pryor Stemmed horizon. Caves in Big Horn Canyon have produced extensive cultural assemblages (Husted 1969). Medicine Lodge Creek has produced a rich cultural level, and there are numerous surface finds of projectile points from Pryor Mountain to the southern end of the Big Horn Mountains. The diagnostic item is a distinctive, alternate-beveled projectile point with a stem and concave base. There are several hypotheses to account for the configuration of alternate beveled points. One idea is that they may be a result of the progressive retouch of blade edges of a projectile point that was originally lenticular in cross section. Thus, one or more stages of alternate beveling may appear on a projectile point during its period of use. Arguments about the function of this projectile-point type are also common. Some argue that its function was as a drill, while others regard it as a projectile point. Both arguments have validity and both may be at least partially right. The distribution and variations of the Pryor Stemmed projectile point have been discussed elsewhere (see Frison 1973).

The Medicine Lodge Creek site produced the diagnostic projectile point discussed earlier (Figure 8.10a) and, as already mentioned, they are common surface finds (see Figure 8.10b). Grinding stones are quite common at this time period at Medicine Lodge Creek, at the Big Horn Canyon rockshelter sites (Husted 1969), and in Schiffer Cave on the North Fork of Powder River on the eastern slopes of the Big Horn Mountains (Frison 1973).

The Pryor Stemmed projectile point is apparently a reliable diagnostic indicator of this cultural manifestation which is limited to the

Big Horn Mountains and the eastern edge of the Big Horn Basin. This restricted distribution is difficult to explain unless ecological barriers were present that cannot be perceived today. An alternative explanation is that some activities did not require use of the diagnostic projectile point, so that it is not present in some areas for this reason. The remainder of the cultural assemblage is not diagnostic and consists of items present in the entire cultural continuum for the area.

The Pryor Stemmed cultural horizon is a continuation of the carefully scheduled hunting-and-gathering orientation, utilizing the entire spectrum of economic resources from the basin floor to timberline and possibly even the alpine areas above this. Seed-grinding stones are quite common, and mountain sheep, mule deer, and an extremely rare bison are the large fauna represented, with a wide variety of small mammals also found. A date on this horizon at Medicine Lodge Creek is 6390 ± 220 B.C. (RL-151); at Schiffer Cave, 6550 ± 160 B.C. (RL-99) and 6410 ± 160 B.C. (RL-100); at a rockshelter (Site 48 JO 303) in the southern Big Horn Mountains, 5850 ± 110 B.C. (A-484) (Haynes, Damon, and Grey 1966). In the Big Horn Canyon caves there are dates of 6090 ± 200 B.C., 6210 ± 180 B.C., and 5610 ± 250 B.C. (Husted 1969: 82). The range of dates is rather large and suggests a long duration for Pryor Stemmed occupations.

A few inches above the Pryor Stemmed level at Medicine Lodge Creek is a poorly defined level, manifested by a small surface fire outlined by thin slabs of burned sandstone, a few chert and quartzite flakes, and some unidentified long bone fragments. A single projectile point (Figure 8.10f) is somewhat different from the Pryor Stemmed type, but a larger sample is necessary before definitive statements can be made. A carbon date from the hearth is 6100 ± 240 B.C. (RL-395). Above the level is a disconformity covering a hiatus of several thousand years. In the disconformity are projectile points diagnostic of the Altithermal period. These are best-known at present from Mummy Cave with radiocarbon dates from 5680 ± 170 B.C. to 3305 ± 140 B.C. (Wedel, Husted, and Moss 1968). Altithermal period occupations will be discussed in a later section.

THE CODY COMPLEX

Through time, the flow of Medicine Lodge Creek has eroded a good portion of the Paleo-Indian deposits at the Medicine Lodge Creek site. Much of this stream activity has been determined by the location of several rockfalls at the site. One major rockfall formed a barrier between the stream and the rock wall of the bluff with a space between where the largest and most complete stratigraphic column of Paleo-Indian deposits formed (Figure 8.6a). In other parts of the site, the stream has cut into cultural deposits, aggraded deposits of stream gravel, and subsequently moved away from the bluff. Other human groups then moved in and the cycle of cutting and deposition was often repeated. Fortunately, the stream did not always remove entire occupation levels.

In the area of the site containing the previously mentioned bone midden and about a foot above it, Medicine Lodge Creek partially cut into a rich Cody complex cultural level. Part of the level was intact, while part was washed somewhat by stream action. Radiocarbon dates have not as yet been obtained for this level but, stratigraphically, it has to be later than the bone midden which was dated at 7640 ± 180 B.C. A large artifact assemblage consisting of projectile points (Figure 8.11a, d), Cody knives (Figure 8.11b, f), gravers, and a wide variety of retouched flake and bone tools was recovered.

Medicine Lodge Creek is about 70 miles from the Horner site. Since the artifact assemblages probably represent the same cultural complex, it would appear that some relationships exist between the two. The hypothesis presented here is that the Cody complex in the Big

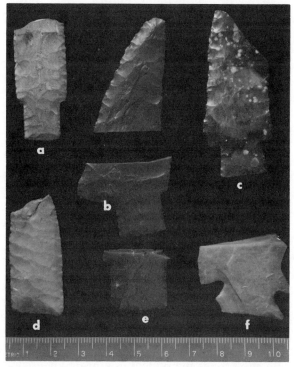

Figure 8.11 Cody complex projectile points and Cody knives (b,f) from the Medicine Lodge Creek site. Projectile-point base (e) and Cody knife (c) from Big Horn Mountain sites.

Horn Basin consisted of one or possibly two or three band-level groups communally hunting bison in the late fall, who, during other parts of the year, were exploiting a number of environments throughout known territories. Artifacts (Figure 8.11c, e) of the Cody complex occur in the Big Horn Mountains, especially in high mountain meadows around water sources. Typologically, they appear to be the same as artifacts at both the Medicine Lodge Creek and Horner sites. There is only limited evidence of bison in the Cody complex level at Medicine Lodge Creek, and very likely they were not plentiful in that particular area. Although it is only 70 miles from the Horner site, it is still in an ecologically distinct area. Cody complex groups apparently were doing more than procuring bison communally for a living; there is evidence in the Big Horn Basin that they were exploiting a great deal of the entire area. The evidence indicates that at least one of the classic Paleo-Indian groups was oriented toward a hunting-and-gathering subsistence base.

Many of the richest cultural levels at the Medicine Lodge Creek site did not produce diagnostic materials. One level produced tools (Figure 8.7a, c) and a base of a projectile point (Figure 8.7b), along with a large quantity of chipped stone. The level is between the one dated at 7410 $\pm$ 380 B.C. and that dated at 6570 $\pm$ 230 B.C. Future work in the site may produce diagnostic material for this level along with sufficient charcoal for a radiocarbon date. Projectile points with the same style of base appear occasionally in surface finds throughout the area; therefore, these projectile points may represent another discrete Paleo-Indian cultural group present in the area. They are as yet too poorly defined to be given definite designation.

One large rockshelter high in the wall of a deep canyon on the eastern slopes of the Big Horn Mountains (Paint Rock Canyon IV; Figure 8.1) demonstrated two occupational levels with radiocarbon dates of 6190 $\pm$ 150 B.C. (RL-391) and 6390 $\pm$ 160 B.C. (RL-381). Mountain sheep and mule deer remains were present in both levels and a rather distinct projectile point was recovered (Figure 8.10e), along with the base of two others with the same general characteristics. A projectile point from an undated level at the Medicine Lodge Creek site (Figure 8.9c) appears to be the same as that shown in Figure 8.10e; the blade edges were reworked, and a similar base was recovered with it. All seem significantly different from other projectile points recovered at the Medicine Lodge Creek site. However, the dates indicate the same time period as the Pryor Stemmed complex, and it is possible that these projectile points are nothing more than a variant. The cave site area is in an ideal mountain sheep and mule deer habitat (Figure 8.12) and probably was a central base for their procurement.

Figure 8.12   Paint Rock Creek IV rockshelter.

The Altithermal Period

The Altithermal period as formalized by Antevs (1955) has long been a subject of controversy. There seems little doubt that the Big Horn Basin and immediately adjacent areas suffered the brunt of the effects of the Altithermal (Albanese 1973, 1974). Evidence to date strongly indicates a period of aridity, although there is no reason to suspect reduced cultural activity in the Big Horn Basin when compared with the Paleo-Indian period.

The first satisfactory evidence of Altithermal occupation of the Big Horn Basin came from Mummy Cave (Wedel, Husted, and Moss 1968), where there is a series of cultural levels with radiocarbon dates from 5880 ± 170 B.C. to 3305 ± 140 B.C. An abrupt change in projectile-point forms from the stemmed and lanceolate styles of the Paleo-Indian to the side-notched styles of the early part of the Altithermal period occurs. Type names were given to these forms (Pahaska Side-Notched, Blackwater Side-Notched) with the names derived from geographical features of the area (Husted and Edgar n.d.). We are beginning now to recognize these early side-notched projectile points in surface finds in the foothills and higher mountain areas. Toward the latter part of the Altithermal period, there are projectile points at Medicine Lodge Creek, Mummy Cave, and the Big Horn Canyon sites that visually are reminiscent of Late Plains Archaic corner-notched styles. Out of context, they are difficult if not impossible to identify properly. To date, there are no samples in existence that are large enough to provide valid statistical studies.

At Medicine Lodge Creek, to date, there is only fragmentary evidence of the early side-notched or Altithermal period occupational levels since either erosion had destroyed most of them or they were deposited during a period of degradation rather than aggradation. Some projectile points were recovered in a stratigraphic context (Figure 8.10g–i), but the charcoal present was insufficient for dating. One small site (Granite Creek Rockshelter) in Shell Canyon, about 30 miles north of Medicine Lodge Creek, produced a stratified occupational sequence. A radiocarbon date on an early side-notched level there is as late as 3440 ± 120 B.C. (RL-390). Similar material was associated with similar dates at Mummy Cave.

At the Lookingbill site near the head of the Wind River (Figure 8.1), a large sample of the early side-notched points was collected. They are stratigraphically in place above the Lovell Constricted level, and the site apparently was a manufacturing area since the entire sequence of manufacture was represented, from the quarried material to finished projectile points. The technological system is from large flake to preform to projectile point through biface reduction. This is quite different from techniques used to manufacture similar-appearing projectile points of the late prehistoric period (approximately A.D. 500 to historic period). In this case, smaller percussion flakes were driven off and the projectile points were shaped by pressure flaking to an outline form, often leaving one side with much of the flat flake face intact, using a pressure retouch to remove the ridge on the back. No dates are yet available from the Lookingbill site.

Another site should be mentioned in the context of the early side-notched cultures. The Hawken site, a bison kill in the Wyoming Black Hills near Sundance, Wyoming, yielded several hundred side-notched projectile points with a radiocarbon date of 4520 ± 140 B.C. (RL-185) (Frison, Wilson, and Wilson, in press). The bison are a large extinct variant, intermediate in size between the *Bison bison antiquus* at the Casper site (Frison 1974) and the modern *Bison bison bison*. There may be relationships here to the Logan Creek materials (Kivett 1962) and possibly also to the Simonsen site (Agogino and Frankforter 1960). Although the Hawken site is 150 miles east of Medicine Lodge Creek in an entirely different ecological area, it helps to demonstrate movement of the early side-notched cultural groups into the entire region at about the same time. The writer does not suggest that the side-notched cultural group living in the Wyoming Black Hills, who possibly were not adversely affected by the Altithermal, were also exploiting the mountain slopes and foothills of the Big Horn Basin.

Although the side-notched forms of projectile points occurred throughout the Altithermal, as is clearly demonstrated at Mummy Cave, toward the end of the Altithermal period there were corner-notched forms as well; these occurred in undated levels at Medicine Lodge Creek, at Big Horn Canyon with a date of 3525 ± 190 B.C. (Husted 1969: 82), and at Mummy Cave with dates of 3440 ± 140 B.C. and 3305 ± 140 B.C. (Husted and Edgar n.d.: 108–138). The corner-notched styles also may be nothing more than part of a range of variation of an entire projectile-point assemblage, which can be demonstrated at the Hawken site (Frison, Wilson, and Wilson, in press).

Summary and Conclusions

The Big Horn Basin has a dated record of over 11,000 years of human occupation. The Fluted Point period is represented by mammoth hunters and a Folsom occupation. The known cultural assemblage, or at least the projectile points associated with the mammoth hunters, is somewhat different from the classic Clovis type but this may be nothing more than a regional variant. The Folsom evidence from one site and several surface finds is, technologically at least, unquestionably that of the classic Folsom although the subsistence base is as yet poorly known. What little evidence there is suggests the utilization of small animals as well as larger ones.

We can find little evidence as yet of the early Plano cultures, such as Agate Basin, Hell Gap, and Alberta in the Big Horn Basin, except for rare surface finds. Evidence for the Hell Gap complex is known for the eastern slope of the Big Horn Mountains at the Sisters Hill site (Agogino and Galloway 1965), but this is in the Powder River Basin and not in the Big Horn Basin. However, at about 8000 B.C., there is an occupational level at the Medicine Lodge Creek site with projectile points that vaguely resemble Plainview. Cultural levels dated between 7600 and 7000 B.C. at Medicine Lodge Creek contain assemblages in which the projectile points at least are not the common Plano types—although some tools, especially sharp-pointed gravers, such as those common in Plano contexts, are present. A wide variety of small mammals, birds, and reptiles were hunted for food; only small numbers of the larger mammals were hunted. Some evidence of seed collecting is also present, suggesting a broadly based hunting-and-gathering orientation.

Between about 6300 and 6600 B.C., there were several cultural levels at Medicine Lodge Creek with projectile points that, in outline form, do vaguely resemble Agate Basin, but technologically they are quite different. In addition, the dates are not comparable with those of

Agate Basin (see Irwin-Williams *et al.* 1973). Several other early cultural groups are represented by cultural levels containing projectile points, tool assemblages, and features at various sites in the Big Horn Basin that, timewise, appear contemporaneous with Plano cultural groups—but the projectile-point types are different. The Cody complex seems to be an exception, although the economic orientation of the Cody complex group at the Medicine Lodge Creek site differs markedly from that at the Horner site about 70 miles away, the type site of the Cody complex. In fact, with the exception of the Horner site, the economic orientation of the early cultural groups at all of the sites in the Big Horn Basin suggests a carefully scheduled hunting-and-

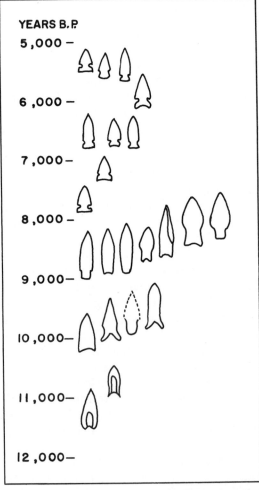

Figure 8.13 Suggested Paleo-Indian and Altithermal period projectile-point sequence for the Big Horn Basin, based on radiocarbon dates and stratigraphy.

gathering economy, centered in and around the mountains and some interior areas of greater topographic relief.

Altithermal period cultures of the Big Horn Basin are manifested by different types of projectile points than the preceding Paleo-Indian period. The Altithermal period saw the introduction of distinctive side-notched projectile points, in contrast to the lanceolate and stemmed projectile points of the Plano period. These side-notched projectile points apparently appear at this time over the entire northwestern Plains and adjacent areas as well. There is no good evidence to indicate greatly reduced human populations in the Big Horn Basin during the Altithermal period, as compared to the Paleo-Indian period. The Altithermal period groups apparently were exploiting approximately the same areas as the Paleo-Indians. Only with the beginning of the post-Altithermal period is there evidence of proliferation of human groups that began to intensively exploit the resources of the interior Big Horn Basin.

This discussion of Big Horn Basin cultural groups is based largely upon projectile-point typology (Figure 8.13) and radiocarbon dates. With the chronology gradually becoming more firmly established, the cultural systematics in terms of seasonality of food procurement activities and other institutional aspects of culture can eventually be added to the chronological framework.

Pecos River Pictographs: The Development of an Art Form

W. W. Newcomb, Jr.

Introduction

A major concentration of prehistoric pictographic art in North America is located in the vicinity of the junction of the Pecos River with the Rio Grande in Val Verde County, southwest Texas. Here, in shelters and beneath overhangs, scoured out of limestone walls in the rugged canyons of the Devils, Pecos, Rio Grande, and their tributaries, are hundreds if not thousands of rock paintings. At some sites, there are only a few figures; but, in larger shelters, jumbled panels of paintings may crowd walls, extending along them for 100 ft. and more (Figure 9.1). Paintings may be diminutive, a few inches in height, or monumental, almost 15 ft. tall, the latter often producing startled, incredulous, or awed reactions in those who see them for the first time. The pictographs are also varied in other respects, reflecting the several purposes of the diversity of peoples who executed them over a period of many millennia. The oldest, most elaborate, and most common rock paintings are known as the "Pecos River style." Of the 95 pictograph sites so far recorded in Val Verde County, 56 have Pecos

Figure 9.1 This watercolor painting by Forrest Kirkland is a scale copy of a 28-ft. section of pictographs in Panther Cave, one of the major rock art sites in the lower Pecos River region. The central figure in this painting is 9 ft. tall. Pictographs extend along the walls and ceiling of this shelter for more than 100 ft.

River style paintings, and a high proportion of the 16 sites at which the rock paintings are too fragmentary or dim to make a stylistic determination probably are also of this style (Parsons 1967). A recent study (Kirkland and Newcomb 1967) has shown that the Pecos River style pictographs followed an orderly pattern of growth and development. This chapter is concerned with the nature of this sequence and its significance to the understanding of changing art forms.

The lower Pecos River region is one of low, rolling, rocky limestone hills, much dissected by steep-sided arroyos and canyons. This is an ecotonal area, on the margins of the Tamaulipan, Chihuahuan, and Balconian biotic provinces, and there is considerable mixing of their fauna and flora (Blair 1950). Average rainfall at Del Rio, on its southeastern side, is about 18 inches, but it falls off sharply to the west, and the long, hot, and windy summers reduce its effectiveness markedly. The lower Pecos River country may have been somewhat more moist during various periods in the last 10 millenniums, but not significantly so in terms of the resources available for exploitation by its prehistoric inhabitants.

On the uplands, the thin soils and meager rainfall support a desert growth of creosote bush, ocotillo, sotol, yucca, cacti, cat's claw, cenizo, nolina, mesquite, and a sparse growth of short grasses (Flyr 1966). The canyon and valley bottoms support a somewhat different flora, with cottonwood, willow, as well as occasional pecans, oaks, Mexican walnut, hackberry, stands of cane, and a heavier growth of grasses. Before the region became the sheep and goat country it is today, grass was undoubtedly a more significant part of the upland flora, and, at least sporadically (probably in winter), it supported bison. Today, the largest indigenous mammals are white-tailed deer and javelinas (collared peccaries). Black bears and wolves are no longer found in the region, and mountain lions (cougars) have been virtually exterminated. Smaller animals include jackrabbits and cottontails, ground squirrels, other rodents, a variety of birds and reptiles, and many insects and other invertebrates. The permanent streams support a diversity of aquatic life, including fish, turtles, and shellfish (Raun 1966: 191–219).

Although the lower Pecos River country might appear to have been harsh, difficult, and unattractive to prehistoric peoples, a more searching appraisal suggests that the presence of three major watercourses, in contrast to the relatively waterless areas to the south and west, must have made it relatively attractive. Also, its location on the margins of three biotic provinces may have given it some peculiar advantages over adjacent regions in the diversity and abundance of its wild foods. In terms of wild food subsistence, it is possible, although unstudied, that it was more productive than better-watered areas to the north and east. In any case, the lower Pecos River country was found quickly by early inhabitants of North America and it was continuously occupied thereafter.

Lower Pecos River Prehistory

Paleo-Indian hunters were the first known humans to occupy the lower Pecos River country. The lowest level in Bonfire Shelter contained remains of extinct species of elephant, camel, horse, and bison in a context suggesting that humans were responsible for their presence (Dibble and Lorrain 1968: 28). Stratigraphically higher in the shelter's deposits were the remains of an extinct form of bison, stampeded or driven off the cliff above the shelter. Among the scrapers, bifaces, and other artifacts scattered among the bison bones were barbless, lanceolate projectile points of Plainview and Folsom types. One charcoal sample from this level was radiocarbon-dated at 8120–8440 B.C., the oldest dated remains at present from the lower Pecos region. Other evidences of Paleo-Indian occupation have been found at the Devil's Mouth site and at several other places in the region (Johnson 1964; Story and Bryant 1966). Paleo-Indians have not been credited with being responsible for pictographic or petroglyphic art elsewhere, and the lower Pecos River pictographs cannot be attributed to them.

The Paleo-Indian occupation of the lower Pecos River region was succeeded by a long and stable Archaic occupation, apparently related to and part of the widespread Western Archaic or Desert Culture (Jennings and Norbeck 1964). Whatever designation is applied to it, this local culture was a conservative, self-contained entity that persisted with little change, at least in its technological component, for many millenniums. Beginning around 7000 B.C., it persisted until about A.D. 1000 (Story 1966: Table 1). The subsistence base was hunting and gathering, with the bulk of the food supply provided by wild plant foods. Chief among these were agave *(Agave lechuguilla)* and Texas sotol *(Dasylirion texanum),* the bulbs and crowns of which were baked in earth ovens. Their flowers, stems, and perhaps other parts also were consumed (Bryant and Williams-Dean 1975). Other plant foods included mesquite beans, prickly pear "pads" and fruit, and a large assortment of other seeds, nuts, and fruits. White-tailed deer were the most important game animals; bison were sporadically and infrequently available; and an assortment of smaller animal remains, from rabbits and rats to lizards and turtles, are found in cultural deposits. Fish bones, especially those of catfish, are found in middens, as are snail shells *(Bulimus),* a terrestrial species. Snail shells and grasshoppers also occur in human coprolites (Bryant and Williams-Dean 1975).

Commonly found in Archaic and later cultural deposits are the seeds and other plant parts of the mescal bean *(Sophora secundiflora),* which contains toxic, narcotic alkaloids, lesser quantities of the hallucinogenic peyote *(Lophophora williamsii),* and also seeds of the Mexican buckeye *(Ungnadia speciosa),* which also may have narcotic or toxic properties. A mescal bean cult, similar to that of historic tribes, may have resulted in the painting of pictographs by these people (Campbell 1958: 159; Kirkland and Newcomb 1967: 65–80).

The basic hunting weapon was the dart or spear propelled by a throwing stick or *atlatl,* parts of which have been found in the cultural deposits of dry shelters. Slightly curved and grooved rabbit sticks have been found, as well as simple digging sticks. Other perishable items recovered from the region's shelters include wooden shovels or scoops, wooden fire hearths, and fire drills. Extensive use was made of plant fibers for sandals of several varieties, matting, basketry, nets, strings, and ropes. Pouches or bags also were woven of vegetable fibers, and the hollowed-out pads of prickly pear cactus, with sewn edges, seem to have been used for the same purpose. Skins were used for bags and leather garments, and fur robes or blankets were made by interweaving fur in strands of cordage. Bone and antler were employed for awls, flakers for chipping flint, and scrapers, needles, beads, and pendants have been recovered. Fragments of stone pipes and what appear to be cane cigarette-holders indicate that smoking was known. Stone mortars and mortars cut into bedrock for grinding seeds and nuts were used, and *metates* or seed-grinding slabs also have been found.

The considerable variety of chipped-stone projectile points, occurring in differing stratigraphic contexts, has served as the basis for subdividing the prehistoric cultural deposits into a number of chronological periods. The most recent chronology, employing a considerable number of radiocarbon dates, and correlating the stratigraphic components at a number of sites, has been proposed by Story (1966: 9–13). Eight periods are established, with Periods II through VI representing the Archaic continuum. Whether the changing morphology of Archaic projectile-point types represents technological advances of some sort or merely stylistic change is unknown, although they do not appear to reflect any basic alterations in the mode of life during the Archaic.

Flat, usually ovate, stream-worn pebbles, painted with black anthropomorphic designs also often are recovered from shelter deposits. These occur throughout the Archaic continuum and into the post-Archaic, and "represent the longest known continuous sequence of any art form in the New World" (Parsons n.d.). Their designs underwent a developmental course that contrasts in some respects with that of the pictographs. An unpublished study (Parsons n.d.) has established six painted pebble styles, Style I dating to the Early Archaic (Story's Time Period II), with pebbles of this type occurring in the three deepest and oldest strata at Eagle Cave (Ross 1965: 160–162). Style V has been dated at Bonfire Shelter at about A.D. 200–500 (Dibble and Lorrain 1968: 51, 61–62), or Period VI in Story's chronology. Fortuitously, but perhaps significantly, Parsons' six painted pebble styles appear to coincide with the chronological periods based on projectile-point types devised by Story (1966: 10–12). Parsons believes that the painted pebbles of Archaic Styles I–V "represent either the torso or the head and torso of a female human being" (n.d.; 39), but that Style VI pebbles, painted in post-Archaic times, represent a human face. He argues persuasively that the painted pebbles are menstrual taboo objects. Unfortunately, there seems to be no connection between the designs (or human figures) on the pebbles and the rock art of the lower Pecos River. Only at one site have possible pebble designs appeared as pictographs. In this case, they appear to represent the reverse side of Style VI pebbles, and they cannot be associated confidently with the other pictographs in this shelter (Kirkland and Newcomb 1967: 53, Plate 18, No. 8).

Around A.D. 1000, the Archaic tradition, at least in a restricted sense, came to an end in the lower Pecos River country. In various other parts of Texas, agriculture, pottery, and the bow and arrow, as indicated by the appearance of small, light projectile points, were introduced. However, the only element of the "Neo-American stage" that penetrated the lower Pecos River country was the bow and arrow. Whether or not a new people or peoples invaded the region is not clear. In addition to the replacement of larger projectile points by smaller points, Pecos River style pictographs were no longer painted, and the painted pebbles (Style VI) took on a new look and, perhaps, a new function. Otherwise, archaeological remains suggest that the old Archaic life style persisted with little change. At the beginning of the historic period, the region was occupied by Coahuiltecans, a poorly known, scattered, somewhat varied medley of band-organized hunters and gatherers of northeastern Mexico and southern Texas (Newcomb 1961: Chapter 2).

In sum, the Archaic culture of the lower Pecos River region was a stable, long-persisting continuum, based on a wild food subsistence that emphasized plant foods. The techniques necessary to process plant foods were simple—seeds, nuts, and other hard substances were ground; coarse, fibrous plants were baked in earth ovens. The subsistence pattern suggests a seminomadic existence, dictated by the availability and harvest time of various foods. The dry shelters appear to have been occupied intermittently but regularly, and there are some indications of habitation in the late spring–early summer (Bryant and Williams-Dean 1975). The kin-based social groups were probably small, perhaps with dispersal in family-sized groups during part of the year, with larger groups gathering for the harvest of certain foods. Ceremonial life, as reflected by pictographs, appears to have been rich and relatively well-organized (Kirkland and Newcomb 1967: 60–65).

Pictographs of the Lower Pecos River Region

That Pecos River style pictographs were executed by people of Archaic culture is indicated by the persistent portrayal in them of throwing sticks (atlatls) and darts, as well as other items, such as rabbit sticks, which were typical of the Archaic tool kit. Archaic remains invariably occur in the same shelters as the Pecos River style pictographs or are nearby, and pigments used in the paintings, crayons, lumps, and pigment-smeared palettes, often are found in Archaic deposits. There is no reason to question the association of Pecos River style pictographs with the local Archaic culture. Unfortunately, no sites have been investigated in which undisturbed cultural materials have covered pictographs. Only one site is known at which this occurred, and, at this site, in Mile Canyon near the hamlet of Langtry, the pictographs at the rear of the small shelter were obscured completely by an accumulation of deposits that measured up to 8 ft. deep. Unfortunately, pot hunters had so disturbed the site that no conclusions could be reached about the age of the cultural deposits (Kirkland and Newcomb 1967: 41).

At present, there is no way of knowing with which part or parts of the Archaic continuum the paintings should be associated. At first glance, it might appear unlikely that a single form of rock painting, even though it underwent a substantial development, would persist for a millennium, let alone five or more. Yet the painted pebbles of these same Archaic peoples, as we have seen, were produced throughout the Archaic, and the Pecos River style pictographs also may have had a spectacularly long history.

Nor is the geographical extent of the Pecos River style pictographs fully known. Most sites are in shelters and under overhangs along the lower Devils and Pecos Rivers, their tributaries, and along adjacent portions of the Rio Grande. But the upper Devils River, as well as other remote areas in Val Verde County have not been surveyed adequately, and virtually nothing is known of their distribution in Mexico. Sites in the Serranias del Burro of northern Coahuila have been reported, but they have not been recorded or studied adequately.

Another pictographic style, named "Red Linear" by Gebhard (1960: 53) and recorded at two sites, also appears to have been the work of Archaic peoples (Kirkland and Newcomb 1967: 94–95; Parsons 1967). Somewhat similar to Pecos River style pictographs, it is probably a product of the same artists, although produced for a different purpose. Several other pictographic styles, attributed to the Archaic, have been discerned by Gebhard (1960: 45–67), but their occurrence is very limited or their reality is questionable, and they need not be examined further.

Much less common than the Pecos River style pictographs, and superimposed over them at one site at least, are paintings in a Red Monochrome style (Gebhard 1960: 12; Kirkland and Newcomb 1967: 41, 81–92). These have been associated with the post-Archaic on the basis of the bows and arrows depicted in them. Neither in technique nor in subject matter do they display any characteristics that would connect them to their forerunners. If the artists who painted them were, as seems likely, descendants of the Archaic culture, the tradition

of painting shelter walls had been abandoned and completely forgotten before their time, or sometime before A.D. 1000. A number of other
scattered pictographs, which may or may not be associated with the
Red Monochrome style, also have been recorded in the lower Pecos
River region, and they apparently are attributable to post-Archaic
cultures. Some pictographs in the region were painted in historic
times, as indicated by guns, horses, churches, and figures in European
clothing.

Pecos River Style Pictographs

Among the most conspicuous and common elements in Pecos River
style pictographs are anthropomorphic beings, variously interpreted
as representing dancers, or mythical beings, and here termed "shamans" after the interpretation given them in a study by Kirkland and
Newcomb (1967). The analysis of the characteristics of 162 of these
figures in this study, meticulously depicted in Kirkland's watercolor
copies of them, and the objects and animals clearly associated with
them, revealed the existence of two major substyles of painting and
possibly two others. The study demonstrated that it was a chronological series, since a number of figures were superimposed over others,
and consequently, the substyles were given "period" designations.
This was a preliminary study, and a more thoroughgoing, definitive
study of this remarkable pictographic style and sequence awaits a
more complete recording of the rock paintings of the region and a
more sophisticated analysis of the data. A limited amount of work has
been accomplished since this study was completed, but the basic
conclusions have been confirmed and amplified (Parsons 1967).

A tentative Period 1 (Figure 9.2) was established for a few
monochromatic, anthropomorphic figures that have been found at
several sites. All are dim, usually vertically elongated, cigar-shaped or
rectangular figures, often lacking legs and distinguishable heads,
although usually possessing arms. They are not accompanied with the
objects in the positions that characterize them in later paintings,
although some objects appear in their vicinity. At one site (Kirkland
and Newcomb 1967: Plate 16, Nos. 1 and 3), later Pecos River style
paintings, apparently of Period 3, are superimposed over them. Little
more can be said to categorize these figures; they may be unfinished
Period 2 figures, peripheral secondary figures in paintings in which the
central figures have been obliterated, or they may represent the
earliest paintings in the Pecos River style series. If they do not
represent the beginnings of Pecos River style pictographs, they must
duplicate in many ways what they were like.

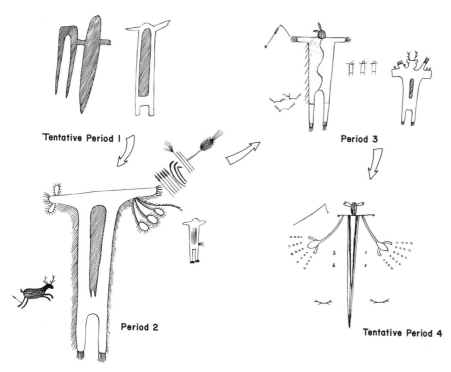

Figure 9.2 Schematic drawings of the Pecos River style shamans.

The shaman figures assume a distinctive form in Period 2 (Figure 9.2). They are usually a single shade of red, elongated, and large; 40% are over 6 ft. tall, and six of them are over 10 ft. in height. They usually are drawn in full-front view, although some figures are shown in profile, a feature seldom found in later paintings. They often lack heads, although not necessarily headdresses, and facial features are never portrayed. Three-quarters lack feet or toes, and more than a third are legless. A few wear a feathered sash low on the body, and a few others wear a distinctive "horn" headdress, both of which are unique to Period 2 figures. More than half of the Period 2 shamans hold an *atlatl* in the right hand with the butt of a feathered dart in place against it. Suspended from the arms of about three-quarters of the figures are objects that usually resemble prickly pear pads, fringed bags, or sticks. In or near the left hand of one-third of the figures are a series of feathered darts, and, in two-thirds of the examples, curved rabbit sticks are portrayed next to them. Next to these are tasseled sticks or other objects, and, to the right of them, extending outward, are a series of lines attached at the far end to an object that again usually appears to be a pouch or prickly object.

In slightly over one-quarter of the Period 2 figures, diminutive deer are associated with the anthropomorphic figures, their bodies often pierced by darts. Cougars occasionally accompany Period 2 figures, but they contrast with the deer by being large relative to the human figures, and they are never pierced by darts. Other anthropomorphic figures are more commonly associated with the shamans than are animals. In some cases, several shamans appear to be jointly engaged in some activity; in others, the peripheral subordinate figures appear to be a supporting cast. Although few Period 2 characteristics are unique, when viewed as a unit, they constitute a distinctive, obvious substyle. At several sites, Period 2 paintings are overpainted by Period 3 pictographs.

Eighty-three, or more than half of the shaman figures Kirkland recorded, were assigned to Period 3 (Figure 9.2). They differ from Period 2 paintings in a number of significant ways. Almost 70% are bi-color, 25% are tri-color, and the use of black is much more common. Almost 90% are under 6 ft. in height, and only 10% lack heads. Legs, feet, and toes are depicted more often than in the earlier period. What appear to be feathers are much employed in head-dresses, and an antlered headdress is associated with an odd variation of the shaman figure. Wide, squared-off "wings" extend outward from either side of the body at shoulder level in this variation, and hands and arms project upward from them. They have a curious resemblance to the old Ford tri-motored airplane, and long since have had this appellation attached to them. The *atlatl* and dart are less often portrayed with Period 3 shamans, and, at the distal end of the dart, three or more short, parallel lines are apt to intersect it at right angles. Whether these lines represent the projectile point, a foreshaft, the method of hafting, or something else is unclear. In any case, these conventionalizations are substituted for the entire dart in many Period 3 paintings.

The various objects associated with Period 3 shamans are more difficult to recognize than their Period 2 counterparts, apparently because they are more simply or hastily drawn. None have all the accouterments that characterized them in the earlier period. Of the Period 3 shamans, 50% have wavy or sinuous lines associated with them. These commonly have been interpreted as snakes, but there are some indications that they are "force lines," extending from a shaman to his human or animal subjects. Period 3 shamans are less frequently associated with animals than in the preceding period, and the head and antlers or only the antlers of deer are employed to depict this animal. There are more peripheral humans than in Period 2; some seem to represent dancers, others are apparently dead warriors, represented by horizontal or upside-down figures, usually transfixed by a dart, or with dart symbols surrounding them. Fallen "warriors" often are accompanied by drawings of birds.

For the most part, Period 3 pictographs are easily distinguished from earlier paintings. They occasionally are superimposed on Period 2 paintings, and, at some sites, there seems to be a tendency toward overpainting of Period 3 figures by other Period 3 figures. No Period 3 paintings are painted over tentative Period 4 paintings, and, so far, no tentative Period 4 paintings have been found that were superimposed over earlier paintings.

Ten paintings of shamans were so conventionalized that they were set apart as a tentative Period 4 (Figure 9.2). Stylistically, they are a step beyond Period 3 shamans, although there is no evidence in the form of overpainting that they were executed later. In the most extreme example (Figure 9.2), the shaman has become a balanced, symmetrical, geometrical design, and only by close inspection does one realize that the *atlatl* and dart are suspended in midair as usual and that much-magnified prickly pouches are suspended from the arms in the familiar way (Kirkland and Newcomb 1967: 57). In general, these figures are symmetrical, polychromatic, use the dart symbol extensively, and streams of red dots or lines (force lines) accompany three of them. In one case, force lines issue from an *atlatl* and cut through a prone figure (Kirkland and Newcomb 1967: 67, Plate 28, No. 1). No Period 4 paintings have been overpainted, nor are any superimposed over other paintings. "Stylistically, then, these few shamans represent the most developed form of Pecos River art, and the probabilities favor their being the most recent of the Pecos River style pictographs" (Kirkland and Newcomb 1967: 58).

Theoretical Considerations

When the nature of the Pecos River style sequence of pictographs is grasped, it becomes obvious that it bears a striking resemblance to that of the Franco–Cantabrian cave art of Europe and, in a general way, conforms to the representational to conventional pattern that has been said to characterize most temporal graphic art sequences. Although increased knowledge may complicate the European cave art sequence, in its simplest terms, it progressed from crude, outlined, monochromatic paintings of animals to skillfully executed, naturalistic, polychrome paintings, to eventual abstraction and simplification. The Texas paintings developed in much the same way, although all of their stages are not yet clearly delineated. That is, there appears to have been an initial stage of groping and experimentation, followed by the appearance of a distinctive, yet still developing, monochromatic representational style in Period 2. Period 3 may be characterized as the classic, polychromatic stage in Pecos River style pictography, which also saw the beginnings of conventionalization. Stylistically, if not temporally, it was followed by a further eradication of nonessentials, which is to say a continuing trend toward conventionalization and abstraction in tentative Period 4.

That the shelter and cave paintings of two separate regions, executed by totally unrelated peoples, separated by thousands of years, followed a broadly similar developmental path serves as a reminder that artistic traditions, like other aspects of culture, are not capricious, helter-skelter expressions of unfettered artists. They are instead regular, step-by-step progressions, each stage or style dependent upon, and an orderly growth from, their predecessors, as in turn they are the foundation on which future developments are based.

To put it in simple terms, suppose that, for one reason or another, a people attempts to portray by means of painting on rock walls a hunter in the act of killing a buffalo. Lacking any experience in painting, the first attempts at such portrayal are bound to be crude and rough. But if such attempts are continued through time, if successive generations persist in attempts to depict in rock paintings hunters killing buffalo, their execution improves. Brushes and paints are apt to be improved, resulting in finer lines and the use of several colors. The artist often learns to include details that his unskilled forebears eschewed, leading to more intricate and complicated works. Discoveries may be made about the techniques of painting—foreshortening, shading, balance, and the other devices artists use to make a two-dimensional illusion approximate a three-dimensional reality. In short, developing painting traditions come to more accurately and clearly approximate the reality of the scenes they are attempting to recreate: It is a representative art.

How far down the representational road a particular painting tradition will travel depends upon the purposes of the art, the perceptual distortions forced upon artists by their culture, the cultural acceptance or rejection of changing or developing artistic styles, technical limitations, and, no doubt, other constraints. The cave art of Europe, for example, apparently went the distance in terms of representational paintings of animals; few, if any, other artists of whatever artistic milieu painted animals more realistically. For the Pecos River artists of Period 2, clearly that intent was to portray the attire of shamans, their accouterments and weapons, and the animals and humans whom they affected or with whom they were associated, as accurately and realistically as their technique permitted. But there was little interest in portraying the human body accurately or completely, as the frequent lack of feet and legs attests, and there may have been an aversion to or a prohibition against delineating the human face.

Before all the technical perfections of representational depiction have been realized, a new tendency and direction usually appears—a new way of portraying the hunter killing buffalo. It may arise out of impatience at painting an entire, faithful rendition of the animal when a few lines or a characteristic part will serve as well. Or, it may arise out of a desire for innovation in circumstances in which the new and different are regarded as praiseworthy; and other possibilities might be suggested. In any case, the new direction is toward conventionalization or abstraction. In the Pecos River sequence, by Period 3 times, among other developments, a kind of shorthand was devised, which is to say the artists abstracted or conventionalized what were to them characteristic or distinctive features of weapons and deer, and let these stand for the whole. Thus, the shorthand depiction of a dart became a line intersected by three or more short, right-angle lines, and a deer's antlers were used to symbolize the entire animal. By tentative Period 4, the tendency was extended to the shamans, and they virtually became geometric figures. Fortunately, there are enough clues in the pictographs to deduce that these represent shamans. There may be others that are unrecognized or for which no clues exist. The audience understood the abstractions, however—a necessity for the paintings to serve their purpose. Very probably, this is a key to understanding why such sequences develop in stages: Quantum leaps would be incomprehensible, small steps are self-evident.

Investigation into the nature of such sequences has lagged, at least in American anthropology, ever since Franz Boas argued that the sequences postulated by late-nineteenth-century evolutionists H. Stolpe, H. Balfour, Karl von den Steinen, and A. C. Haddon were defective. Boas cited F. W. Putnam as the first investigator

> to propound clearly the theory that conventional designs develop from attempts at realistic representations, which gradually degenerate so that ultimately a purely conventional design remains, in which the realistic origin can hardly be recognized [Boas 1908: 321].

Aside from his amazingly precise, though of course inadvertent, description of the Pecos River style pictographic sequence, Boas contended quite properly that Putnam's series of decorative designs on the pottery of Chiriqui Indians, Haddon's series of arrows from the Torres Straits, decorated with carvings representing crocodiles, and others, were in essence typological classifications, not necessarily temporal sequences. But Boas was not content to let the matter rest there. He attempted to discredit the universality of the representational to conventional sequence by showing in a study of Alaskan needlecases that the reverse sequence also occurred (Boas 1908). The study has been long held up as the classic refutation of the old evolutionist position (see, for example, Bunzel 1938: 578; Herskovits 1948: 395–398; Hoebel 1972: 637–638), but it is flawed in several ways. The needlecases Boas described were museum specimens and their temporal relationships were assumed not given, so that his study might be faulted on the same grounds he applied to others. But more crucially, Boas did not demonstrate a sequence from conventional to representational, but rather that

> various parts of the flanged needlecase excite the imagination of the artist; and a geometrical element here or there is developed by him, in accordance with the general tendencies of Eskimo art, into the representation of whole animals or of parts of animals [1908: 337].

This is not sequential development, only variation on a theme. The theme was the presumably old, conventional type of needlecase, with geometric embellishments, to which a later generation of artists added an assortment of more or less representational animals. Boas saw no regularity or order here, only questions about the inner motivations of the artists, invoking "play of the imagination" (1908: 337), "tendencies . . . active in the human mind" (1908: 341), and "other psychic processes" (1908: 341) to account for the variety of representative animal forms they added to the needlecases.

The observation that all men, including primitive artists, possess the ability to see an elephant in a cloud formation, a butterfly in an ink blot, or an animal or human in some geometric figure or in the shape of a utilitarian tool is, of course, valid. Artists and artisans of many cultures seize upon these suggestive forms, carving animal likenesses on hoe handles and converting geometric figures into human visages, and the like. But this is not comparable to and is not the same as the growth through time of a specific art form, whether it be decorative or pictographic. Once a manner of decorating an object or painting a likeness of some sort on a cave wall has become established, future practitioners of the art base their own renditions and variations on what is familiar to them. It may be as close a copy as they can manage, or it may be an "improvement" and a step removed from the traditional, but it is as intimately related to its predecessor as the son is to the father. Not only is this relationship logical in terms of what is known about the growth and development of any segment of culture, but it is the only one that is observed empirically.

More specifically, if a temporal sequence of related forms is

A–B–C–D, or even D–C–B–A, each form is invariant in that C and A are always separated by B. To put it another way, forms (or styles) close or adjacent to one another in a series share more characteristics with each other than they do with forms farther removed in the series. In a predictive (and practical) sense, if the directional development of the sequence is known, missing forms can be reconstructed. Or, if a sequence of forms has been established, they can be utilized as time or period markers. The imposition of named styles or periods (A, B, C, D, etc.) to a developmental sequence of art forms is artificial in that they may not precisely reflect all the gradations between forms. Thus, a number of Pecos River style shamans could not be assigned "period" designations because they exhibited characteristics that were transitional between periods (Kirkland and Newcomb 1967: 44). This situation is to be expected, particularly if categories are gross and the gradations between forms are many.

Although Boas failed to demonstrate a conventional to representational sequence in Alaskan needlecases, this does not negate the possibility of such sequences in other art forms. Oddly, the development of painted pebble designs in the lower Pecos River region seems to provide just such a sequence. The earliest painted pebbles, Style I in Parsons' series (Parsons n.d.), appear to exhibit purely geometric designs, Style V designs are rather obviously anthropomorphic, and Style VI pebbles, as we have seen, are fairly realistic portrayals of human faces. The problem lies in assuming that the early styles are geometric, when in fact they may have been attempts, following Parsons' interpretation, to realistically portray human torsos, female sex organs, menstrual pads, or something else. On the other hand, if the painted pebbles were personal items, used privately, perhaps in some magical context, there would be no need for them to be representational because their meaning did not have to be communicated or shared with others, at least in any specific sense. Actually, painted pebbles are tremendously varied, a situation one might expect with "private" art objects.

In general, the conventionalized to representational sequence occurs infrequently in any developmental series. This opinion is based on the supposition that most artists set out to draw, paint, chisel, or mold some actual object or scenes in their physical and cultural universes. They are not and need not be prompted by a suggestive form or object in or on the medium with which they are working. The conventional to representational sequence is also more likely to occur in some forms of artistic expression than in others. The cave wall rarely suggests the figures or scenes the artist paints upon it. But the weaver, the toolmaker, and other artisans, because of the form, texture, natural pattern, or other intrinsic features of their materials frequently are stimulated to embellish them in one way or another. But even in these instances, a developmental sequence may not be initiated. The shape of a tool may, for example, suggest a bird, and the artist may convert it into a more realistic bird form. But he does not necessarily inaugurate a series that, through time, produces more and more realistic birds.

Since these developmental sequences of art forms seem usually to proceed from representational to conventional, but may sometimes reverse the direction, the question of whether or not the process may be cyclical inevitably arises. One might hypothesize, for example, that the next step beyond a geometrical Pecos River style Period 4 shaman would be a more realistic interpretation. Assuming that shaman painting was to continue, there was obviously no other direction it could take. Presumably, then, the sequence might return to a representational stage of depicting shamans.

Finally, developmental sequences, like those of the Pecos River style pictographs, deserve more intensive study than they have received. They were stunted in the stampede to refute evolutionary studies; they have languished since, unnecessarily and for far too long. Not only might such studies aid in reconstructing specific cultures and cultural sequences, but they promise to yield fruitful results in better understanding the aesthetic aspects of culture. In this context, exotic art, such as that found on shelter walls of the Pecos River country, is so far removed from our own artistic heritage and aesthetic biases that its study would seem to offer a rare opportunity to achieve detachment and objectivity.

References for Part II

Adams, R. M., and W. M. Walker
   1942   Archaeological Survey of New Madrid County, Missouri. *Missouri Archaeologist* **8**:1–23.
Agogino, G. A., and W. O. Frankforter
   1960   A Paleo-Indian Bison Kill in Northwestern Iowa. *American Antiquity* **25**:414–415.
Agogino, G. A., and E. Galloway
   1965   The Sisters Hill Site: A Hell Gap Site in North Central Wyoming. *Plains Anthropologist* **10**:190–195.
Albanese, J. P.
   1973   The Holocene Climate in the Northern Plains Area of Wyoming and Montana. Paper presented at the 31st Plains Conference, Columbia, Missouri, November 22–24.
   1974   Holocene Alluvial Chronology and Climate Change on the Northwestern Plains. Paper presented at the 3d Biennial Meeting, University of Wisconsin, Madison, Wisconsin, July 30–August 1.
Antevs, E.
   1955   Geologic Climate Dating in the West. *American Antiquity* **20**:317–335.
Arkansas Gazette
   1927a   Town of Eudora is Refugee Center. *Arkansas Gazette*, April 29, 1927. Little Rock.
   1927b   Another Big Lake Levee Gives Way. *Arkansas Gazette*, May 3, 1927. Little Rock.
Baity, E. C.
   1973   Archaeoastronomy and Ethnoastronomy So Far. *Current Anthropology* **14**:389–431.
Beauchamp, W. M.
   1900   Aboriginal Occupations of New York. *New York State Museum Bulletin* No. 32, Albany.
Beckwith, T.
   1911   *The Indian or Mound Builder.* Cape Girardeau, Missouri: Naeter Brothers.
Binford, L. R.
   1962   Archaeology as Anthropology. *American Antiquity* **28**:217–225.
   1971   Mortuary Practices: Their Study and Their Potential. In Approaches to the Social Dimensions of Mortuary Practices, edited by J. A. Brown. *Memoirs of the Society for American Archaeology* **25**:6–29.

Blair, W. F.
  1950 The Biotic Provinces of Texas. *Texas Journal of Science* **2**:93–115.
Boas, F.
  1908 Decorative Designs of Alaskan Needlecases: A Study in the History of Conventional Designs, Based on Materials in the U.S. National Museum. *Proceedings of the United States National Museum* **34**:321–344.
Brain, J. P.
  1970 Winterville: A Case Study of Prehistoric Culture Contact in the Lower Mississippi Valley. Ph.D dissertation, Yale University. University Microfilms No. 70-15,680, Ann Arbor.
Braun, E. L.
  1950 *Deciduous Forests of Eastern North America*. Philadelphia: Blakiston.
Brose, D.
  1972 An Initial Summary of the Late Prehistoric Period in Northeastern Ohio. Paper presented at the 1972 Central States Anthropological Society Symposium, "Late Prehistory in the Lake Erie Drainage Basin."
Brown, J. A.
  1971a Introduction. In Approaches to the Social Dimensions of Mortuary Practices, edited by J. A. Brown. *Memoirs of the Society for American Archaeology* **25**:1–5.
  1971b The Dimensions of Status in the Burials at Spiro. In Approaches to the Social Dimensions of Morturary Practices, edited by J. A. Brown. *Memoirs of the Society for American Archaeology* **25**:92–112.
Bryant, V. M., Jr., and G. Williams-Dean
  1975 The Coprolites of Man. *Scientific American* **232**:100–109.
Bunzel, R.
  1938 Art. In *General Anthropology*, edited by Franz Boas. Boston: D. C. Heath. Pp. 35–588.
Campbell, T. N.
  1958 Origin of the Mescal Bean Cult. *American Anthropologist* **60**:156–160.
Carter, C. T. (Editor)
  1953 *The Territory of Arkansas, 1819–1825*. Volume 19 of *The Territorial Papers of the United States*. Washington: U.S. Government Printing Office.
Davis, E. M. (Editor)
  1961 Proceedings of the Fifth Conference on Caddoan Archeology. *Bulletin of the Texas Archeological Society*, Vol. 31 for 1960: 3–151.
Dibble, D. S., and D. Lorrain
  1968 Bonfire Shelter: A Stratified Bison Kill Site, Val Verde County, Texas. *Texas Memorial Museum Miscellaneous Papers* No. 1.
Engelbrecht, W.
  1971 A Stylistic Analysis of New York Iroquois Pottery. Ph.D. dissertation, University of Michigan, Ann Arbor.
  1972 The Reflection of Patterned Behavior in Iroquois Pottery Decoration. *Pennsylvania Archaeologist* **42**:1–15.
  1974 The Iroquois: Archaeological Patterning on the Tribal Level. *World Archaeology* **6**:52–65.
  1975 Ceramic Patterning between New York Iroquois Sites. Paper presented at the 1975 Annual Meeting of the New York State Archaeological Association.
Evans, D. R.
  1970 Exploratory Investigations at a Thousand Year Old Fortified Indian Town Site between New Madrid and Lilbourn, Missouri. *Missouri Archaeological Society Newsletter* **242**:1–3.

1971   Excavation Progress at the Lilbourn Site. *Missouri Archaeological Society Newsletter* **251**:1–5.

Fenton, W. N.
1940   Problems Arising from the Historic Northeastern Position of the Iroquois. *Smithsonian Miscellaneous Collections* **100.** Washington, D.C.

Ferguson, J. L., and J. H. Atkinson
1966   *Historic Arkansas.* Little Rock: Arkansas History Commission.

Fisk, H. N.
1944   Geological Investigation of the Alluvial Valley of the Lower Mississippi River. *U.S. Army Corps of Engineers, Mississippi River Commission, Publication* No. 52. Vicksburg, Mississippi.

Flint, T.
1833   *The History and Geography of the Mississippi Valley, to which is Appended a Condensed Physical Geography of the Atlantic United States and the Whole American Continent.* 3d ed. 2 vols. Cincinnati, Ohio: E. H. Flint.

Flyr, D.
1966   The Contemporary Vegetation of the Amistad Reservoir Area. In A Preliminary Study of the Paleoecology of the Amistad Reservoir Area, assembled by Dee Ann Story and Vaughn M. Bryant, Jr. Final Report of Research under the Auspices of the National Science Foundation. Pp. 33–60. Mimeograph.

Fowler, M. L.
1969   The Cahokia Site. In Explorations into Cahokia Archaeology, edited by M. L. Fowler. *Illinois Archaeological Survey Bulletin* No. 7. Pp. 1–30.

Ford, J. A.
1961   Menard Site: The Quapaw Village of Osotouy on the Arkansas River. *American Museum of Natural History Anthropological Papers* **48**: Part 2.

Ford, J. L., and M. A. Rolingson
1972   Site Destruction due to Agricultural Practices in Southeast Arkansas. In Site Destruction due to Agricultural Practices in Southeast Arkansas and in Northeast Arkansas, edited by Janet L. Ford, Martha A. Rolingson, and Larry D. Medford. *Arkansas Archeological Survey, Research Series* No. 3. Pp. 1–40. Fayetteville.

Frankenfield, H. C.
1923   The Spring Floods of 1922. *U.S. Department of Agriculture, Weather Bureau, Monthly Weather Review*, Supplement No. 22. Washington, D.C.

Frison, G. C.
1973   Early Period Marginal Cultural Groups in Northern Wyoming. *Plains Anthropologist* **18**:300–312.
1974   *The Casper Site: A Hell Gap Bison Kill on the High Plains.* New York: Academic Press.
n.d.   The Lookingbill Site: A High Altitude Paleo-Indian and Altithermal Period Site in Wyoming. Manuscript on file at the Department of Anthropology, University of Wyoming, Laramie.

Frison, G. C., M. Wilson, and D. Wilson
In press   Fossil Bison and Artifacts from an Early Altithermal Period Arroyo Trap in Wyoming. *American Antiquity* **41.**

Gebhard, D.
1960   Prehistoric Painting of the Diablo Region: A Preliminary Report. *Roswell Museum and Art Center, Publications in Art and Science* No. 3.

Gregory, H. F., Jr.
1969   Plaquemine Period Sites in the Catahoula Basin: A Cultural Microcosm in East Central Louisiana. *Louisiana Studies* **8**:111–134.

Griffin, J. B.
  1944   The Iroquois in American Prehistory. *Papers of the Michigan Academy of Science, Arts and Letters* **34.**
  1946   Cultural Change and Continuity in Eastern United States Archaeology. In Man in Northeastern North America, edited by F. Johnson. *Papers of the Robert S. Peabody Foundation for Archaeology* **13.** Andover, Massachusetts.
  1952   *Archeology of Eastern United States,* edited by J. B. Griffin. Chicago: University of Chicago Press.
  1967   Eastern North American Archaeology: A Summary. *Science* **156:**175–191.
Griffin, J. B., and A. Spaulding
  1952   The Central Mississippi Valley Archaeological Survey, Season 1950. *Prehistoric Pottery of the Eastern United States* **2:**1–7.
Guthe, A. E.
  1955   The Hummel Site (Can 23-3). *Museum Service* (Bulletin of the Rochester Museum of Arts and Sciences).
  1958   The Late Prehistoric Occupations in Southwestern New York: An Interpretive Analysis. *New York State Archaeological Association* **14**(1). Rochester.
Hally, D. J.
  1966   Post-Coles Creek Cultural Development in the Upper Tensas Basin in Louisiana. *Proceedings of the 23d Southeastern Archaeological Conference, Bulletin* No. 6. Pp. 36–40. Morgantown.
  1972   The Development of Mississippian Culture in the Upper Tensas Basin of Louisiana. Paper presented at the Society for American Archaeology meetings, Miami, Florida, May 5.
Harrington, M. R.
  1922   A Mid-Colonial Seneca Site in Erie County. In The Archaeological History of New York, edited by A. C. Parker. *New York State Museum* Nos. 235–236. Albany.
Hayes, C. F.
  1962   Another Prehistoric Iroquois Site in the Bristol Hills, New York. *Museum Service* (Bulletin of the Rochester Museum of Arts and Sciences).
  1963a The Excavation of Two Iroquois Structures. *Museum Service* (Bulletin of the Rochester Museum of Arts and Sciences).
  1963b Prehistoric Iroquois Studies in the Bristol Hills, New York: A Summary. *Pennsylvania Archaeologist* **33.**
Haynes, C. V.
  1970   Geochronology, Man-Mammoth Sites and Their Bearing on the Origin of the Llano Complex. In Pleistocene and Recent Environments of the Central Great Plains, edited by Wakefield Dort, Jr. and J. Knox Jones, Jr. *Department of Geology, University of Kansas, Special Publication* No. 3.
Haynes, C. V., Jr., P. E. Damon, and D. C. Grey
  1966   Arizona Radiocarbon Dates VI. *Radiocarbon* **8:**1–21.
Healan, D. M.
  1972   Surface Delineation of Functional Areas at a Mississippian Ceremonial Center. *Memoir of the Missouri Archaeological Society* **10.**
Heidenreich, C. E.
  1971   *Huronia—A History and Geography of the Huron Indians, 1600–1650.* McClelland and Stewart.
Heidenreich, C. E., *et al.*
  1968   Maurice and Robitaille Sites: Environmental Analysis. In Paleoecology and Ontario Prehistory, edited by W. Hurley and C. E. Heidenreich. *Department of Anthropology, University of Toronto, Research Report* No. 1. Pp. 112–154.

Heidenreich, C. E., and V. A. Konrad
   1973   Soil Analysis at the Robitaille Site—Part II: A Method Useful in Determining the Location of Longhouse Patterns. *Ontario Archaeology* **20**:33–62.
Heidenreich, C. E., and S. Navratil
   1973   Soil Analysis at the Robitaille Site—Part I: Determining the Perimeter of the Village. *Ontario Archaeology* **20**:25–32.
Herskovits, M. J.
   1948   *Man and His Works.* New York: Alfred A. Knopf.
Hesey, H. W., and P. J. Witmer
   1964   The Shenk's Ferry People, A Site and Some Generalities. *Pennsylvania Archaeologist* **34**.
Hoebel, E. A.
   1972   *Anthropology: The Study of Man.* 4th ed. New York: McGraw-Hill.
Houck, L.
   1908   *A History of Missouri.* Vol. 1. Chicago: R. R. Donnelley.
Howard, J. H.
   1968   The Southeastern Ceremonial Complex and Its Interpretation. *Memoir of the Missouri Archaeological Society* **6**.
Husted, W. M.
   1969   Bighorn Canyon Archeology. *Smithsonian Institution, River Basin Surveys Publications* No. 12.
Husted, W. M., and R. Edgar
   n.d.   The Archeology of Mummy Cave, Wyoming: An Introduction to Shoshonean Prehistory. Manuscript on file at the Department of Anthropology, University of Wyoming, Laramie.
Irwin-Williams, C., H. Irwin, G. Agogino, and C. V. Haynes
   1973   Hell Gap: Paleo-Indian Occupation on the High Plains. *Plains Anthropologist* **18**:40–53.
Jennings, J. D., and E. Norbeck (Editors)
   1964   *Prehistoric Man in the New World.* Chicago: University of Chicago Press.
Jepsen, G. L.
   1953   Ancient Buffalo Hunters of Northwestern Wyoming. *Southwestern Lore* **19**:19–25.
Johnson, L., Jr.
   1964   The Devil's Mouth Site: A Stratified Campsite at Amistad Reservoir, Val Verde County, Texas. *Archeology Series* No. 6. Austin: University of Texas, Department of Anthropology.
Kinsey, W. F.
   1960   Additional Notes on the Albert Ibaugh Site. *Pennsylvania Archaeologist* **30**.
Kirkland, F., and W. W. Newcomb Jr.
   1967   *The Rock Art of Texas Indians.* Austin: University of Texas Press.
Kivett, M. F.
   1962   The Logan Creek Complex. Paper presented at the 20th Plains Anthropological Conference, Lincoln, Nebraska.
LaMarche, V. C., Jr.
   1974   Paleoclimatic Inferences from Long Tree-Ring Records. *Science* **183**:1043–1048.
Lamb, H. H.
   1966   On the Nature of Certain Climatic Epochs which Differed from the Modern (1900–1939) Normal. In *The Changing Climate, Selected Papers.* London: Methuen. Pp. 58–112.

Larson, L. H., Jr.
  1971 Archaeological Implications of Social Stratification at the Etowah Site, Georgia. In Approaches to the Social Dimensions of Mortuary Practices, edited by J. A. Brown. *Memoirs of the Society for American Archaeology* **25:**58–67.

Lee, T. E.
  1950 A Preliminary Report on an Archaeological Survey of Southwestern Ontario in 1950. *National Museum of Canada Bulletin* No. 126.

Lemley, H. J., and S. D. Dickinson
  1937 Archaeological Investigations on Bayou Macon in Arkansas. *Bulletin of the Texas Archeological and Paleontological Society* **9:**11–47. (Reprinted in *Arkansas Archeologist* **5:**21–39 (1964).

Lenig, D.
  1965 The Oak Hill Horizon and Its Relation to the Development of Five Nation Iroquois Culture. *New York State Archaeological Association, Research Transactions* **15.** Albany.

Lewis, R. B.
  1972 Land Leveling Salvage Archaeology in Portions of Stoddard and Scott Counties, Missouri: 1969. Unpublished report submitted to the National Park Service.
  1973 Mississippian Period Settlement Locations and Subsistence in Southeast Missouri: 1969. Unpublished report submitted to the National Park Service.

Lischka, J. J.
  1973 Preliminary Report on Test Excavations of Prehistoric Sites in the Felsenthal National Wildlife Refuge, 1972. Manuscript on file at the Arkansas Archeological Survey, Fayetteville.

MacNeish, R. S.
  1952a Iroquois Pottery Types. *National Museum of Canada Bulletin* No. 124.
  1952b The Archeology of the Northeastern United States. In *Archeology of Eastern United States*, edited by J. B. Griffin. Chicago: University of Chicago Press. Pp. 46–58.
  1958 Preliminary Archaeological Investigations in the Sierra de Tamaulipas. *Transactions of the American Philosophical Society* **48,** Pt. 6.

Marshall, R. A.
  1965 An Archaeological Investigation of Interstate Route 55 through New Madrid and Pemiscot Counties, Missouri, 1964. *Highway Archaeology Report* **1.**

McDonald, L. L.
  1974 Opal Phytoliths as Indicators of Plant Succession in North-central Wyoming. Master's thesis, University of Wyoming, Laramie.

McGimsey, C. R.
  1964 A Report on the Quapaw in Arkansas Immediately Prior to the Treaty of 1818. Manuscript on file at the University of Arkansas Museum, Fayetteville.

Moore, C. B.
  1908 Certain Mounds of Arkansas and of Mississippi. Part I: Mounds and Cemeteries of the Lower Arkansas River. *Journal of the Academy of Natural Sciences of Philadelphia* **13:**479–605.
  1909 Antiquities of the Ouachita Valley. *Journal of the Academy of Natural Sciences of Philadelphia* **14:**7–170.
  1911 Some Aboriginal Sites on Mississippi River. *Journal of the Academy of Natural Sciences of Philadelphia* **14,** Part 3: 365–480.

Moore, D. M.
  1960 *Trees of Arkansas.* Rev. ed. Little Rock: Arkansas Forestry Commission.

Newcomb, W. W., Jr.
  1961 *The Indians of Texas from Prehistoric to Modern Times.* Austin: University of Texas Press.
Nimmo, B. W.
  1971 Population Dynamics of a Wyoming Pronghorn Cohort from the Eden-Farson Site, 48 SW 304. *Plains Anthropologist* **16**:285–288.
Noble, W. C.
  1968 Iroquois Archaeology and the Development of Iroquois Social Organization. Ph.D. dissertation, University of Calgary.
  1975a Van Besien (AfHd-2): A Study in Glen Meyer Development. *Ontario Archaeology* No. 24.
  1975b Corn and the Development of Village Life in Southern Ontario. *Ontario Archaeology* No. 25.
  1975c The Neutral Indians. *Grimsby Historical Society Centennial Volume.* Toronto.
Noble, W. C., and I. I. Kenyon
  1972 A Probable Glen Meyer Village in Brant County Ontario. *Ontario Archaeology* No. 19.
Orr, K. G.
  1952 Survey of Caddoan Area Archeology. In *Archeology of Eastern United States,* edited by James B. Griffin. Chicago: University of Chicago Press. Pp. 239–255.
Parker, A. C.
  1907 Excavations in an Erie Village and Burial Site at Ripley, Chautaugua County, New York. *New York State Museum Bulletin* No. 117.
Parsons, M. L.
  1967 Notes on the Texas Memorial Museum Pictograph Survey. Unpublished notes on file at the Texas Memorial Museum, Austin, Texas.
  n.d. Painted Pebbles: A Stylistic and Chronological Analysis. Mimeographed report on file at the Texas Memorial Museum, Austin, Texas.
Patterson, J. L.
  1971 Floods in Arkansas, Magnitude and Frequency Characteristics through 1968. *Arkansas Geological Commission, Water Resources Circular* No. 11. Little Rock.
Peebles, C. S.
  1971 Moundville and Surrounding Sites: Some Structural Considerations of Mortuary Practices II. In Approaches to the Social Dimensions of Mortuary Practices, edited by J. A. Brown. *Memoirs of the Society for American Archaeology* **25**:68–91.
Pendergast, J. F.
  1962 The Crystal Rock Site: An Early Onondaga-Oneida Site in Eastern Ontario. *Pennsylvania Archaeologist.*
  1965 Three Prehistoric Iroquois Components in Eastern Ontario. *National Museum of Canada Bulletin* No. 208.
  1966 The Berry Site. Contributions to Anthropology 1963–1964. *National Museum of Canada Bulletin* No. 206.
  n.d. An *In-Situ* Hypothesis to Explain the Origin of the St. Lawrence Iroquoians. Mimeographed report.
Pendergast, J. F., and J. Trigger
  1972 *Cartier's Hochelaga and the Dawson Site.* McGill: Queen's University Press.
Phillips, P.
  1970 Archaeological Survey in the Lower Yazoo Basin, Mississippi, 1949–1955. *Papers of the Peabody Museum of Archaeology and Ethnology* No. 60. Cambridge, Massachusetts.

Phillips, P., J. A. Ford, and J. B. Griffin
  1951 Archaeological Survey in the Lower Mississippi Alluvial Valley, 1940–1947. *Papers of the Peabody Museum of American Archaeology and Ethnology* No. 25. Cambridge, Massachusetts.

Porter, J. W.
  1969 The Mitchell Site and Prehistoric Exchange Systems at Cahokia: A.D. 1000 ± 300. In Explorations into Cahokia Archaeology, edited by M. L. Fowler. *Illinois Archaeological Survey Bulletin* 7:137–164.

Potter, W. B.
  1880 *Archaeological Remains in Southeastern Missouri. Contributions to the Archaeology of Missouri by the Archaeological Section of the St. Louis Academy of Science. Part I. Pottery.* Salem: George A. Bates.

Pratt, P. P.
  1961 The Bigford Site: Late Prehistoric Oneida. *Pennsylvania Archaeologist* **30.**
  1963 A Heavily Stockaded Late Prehistoric Oneida Iroquois Settlement. *Pennsylvania Archaeologist* **33.**

Price, J. E.
  1973 Settlement Planning and Artifact Distribution on the Snodgrass Site, and Their Socio-Political Implications in the Powers Phase of Southeast Missouri. Ph.D. dissertation, University of Michigan, Ann Arbor.

Putnam, F. W.
  1875 Additions to the Museum, 1874. *Annual Report of the Trustees of the Peabody Museum of American Archaeology and Ethnology* 8:14–55.

Quimby, G. I.
  1951 The Medora Site, West Baton Rouge Parish, Louisiana. *Field Museum of Natural History, Anthropological Series* **24.**

Raun, G. G.
  1966 Vertebrate Paleofauna of Amistad Reservoir. In A Preliminary Study of the Paleoecology of the Amistad Reservoir Area, assembled by Dee Ann Story and Vaughn M. Bryant, Jr. Final Report of Research under the Auspices of the National Science Foundation. Pp. 209–220. Mimeograph.

Redfield, A.
  n.d. The Dalton Project. Manuscript on file at the Peabody Museum, Harvard University, Cambridge; Arkansas Archeological Survey, Fayetteville; University of Missouri, Columbia; and American Museum of Natural History, New York.

Reed, N. A.
  1969 Monks and Other Mississippian Mounds. In Explorations into Cahokia Archaeology, edited by M. L. Fowler. *Illinois Archaeological Survey Bulletin* 7:31–42.

Reher, C. A.
  1974 Population Study of the Casper Site Bison in the Casper Site. In *A Hell Gap Bison Kill on the High Plains,* edited by George C. Frison. New York: Academic Press.

Ridley, F.
  1952a The Huron and Lalonde Occupations of Ontario. *American Antiquity* **17.**
  1952b The Fallis Site, Ontario. *American Antiquity* **18.**

Ritchie, W. A.
  1952 The Chance Horizon, an Early Stage of Mohawk Cultural Development. *New York State Museum Circular* No. 29.
  1969 *The Archaeology of New York State.* Garden City, New York: Natural History Press.

Ritchie, W. A., and R. E. Funk.
　1973　Aboriginal Settlement Patterns in the Northeast. *New York State Museum and Science Service Memoir* No. 20. Albany.

Ritchie, W. A., D. Lening, and P. S. Miller
　1953　An Early Owasco Sequence in Eastern New York. *New York State Museum Circular* No. 32.

Ritchie, W. A., and R. S. MacNeish
　1949　The Pre-Iroquoian Pottery of New York State. *American Antiquity* **15.**

Rolingson, M. A.
　1971　The Ashley Point. *The Arkansas Archeologist* **12:**50–52.
　1972　Report on the Preliminary Site Survey of the Felsenthal National Wildlife Refuge, 1971. Manuscript on file at the Arkansas Archeological Survey, Fayetteville.
　n.d.　The Bayou Bartholomew Project. Manuscript in preparation.

Ross, R. E.
　1965　The Archaeology of Eagle Cave. *Papers of the Texas Archeological Salvage Project* No. 7.

Saucier, R. T.
　1967　Geological Investigation of the Boeuf-Tensas Basin, Lower Mississippi Valley. *U. S. Army Corps of Engineers, Waterways Experiment Station, Technical Report* No. 3-757.
　1968　A New Chronology for Braided Stream Surface Formation in the Lower Mississippi Valley. *Southeastern Geology* **9:**65–76.
　1974　Quarternary Geology of the Lower Mississippi Valley. *Arkansas Archeological Survey, Research Series* No. 6.

Saucier, R. T., and A. R. Fleetwood
　1970　Origin and Chronologic Significance of Late Quaternary Terraces, Ouachita River, Arkansas and Louisiana. *Geological Society of America Bulletin* **81:**869–890.

Saxe, A. A.
　1971　Social Dimensions of Mortuary Practices in a Mesolithic Population from Wadi Halfa, Sudan. In Approaches to the Social Dimensions of Mortuary Practices, edited by J. A. Brown. *Memoirs of the Society for American Archeology* **25:**39–47.

Schock, J. M.
　1972　Southwestern New York: The Chautauqua Culture and Other Late Woodland Occupations. Paper presented at the 1972 Central States Anthropological Society Symposium, "Late Prehistory in the Lake Erie Drainage Basin."
　1974　The Chautauqua Phase and Other Late Woodland Sites in Southwestern New York. Ph.D. dissertation, SUNY–Buffalo.

Shelford, V. E.
　1963　*The Ecology of North America.* Urbana: University of Illinois Press.

Story, D. A.
　1966　Archeological background. In A Preliminary Study of the Paleoecology of the Amistad Reservoir Area, assembled by Dee Ann Story and Vaughn M. Bryant, Jr. Final Report of Research under the Auspices of the National Science Foundation. Pp. 7–30. Mimeograph.

Story, D. A., and V. Bryant, Jr.
　1966　A Preliminary Study of the Paleoecology of the Amistad Reservoir Area. Final Report of Research under the Auspices of the National Science Foundation. Mimeograph.

Stothers, D. M.
　1973　The Princess Point Complex. Paper presented at the 1972 Central States

Anthropological Society Symposium, "Late Prehistory in the Lake Erie Drainage Basin."

Stothers, M. W.
1970 The Princess Point Complex. *Archaeological Notes, D. A. S. Monthly Newsletter* No. 70.

Suhm, D. A., and E. B. Jelks.
1962 Handbook of Texas Archeology: Type Descriptions. *Texas Archeological Society Special Publication* No. 1.

Suhm, D. A., and A. D. Krieger
1954 An Introductory Handbook of Texas Archeology. *Bulletin of the Texas Archeological Society* **25.**

Swanton, J. R.
1911 Indian Tribes of the Lower Mississippi Valley and Adjacent Coast of the Gulf of Mexico. *Bureau of American Ethnology, Bulletin* **43.**
1928 Aboriginal Culture of the Southeast. *42nd Annual Report of the Bureau of American Ethnology.* Pp. 673–726.
1939 Final Report of the United States De Soto Expedition Commission. *House Document* No. 71. U.S. Government Printing Office, Washington, D.C.
1952 The Indian Tribes of North America. *Bureau of American Ethnology, Bulletin* **145.** Washington, D.C.

Thomas, C.
1894 Report on Mound Explorations of the Bureau of Ethnology. *Twelfth Annual Report of the Bureau of Ethnology, 1890–1891.* Washington, D.C.: U.S. Government Printing Office.

Thwaites, R. G. (Editor)
1905 Nuttall's Travels into the Arkansas Territory, 1819. In *Early Western Travels, 1748–1846.* Vol. 13. Cleveland: Arthur H. Clark.

Trigger, B. G.
1968 The Determinants of Settlement Patterns. In *Settlement Archaeology*, edited by K. C. Chang. Palo Alto, California: National Press Books. Pp. 53–78.

Tuck, J. A.
1970 Iroquois Cultural Development in Central New York. Ph.D. dissertation, University of Syracuse.
1971 *Onondaga Iroquois Prehistory—A Study in Settlement Archaeology.* Syracuse: Syracuse University Press.

U.S. Army Corps of Engineers
1966 Bayou Bartholomew and Tributaries, Arkansas and Louisiana. Report referred to the Committee on Public Works. *House Document* No. 506. Washington, D.C.: U.S. Government Printing Office.

Walker, D. N.
1975 A Cultural and Ecological Analysis of the Vertebrate Fauna from the Medicine Lodge Creek Site (48 Bh 4990). Master's thesis, University of Wyoming, Laramie.

Walker, W. M., and R. M. Adams
1946 Excavations in the Matthews Site, New Madrid County, Missouri. *Transactions of the St. Louis Academy of Science* **31:**71–120.

Weber, J. C.
1973 The Pawpaw Site (3 Ou 22): A Report on Excavations in Area Four. Manuscript on file at the Arkansas Archeological Survey, Fayetteville.

Wedel, W. R., W. M. Husted, and J. H. Moss
1968 Mummy Cave: Prehistoric Record from Rocky Mountains of Wyoming. *Science* **160:**184–186.

Whallon, R.
1968   Investigations of Late Prehistoric Social Organization in New York State. In *New Perspectives in Archeology*, edited by S. R. Binford and L. R. Binford. Chicago: Aldine Press.
1972   A New Approach to Pottery Typology. *American Antiquity* **37**:13–33.

White, M. E.
1961   Iroquois Culture History in the Niagara Frontier Area of New York State. *Museum of Anthropology, University of Michigan Anthropological Papers* No. 16.
1967   An Early Historic Niagara Frontier Cemetery in Erie County, New York. *New York State Archaeological Association* **16.**
1972a   On Delineating the Neutral Iroquois of the Eastern Niagara Peninsula of Ontario. *Ontario Archaeology* No. 17:62–74.
1972b   Late Woodland Archaeology in the Niagara Frontier of New York and Ontario. Paper presented at the 1972 Central States Anthropological Society Symposium, "Late Prehistory in the Lake Erie Drainage Basin."
1973   Prehistoric Iroquois Population Shifts. Paper presented at the 1973 Annual Meeting of the New York State Archaeological Association.

Willey, G. R.
1966   *An Introduction to American Archaeology.* Vol. 1. *North and Middle America.* Englewood Cliffs, New Jersey: Prentice-Hall.

Willey, G. R., and P. Phillips.
1958   *Method and Theory in American Archaeology.* Chicago: University of Chicago Press.

Williams, J. R.
1964   A Study of Fortified Indian Villages in Southeast Missouri. Master's thesis, University of Missouri, Columbia.
1967   Land Leveling Salvage Archaeological Work in Southeast Missouri: 1966. Unpublished report submitted to the National Park Service.
1968   Southeast Missouri Land Leveling Salvage Archaeology: 1967. Unpublished report submitted to the National Park Service.
1972   Land Leveling Salvage Archaeology in Missouri: 1968. Unpublished report submitted to the National Park Service.

Williams, S.
1954   An Archaeological Study of the Mississippian Culture in Southeast Missouri. Ph.D. dissertation, Yale University.
1964   The Aboriginal Location of the Kadohadacho and Related Tribes. In *Explorations in Cultural Anthropology*, edited by Ward H. Goodenough. New York: McGraw-Hill. Pp. 545–570.
1966   Interim Statement on Upper Tensas Basin Research, 1963–1964. Mimeographed paper on file at the Peabody Museum, Harvard University, Cambridge, Massachusetts.

Wintemberg, W. J.
1928   Uren Prehistoric Village Site, Oxford County, Ontario. *National Museum of Canada Bulletin* **51.**
1936   The Roebuck Prehistoric Village Site, Grenville County, Ontario. *National Museum of Canada Bulletin* **83.**
1939   Lawson Prehistoric Village Site, Middlesex County, Ontario. *National Museum of Canada Bulletin* **94.**
1946   The Sidey-Mackay Site. *American Antiquity* **11.**
1948   The Middleport Prehistoric Village Site. *National Museum of Canada Bulletin* **109.**

Witthoft, J.
 1959 Ancestry of the Susquehannocks. In *Susquehannock Miscellany*, edited by J. Witthoft and W. F. Kinsey. Harrisburg: Pennsylvania Historical and Museum Commission.

Witthoft, J., and W. F. Kinsey
 1959 A Susquehannock Cemetery: The Ibaugh Site. In *Susquehannock Miscellany*, edited by J. Witthoft and W. F. Kinsey. Harrisburg: Pennsylvania Historical and Museum Commission.

Wittry, W. L.
 1969 The American Woodhenge. In Explorations into Cahokia Archaeology, edited by M. L. Fowler. *Illinois Archaeological Survey Bulletin* **7**:43–48.

Wray, C. F.
 1973 Manual for Seneca Iroquois Archaeology, Cultures Primitive. Rochester.

Wray, C. F., and H. L. Schoff
 1953 A Preliminary Report on the Seneca Sequence in Western New York, 1550–1687. *Pennsylvania Archaeologist* **23**.

Wright, J. V.
 1960 The Middleport Horizon. *Anthropologia* **2**.
 1966 The Ontario Iroquois Tradition. *National Museum of Canada Bulletin* **210**.
 1972 Ontario Prehistory. National Museum of Man, National Museums of Canada.

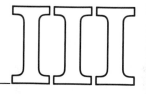

Patterns of
Mesoamerican
Urbanism

10

Evolution of the
Public Building
in Formative Oaxaca*

Kent V. Flannery   Joyce Marcus

Preface

This essay is submitted in honor of James B. Griffin, who has been, to
use his own salty and original phrase, "the best damn boss we ever
had." Knowing that Mesoamerica was one of his early loves, we have
chosen that area. Knowing his dislike for papers that are mostly
"horsefeathers," we have written this chapter with an emphasis on
data. And finally, knowing his long-term interest in cultural evolution,
we have framed our data in those terms.

Introduction

One of the most fascinating periods of Mesoamerican prehistory is
that between 2000 B.C. and A.D. 1. These two millennia saw the

* Our research in the Valley of Oaxaca was supported by National Science Foundation
grants GS-42568, GS-2121, and GS-1616. Permission was granted by the Instituto
Nacional de Antropología e Historia, Mexico. We are grateful to both these institutions, as well as the Centro Regional de Oaxaca and its director, Manuel Esparza.

establishment of village life, the origins of social ranking, and the rise of the state. It was a time of great sociopolitical change, with important clues to this change provided by the evolution of public architecture during the period. For public buildings indirectly reflect sociopolitical institutions, and, as these institutions evolved, they were reflected in the architecture of their times.

The Valley of Oaxaca, lying at an elevation of 1550 m in the southern highlands of Mexico, has proved a particularly favorable locale in which to study this evolution archaeologically. The semiarid environment of Oaxaca fosters the preservation of clay floors, adobe walls, postmolds, stucco, mortar, and other architectural features. In addition, the prehistoric Zapotec Indians of that region seem to have been precocious architects. For example, the Valley of Oaxaca has provided some of Mesoamerica's oldest specimens of formal architecture and some of its earliest examples of lime plaster, adobe brick, and stonemasonry.

It will come as no surprise that public architecture was rare to absent at the start of the period under consideration. This was a time of seminomadic hunting-and-gathering bands, and such bands rarely perform communal activities that require the maintenance of permanent public buildings. Most frequently, they engage in unscheduled, time-independent communal rituals which occur when favorable environmental conditions permit larger-than-usual groups to reside together for longer-than-usual periods. These ad hoc ceremonies (initiation, dances or other ritual activity, athletic competition) may be contrasted with the scheduled, time-dependent, or "calendric," rituals of sedentary agricultural villages (Flannery 1972). Among village farmers in Mesoamerica, where harvests occur at predictable times of the year, there were communal activities that followed agricultural, religious, or political calendars with marked temporal regularity, and whose performance took place in permanently maintained buildings. Carved monuments indicate that the typical Mesoamerican 260-day ritual calendar (the numbers 1 to 13 were combined with 20 day names; the 261st day would then be the same as the first day of the cycle) was in use in Oaxaca by at least 500 B.C. (Marcus, in press a). Finally, it is also no surprise that, by A.D. 1, there were many different kinds of public buildings in use—reflecting a rich variety of public institutions with ceremonies underwritten by the Zapotec state, whose capital was the mountaintop city of Monte Albán (Bernal 1965).

"Public Space" in the Preceramic Era

To set the stage for the origins of public architecture in Mesoamerica, we must go back to the preceramic hunting-and-gathering era, some 5000 years before Christ. As of this writing, no formal architecture, public or otherwise, is known from this remote epoch. However, there are features in open-air preceramic sites that suggest that, even at that period, some space was set aside for ritual or communal activity.

The site of Gheo-Shih, an open-air camp on the north bank of the Rio Mitla in the Valley of Oaxaca, lies on a fan of indurated sand alluvium that was evidently occupied between 5000 and 4000 B.C. Gheo-Shih covers about 1.5 ha (hectares), qualifying as a "macroband camp" in MacNeish's (1964) settlement typology. Because it lies in a zone of mesquite thickets, which bear pods in July and August, we assume it was occupied during the rainy season. Gheo-Shih well may be the seasonal encampment of the entire local group of hunters or incipient cultivators occupying the Mitla region. Although no actual huts could be defined, excavator Frank Hole found many circular or oval concentrations of artifacts which may reflect small shelters of some kind (Flannery *et al.* 1970: 22–24).

The most interesting feature at Gheo-Shih, however, consisted of two parallel lines of boulders running northwest–southeast for about 20 m. The space between them, which was 7 m wide, had been swept clean and contained virtually no artifacts. To either side of the cleared area, however, artifacts were abundant. The boulder lines ended without turning a corner, at which point tool scatters began again (Figure 10.1).

Although the function of this cleared and boulder-lined area is unknown, similar features are known from the camps of ethnographically documented hunters and gatherers. Many band-level societies of the Great Basin cleared "dance grounds" for use at their larger encampments. In one of the most impressive examples from the literature, the !Kung Bushman of the Kalahari clear a "dance path" a quarter of a mile long, which leads from their camp to a circular area where young boys are initiated (cf. Fraser 1968: Figure 16).

Whatever the function of this feature at Gheo-Shih, two observations can be made. First, it can be assumed from its placement in the heart of the camp that whatever activity was performed there was observed by all members of the local group; it could not have been used for "secret" rites in the manner of a kiva, for example. Second, this kind of impermanent feature is likely to be used for ad hoc ritual, requiring no long-term maintenance or architectural skill.

"Public Space" at 1500 B.C.

Because of the vagaries of the archaeological record, we cannot trace the activities of the occupants of the Valley of Oaxaca between

Figure 10.1 Gheo-Shih, Oaxaca. Crossing the photo from left to right are parallel lines of boulders outlining a cleared area of some 20 by 7 m in the preceramic campsite. Estimated date: 5000–4000 B.C.

2800 and 1600 B.C. We pick up the sequence again during a period of early, undecorated monochrome pottery which is probably the Oaxacan equivalent of the Purrón complex (cf. MacNeish, Peterson, and Flannery 1970: Chapter 2). The only open-air site known to have been occupied at that time is San José Mogote, some 10 km north of the city of Oaxaca and the ruins of Monte Albán. The presence of at least one house constructed of wooden posts with cane wattle, clay daub, and a layer of whitewash suggests that San José Mogote was already a permanent hamlet by around 1600 B.C.

No public architecture so far has been recovered from this early village period. At the transition from this Oaxacan variant of the Purrón phase to the subsequent Tierras Largas phase, our next evidence appears. Since we have no associated radiocarbon dates, we can only estimate this transition at around 1500 B.C. The evidence, vaguely reminiscent of the cleared area at Gheo-Shih, consists of an open area (perhaps 7 m wide from west to east), set apart from the residential areas of the hamlet by a double line of staggered posts (Figure 10.2, left). In some places, this double line of posts was reinforced by a row of heavy stone slabs set on edge (Figure 10.2, right). The orientation of this enclosure, which contained no architec-

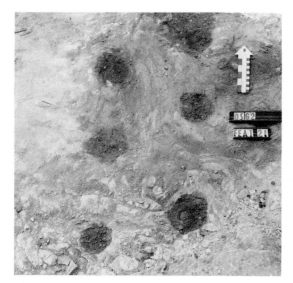 

Figure 10.2 San José Mogote, Oaxaca: archaeological evidence of a cleared area, set off from the residences by means of a double line of staggered posts. Left, Feature 21, a series of postmolds from the west side of the cleared area. Right, Feature 66, a series of postmolds accompanied by heavy stone slabs along the east side of the cleared area. Estimated date: 1500 B.C.

ture and was nearly free of artifacts, was slightly west of true north—perhaps our first example of an orientation that was to characterize later Oaxacan public buildings for the next 1000 years.

Public Buildings of the Tierras Largas Phase

Our first actual public buildings appear in the early part of the Tierras Largas phase, and date to approximately 1500–1300 B.C. By this period, San José Mogote was a hamlet covering at least 1.5–2.0 ha on the tip of a low piedmont spur overlooking the Atoyac River. In the western part of this hamlet, an area of at least 15 by 18 m had been set aside for the construction of public buildings; no ordinary residences were found in this area.

We have evidence for only one type of public building in the early Tierras Largas phase. At least eight examples of that type occurred at San José Mogote; however, we do not believe that there would ever have been more than one in use at any one moment. Rather, the eight examples seem to represent a chronological series of structures built, repaired, replastered, renovated, and eventually abandoned in favor of a new structure, on virtually the same spot for hundreds of years. In

some cases, the new building was set directly over its predecessor and
given a plan so similar that the corners and other internal features
virtually overlapped.

Each of these structures was a rectangular, one-room building
whose walls had a core of upright pine posts. In some cases, the posts
were set 85–90 cm apart; in others, they might be only 20–30 cm apart.
Structure 6, our most complete example, was roughly 4.4. by 5.4. m in
extent (Figure 10.3). This structure would have required at least 20
posts, and some may have needed as many as 40.

The posts frequently were set 30 cm into bedrock. A platform of
crushed volcanic tuff, clay, lime, and sand was then built up to level
and support the floor. Bundles of canes were lashed into the spaces
between the posts, and clay (reinforced with sand and crushed tuff)
was daubed over the walls. Both floor and walls then were coated with
pure white lime stucco and smoothed; in places, as many as four
replasterings were visible. Where preservation was good, the lower 40

Figure 10.3 Remains of Structure 6 at San José Mogote, an early Tierras Largas phase
public building. In the center is a storage pit that contained powdered lime for making
stucco; to the left of the pit is the base of a probable altar. Workmen are shown
constructing a protective stone wall outside the area of the pre-Columbian building.
Date: 1350 B.C.

cm of the wall appeared to have been expanded into a low bench which ran around the inside of the room.

Two features occurred in these buildings with stereotyped regularity. Set against the south wall was a low rectangular platform, possibly a step, but more likely an altar of some kind; the one in Structure 6 had been rebuilt three times. Directly north of this altar appeared a storage pit, incorporated into the original floor of the room and coated with the same white stucco. In three cases, these pits were filled with powdered lime of the very type used for the plastering and replastering of the room.

Stone Terraces, Stairways, and Carved Stones of the San José Phase

Buildings of the type just described were still made during the subsequent San José phase (1150–850 B.C.), though during this period, their stucco was more frequently yellow than white. They were soon joined, however, by public buildings of other types. Near the east edge of San José Mogote, a gentle slope that once had been covered with ordinary residences was converted into a series of stepped terraces, faced with stones set in hard puddled adobe clay. The westernmost terrace rose in two stages to a height of 3 m; the easternmost was lower, but had two small stairways made from stone slabs on its downhill face (Figure 10.4). This latter terrace, called Structure 2, had a facing of several tiers of heavy volcanic tuff boulders and limestone slabs. Below it were found two carved stones, Monuments 1 and 2, which originally may have been set in an upper tier of the terrace. Tentatively, Monument 1 seems to depict the head of a jaguar or other feline, while Monument 2 represents a raptorial bird. Dating between 1000 and 900 B.C., they are, for the moment, the oldest carved stones from the Valley of Oaxaca.

Adobe Platforms of the San José and Guadalupe Phases (1150–650 B.C.)

During the Early Formative San José phase, public buildings evolved in both size and diversity. While white-plastered wattle and daub remained in favor for the buildings themselves, now these structures often were set on platforms of stone and adobe and sometimes were equipped with stairways. The standard adobe of the period was round to oval in plan, and planoconvex, or "bun-shaped," in cross section.

Figure 10.4 Structure 2 at San José Mogote, a San José phase stonemasonry terrace with stairways. Workmen are removing overburden in the area where carved stones (Monuments 1 and 2) were discovered. Date: 1000–900 B.C.

Several stone-and-adobe platforms occurred at San José Mogote, the most fully investigated being Structure 8 (Figure 10.5). Dating to terminal San José or earliest Guadalupe times (900–800 B.C.), the building was oriented 8° west of north. The east side (which appeared to be the front) was a wall more than a meter wide, composed of several layers of undressed field stones. Running west from this were retaining walls of planoconvex adobes, which apparently represented the northern and southern limits of the structure. In places, the adobes were preserved to a height of four courses totaling 70 cm and capped with a thick floor of puddled adobe clay. The area between the retaining walls had been filled with hundreds of basketloads of earth. A few postholes were all that remained of the building that had once stood on the platform.

Dating to roughly the same time period was Platform 4 at Barrio del Rosario Huitzo, 25 km north of Oaxaca City. This was a structure 2 m high and more than 15 m wide, also oriented 8° west of north. The sloping outer wall was of boulders or cobbles set in puddled adobe clay, while the interior had earthen fill retained by high walls of planoconvex adobes. Here we recovered fragments of a massive burned building of wattle and daub (without stucco) and two heavy pine posts, one of which gave a radiocarbon date of 850 B.C.

Figure 10.5 South end of Structure 8 at San José Mogote, the platform for a public building of late San José or early Guadalupe times. Earthen fill was enclosed by a low stonemasonry wall (left, foreground) and strengthened by retaining walls of bun-shaped adobe brick (right, background). Date: 900–800 B.C.

By 700 B.C., the Guadalupe phase architects had truly mastered the use of planoconvex adobe. Stratigraphic Zone C at Huitzo produced Platform 3, perhaps one of the best examples of their work (Figure 10.6). This was a platform 1.3 m high and 11.5 m long east–west, built of earthen fill between adobe retaining walls, and covered with white stucco. Oriented 8° west of north, the structure had a stairway 7.6 m wide which faced north onto a white-stuccoed patio floor; each of the three steps in the stairway was built up over a double row of bun-shaped adobes. To the east and west, attached to Platform 3 by low benches perhaps a meter long, were remnants of what appeared to be other platforms, running north into an unexcavated area. Thus, Platform 3 may be the southernmost of a group of three or four public buildings grouped around a common courtyard, an extremely common feature of later Oaxacan sites.

Acropolis and Plaza in the Rosario Phase

Two of the architectural advances of the Rosario phase (650–500 B.C.) were rectangular adobe bricks and cut-stone facades. Two large

Figure 10.6 Work in progress on the surviving northern part of Platform 3 at Barrio del Rosario Huitzo, a Guadalupe phase public building. Bun-shaped adobes underlie the stairway and reinforce the earthen fill below the plastered, puddled adobe surface. Date: 700–600 B.C.

buildings of the terminal Rosario–early Monte Albán Ia phase were found at Huitzo, stratigraphically covering the Guadalupe phase structures already described. The oldest of these, Platform 2, was a massive earthen platform (more than 20 m long) with retaining walls of stone and rectangular adobe. An adult (apparently sacrificial) burial, oriented 8° west of north like the platform, occurred under one retaining wall.

By far the most impressive constructions of the Rosario phase, however, occurred atop Mound 1 at San José Mogote. Here the middle to late Rosario phase architects produced a veritable acropolis of monumental buildings around a common plaza that overlooks the rest of the site from a height of nearly 15 m; at least one of these buildings, Structure 19, was 20 m by 28 m and up to 2 m high. Structure 14, on the east side of the patio, rises in places to a height of over 3 m. Its outer facing is roughly cut limestone blocks, often weighing more than a ton, which had to be transported from quarries some 5 km away (Figure 10.7). A carved stone, Monument 3, served as the threshold for a corridor between Structures 14 and 19.

The Great Plaza at Monte Albán

The Rosario phase acropolis on Mound 1 at San José Mogote is our first example of a complex of Middle Formative public buildings removed from the heart of the village and raised to a new position some 15 m above. This acropolis would have been visible for many kilometers, yet the buildings themselves now may have been of more limited access to members of the community. This trend was developed still further by the founding, some time around 500 B.C., of Monte Albán on a mountaintop 400 m above the valley floor. Monte Albán was visible at even greater distances than Mound 1 at San José Mogote, yet removed still farther from the populace at large. Moreover, a recent ekistic or traffic flow analysis of Monte Albán conducted by Richard Blanton (personal communication) shows the great plaza at that site to be located in one of the areas of lowest accessibility, not served by any of the main pre-Columbian roads on the site.

We will mention only briefly the great plaza at Monte Albán, because it has been described well in previous publications (Acosta 1965; Bernal 1965; Paddock 1966). Although limited by the natural boundaries of the ridge on which it lies, the plaza itself is about 300 m north–south and 150 m east–west. The South Platform, at one end, apparently supported temples; the North Platform, at the other end, had a vast complex of residences and public buildings. Flanking the plaza on the east and west were buildings constructed over natural

Figure 10.7 Lower courses of Structure 14 at San José Mogote, a Rosario phase public building with outer walls of huge limestone blocks. Estimated date: 600 B.C.

rock outcrops; Buildings G, H, I, and J were on similar outcrops in the center of the plaza.

Unfortunately, due to Classic period overburden, it has never been clear how much of the great plaza belongs to the earliest, or Monte Albán I, phase (500–100 B.C.). Deeply buried structures in the North Platform and in the Building of the Danzantes on the southwest corner of the plaza date to this period. However, most authorities do not believe the outlines of the plaza were established until Monte Albán II. During the latter period, similar ceremonial plazas were also built at secondary centers like San José Mogote.

Functional Differentiation in the Terminal Formative: Palaces, Temples, and Ballcourts

During the Monte Albán II phase (100 B.C.–A.D. 100), corresponding to the Terminal Formative or Protoclassic period elsewhere in Mesoamerica, Oaxaca reached still another level of complexity. Perhaps the most striking aspect of this level was the appearance of a whole series of clearly recognizable and functionally distinct public buildings, for which a preliminary typology can be presented. This is also the first period for which an actual *palace* or royal residence can be recognized, as distinct from the multifamily apartment complexes occupied by other persons of high rank.

A. One important Monte Albán II type is a rectangular temple with a main chamber, vestibule, and columns to either side of the doorway (Figure 10.8). The best-preserved is the important temple discovered by Caso (1935) within Mound X, which lies northeast of the great plaza at Monte Albán. This structure, built atop a platform with a stairway on the south side, measures 10 by 8 m. The vestibule doorway, flanked by single columns on either side, measures just over 4 m. From here, one crosses 2 m of vestibule and steps up into the slightly elevated main chamber. The latter measures 8 by 3 m and has a 2-m doorway, once again flanked by single columns on either side. The walls of the temple are of rectangular adobe, over a stonemasonry

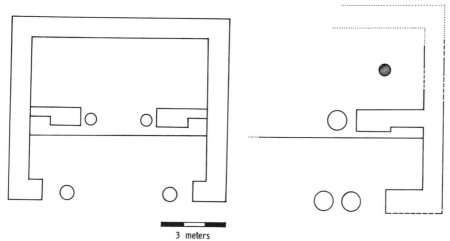

3 meters

Figure 10.8 Ground plans of rectangular, two-room temples of the Monte Albán II period. Left, the temple in Mound X at Monte Albán. Right, partial remains of Structure 13 at San José Mogote. The white circles are column bases; the small shaded circle is a plastered basin in the floor of Structure 13. Estimated date: 100 B.C.–A.D. 100.

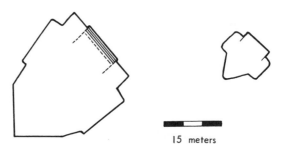

15 meters

Figure 10.9 Examples of arrowhead-shaped buildings of the Monte Albán II period. Left, Building J at Monte Albán. Right, building in Mound O at Caballito Blanco. Estimated date: 100 B.C.–A.D. 100. [Redrawn from Paddock (1966: Figure 89).]

foundation 1 m high. The columns are made of small stones set in clay mortar and vary in diameter between 82 cm (vestibule) and 57 cm (main chamber).

In 1974, we discovered a similar temple, Structure 13, on Mound 1 at San José Mogote. Although poorly preserved, Structure 13 appears to be half again as large as its Mound X counterpart—perhaps because it was a major temple at San José, while Mound X was peripheral to the main temples at Monte Albán. Assuming that Structure 13 was symmetrical and had roughly the same proportions as the Mound X temple, its size would have been at least 15 by 8 m. In addition to its greater size, Structure 13 had pairs of columns to either side of the vestibule doorway. Like the temple on Mound X at Monte Albán, it was oriented to the cardinal points.

B. Arrowhead-shaped buildings are another recognizable type during Monte Albán II (Figure 10.9). By far the best-known is Building J in the great plaza at Monte Albán, but a smaller version has been found in Mound O at Caballito Blanco some 50 km to the east (Paddock 1966). Both buildings are distinctive in their arrowhead-shaped ground plan and their atypical orientation; whereas other major structures at Monte Albán and Caballito Blanco are aligned within a few degrees of north–south, the arrowhead-shaped buildings have stairways facing northeast.

Traditionally, Building J has been described in the literature as an "observatory," and astronomical functions have been suggested to explain both its peculiar shape and its orientation (cf. Aveni and Linsley 1972). We see little evidence from which to infer such a function. Moreover, the "observatory" interpretation fails to account for one of the most interesting features of Building J, namely, the series of more than 40 "conquest slabs" set in its outer face. Alfonso Caso (1947) defined these slabs as having the following elements carved on them:

1. A "hill" or *cerro* glyph which signifies "place."
2. A group of glyphs, usually above the "hill" sign, which apparently represent the name of a place.
3. A human head with closed eyes, upside down beneath the "hill" sign, presumably representing a dead or subjugated ruler of that place.
4. A hieroglyphic text which, in its most complete form, includes a year, month, and day, as well as other glyphs of unknown meaning [Marcus, in press a].

Any interpretation of Building J at Monte Albán must consider these Period II slabs, which suggest a list of conquered or tributary places rather than a series of astronomical observations. Unfortunately, Mound O at Caballito Blanco has no carved stones, and its function is therefore even less clear than Building J. The arrowhead-shaped building in Mound O is 9 by 10 m in maximum extent, while Building J is three times larger (27 by 32 m).

C. Ball courts are another of our Terminal Formative building types; in the Valley of Oaxaca, they occur as early as Monte Albán II. Our oldest complete example, the ballcourt in Mound 7s at San José Mogote, was excavated by Chris Moser in 1974 (Moser n.d.). Ballcourts of equivalent age were present at Monte Albán, but their remains are incompletely known because of superimposed later constructions (Acosta 1965: 824). The upper stage of the ballcourt in the great plaza at Monte Albán, presently reconstructed for viewing by tourists, dates to Period III.

Oaxacan ballcourts generally have the shape of a Roman numeral I (Figure 10.10), with great sloping *taludes* or inclined surfaces rising from the central axis. The courts have a north–south orientation, and lack the rings seen in Maya ballcourts. The dimensions of Mound 7s at San José Mogote and the main plaza at Monte Albán are so similar that the use of a standard plan is suggested. The dimensions are:

	Mound 7s, San José Mogote	Great Plaza, Monte Albán
Maximum length:	41.5 m	41 m
Maximum width:	24.2 m	24 m
Central court, between *taludes:*	27.2 m	26 m

Summary and Conclusions

The evolution of public architecture in the Valley of Oaxaca (Figure 10.11) sheds light on the evolution of society as well. Even in the hunting–gathering period, a part of the community was set aside as "public" space. However, no activity performed in this space seems to

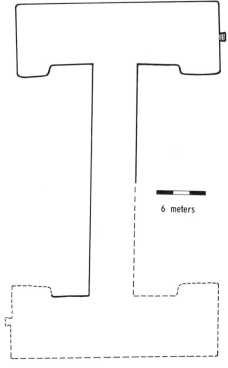

6 meters

Figure 10.10 Ballcourt of the Monte Albán II period, Mound 7s, San José Mogote. Dashed lines indicate the presumed outline of the unexcavated parts of the court. Estimated date: 100 B.C.–A.D. 100. [From a drawing by Chris L. Moser (n.d.).]

have required the maintenance of a permanent building, and the space was accessible to all. During the Early Formative, some villages had standardized public buildings in areas set aside from the ordinary residences but readily accessible to them. Little is known of the precise functions of these buildings, because they do not show the diversity and specialization of later periods. They might thus be called "generalized" public buildings.

During the Middle Formative, two new trends began to separate the public building from its community. First, such buildings were placed in groups of three or four, facing inward on a common courtyard rather than out toward the rest of the village. Second, at least some were placed on low hills overlooking the community, rather than among the ordinary residences. Perhaps the ultimate step in this direction came with the founding of Monte Albán on a 400-m mountaintop, with its main plaza located in one of the more remote areas of the city in terms of urban road networks. One possible implication is that access to at least some public buildings was now limited to the elite or to religious specialists.

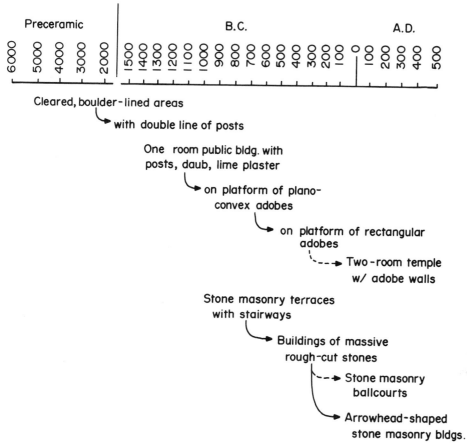

Figure 10.11 History and evolution of the public building in the Valley of Oaxaca, based on information available in 1975. Arrows indicate hypothetical development of one building type out of another; dashed lines are more tentative than solid lines.

In the Terminal Formative, public buildings were diversified into several types, including two-room temples with columns, arrowhead-shaped buildings, and ballcourts. Clearly, the activities carried on in these buildings must have been very different, presumably reflecting different sociopolitical institutions and different sets of personnel. Such architectural complexity is one archaeological manifestation of state organization.

Acknowledgment

We would like to thank Horst Hartung for a useful critique of an earlier version of this chapter.

11

The Origins of Monte Albán*

Richard E. Blanton

Introduction

This chapter concerns Monte Albán, an archaeological site in Oaxaca, Mexico, which was one of the largest cities in the New World during the Mesoamerican Classic period. A set of hypotheses surrounding the city's origin is presented. In particular, I will discuss certain features of the relationships between the foundation and early growth of Monte Albán and the evolution of states in the Valley of Oaxaca. I shall argue that the foundation and early growth of the city are best viewed as epiphenomena reflective of the evolutionary changes proceeding during the Formative period among cultural systems in the Valley of Oaxaca. First, however, I shall give a brief background to the information utilized.

In 1971, I helped initiate a long-term project, the "Valley of Oaxaca Settlement Pattern Project," which has as its goals the location,

---

* The first version of this chapter was read at the 1974 meeting of the International Congress of Americanists, in a symposium titled "City and State in Prehispanic America," organized by Edward Calnek.

description, and surface collection of all prehispanic sites in the valley
and the analyses of these data to better understand the processes
involved in evolutionary changes in the valley's cultural systems.
Although the project is still in its infancy, much fieldwork has been
accomplished, including the mapping, description, and surface collection of Monte Albán; the preliminary settlement pattern survey
(Figure 11.1) of the Etla (north) arm of the valley (done by Dudley
Varner); and the intensive settlement pattern survey (Figure 11.1) of
the valley's central region (done by Steve Kowalewski). This work has
produced roughly 30,000 pages of completed survey forms and maps
describing Monte Albán, as well as descriptions and surface collections of over 500 other archaeological sites, ranging from 1300 B.C. to
A.D. 1500. These data now are being organized, coded, and analyzed by
this author, Steve Kowalewski, Charles Spencer, Dudley Varner,
James Neely, and Carl Kuttruff.

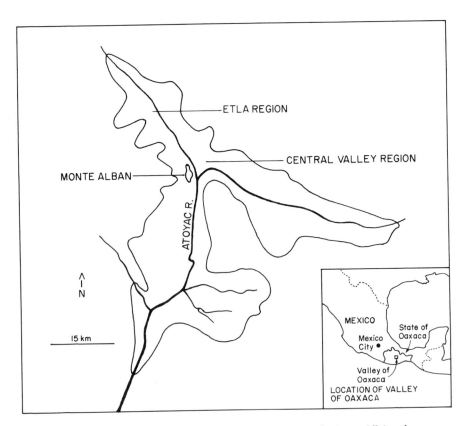

Figure 11.1 The Valley of Oaxaca, showing the location of Monte Albán, the survey
regions, and the location of the valley in Mexico.

Background to the Establishment of Monte Albán

Very little is known about the causal factors involved in state formation in the Valley of Oaxaca or about the socioenvironmental stresses that selected for the growth of more centralized systems. We can, however, generally characterize the gradual changes in valley societies during the Formative period which culminated in the evolution of states, cities, and, eventually, empire (cf. Bernal 1965; Caso, Bernal, and Acosta 1967; Flannery *et al.* 1967; Flannery 1970). For our purposes, the most important of these changes are: *(1)* overall growth of the human population which, at some times, approaches the agricultural limits of the valley (Kirkby 1973; Kowalewski 1974); *(2)* a gradual increase in the number of communities (in the Etla Region, Varner found fewer than 10 sites dating to around 1300 B.C. but 54 that had been occupied during the Terminal Formative period); and *(3)* an increase through time in community variability. Specifically, the valley settlement pattern was increasingly characterized by a hierarchy of communities ranging from small villages to large towns that contained large-scale civic–ceremonial architecture. Tierras Largas, probably typical of most small Formative villages in the area, was test excavated by Marcus Winter (1973), who discovered that it had maintained a stable size of 5 to 10 households during the long span from 1400 to 300 B.C. In contrast, San José Mogote, another valley site, began as a small community of about 3 ha (hectares) around 1400 B.C. but gradually grew, so that, by 1000 B.C., it covered an area of 20 ha, and, by the end of the Formative period, it covered over 100 ha (Flannery 1970). Whereas Tierras Largas had little or no public architecture, San José Mogote contained, as early as 1400 B.C., an area of public architecture covering at least 240 m²; by the end of the Formative, it had huge public buildings covering thousands of square meters. One public building, the *Mogote del Cacique*, is a high mound, 80 m by 80 m at the base, which defines the southern border of a 300-m-long plaza (Flannery 1970).

Although additional archaeological excavation is required to delineate the dimensions and nature of changes in valley societies during the Formative, the settlement pattern data allow us to infer that valley societies were becoming more complex (in the sense of having more parts, subparts, and ties between parts), were increasing in size, and were characterized by increasing social stratification and centralization of power.

Prior to about A.D. 300, there is no evidence that the Valley of Oaxaca was a single sociopolitical unit. Instead, during the Formative period, the valley population probably was organized into a series of discrete, largely autonomous units, each consisting of a center plus its dependent communities. Even during the Terminal Formative, there were several regional, independent iconographic and epigraphic styles in the valley—surely an indicator of the presence of discrete systems (Marcus n.d.). As the settlement pattern data are gathered, we should be able to determine the spatial and temporal parameters of each system in question and characterize changes in it through time.

The Establishment of Monte Albán

Monte Albán was established during the early Monte Albán I ceramic phase, approximately 500–400 B.C. (Table 11.1). Initially, it consisted of several closely spaced but discrete areas of settlement, covering a maximum area of slightly less than 1 km², located on the top of a high hill near the center of the valley (Figure 11.1). Although the ceramic analysis is not complete, the evidence indicates that the site was neither exclusively a ceremonial locality nor a purely extractive site. The full range of domestic wares of the phase seem to

Table 11.1 **Chronological Divisions Mentioned in the Text**

Mesoamerican periods	*Valley of Oaxaca designations*	*Approximate chronology*
Postclassic	Monte Albán V	A.D. 1500
	....	A.D. 1200
	Monte Albán IV	
	....	A.D. 900
Classic	Monte Albán IIIb	
	Monte Albán IIIa	
	....	A.D. 300
Late and Terminal Formative	Monte Albán II	
	....	200 B.C.
	Late Monte Albán I	
	Early Monte Albán I	
	....	500 B.C.
Middle Formative	Rosario phase	
	Guadalupe phase	
	....	850 B.C.
Early Formative	San José phase	
	....	1150 B.C.
	Tierras Largas phase	
	....	1400 B.C.

be present in the surface collections, probably indicating full-time occupation by households.

Prior to early Monte Albán I, this locality was not occupied on a full-time basis. Monte Albán was not unique in this sense; in the Etla Region, Varner found 48 sites with evidence of early Monte Albán I occupation, in contrast to 14 sites that were occupied during the preceding Guadalupe phase (Varner 1974). In the Central Valley Region, Kowalewski found 8 Guadalupe and Rosario phase sites (Middle Formative), but located 35 sites with early Monte Albán I occupations (Kowalewski 1974).

Based on the results of our valley surveys as well as those of Flannery and his associates, we know there were basically five kinds of communities during the early Monte Albán I phase: *(1)* towns, such as San José Mogote, typically located adjacent to highly productive agricultural land, which were probably the administrative and economic centers of local systems; *(2)* villages, such as Tierras Largas, located adjacent to well-watered deep alluvial soils; *(3)* villages, high in the piedmont zone, located adjacent to perennial streams where simple canal irrigation would have been feasible (Flannery *et al.* 1967); *(4)* small "ceremonial centers" on hilltops near the piedmont sites and probably closely associated with them (Flannery *et al.* 1967); and *(5)* communities involved in the specialized production of some locally available resource, such as the salt-making site excavated at Fábrica San José (Drennan 1972). Monte Albán is unique because it does not fit into any category. It has no convenient access to the water and deep soils of the low or high alluvium zones. If access to these zones had been desired, one might predict that the earliest settlement would have been on the east ridge of the main hill, a ridge that terminates near a large expanse of low alluvium south of what is now Oaxaca City. Our survey has shown that this arm of Monte Albán was not colonized until the Classic period and was one of the last areas of the hill to be utilized for settlement (Blanton 1973). Early Monte Albán is not located, as were a number of valley sites, near a perennial stream suitable for irrigation; in fact, procuring water for drinking and other household uses must have been a problem. Finally, there is no resource in the vicinity of the site which could have been extracted for export. Clearly, Monte Albán cannot be easily placed into any of our early Monte Albán I site categories. It is also much larger than any other newly established early Monte Albán I community. The largest such site in the Etla Region is 41 ha (Varner 1974). The largest such site in the Central Valley Region covers 15 ha (Kowalewski 1974). Monte Albán during this period covered about 100 ha.

Because of the site's location near the confluence of the three arms of the valley and central to the valley's population, one might guess that it would have been ideally located as a central valley market. After all, the current central valley market is located in nearby Oaxaca City, at the base of Monte Albán. However, the site is in one of the least likely spots for a market place—on top of a steep-sided mountain roughly 1000 ft. above the valley floor. Data concerning road patterns and the distribution and abundance of workshops lead me to suggest that the city never served as an important market or production center (Blanton 1973). Monte Albán thus contrasts strongly with its contemporary, Teotihuacán. There, Millon found over 500 workshops and a large feature near the city's center, the "Great Compound," which, he argues, was a large market area (Millon 1973).

From the preceding, I feel there is no simple or obvious explanation for why Monte Albán was established or why it was established where it was. Monte Albán may be one of a genre of human communities whose locations often cannot be simply understood, communities that have as their special function decision making on a regional level or intermediation between localized systems. I do not necessarily mean to imply that Monte Albán was, at that time, a regional capital. Decision making and intermediation on a regional level can occur in the absence of centralization of power at the center where this intermediation takes place. Early Athens, for example, was not a large city and center of government, although it later became one as a result of the unification efforts of Theseus and Pericles. According to Thucydides:

> Most of them had been always used to living in the country. . . . From very early times this way of life had been especially characteristic of the Athenians. From the time of Cecrops and the first kings down to the time of Theseus the inhabitants of Attica had always lived in independent cities, each with its own town hall and its own government. Only in times of danger did they meet together and consult the King at Athens; for the rest of the time each state looked after its own affairs and made its own decisions. There were actually occasions when some of these states made war on Athens . . . [Thuc., Peloponnesian War II, 2; Warner 1954: 106].

Because communities of this type—that is, those specializing in some kind of intermediation and decision making on a regional level—often are inhabited largely by specialists and typically are not self-supporting, their locations need not make sense in terms of local agricultural or other resources. Mecca, for example, was founded in A.D. 400 by members of the Koreish tribe in a location described by a pre-Islamic poet (Essad Bey 1936: 44):

> If Mecca had any attractions to offer, Himyarite princes at the head of their armies would have long since hurried there. There winter and summer are equally desolate. No bird flies over Mecca, no grass grows. There are no wild beasts to be hunted.

Mecca became an important regional center because of the establishment there, by the Koreish, of a sacred area, the Ka'ba, where members of different tribes could articulate in a noncombatant atmosphere. J. Wellhausen (Wolf 1951: 338) described the importance of sanctuaries like Mecca as follows:

> Within the tumultuous confusion which fills the desert the festivities at the beginning of each season represent the only enjoyable periods of rest. A peace of God at this time interrupts the continuous feuds for a fair period of time. The most diverse tribes which otherwise did not trust each other at all, make common pilgrimage to the same holy places, without fear, through the land of friend and foe. Trade raises its head, and general and lively exchange results. . . . The exchange of commodities is followed by an exchange of ideas. A community of ideological interest develops that comprises all of Arabia.

Brasilia and Washington, D.C., are further examples of this phenomenon—Brasilia is located in the middle of virgin jungle, and Washington was founded far south of the main cities of New York, Boston, and Philadelphia, in a completely undeveloped forested area where, according to Morison (1965: 360), "The red clay soil . . . became dust in dry weather and liquid cement in every rain, after which swarms of mosquitos spread malaria." Centers of this type often may be located in marginal and "neutral" localities. They need not be placed in locations suitable for them to function as commercial central places, break-of-bulk points, or the like.

I would argue that a community was established at Monte Albán, during the early Monte Albán I phase, perhaps by agreement of the elites of the various autonomous societies in the valley as a place where specialists in regional decision making would reside. If this were true, then its location—central to the valley as a whole but not close enough to valuable agricultural land or some other resource to present a threat to the resource base of any existing community—is no longer difficult to understand.

If Monte Albán was such a community, it may be easier to explain why, as far as we can tell from surface evidence alone, the early Monte Albán I site consists of three closely spaced but discrete areas. The members of the community would have been close together to facilitate communication but could maintain their ethnic identities by living in separate localities on the hilltop. This hypothesis is relatively easy to test by analysis of design motifs on pottery, figurine styles, and the like. We might predict, using a simple gravity model (Haggett 1965: 35; Olsson 1965), or some comparable statistic, that a given portion of the Monte Albán site would show an unusually high degree of interaction with one of the large centers in the valley: the center whose representatives lived there. However, the archaeological testing of hypotheses regarding the early role of Monte Albán will be difficult because of the heavy overburden consisting of the deposition from later occupations of the site.

Another important problem is why Monte Albán was established when it was, rather than earlier or later. Again, the information necessary to resolve this problem is not now available, nor is it likely to be in the near future. Several factors, however, may have been important. As I have pointed out, societies in the valley were becoming increasingly larger, more complex, and more centralized. These changes seem to have been particularly rapid during the early Monte Albán I phase. During this time of rapid sociocultural change in the valley, I suggest, the kinds of "border mechanisms" or media through which information and materials were exchanged between systems became inadequate to handle the rapid increase in complexity of intersystemic articulation, so that new mechanisms were developed. We may infer, on the basis of ethnographically known primitive societies, that the "border mechanisms" in the Early Formative were like those associated with "tribes" and "chiefdoms," such as "trade partners" (cf. Flannery 1968; Harding 1967; Sahlins 1972) and inter-marriage of elites across systemic boundaries (cf. Flannery 1968; Leach 1965). The latter has been documented, through an analysis of codices, as the key mechanism of intersystemic articulation between the small "kingdoms" of the Mixteca in prehispanic times (Spores 1974). As societies in the valley grew in size and complexity, however, these mechanisms alone may have proved to be inadequate. Given conditions such as these, elites may have appointed specialists to deal exclusively in "border" problems. The product of this, I argue, was the formation of Monte Albán as a community of specialists involved in decision making at the regional level. The difficulties involved in decision making on this level may have been increasing at that time also because societies in other parts of Mesoamerica, particularly in the Valley of Mexico, also were changing rapidly (cf. Blanton 1972a, b; Parsons 1971a; Sanders 1965). Traditional mechanisms of interregional interaction may have been replaced or may have required some kind of reorganization, adding to the need for specialists. Testing these hypotheses could involve: (1) demonstrating which "border mechanisms" were present during the early part of the Formative (the work of Flannery and his associates already has contributed much in this area), (2) demonstrating that these mechanisms are generally inadequate once systems grow beyond a certain level of size and complexity, and (3) demonstrating that these societies exceeded those limits during the early Monte Albán I phase.

The Later Growth of Monte Albán

Early Athens and early Mecca, both used here as somewhat analogous to early Monte Albán, became cities which were both the political and religious centers of states. During the latter part of the Formative period, Monte Albán increased greatly in size (to over 4 km²) and had a large defensive wall, reservoirs, and an irrigation system (Blanton 1973; Neely 1972). For that time period, Monte Albán was one of several large, competing centers in the valley. Later, during the Classic period, other valley centers apparently lost their importance, while Monte Albán continued to grow, reaching a maximum extent during the "Late Classic" of about 7.5 km² (Blanton 1973), making it one of the largest prehispanic cities in all of Mesoamerica. The bases for this reorganization of valley societies and growth of Monte Albán are virtually unknown now, but analyses now in progress will, hopefully, throw new light on them.

Conclusions

I have presented the following set of hypotheses:

1. The factors that determined the locations and functions of new communities during the early Monte Albán I phase in the Valley of Oaxaca are not relevant to Monte Albán. It is unique locationally, and, therefore, it was unique functionally.

2. Monte Albán was probably not self-sufficient agriculturally because the steep, dry slopes of the mountain would have been too marginal for cultivation at the time of its founding (Kirkby 1973; Figure 51, passim). In addition, there is no resource there that could have been extracted for export, and the isolated, hilltop location of the site indicates that it was not a central valley market.

3. The top of Monte Albán, central to the valley as a whole, but away from existing large centers, may have been an ideal location for the formation of a community of specialists involved in regional or interregional decision making. As I pointed out earlier, communities of this genre often are located away from existing centers, in a "neutral" locality. Washington, D.C., and Brasilia are good examples.

4. Early Monte Albán may have been analogous to pre-Islamic Mecca as a locality where members of different tribes could associate freely. It may have been designated as a sacred place, like the Ka'ba, where representatives of the various valley societies could interact in a peaceful atmosphere.

5. Monte Albán was established as a special "border mechanism" during the early Monte Albán I phase because, in the context of rapid evolutionary change and growth in valley societies, traditional media for the exchange of information and materials had proved to be inadequate, so that specialists had to be appointed. A further problem for elites at that time was the similarly rapid change in societies in other Mesoamerican regions, perhaps necessitating the institution of new means of intersystemic interaction at this level also.

Archaeological testing of hypotheses of this sort is difficult at best, but the settlement pattern work we are doing, in combination with the excavation projects directed by Flannery, are contributing a vast amount of new data pertinent to an understanding of early Monte Albán. We already are able to use simple gravity models and similar statistics to determine whether or not portions of early Monte Albán had close ties with specific valley centers. This will help us decide whether or not each valley "capital" had a group of representatives living on Monte Albán.

Acknowledgments

The ideas presented here were developed as a result of stimulating conversations with Kent Flannery, Ignacio Bernal, and Melvin Ember. All interpretative errors, however, are mine.

12

The Role of Chinampa Agriculture in the Food Supply of Aztec Tenochtitlan*

Jeffrey R. Parsons

Introduction

This chapter discusses a specific case of the general problem of food supply in preindustrial urbanized societies. Most such societies must cope with transporting bulky foodstuffs to concentrated population centers incapable of sustaining themselves from their immediate environs. Predictable responses to such food supply problems would include *(1)* improvement of transportation facilities, *(2)* extension of trade and tributary networks, and *(3)* expansion of local food production by means of technological innovations, bringing new land into cultivation and increasing labor inputs. In situations in which the transportation potential is especially restricted, the intensification of food production in areas close to primary consuming centers is particularly expectable.

Here we will consider the Aztec state during the fifteenth and early

* Our fieldwork during 1969 and 1972 was supported by the National Science Foundation (Grant GS-31911) and the Ford Foundation.

sixteenth centuries A.D. (Table 12.1). The heartland of this polity was
the Valley of Mexico, an internal drainage basin of some 7000 km²
(Figure 12.1) with a probable population of some 1.0–1.2 million
people at Spanish contact (Sanders 1971). With a surface area of
about 12 km² and a population recently estimated at between 150,000
and 200,000 (Calnek 1973), Tenochtitlan was the largest and most
powerful urban center within the Aztec state. Another important
urban center at Texcoco covered some 4 km² and probably contained
approximately 20,000–30,000 people (Sanders 1971; Parsons 1971a). A
third group of some five urban communities averaged about 15,000
persons each (Sanders 1971). The lowest tier of nucleated population
centers, numbering about 40, had average populations of 4000–5000
(Sanders 1971). Perhaps half of the total population resided in
dispersed rural settlements widely distributed throughout the basin.

Many urban centers, including most of the largest, were situated
around the shores of a series of interconnected shallow lakes in the
center of the basin (Figure 12.1). Tenochtitlan itself occupied an island
in saline Lake Texcoco. Lake Xaltocan–Zumpango, to the north, and
Lake Chalco–Xochimilco, to the south, were situated at slightly higher
elevations and drained into Lake Texcoco. Although the lake system
afforded a ready transportation–communication artery, there were no
other navigable waterways—overland transport was restricted to
human carriers.

Tenochtitlan clearly occupied a very special place in the Aztec state
heartland. Its great size (apparently at least five times larger than

Table 12.1 Late Postclassic Chronology, Valley of Mexico[a]

Absolute chronology	Phases	
	Griffin and Espejo (1947)	Inst. Nac. de Antro. e Hist.
1520	Tlatelolco	Aztec IV
	Tenochtitlan	Aztec III
1400	Tenayuca	Aztec II
	Culhuacan	Aztec I
1200 A.D.		

[a] The absolute chronology has not been firmly established. Dates given here
are adapted from best approximations and current usage. Charlton's (1972)
work indicates that some ceramic types associated with the Aztec III and IV
phases continued to be produced and used during the Early Colonial period.

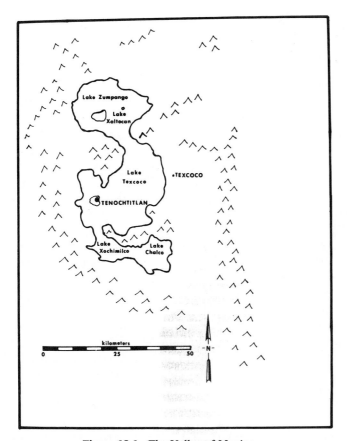

Figure 12.1 The Valley of Mexico.

Texcoco, its closest rival) and obvious significance at the time of Spanish conquest are indicative of its dominant role during the last century of the prehispanic era. Furthermore, unlike nearly every other Late Postclassic urban center in the Valley of Mexico, Tenochtitlan lacked a productive agricultural zone of any significance in its immediate environs (Calnek 1972). Because of its unusually large size and lack of direct access to its subsistence base, the provisioning of Tenochtitlan thus would have presented a number of special problems for the Aztec state.

Using ethnohistoric sources, Calnek (in press) has developed a model for the organization of Tenochtitlan's food supply. He distinguishes three separate mechanisms that provided foodstuffs to the Aztec capital: tribute from subject provinces, trade within a complex market system, and "rent" from landed estates for the support of important administrative personnel (the "owners" of the estates) resident in Tenochtitlan. Calnek finds that landed estates were created in two general ways: *(1)* by the expropriation of land in conquered areas in and around the Valley of Mexico; and *(2)* by creating new agricultural land, primarily by means of large-scale drainage of swampy ground and the subsequent formation of highly productive chinampa plots in the Chalco–Xochimilco lakebed in the southern Valley of Mexico. Officials residing in Tenochtitlan received rights to production from specific tracts of such land. The actual cultivation was supervised by state-appointed administrators (not the "owners") who resided in the general area of the estate and who directed the activities of resident tenant laborers. These tenants existed outside the traditional communal *calpulli* framework. Lacking access to communal resources of the *calpulli* unit, such tenants constituted another kind of state dependent. Rents in kind were delivered by the tenant cultivators to the estate "owners" at their residences in Tenochtitlan. All indications point to the reigns of Itzcoatl (A.D. 1426–1440) and Motechuzoma Ilhjicamina (A.D. 1440–1467) as the principal period during which large-scale conquest, land reclamation, and chinampa construction were initiated and carried out (Calnek, in press: 4–5).

The objective of this chapter is to consider further the role of chinampa agriculture in the food supply of Tenochtitlan in the light of our recent archaeological survey of the Chalco–Xochimilco lakebed (Parsons 1973). This work, together with Sanders' (1957) and Armillas' (1971) earlier studies in parts of the same area, complement Calnek's archival research. Armillas (1971: 660) has provided an estimate of the total area once covered by chinampa plots in the Chalco–Xochimilco lakebed, and his pioneering surveys suggest that their primary construction and utilization occurred between A.D. 1400 and 1600. Sanders' ethnographic studies of contemporary chinampa productivity provide a base for inferring the total carrying capacity of the prehispanic chinampa system. Our detailed surface surveys make it possible to estimate total population of the chinampa district at several points in the prehispanic period as well as to infer certain aspects of the organization of chinampa cultivation. In the remainder of this chapter, I shall attempt to integrate these various lines of evidence in order to develop a more complete model of the role of chinampa cultivation in the food supply of Tenochtitlan during the last century before Spanish conquest. The principal tasks will be to estimate the surplus productive capacity of the Chalco–Xochimilco chinampa district during this period and to infer the disposition of this surplus.

The Chronology of Chinampa Construction and Utilization in Lake Chalco–Xochimilco

Chronological inferences are based primarily upon Armillas' (1971) selective surveys in parts of the old lakebed and around its edges and upon our own complete surface reconnaissance in the same area over all ground not presently occupied by modern construction (see Parsons 1971a: 16–21, and Parsons 1974: 84–87, for discussions of survey methodology). Despite its deep alluvial soil cover, the Chalco–Xochimilco lakebed seems to have had very little soil deposition over the past 3000 years. Early Formative (around 1200–800 B.C.), Middle Formative (around 800–500 B.C.), and Late Formative (around 500–200 B.C.) occupations can be found in relatively undisturbed condition at and near the present ground surface in a few localities (Parsons 1973; Armillas 1971; Tolstoy 1972). Late Postclassic housemounds in fair to good condition are found rising above the ground surface throughout the entire area. Further north, in the southeastern corner of Lake Texcoco, the undisturbed remains of an *in situ* mammoth recently have been found at the modern ground surface (Mirambell 1972). The abundance of ancient occupational traces at the modern surface of the old lakebed indicates that a thorough, systematic survey, such as our own, would produce a fairly complete delineation of prehistoric settlement.

Our surveys have confirmed Armillas' impression that almost all occupation within the Chalco-Xochimilco lakebed dates to A.D. 1400–1600 (Aztec III, Aztec IV, and Early Colonial phases, Figure 12.2). As Armillas noted, there is also a little Aztec II material in parts of the lakebed area (Figure 12.3), but most Aztec I–II occupation is confined to islands within the lakebed and to higher ground around the edges of the lakeshore. These distributional patterns indicate that there was extremely limited occupation within the chinampa zone prior to Aztec III times, with a very substantial occupation of this zone in the Aztec III–IV and Early Colonial periods (ca. A.D. 1400–1600). Such an occupational pattern fits nicely with Calnek's ethnohistorically derived assignment of principal swamp drainage and chinampa construction to the period A.D. 1426–1467.

Late Postclassic Settlement and Population in Lake Chalco–Xochimilco

Although most of the Chalco–Xochimilco lakebed was still clear of modern occupation during the 1972 field season, there was consider-

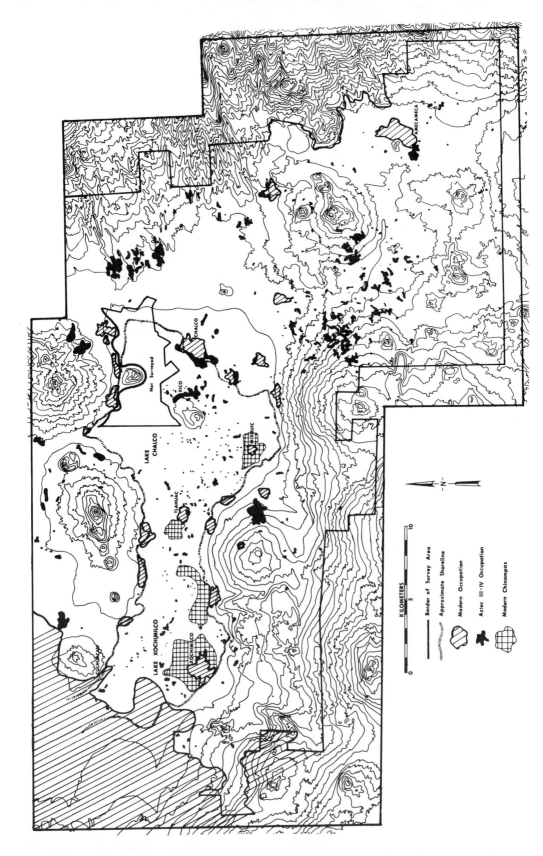

Figure 12.2 Aztec III–IV settlement, southern Valley of Mexico.

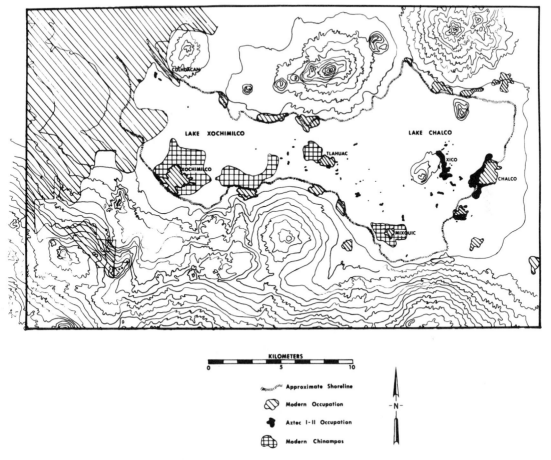

Figure 12.3 Aztec I–II settlement, Chalco–Xochimilco lake bed.

able nucleated modern construction around the margins of Lake Xochimilco and, to a lesser degree, around Lake Chalco (Figures 12.2, 12.3). There are several substantial modern towns within or around the lakebed that occupy the same locations as Late Postclassic centers: Xochimilco, Tlahuac (Cuitlahuac), Mixquic, Culhuacan, and Chalco. There are also large areas of modern chinampas around Xochimilco, Mixquic, and Tlahuac, where it was not possible to carry out systematic reconnaissance (Figures 12.2, 12.3). The archaeological control for lakeshore settlement, for modern chinampa zones, and for urban centers in and around Lake Chalco–Xochimilco is thus some-what deficient. We must rely on ethnohistoric sources for an adequate estimation of Late Postclassic population in these parts of the survey area.

Archaeological occupation is manifested in several ways. Often there are distinctive, well-preserved mounds with abundant surface pottery. These mounds generally measure between 10 and 20 m in diameter and 1 or 2 m high. A majority of sites within the lakebed zone consist of these mounds, either isolated or in small clusters of two to five structures. In some intensively plowed areas, there are relatively few mounds, but concentrations of surface pottery up to several hundred meters in diameter can readily be delineated on the ground surface. These sherd concentrations probably represent the loci of former mounds and mound clusters, now completely flattened and obliterated by modern plowing. In a few cases, there are large, continuously built up archaeological zones with length–width dimensions up to several hundred meters and elevations between 1 and 3 m. These occur around the edges of some of the modern towns which were also large centers in Late Postclassic times (Chalco, Tlahuac, Culhuacan; Figures 12.2, 12.3). A nearly intact site of this character occurs around the northeastern margins of Xico Island in eastern Lake Chalco, where a modest Late Postclassic center has not been covered with modern occupation.

Aztec III–IV occupation in the Chalco–Xochimilco lakebed falls into two distinctive settlement types (Figure 12.2). First, there are a series of nucleated centers around the edges of the lakeshore (Chalco, Culhuacan), or within the lakebed on natural islands or artificial platforms (Xico, Tlahuac, Mixquic, and Xochimilco). Although we have no archaeological data for Mixquic and Xochimilco, ethnohistoric sources (Sanders 1971) clearly indicate the existence and importance of these two centers during the fifteenth and sixteenth centuries. Where archaeological data are available (at all centers except Xochimilco and Mixquic), all these lakebed centers show substantial Aztec I–II occupation intermixed with similar quantities of Aztec III–IV material.

Second, there are 148 small sites—often a single mound or small sherd concentration, sometimes a cluster of two to five mounds or more extensive sherd debris—scattered widely throughout the old lakebed. Virtually all have Aztec III–IV occupations, but only a few show secondary Aztec II material (Figure 12.3). (We have located Aztec I pottery only around the edges of Chalco, Xico, Tlahuac, and Culhuacan.) In a few places, where modern plowing has not occurred, preserved mounds occur in close constructional association with well-preserved ancient chinampa fields (Figure 12.4); these locations have been noted previously by Armillas (1971).

An estimate of the Aztec III–IV population within the Chalco–Xochimilco lakebed should approximate the number of people whose subsistence derived principally from chinampa cultivation. The dif-

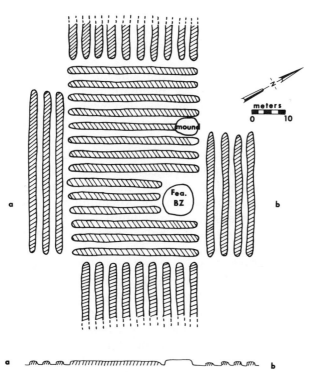

Figure 12.4 Plan of well-preserved ancient chinampas and associated Aztec III–IV mounds.

ference between this figure and the total potential carrying capacity of the chinampa zone should provide a measure of the maximum surplus potentially available for rent, tribute, storage, trade, and so on during Aztec III–IV times. The reader is referred to earlier discussions (Parsons 1971a: 21–24; Blanton 1972: 18–21) for the specific procedures followed in making population estimates from archaeological surface remains. Basically, this involves measuring the surface area (in hectares) over which surface pottery and mounds occur, and multiplying this area by a density figure (people per hectare) deemed appropriate on the basis of the relative abundance of archaeological surface debris. In cases in which distinct mounds are preserved, we estimate that each mound represents 5 to 10 people. We have considered such population estimates to be most meaningful as indices of relative population by means of which different prehistoric periods can be compared demographically. However, our population estimates for Late Postclassic Texcoco and its environs in the eastern Valley of Mexico (Parsons 1971a) correspond fairly closely to independent calculations for the same area derived from ethnohistoric sources (Sanders 1971). Crude as it is, our method seems to have some validity as a measure of absolute population for the Late Postclassic period.

For the 148 small sites in the Chalco–Xochimilco lakebed, we calculate a total Aztec III–IV population of 3670 (Table 12.2). To account for sites of this character that probably remain hidden by modern occupation, another 15% might be added. This brings the total Aztec III–IV lakebed population residing in small, scattered sites to 4220. To this figure must be added those inhabitants of larger centers in the lakebed and around its edges who were probably dependent on chinampa cultivation for most of their subsistence (Table 12.3), including the entire populations of Xochimilco, Tlahuac, Xico, and Mixquic—these centers have only limited access to non-chinampa land. On the other hand, both Chalco and Culhuacan have immediate access to substantial areas of non-chinampa land. We would estimate that perhaps half of Culhuacan's and one-fifth of Chalco's population may have been dependent primarily upon chinampa cultivation. We have added an additional 20% (Table 12.3) to account for residents of smaller lakeshore communities that may have remained unidentified archaeologically because of modern settlement who would also have been dependent to some degree upon chinampa cultivation.

In summary, there are two distinct Aztec III–IV settlement types in Lake Chalco–Xochimilco: (1) 148 small sites, most of them with fewer than 50 inhabitants, scattered widely over the lakebed; and (2) 6 nucleated centers with populations ranging between 2000 and 15,000. The small, dispersed sites are very predominantly Aztec III–IV, with only a minor Aztec II component. The larger centers are mixed Aztec I–II–III–IV (no archaeological data are available for Mixquic or Xochimilco). Some 4220 people in scattered, small sites, and 32,400 people in larger centers, were fully dependent upon chinampa cultivation for their subsistence during Aztec III–IV times.

The Carrying Capacity of Sixteenth-Century Chinampa Agriculture

Sanders (Sanders, Parsons, and Logan n.d.: 105 [cited in Calnek 1972: 111]) has calculated that 1 ha (hectare) of intensively cultivated chinampa can support between 15 and 20 people at a subsistence level comparable to that of modern rural inhabitants of Central Mexico

Table 12.2 **Small Lakebed Aztec III–IV Sites: Distribution by Population Size**

Site population	10	15	20	30	40	50	60	80	90	100	150	160	250
Number of sites	82	14	17	9	5	10	1	2	1	3	1	2	1

Table 12.3 **Population Estimates for Aztec III–IV Centers in and around Lake Chalco–Xochimilco**

Center	Total population	Source	Population probably dependent on chinampas
Culhuacan	4,000	Blanton (1972b: 164)	2,000
Tlahuac	3,000	Area of modern community multiplied by 50 people/ha. Population estimate questionable.	3,000
Mixquic	2,000	Area of modern community multiplied by 50 people/ha. Population estimate questionable.	2,000
Xochimilco	15,000	Sanders (1971: 449–450).	15,000
Xico	2,500	Parsons (1971b).	2,500
Chalco	12,500	Parsons (1971b). Only the west side of the Aztec town is free of modern occupation. This population estimate assumes Aztec occupation underlies all of the modern town.	2,500
Total population dependent on chinampa cultivation			27,000
Plus 20%			5,400
Total			32,400

(about 160 kilos of maize per average person per average year). Armillas (1971: 660) has measured the physical remains of old chinampa plots on the Chalco–Xochimilco lakebed over a total area of about 120 km². To allow for uncultivated canals and pools within this zone, he suggests that a figure of about 90 km² (9000 ha) would approximate the amount of productive chinampa land. We might reasonably increase this figure to about 9500 ha to allow for areas where chinampa traces may have been obliterated prior to Armillas' survey (Armillas 1971: 655).

If we use an average carrying capacity of 15–20 people per ha and a figure of 9500 cultivable ha of chinampa land, the total carrying capacity for the Lake Chalco–Xochimilco chinampa zone in the early sixteenth century would be 140,000 to 190,000 people. Likewise, we can approximate the average annual yield for 1 ha of cultivated chinampa as equivalent to 2400–3200 kilos of maize (with a subsistence level of 160 kilos per person per year). This would not seem to be an unreasonable estimate of average productivity in view of Sanders' (1957: 84–85) observation that some commercially operated modern chinampas are capable of producing up to 4000 kilos of maize annually. To simplify our calculations, I will assume an average annual productivity equivalent to 3000 kilos of maize per hectare of chinampa land. The entire 9500 ha of cultivated chinampa thus might have been capable of a maximal annual production of 28,500,000 kilos of grain.

At least two additional factors should be considered in estimating productivity and carrying capacity of the Chalco–Xochimilco chinampa district: *(1)* nutritional requirements and *(2)* labor requirements for chinampa cultivation. While 160 kilos of maize per year may supply a high proportion of an average person's basic dietary needs, certain other essential nutrients must be supplied from other sources. At the risk of great oversimplification, we will assume that the complete nutritional needs of an average individual can be met by the equivalent of 200 kilos of maize per year (that is, an annual maize surplus of 40 kilos per person that can be exchanged for other items; or, the production of other foods on land that, if planted to maize, would produce 40 kilos annually).

To be more realistic, of course, we should consider the actual dietary needs of an average individual and proceed to calculate the productivity of each major food item. In practice, this is virtually impossible to do, since we are unable to locate systematic productivity data for any crop except maize. Although we can calculate chinampa productivity only in terms of maize, we do not mean to imply that maize was the only crop cultivated in the chinampas. Hopefully, we are more or less correct in assuming that the land and labor involved in the annual production of 200 kilos of maize would supply the total subsistence needs of an average individual during Aztec III–IV times.

All detailed descriptions of modern chinampa cultivation (Sanders 1957; West and Armillas 1950) emphasize its labor intensity. To maintain high levels of productivity, continuous hand labor must be expended throughout an annual cycle—for example, irrigating, fertilizing, soil preparation, weeding, transplanting. Long-term fertility maintenance also requires careful crop rotation. Sanders (1957: 89) has noted particularly the importance of systematic rotation of maize with chile and tomato in early twentieth-century chinampa cultivation. He also emphasizes the very detailed knowledge concerning crop sequences and rotations that successful chinampa cultivation demands. Only by means of these labor-intensive techniques can chinampa land be kept in continuously high production with little or no fallowing.

The area of chinampa land that one adult laborer can effectively cultivate is difficult to estimate from published accounts. Sanders (1957: 80) states that, in a hypothetical situation in which continuous hand watering is required, one man probably would be unable to cultivate more than a half hectare at any one time. The need for hand watering is considerably alleviated by normal rainfall during the summer months, but there are a variety of other time-consuming tasks that must be carried out. We will assume that one fully effective laborer can cultivate .75 ha of chinampa land during an annual cycle.

These considerations reduce the maximal carrying capacity of the 9500 cultivable ha of chinampa land in Lake Chalco–Xochimilco to 142,000 people (with a total annual productivity equivalent to 28,500,000 kilos of maize and a subsistence need equivalent to 200 kilos of maize per average person per average year). Such productivity would demand a labor force of about 12,700 people (with 9500 cultivable ha and each laborer working .75 ha of chinampa land annually).

The Aztec III–IV Surplus Productive Capacity of the Chalco–Xochimilco Chinampa Zone

We have calculated that some 36,620 people residing within the Chalco–Xochimilco lakebed zone were dependent upon chinampa cultivation during Aztec III–IV times (Table 12.4). If each consumed the equivalent of 200 kilos of maize per year, this population would require the equivalent of 7,324,000 kilos of maize annually. With an average annual production equivalent to 3000 kilos of maize per ha of chinampa, this much grain could have been produced on a cultivated area of 2440 ha. These figures probably represent minimal estimates of the food requirements of the resident Aztec III–IV lakebed population since they do not consider any nonsubsistence activities that would have to be underwritten largely by local agricultural production, particularly in the case of the larger centers—for instance, storage of surplus as a buffer against poor harvests, paying tribute to higher levels within the Aztec state, and participating in regional exchange networks.

It seems reasonable to consider only the larger centers in estimating the amount of chinampa land necessary to underwrite the nonsubsistence needs of the Aztec III–IV population residing within the chinampa zone. Needs of the scattered rural population are likely to have been so few as to be negligible in our overall calculations. As a first step, we will add another 20% to the estimate of the needs of the 32,400 people residing in the larger lakebed centers who were dependent on chinampa cultivation for subsistence. This adds the equivalent of 6480 people (or 430 ha at a productivity equivalent to 3000 kilos of maize per year) and raises the overall needs of the resident Aztec III–IV lakebed population to the productive capacity of 2870 ha of cultivated chinampa land (2440 plus 430; Table 12.4).

Table 12.4 **Calculations of Surplus Capacity**

A. Lakebed population dependent on chinampa cultivation

a. Tenants on landed estates		4,220
b. Nontenants in nucleated centers		32,400
c. Total		36,620

B. Annual food requirements of resident lakebed population (expressed in terms of maize)	*kilos*	*hectares of chinampa*
a. One average person	200	
b. Subsistence needs of tenant population (4,220 × 200)	840,000	280
c. Subsistence needs of nontenant population (32,400 × 200)	6,480,000	2,160
d. Nonsubsistence needs of nontenant population (.2 × 32,400 × 200)	1,296,000	430
e. Total	8,610,000	2,870

C. Total annual productivity of Chalco–Xochimilco chinampas (expressed in terms of maize)		*kilos*
a. 1 ha		3,000
b. 9,500		28,500,000

D. Surplus capacity (expressed in terms of maize)	*kilos*	*hectares of chinampa*
a. Total productive capacity	28,500,000	9,500
b. Needs of local population	8,610,000	2,870
c. Surplus	19,980,000	6,630

With 2870 ha required for the food supply of the Aztec III–IV population resident within the Chalco–Xochimilco lakebed, there would have remained an additional 6630 ha of cultivable chinampa land potentially available for other uses (out of a total of 9500 ha). With an annual productivity equivalent to 3000 kilos of maize per ha, this amount of chinampa could have produced the equivalent of 19,890,000 kilos of maize per year. The equivalent of this much maize could have been available every year as surplus from the Chalco–Xochimilco chinampa zone. This figure should be regarded as an absolute maximum, as it assumes full productivity over the total area formerly covered by chinampas in Lake Chalco–Xochimilco (see Table 12.4 for a summary of these calculations).

Of critical importance in any estimate of surplus productive capacity is the matter of labor input. We have assumed already that one effective laborer can cultivate no more than .75 ha of chinampa land at high productivity. On this basis, we earlier calculated that a labor force of some 12,700 people would be needed to work the 9500 ha of chinampa land at this high level of productivity. Thus, roughly a third of the total Aztec III–IV population of 36,620 people living within the Chalco–Xochimilco lakebed would have been fully engaged in chinampa cultivation for this production to be feasible. This is not an unreasonable proportion, but it would suggest a high degree of full-time participation in chinampa cultivation by most effective laborers residing within the Chalco–Xochimilco lakebed in Aztec III–IV times.

A Model of Late Postclassic Food Production in the Chinampa Zone

Before developing the model more completely, I shall present its major points in summary form.

SUMMARY OF THE MODEL

At the outset of the Late Postclassic (Figure 12.3, ca. A.D. 1200, Aztec Phase I), nucleated communities began to develop around the edges of Lake Chalco–Xochimilco and on natural islands within its borders (Chalco, Xico, Tlahuac, Culhuacan, and probably Mixquic and Xochimilco). Residents of these communities probably undertook localized swamp drainage and chinampa construction within fairly restricted zones in their immediate environs near the lakeshore and around natural islands. Some minor additional drainage and chinampa construction was probably undertaken during Aztec II times, but the great bulk of the lakebed remained as unreclaimed swampy terrain until the Aztec III phase.

In Aztec III times (fifteenth century), with the expansion of the Aztec state and the ascendancy of Tenochtitlan, large-scale drainage projects within the main Chalco–Xochimilco lakebed were planned and undertaken. Most of the older chinampas also were incorporated into the large drainage and water-control system associated with large-scale chinampa agriculture of the fifteenth and sixteenth centuries. The state's purpose in undertaking and maintaining large-scale chinampa cultivation was to provide for the subsistence requirements of a large number of non-food producers at Tenochtitlan. Food supplies from the Chalco–Xochimilco chinampas were acquired by Tenochtitlan in three different ways. *(1)* Approximately 2000 ha of chinampa land were cultivated by dependent tenant farmers living in small house clusters and isolated residences scattered widely throughout the chinampa zone where they had ready access to their assigned fields. The annual surplus production of these resident tenants (the equivalent of about 2535 metric tons of maize) was appropriated as "rent" by state officials in Tenochtitlan. *(2)* Approximately 800 metric tons of grain were obtained each year in the form of tribute from nontenant chinampa cultivators residing in large, nucleated communities. *(3)* These same nontenant cultivators annually produced the equivalent of another 16,555 metric tons of maize that were absorbed by Tenochtitlan through the market system.

During the last prehispanic century, chinampa cultivation was intimately tied into the large water-control system constructed, maintained, and managed by the Aztec state (whose principal focus was at Tenochtitlan). This meant an increased measure of dependence upon Tenochtitlan for older chinampa communities in Lake Chalco–Xochimilco. Such dependence may have been an important element in the new level of political dominance achieved by Tenochtitlan during the fifteenth and early sixteenth centuries.

EXPLICATION OF THE MODEL

There is no direct evidence that the inhabitants of Xico, Chalco, Mixquic, Tlahuac, Culhuacan, and Xochimilco practiced chinampa cultivation in Aztec I–II times. However, the locations of these nucleated sites (particularly Mixquic, Xico, and Tlahuac, where substantial populations were situated far from higher, well-drained ground) is certainly suggestive of localized drainage and chinampa cultivations. Actually, such localized activity well may have been initiated earlier around Xico Island and at a few other places around the lakeshore where pre-Aztec occupation occurs (Armillas 1971; Parsons 1971b, 1973). The scarcity of Aztec I–II occupation throughout the main Chalco–Xochimilco lakebed strongly suggests the very limited significance of chinampa cultivation over most of the lakebed zone prior to the fifteenth century.

As previously noted, available archaeological and ethnohistorical evidence indicates an Aztec III date for large-scale chinampa construction and utilization. Continued occupation in Aztec III–IV times at the older Aztec I–II lakebed–lakeshore centers suggests a continuation of chinampa cultivation in these locations. On the other hand, the Aztec III–IV settlement pattern over the rest of the lakebed is so distinct from that of the antecedent Aztec I–II as to suggest distinctive exploitative systems for the two periods. The principal contrast is between *(1)* the sizable nucleated population centers established on natural and artificial islands in Aztec I–II times which continued to be occupied through the Aztec III–IV period, and *(2)* the completely dispersed pattern of small Aztec III–IV house clusters and individual residences over the main lakebed. As Armillas (1971) has observed, the overall uniformity in chinampa size and orientation throughout the

Chalco–Xochimilco lakebed is indicative of a massive, planned constructional effort carried out within a fairly short period of time. Similarly, the sophisticated technology for controlling critical water levels throughout the large chinampa zone demanded considerable engineering skill as well as a planned, unified operation (Palerm 1955; Blanton 1972b). Certainly chinampa construction and management during Aztec III–IV times is best characterized as large-scale and state-directed. Calnek's (in press) ethnohistoric studies lend additional credence to this hypothesis.

The scattered, small-site component of the observed Aztec III–IV settlement pattern conforms well with the expectations of Calnek's ethnohistoric model of dependent tenant cultivators, existing outside the traditional communal *calpulli* framework, working state-created and state-owned chinampa plots under direct state supervision. If we postulate that the small Aztec III–IV sites scattered over the Chalco–Xochimilco lakebed represent the residences of these dependent tenants, then we can approximate their population at 4220 (Table 12.4). Such a group would require about 280 ha of cultivated chinampa land for its own subsistence (at a productivity level of 3000 kilos of maize per ha per year). While the demographic structure of this hypothetical tenant population remains unknown, it seems unlikely that many more than about 1500 people (about 40%) would have been capable of fully effective agricultural labor—assuming we are dealing with nuclear family or extended family residential patterns. These 1500 effective laborers should have been capable of working about 1125 ha of chinampa land annually, including the 280 ha required for their own subsistence. Thus, the production of some 845 ha of chinampa land, equivalent to 2535 metric tons of maize, should have been directly available for state appropriation each year as rent from landed estates in the Chalco–Xochimilco lakebed.

To this point, we have accounted for the use of some 3715 ha of chinampa land: 1125 ha cultivated by resident dependent tenants (with the production of about 280 ha necessary for their own subsistence needs, and the production of about 845 ha available as rent to inhabitants of Tenochtitlan); and another 2590 ha required for the needs of the resident nontenant lakebed population (32,400 people, Table 12.4). This leaves a maximum of about 5785 ha (out of a total of 9500 ha) whose productivity might be considered as surplus that could be absorbed by the Aztec state through mechanisms other than rent from landed estates. At a level of productivity equivalent to 3000 kilos of maize per year, this could have provided Tenochtitlan with the equivalent of an additional 17,355 metric tons of maize annually.

Calnek (1973: 192) estimates Tenochtitlan's urban population at 150,000 to 200,000 in the early sixteenth century. Although this is a considerably higher figure than some other recent estimates (Sanders [1971] estimates a maximum of 72,000–82,000), we will assume that Calnek's estimate is correct. A population of 150,000 would require the equivalent of about 30,000 metric tons of maize annually for its subsistence needs (assuming an average individual requires the equivalent of 200 kilos of maize per year). A population of 200,000 would consume about 40,000 metric tons per year. If Calnek's (1972) convincing argument for the very limited local agricultural capacity of Tenochtitlan is correct, then nearly all of this produce must have derived from outside the immediate vicinity of the Aztec capital. We have calculated previously that the dependent tenant cultivators residing on landed estates in the Chalco–Xochimilco chinampa zone should have been capable of delivering the equivalent of about 2535 metric tons of maize to Tenochtitlan annually (Table 12.5). If all this

Table 12.5 **Disposition of Chinampa Surplus (Expressed in Terms of Maize)**

	kilos
A. Tenochtitlan's annual subsistence requirements	
a. Population of 150,000	30,000,000
b. Population of 200,000	40,000,000
B. Maximum total annual surplus from chinampas (6630 ha × 3000 kilos/ha)	19,890,000
C. Annual rent to Tenochtitlan from landed estates in chinampa district (845 ha × 3000 kilos/ha)	2,535,000
D. Annual tribute to Tenochtitlan from chinampa district (estimated from *Codex Mendoza*)	800,000
E. Annual tribute to Tenochtitlan from non-chinampa areas (estimated from *Codex Mendoza*)	15,200,000
F. Total supplied to Tenochtitlan from chinampa area as rent and tribute (C plus D)	3,335,000
G. Total supplied to Tenochtitlan as rent from landed estates in chinampa district and total tribute (E plus F)	18,535,000
H. Annual rent to Tenochtitlan from landed estates in central Mexico outside chinampa district	?
I. Total annually required by Tenochtitlan over and above rent from landed estates in chinampa district and total tribute	
a. 150,000 people (A[a] minus G)	11,465,000
b. 200,000 people (A[b] minus G)	21,465,000
J. Maximum potential surplus annually available through market from chinampa district, over and above rent and tribute (B minus F)	16,555,000
K. Capacity of chinampa district to supply Tenochtitlan's annual subsistence requirements	
a. 150,000 people (J minus I[a]); excess	5,090,000
b. 200,000 people (J minus I[b]); deficit	4,910,000
L. Foodstuffs required by state to underwrite nonsubsistence activities	?

material were used for subsistence, an additional 27,465–37,465 metric tons still would have been required each year (30,000 minus 2535; and 40,000 minus 2535).

Probably this additional quantity of foodstuffs was supplied through tribute and trade networks. A rough approximation of the amount of foodstuffs appropriated by Tenochtitlan as tribute from the Chalco–Xochimilco chinampa zone can be derived from ethnohistoric studies (Molins 1954–55; Barlow 1949). Using Barlow's study of the *Codex Mendoza*, Molins has quantified the amount of grain that entered Tenochtitlan from various parts of its tributary domain at the time of the Spanish conquest. Molins calculates an annual figure of 19,000 metric tons (86 *trojes*) of maize, beans, chian, and huauhtli. Calnek (in press: 11) suggests that, although this figure may be a little high, it was probably no lower than about 15,000 metric tons. We shall use a figure of 16,000 metric tons for our calculations. This grain tribute derived from an area far more extensive than the Chalco–Xochimilco chinampa district. However, using Molins' and Barlow's distribution maps and figures, one can estimate crudely the proportion of the total grain tribute that derived from the chinampa zone.

From Barlow's (1949) map, the Petlatalco tributary province seems to approximate the Chalco–Xochimilco lakebed zone with a slight extension northward. We shall use the Petlatalco food tribute to approximate the food tribute paid by the chinampa district to Tenochtitlan. Expressed in the *Codex Mendoza's* sixteenth-century measure, Tenochtitlan's total annual grain tribute amounted to a total of 86 *trojes*, of which some 4 *trojes* (about 5%) derived from the Petlatalco tributary province. If 86 *trojes* are equivalent to about 16,000 metric tons, then the annual food tribute to Tenochtitlan from the Chalco–Xochimilco chinampa zone should be roughly 800 metric tons (5% of 16,000). If we can assume that, in terms of their land and labor requirements, metric tons of maize are equivalent to metric tons of beans, chian, and huauhtli, then the potential annual chinampa surplus, unaccounted for by either rent or tribute, would have been equivalent to about 16,555 metric tons of maize (Table 12.5).

To summarize, we calculate that the chinampa district supplied the equivalent of about 3335 metric tons of maize annually to Tenochtitlan in the form of rent and tribute (2535 tons as rent and 800 tons as tribute). To supply Tenochtitlan's subsistence needs, an additional 26,665–36,665 metric tons per year still had to be generated (out of a total subsistence need equivalent to 30,000–40,000 metric tons of maize for a population of 150,000 to 200,000 people). Of this, we estimate that about 15,200 metric tons of foodstuffs (16,000 minus 800) were acquired annually from tributary provinces outside the Chalco–Xochimilco chinampa district (Table 12.5). This means that between 11,465 and 21,465 metric tons of foodstuffs (calculating by subtracting 15,200 from 26,665 and 36,665) must have been supplied each year through mechanisms other than rent and tribute—that is, through the market system (Table 12.5).

The potential annual surplus from the Chalco–Xochimilco chinampa zone (over and above rent, tribute, and local needs), equivalent to about 16,555 metric tons of maize (Table 12.5), thus could have supplied all, or most, of Tenochtitlan's remaining subsistence needs (Table 12.5). With an urban population of 150,000, there would have been a potential excess equivalent to about 5090 metric tons of maize (16,555 minus 11,465) available each year for nonsubsistence needs of the Aztec state (such as storage, long-distance trade, military operations, higher standards of living for certain elite strata, and so on). With an urban population of 200,000, a minimum of about 4910 metric tons of grain (16,655 minus 21,465) would have been acquired from sources outside the chinampa zone to supply Tenochtitlan's subsistence needs (Table 12.5). Rent from landed estates in other parts of the Valley of Mexico (Calnek, in press), outside the chinampa zone, probably could have provided this additional produce. At the moment, we have no way of estimating the amount of foodstuffs potentially available to Tenochtitlan from this latter source.

Table 12.5 summarizes the rather complex numerical calculations concerning the disposition of chinampa surplus. These figures suggest that a population of 150,000 or slightly higher would have been reasonable for Tenochtitlan in terms of the productive capacity of the Valley of Mexico and the Aztec state's unknown, but expectable, needs for agricultural produce to underwrite a variety of nonsubsistence activities. A population approaching 200,000 also could have been supported but would have placed more severe strains on Tenochtitlan's capacity to feed itself.

We are convinced that all, or most, of the foodstuffs entering Tenochtitlan each year through the market system (equivalent to about 16,555 metric tons of maize; Table 12.5) must have derived from the Chalco–Xochimilco chinampa district. Although we cannot presently demonstrate it, we doubt that any additional food surplus for the supply of Tenochtitlan could have been generated elsewhere in the Valley of Mexico outside the chinampa zone. The surplus capacity of most of the remaining valley probably is represented by the many thousands of metric tons of foodstuffs acquired annually by Tenochtitlan as tribute from outside the chinampa area. Barlow (1949) and Molins Fabrega (1954–1955) have shown that a high proportion of this total food tribute derived from within the Valley of Mexico. To this tribute must be added the rent appropriated from the landed estates outside the chinampa area, which Calnek (in press) reports scattered throughout the Valley of Mexico. The existence of numerous large, nucleated population concentrations elsewhere through the valley would have created high demands for foodstuffs almost everywhere. With its relatively low resident population and high productive potential, the Chalco–Xochimilco chinampa district was probably the only sizable area within the entire Valley of Mexico capable of producing a large food surplus for use in Tenochtitlan during Aztec III–IV times. Furthermore, as Armillas (1971) has pointed out, the chinampa district was the only rich agricultural area in the Valley of Mexico whose total productivity was directly accessible to the Tenochtitlan urban population by water transport: Literally every field was on a navigable canal. This fact is particularly important in view of the very limited development of overland transport in prehispanic times.

As Sanders (1952, 1956) and Calnek (1972) have stated, the acquisition of such a large proportion of its food supply through a market structure probably would have required a high degree of complementary craft specialization within the Tenochtitlan urban population. With such a high degree of complementary occupational specialization—that is, intensive chinampa cultivation on the part of Lake Chalco–Xochimilco residents, and craft activities on the part of the Tenochtitlan urban population—an urban population of up to 200,000 people could have been sustained by means of the rent–tribute–market mechanisms sketched earlier.

Finally, there is another aspect of chinampa cultivation that should be briefly developed here. Most chinampa land, including that utilized by nontenant cultivators, had been created by large-scale drainage projects undertaken by the Aztec state in the fifteenth century. Furthermore, the continued operation and maintenance of the entire chinampa system was possible only through a massive system of dams, sluice gates, gates, and canals that regulated the water level within narrow limits throughout the entire Chalco–Xochimilco lakebed (for example, Blanton 1972b: 172–173; Palerm 1955: 36–38). This critical water-control system was so large, complex, and interconnected that it almost certainly was managed directly by the Aztec state.

If this is a valid assessment of the situation, a special kind of relationship between chinampa agriculturalists and the Aztec state is implied. We have argued that surplus production from chinampa agriculture (equivalent to about 16,555 metric tons of maize annually) was exchanged through the market structure for a wide variety of necessary craft products. Given the critical significance of the state presence in chinampa operation, the apparent intensity of chinampa cultivation may reflect the concern of the Aztec state with insuring an adequate subsistence base for its principal urban center. Because most chinampa cultivation of the fifteenth and sixteenth centuries could not function without direct state management of critical water-control apparatus, the state probably could have issued directives concerning productivity and disposition of produce with reasonable assurance that such directives would be followed. The relatively low Aztec III–IV population of the rich Chalco–Xochimilco chinampa zone likewise may be a manifestation of the Aztec state's great concern with reserving the bulk of chinampa production for the needs of the Tenochtitlan urban community. Specifically, the extremes of regional population build-up observed in other areas of the Valley of Mexico (Parsons 1971a; Sanders 1965, 1971) may have been deliberately prohibited within this critical chinampa district whose surplus production was so essential for Tenochtitlan's food supply.

Summary and Conclusions

Tenochtitlan's total subsistence needs in the early sixteenth century would have amounted to the equivalent of 30,000–40,000 metric tons of maize annually. An undetermined additional quantity of foodstuffs certainly would have been required by the Aztec state to underwrite a variety of nonsubsistence activities. We have argued that the Chalco–Xochimilco chinampa district annually supplied Tenochtitlan with 19,840 metric tons of foodstuffs, as follows: (1) the equivalent of some 2535 metric tons of maize through the payment of rent from landed estates; (2) another 800 metric tons or so in the form of tribute payments; and (3) the equivalent of another 16,555 metric tons of maize through the market structure (Tables 12.4–5). Thus, our model posits that between a half and two-thirds of Tenochtitlan's total subsistence requirements were supplied by the Chalco–Xochimilco chinampa area. Tenochtitlan acquired most of its remaining foodstuffs as tribute from subject populations in and around the Valley of Mexico (but outside the chinampa district) and as rent from landed estates in the same general area. Within our model, the market institution assumes an especially critical role, for it structured the intake of at least 40% of Tenochtitlan's total food supply.

We stress that the model developed here is meant only to be suggestive of how we might proceed in the future. At this stage, we still do not control enough variables to adequately simulate the chinampa's role in Tenochtitlan's food supply system. Particularly distressing is the number of incompletely tested assumptions we have had to make concerning the basic parameters of productivity, labor inputs, and population.

Our basic assumptions are *(1)* that 9500 ha is a reasonable approximation of the amount of cultivable chinampa land available in Aztec III–IV times within the Chalco–Xochimilco lakebed; *(2)* that all 9500 ha were cultivated simultaneously and continuously at a high level of productivity in Aztec III–IV times; *(3)* that 1 ha of chinampa can produce the equivalent of 3000 kilos of maize per year; *(4)* that one fully effective laborer can intensively cultivate about .75 ha of chinampa land during an annual cycle; *(5)* that only people residing within the chinampa zone were involved in chinampa cultivation; *(6)* that half the population of Culhuacan and one-fifth of the population of Chalco were dependent upon chinampa cultivation for their subsistence in Aztec III–IV times; *(7)* that our archaeologically derived population estimate for the small Aztec III–IV sites scattered over the Chalco–Xochimilco lakebed should be increased by 15% to more closely approximate reality; *(8)* that our original estimate of the chinampa-dependent population living in Aztec III–IV lakebed–lakeshore centers should be increased by 20% to account for obscured sites; *(9)* that a level of production equivalent to the subsistence needs of an additional 20% of the chinampa-dependent population residing in Aztec III–IV lakebed–lakeshore centers should be added to take into account the nonsubsistence needs of these centers; *(10)* that Tenochtitlan's population at Spanish contact was between 150,000 and 200,000 people; *(11)* that the small Aztec III–IV sites scattered throughout the chinampa zone represent family household residences and that no more than 40% of such a population would have been capable of fully effective agricultural labor; *(12)* that the annual subsistence needs of an average individual during Aztec III–IV times were equivalent to 200 kilos of maize; *(13)* that the *Codex Mendoza* provides a reasonable estimate of the foodstuffs that entered Tenochtitlan as tribute in the early sixteenth century and that such tribute was distinct from rent payments from landed estates worked by dependent tenant cultivators; *(14)* that all surplus production from the chinampa zone was absorbed by Tenochtitlan; and *(15)* that Tenochtitlan was incapable of producing any significant part of its own subsistence needs within its immediate environs.

We believe these are reasonable assumptions, given the present state of knowledge about chinampa agriculture and Aztec III–IV polity, population, and settlement distribution. However, any significant changes in one or several of these critical demographic and productivity parameters could force major revisions in our model. At this point, several assumptions seem to be more problematical than others. In particular, we would point to the estimates of *(1)* Tenochtitlan's population, *(2)* the total area of chinampas under cultivation, *(3)* the area of chinampa land that one fully effective laborer could cultivate during an annual cycle in the fifteenth and sixteenth centuries, and *(4)* the quantity of foodstuffs that entered Tenochtitlan in the form of tribute as opposed to trade and rent. The two most recent estimates of Tenochtitlan's population differ considerably: Sanders' (1971) estimate of 72,000–82,000 and Calnek's (1973) estimate of 150,000–200,000. We have argued here that Calnek's estimates seem reasonable. If, on the other hand, Tenochtitlan's population more closely approached Sanders' lower estimate, then our model as presently structured does not account for the disposition of very sizable potentially available food surpluses.

Although an area of 9500 ha may be a reasonable figure for the total cumulative area devoted to cultivated chinampas in the Chalco–Xochimilco lakebed, it may be misleading to think of this much land ever being in production simultaneously. Armillas (1971: 658) has noted the ongoing construction of chinampas in Early Colonial times—surely these also are included within our estimates. Any significant reduction in the area of chinampa land will reduce the surplus available for consumption at Tenochtitlan and will force us to look elsewhere for some of that center's subsistence needs.

For the critical parameter of labor inputs, we have only Sanders' (1957: 80) statement that continual hand water probably would limit a man's cultivation capacity to .50 ha. This was the sole basis for our suggestion that .75 ha might be a reasonable approximation of the amount of chinampa land one person might be able to cultivate at a fairly high level of productivity within an annual cycle. Raising or lowering this estimate significantly would seriously affect the surplus capacity of the chinampa zone.

Throughout this discussion, following Calnek (in press), we have assumed that tribute from subject populations and rent from landed estates are two different categories of food intake for Tenochtitlan and that both are distinct from a third category: trade. This seems inherently logical to the Western mind, but I am not wholly convinced that we can assume Aztec administrators would have conceptualized these same distinctions in thinking about Tenochtitlan's food supply— particularly since we still understand relatively little about how rent, tribute, and trade actually operated. This is a major question, demanding insights into the Aztec economy that we do not possess. For our present purposes, this matter affects our model only insofar as it bears upon our assumption that the *Codex Mendoza* provides an adequate measure of Tenochtitlan's food tribute and that no materials derived as rent or trade appear in this document.

The small quantity of food apparently acquired by Tenochtitlan each year as tribute from the Chalco–Xochimilco chinampa zone (probably about 800 metric tons) is somewhat surprising in view of the much more substantial quantities of food tribute coming from other (less productive) parts of the Valley of Mexico. We take this to mean that food tribute was a relatively unimportant aspect of the chinampa district's contribution to Tenochtitlan's food supply. Frankly, this is puzzling. However, such a small quantity probably indicates that, for the chinampa zone at least, food supplies acquired through rent or trade were not being listed in the *Codex Mendoza*.

Our model imposes a great burden upon the market in the organization of Tenochtitlan's food supply. It is unfortunate that our understanding of the Aztec market as a redistributional institution remains so deficient. We know of no significant advances in the study of the Aztec market since the work of Katz (1966) and Sanders (1956). Any further refinement of our understanding of Tenochtitlan's food supply also will demand renewed study of its market system.

Acknowledgments

I am grateful to Pedro Armillas and William Sanders for much information about the chinampa zone. Our archaeological survey was carried out with the able assistance of J. Appell, M. Baylis, E. Brumfiel, A. Carr, T. D'Altroy, R. Ekstein, J. Elias, M. Esplin, B. Jaffee, K. Mauer, W. Mindell, M. Parsons, E. Prahl, Y. Schreuder, A. Wenke, R. Wenke, K. Wilcox, D. F. Wilson, D. J. Wilson, and D. Wolf. I have received constructive criticisms from Mary Parsons and Elizabeth Brumfiel. The deficiencies of this chapter may, in part, result from my failure to follow some of their advice.

References for Part III

Acosta, J. R.
  1965 Preclassic and Classic Architecture of Oaxaca. In *Handbook of Middle American Indians*, edited by Gordon R. Willey. Vol. 3. Austin: University of Texas Press. Pp. 814–836.

Armillas, P.
  1971 Gardens on Swamps. *Science* **174:**653–661.

Aveni, A. F., and Linsley, R. M.
  1972 Mound J, Monte Albán: Possible Astronomical Orientation. *American Antiquity* **37:**528–540.

Barlow, R. H.
  1949 The Extent of the Empire of the Culhua Mexica. *Ibero-Americana* No. 28. Berkeley: University of California Press.

Bernal, I.
  1965 Archaeological Synthesis of Oaxaca. In *Handbook of Middle American Indians*, edited by Gordon R. Willey. Vol. 3. Austin: University of Texas Press. Pp. 788–813.

Blanton, R.
  1972a Prehispanic Adaptation in the Ixtapalapa Region, Mexico. *Science* **175:**1317–1326.

  1972b Prehispanic Settlement Patterns of the Ixtapalapa Peninsula Region, Mexico. *Pennsylvania State University Occasional Papers in Anthropology* No. 6.

  1973 The Valley of Oaxaca, Mexico, Settlement Pattern Project, 1971 and 1972 Field Seasons. Mimeographed report submitted to the Instituto Nacional de Antropología e Historia and the National Science Foundation.

Calnek, E.
  1972 Settlement Pattern and Chinampa Agriculture at Tenochtitlan. *American Antiquity* **37:**104–115.

  1973 The Localization of the Sixteenth Century Map Called the Maguey Plan. *American Antiquity* **38:**190–195.

  In press The Organization of Urban Food Supply Systems: The Case of Tenochtitlán. Mimeographed copy prepared for publication in *Atti del XL Congresso Internazionale degli Americanisti*, December 1974.

Caso, A.
  1935 Las Exploraciones en Monte Albán: Temporada 1934–1935. *Publicación* No. 18. Instituto Panamericano de Geografía e Historia, México, D.F.

259

1947   Calendario y Escritura de las Antiguas Culturas de Monte Albán. In *Obras Completas de Miguel Othón de Mendizábal* 1:115–143. México, D.F.

Caso, A., I. Bernal, and J. R. Acosta
1967   La ceramica de Monte Albán. *Memorias del Instituto Nacional de Antropología e Historia* **13**. Mexico City, Mexico.

Charlton, T.
1972   Population Trends in the Teotihuacan Valley, A.D. 1400–1969. *World Archaeology* **4**:106–123.

Drennan, R. D.
1972   Excavations at Fábrica San José, Oaxaca, Mexico, January–July, 1972. Mimeographed report submitted to the Instituto Nacional de Antropología e Historia and the National Science Foundation.

Essad Bey
1936   *Mohammed.* London: Longmans Green.

Flannery, K. V.
1968   The Olmec and the Valley of Oaxaca: A Model for Interregional Interaction in Formative Times. In *Dumbarton Oaks Conference on the Olmecs*, edited by Elizabeth Benson. Washington: Dumbarton Oaks Research Library. Pp. 79–110.
1972   Summary Comments: Evolutionary Trends in Social Exchange and Interaction. In Social Exchange and Interaction, edited by Edwin N. Wilmsen. *Anthropological Papers, Museum of Anthropology, University of Michigan* No. 46. Pp. 129–135.

Flannery, K. V., A. V. T. Kirkby, M. J. Kirkby, and A. Williams, Jr.
1967   Farming Systems and Political Growth in Ancient Oaxaca. *Science* **158**:445–454.

Flannery, K. V., M. C. Winter, S. Lees, J. Neely, J. Schoenwetter, S. Kitchen, and J. C. Wheeler
1970   Preliminary Archeological Investigations in the Valley of Oaxaca, Mexico. Mimeographed report submitted to the Instituto Nacional de Antropología e Historia and the National Science Foundation.

Fraser, D.
1968   *Village Planning in the Primitive World.* New York: George Braziller.

Griffin, J. B., and A. Espejo.
1947   La Alfarería Correspondiente al Último Período de Ocupación Nahua del Valle de México. *Memorias de la Academia Mexicana de la Historia* **6**(2).

Haggett, P.
1965   *Locational Analysis in Human Geography.* New York: St. Martin's Press.

Harding, T.
1967   *Voyagers of the Vitiaz Straits.* Seattle: University of Washington Press.

Katz, F.
1966   Situación Social y Económica de los Aztecas durante los Siglos XV y XVI. *Universidad Nacional Autónoma de México, Instituto de Investigaciones Históricas, Serie de la Cultura Náhuatl, Monografía* **8**. (Original German edition published in 1956.)

Kirkby, A. V. T.
1973   The Use of Land and Water Resources in the Past and Present Valley of Oaxaca, Mexico. *Memoirs of the Museum of Anthropology, University of Michigan* No. 5.

Kowalewski, S. A.
1974   Ancient Settlement Patterns in the Central Valley of Oaxaca, Mexico. Mimeographed paper read for the 73rd Annual Meeting of the American Anthropological Association.

Leach, E. R.
1965   *Political Systems of Highland Burma.* Boston: Beacon Press.
MacNeish, R. S.
1964   Ancient Mesoamerican Civilization. *Science* **143:**531–537.
MacNeish, R. S., F. A. Peterson, and K. V. Flannery.
1970   *Ceramics.* Vol. 3 of *The Prehistory of the Tehuacán Valley.* Austin: University of Texas Press.
Marcus, J.
n.d.   Report to the Ford Foundation on summer field work in the Valley of Oaxaca, Mexico. Mimeograph.
In press a   The Iconography of Militarism at Monte Albán and Neighboring Sites. In *The Origins of Religious Art and Iconography,* edited by Henry B. Nicholson. Los Angeles: Latin American Research Center, U.C.L.A.
In press b   The Size of the Early Mesoamerican Village. In *The Early Mesoamerican Village,* edited by K. V. Flannery. New York: Academic Press.
Millon, R.
1973   *Urbanization at Teotihuacán.* Vol. I. Austin: University of Texas Press.
Mirambell, L.
1972   Una Osamenta Fosil en el Ex-lago de Texcoco. *Boletín, Instituto Nacional de Antropología e Historia, Época* **2:**9–16.
Molíns Fábrega, N.
1954–   El Códice Mendocino y la Economía de Tenochtitlán. *Revista Mexicana de*
1955   *Estudios Antropológicos* **14:**303–335.
Morison, S. E.
1965   *The Oxford History of the American People.* New York: Oxford University Press.
Moser, C. L.
n.d.   Excavations in Mound 7s, San José Mogote, 1974. Unpublished manuscript on file at the Museum of Anthropology, University of Michigan, Ann Arbor.
Neely, J. V.
1972   Prehistoric Domestic Water Supplies and Irrigation Systems at Monte Albán, Oaxaca, Mexico. Mimeographed paper read for the 1972 Annual Meeting of the Society for American Archaeology.
Olsson, G.
1965   Distance and Human Interaction: A Review and Bibliography. *Regional Science Research Institute Bibliography Series* No. 2. Philadelphia.
Paddock, J.
1966   Oaxaca in Ancient Mesoamerica. In *Ancient Oaxaca,* edited by John Paddock. Palo Alto: Stanford University Press. Pp. 83–242.
Palerm, A.
1955   The Agricultural Bases of Urban Civilization in Mesoamerica. In *Irrigation Civilizations: A Comparative Study,* edited by Julian Steward. Washington: Pan American Union.
Parsons, J. R.
1971a   Prehistoric Settlement Patterns of the Texcoco Region, Mexico. *Memoirs of the Museum of Anthropology, University of Michigan* No. 3.
1971b   Prehispanic Settlement Patterns in the Chalco Region, Mexico: 1969 Season. Paper on file at The Museum of Anthropology, University of Michigan, Ann Arbor.
1973   Reconocimiento Superficial en el sur del Valle de México: Temporada de 1972. Paper on file at The Museum of Anthropology, University of Michigan, Ann Arbor.

1974   The Development of a Prehistoric Complex Society: A Regional Perspective from the Valley of Mexico. *Journal of Field Archaeology* **1–2**:81–108.

Sahlins, M.
1972   *Stone Age Economics*. Chicago: Aldine-Atherton.

Sanders, W. T.
1952   El Mercado en Tlatelolco, un Estudio de Economía Urbana. *Tlotoani* **1**:14–16.
1956   The Central Mexican Symbiotic Region: A Study in Prehistoric Settlement Patterns. In Prehistoric Settlement Patterns in the New World, edited by Gordon Willey. *Viking Fund Publications in Anthropology* No. 23. Pp. 115–127.
1957   Tierra y Agua: A Study of the Ecological Factors in the Development of Mesoamerican Civilizations. Ph.D. Dissertation, Harvard University.
1965   Prehistoric Cultural Ecology of the Teotihuacán Valley, Mexico. State College, The Pennsylvania State University. Mimeograph.
1971   The Population of the Teotihuacán Valley, the Basin of Mexico, and the Central Mexican Symbiotic Region in the 16th century. In The Natural Environment, Contemporary Occupation and 16th Century Population of the Valley. *Pennsylvania State University, Occasional Papers in Anthropology* No. 3. Pp. 385–457.

Sanders, W. T., J. Parsons, and M. Logan
n.d.   Ecological Adaptation and Cultural Evolution in the Basin of Mexico, 1200 B.C.–A.D. 1519. Manuscript submitted for publication to the University of New Mexico Press.

Spores, R.
1974   Marital Alliance in the Political Integration of Mixtec Kingdoms. *American Anthropologist* **76**:297–311.

Tolstoy, P.
1972   Excavations and Environmental Research in the Lake Chalco Basin, Mexico. Mimeographed grant proposal submitted to the National Science Foundation, Department of Anthropology, Queens College (CUNY), New York.

Warner, R.
1954   *Thucydides: The Peloponnesian War*. Harmondsworth: Penguin.

West, R., and P. Armillas
1950   Las Chinampas de Mexico—Poesia y Realidad de los "Jardines Flotantes." *Cuadernos Americanos* **2**:165–182.

Winter, M.
1973   Tierras Largas: A Formative Community in the Valley of Oaxaca, Mexico. Ph.D. dissertation, University of Arizona, Tucson.

Wolf, Eric
1951   The Social Organization of Mecca and the Origins of Islam. *Southwestern Journal of Anthropology* **7** (4):329–356.

Biotic Considerations
in Prehistoric
Adaptation

13

Early Plant Husbandry in Eastern North America

Richard A. Yarnell

A list of all plants that were encouraged, tended, protected, propagated, altered, or extended in range or habitat by Native Americans in eastern North America for their own benefit would be lengthy. Included would be amaranths, carpetweed, knotweeds, maygrass, maypop, milkweeds, pokeweed, purslane, Jerusalem artichoke, ragweeds, wild rice, grapes, persimmon, plums, American lotus, sweet flag, Indian hemp, nettles, and others. The evidence for including many of these plants is incomplete at best, but the archaeological and ethnological data indicate that the Indians had developed rather close ecological interrelationships with many plant species before the time of European contact.

On the other hand, there are only a few plants for which there is good evidence of prehistoric cultigen status in the East (temperate eastern North America, primarily the deciduous forest region and, most especially, the sector from Tennessee and Arkansas to Ohio and Missouri). The most obvious are maize, common bean, pepo squash, bottle gourd, and tobacco, none of which were locally domesticated in the East. In addition, there are two or three plants that apparently were locally domesticated. These include a sunflower (*Helianthus annuus* L.), sumpweed (*Iva annua* L.), and perhaps also a species of Chenopodium.

Domestication of sunflower and sumpweed (a marsh elder) probably began during the second or third millennium B.C. Also, garden produce probably achieved major significance in subsistence during the first millennium B.C. in some locations, although the evidence is still somewhat sketchy (Yarnell 1972, 1974, in press). During this period, the first foreign cultigens, squash (*Cucurbita pepo* L.) and bottle gourd (*Lagenaria siceraria* Standl.), appeared.

Introduction of these cucurbits from Mexico may have been by way of the Southwest or by some as yet unknown more direct route. Transport through Louisiana northward up the Mississippi Valley is a possibility. Further speculation on the route of introduction must await collection and analysis of plant remains from Poverty Point sites and from Late Archaic sites in the southern and central Plains regions.

The tobacco (*Nicotiana rustica* L.) grown in the East prehistorically does not appear in the archaeological record of the Southwest until after the time of Spanish invasion. There is some prehistoric archaeological evidence of tobacco from New Mexico and Arizona, but all the identifications are of *Nicotiana attenuata* (Yarnell, in press). Neither the route nor the time of introduction of *N. rustica* into the East is known, but it seems to have bypassed the Southwest, presumably traveling directly from Mexico across Texas or the northeast Gulf of Mexico. Unfortunately, we have no clue to the time of this introduction, except that unambiguous archaeological remains of tobacco in the East do not antedate the Late Woodland.

The bottle gourd and pepo squash were present in Tamaulipas 4000 to 5000 years before their arrival in the East, but the oldest evidence of cucurbit in the Southwest is no earlier than it is in the East. Cutler and Whitaker (1961: 483) have concluded that the earliest Southwestern records of pepo squash and bottle gourd are from the 300 B.C. levels of Cordova and Tularosa caves in New Mexico. This is somewhat later than the earliest records in the East. However, C. E. Smith (1968: 257) indicates that squash was present as early as maize at Bat Cave in New Mexico; unfortunately, the date of the earliest Bat Cave maize is not known.

The earliest Bat Cave radiocarbon date accepted by Mangelsdorf, Dick, and Cámaro-Hernández (1967: 4) is 912 B.C. ± 250. This dates wood from the lowest maize level. On the basis of comparisons between the earliest Bat Cave maize, maize from the Guerra phase of Romero's Cave in Tamaulipas, and maize from the Tehuacan caves, they conclude that the earliest Bat Cave maize is no earlier than 2300 B.C. and may be several centuries later. On the basis of proximity, comparison to the Tamaulipas maize probably would be more appropriate for dating purposes, and the earliest Bat Cave maize would be no earlier than 1800 B.C.

Irwin-Williams (1973) reports that maize appeared in the Arroyo Cuervo region of New Mexico during the Armijo phase of the Oshara tradition. This phase lasted from 1800 B.C. to 800 B.C. Maize pollen occurs in the En Medio shelter in New Mexico in levels dating back to about 1600 B.C. (Irwin-Williams and Tompkins 1968; Irwin-Williams, personal communication).

Smith's record of Bat Cave squash is presently the only indication of cucurbit husbandry in the Southwest earlier than about 300 B.C. The most recent data indicate that maize, and presumably also squash, were introduced into the Southwest early in the second millennium B.C. but that the bottle gourd may not have arrived until much later.

My own interpretation of recent evidence is that early second millennium B.C. was the approximate time of initiation of sunflower–sumpweed domestication in the East. If this is true, a direct relationship probably did not exist between the early sequences of plant husbandry in the East and the Southwest. There may, however, have been other factors that influenced developments in both regions so that people in the East and also in the Southwest were receptive to innovations leading to substantial change in their basic subsistence patterns. Such factors could have directly or indirectly involved natural environment or repercussions of developments taking place in Mexico. Reported investigations have not yet produced results that allow us to go beyond such speculation.

Plant remains relevant to inquiries about early plant husbandry in eastern North America have been recovered from Salts Cave and Mammoth Cave in central Kentucky, from the Riverton site in the Wabash Valley of Illinois, from the Higgs and Westmoreland–Barber sites in eastern Tennessee, from the Collins site in northeastern Missouri, from the Newt Kash Hollow shelter and probably other rock shelters of eastern Kentucky, from the Leimbach site in northern Ohio, and possibly from a few other sites.

Some of the earliest radiocarbon dates on materials in close association with evidence of plant husbandry are from Salts Cave. The materials were recovered during Watson's excavation into the floor of the Salts Cave Vestibule, where a series of 23 natural levels were exposed in one trench. Cultigen remains were recovered from Level 4 to Level 8 and from Levels 10 and 11. Plant food remains from below Level 11 include only hickory nutshell, chenopodium seeds, and maygrass seeds. The dates are not from the trench that produced the main collection of plant remains (Quadrant IV of Trench J) but from three contiguous trenches nearby (E, G, and H). Correlations between groups of levels in the various trenches have been derived through stratigraphic interpretation (Watson 1974: 82). On this basis, there are dates of 1410 B.C. ± 110 and 1540 B.C. ± 220 for Trench J, Quadrant IV Levels 3 and 4, and dates of 710 B.C. ± 100, 990 B.C. ± 120, and 1460 B.C. ± 220 for Levels 5 to 13 (Watson 1974: 236). This inversion of the expected vertical sequence of dates is difficult to interpret. The two later dates are from the same level of one trench, whereas the three clustered earlier dates are from different trenches. This indicates an intensity of activity at approximately 1500 B.C. Although the interpretation is open to question, one may infer that part of the sequence of plant remains from Levels 11 through 4 in Trench J was deposited during the middle of the second millennium B.C.

Of even greater significance is the fact that cultigen sunflower and sumpweed seeds and many chenopodium seeds are present throughout the sequence although there is no evidence of squash below Level 5 and no evidence of gourd below Level 4. There is a radiocarbon date of 620 B.C. ± 140 on a human paleofecal specimen containing gourd seeds. The specimen was collected well into the interior of Salts Cave (Watson 1974: 236). If this date is approximately correct and if we assume that squash and gourd were introduced into central Kentucky at approximately the same time, it follows that Level 5 of Trench J-IV was deposited not much later than 600 B.C. and perhaps somewhat earlier. In any case, it is possible that these cucurbits were adopted by a people who already were cultivating gardens in which they planted sunflower, sumpweed, and possibly chenopodium, as well as foraging for various other foods. However, there is very recent preliminary evidence that squash was present in Kentucky before 2000 B.C. at two "Indian Knoll" sites (G. Crawford, personal communication).

The inference that sunflower and sumpweed were planted in cultivated plots is based on considerations of seed size and geographic range of species (Yarnell 1972, in press). Because of its habit of growing in highly disturbed ground, chenopodium likely grew in the cultivated plots also. Some progress is being made toward determining the specific taxonomic status of this plant. Electron microscopic examination has determined that it is not *Chenopodium album* or *C. hybridum* (incorrect identifications previously made by me). The seeds are very similar to those of *C. nuttaliae*, a Mexican cultigen, to *C. quinoa*, an Andean cultigen, and to *C. bushianum*, which is native to eastern North America and is probably the correct identification of the species eaten by the central Kentucky cave dwellers (Hugh Wilson, personal communication).

This information leads to various speculations regarding the prehistoric relationships of chenopodium to people in terms of ecology, phytogeography, and the domestication process. There are strong indications that it was a staple food in the Late Archaic and Woodland period diets in the region from southern Illinois to Ohio and northern Alabama, especially in central Kentucky, where it appears to have been the dominant food source at times during the period of 1500 B.C. to 300 B.C. or later (Struever and Vickery 1973; Marquardt 1974; Stewart 1974; Yarnell 1974, in press). It is suggested that chenopodium differed significantly in its early relationships to eastern people from other weedy food plants, such as amaranth, knotweed, pokeweed, and purslane. Seeds or greens of these less important food plants were collected or harvested in the disturbed habitats where they grew, perhaps in gardens, but we have no evidence to indicate that they were significantly involved in more developed plant husbandry relationships. The activities of people probably had at least incidental effects of increasing the availability of these food plants, but we have no clear indications that propagation was ever intentional.

A possible distinction between chenopodium and other weedy food plants is that it may have grown as a volunteer in garden plots under active cultivation at the time, whereas the other plants may have taken over former garden plots. There are records, however, indicating that purslane (*Portulaca oleracea* L.) grew in cultivated plots of the Aztecs and also the Huron (Chapman, Stewart, and Yarnell 1974). This is similar to the situation reported for the Jerusalem artichoke (*Helianthus tuberosus* L.) by Parker (1910: 105–106): Although it grew in the Iroquois fields, it was a volunteer which was utilized as a tuber food.

Maygrass (*Phalaris caroliniana* Walt.) is another agricultural weed that furnished an important part of the Early Woodland diet in central Kentucky and for which we have no good reason to infer that planting was intentional. However, it was an abundant source of food, judging from the paleofeces, in late spring or early summer, rather than during the regular harvest season (Marquardt 1974; Stewart 1974; Yarnell 1974).

There is good evidence from the lower Illinois Valley that knotweed (*Polygonum*) was an especially important food source during the first millennium A.D. (Struever and Vickery 1973). In fact, the seeds of this plant, which may have been a garden product, rival those of chenopodium in abundance and may have occupied a position in the diet equal or perhaps superior to chenopodium in Illinois.

There is recently discovered evidence that squash was present at the Late Archaic Riverton site in Illinois late in the second millennium B.C. During the reexamination of unidentified plant remains from Feature 8a, a small carbonized fragment of *Cucurbita* rind was discovered. A single sunflower seed from this feature is longer than the maximum length of wild sunflower seeds, just below the upper limit of the range of ruderal sunflower seeds, and just above the lower limit of the range of cultigen sunflower seeds. It is well within the length range but below the mean for seeds from Salts Cave, although its width is greater than the Salts Cave mean seed width (Yarnell, in press).

The Higgs site in eastern Tennessee has provided a sample of 110 carbonized sunflower seeds from a Terminal Archaic feature with a radiocarbon date of 900 B.C. ± 85. A corroborating date of 780 B.C. was obtained from an adjacent feature. The mean size of 24 measurable seeds is slightly larger than the mean for carbonized seeds from the Salts Cave Vestibule excavations (Brewer 1973; McCollough and Faulkner 1973: 65). Although the correlation is imperfect, both sunflower and sumpweed seeds generally increase in size through time. Because the Higgs sunflower seeds are larger than those from Salts Cave, this is an indication that the Higgs sunflower is of more recent origin than those from the earlier strata of the Salts Cave sequence.

A single carbonized sunflower seed has been recovered by Charles Faulkner from an undated Terminal Archaic feature of another site in eastern Tennessee. This seed, from the Westmoreland–Barber site (40 Mi 11), is 6.1 by 2.6 mm. The original achene probably was approximately 8.0 by 3.6 mm.

Evidence indicating Late Archaic plant husbandry still is not abundant. However, the interpretation may be advanced that sunflower and sumpweed were established as garden crops near tributaries of the lower Ohio River soon after the introduction of cucurbits into the region in the third millennium B.C. Squash and gourd probably were carried up the Mississippi Valley, or down valleys across the Plains, to the vicinity of the mouth of the Ohio River and thence eastward.

There is evidence that plant husbandry was somewhat more widespread in the East by the middle of the first century B.C. Sumpweed was present at the Collins site in northeastern Missouri by about 600 B.C. (W. E. Klippel, personal communication; Yarnell 1972). Sunflower, sumpweed, and perhaps cucurbits apparently had arrived also in eastern Kentucky by this time. Squash was present at the Leimbach site in northern Ohio by about 500 B.C. (O. C. Shane, personal communication) and possibly also at the Schultz site near Saginaw, Michigan (cf. Wright 1964: 20). Some of the cucurbit, sunflower, and sumpweed remains recovered from rock shelters in central Ohio, eastern Kentucky, and the Ozarks may be from the middle to latter part of the first millennium B.C., but the dating is questionable or uncertain.

Struever and Vickery (1973) report maize from the Early Woodland component of the Leimbach site. The plant remains from this site were sent to me by Orrin C. Shane III for analysis. Maize kernels were found in a number of samples of the Late Woodland occupation debris and from one sample identified as Early Woodland. This latter sample was taken from a level only 2 inches below deposits identified as Late Woodland. Unless additional Early Woodland samples containing maize exist, it seems premature to accept this as a valid example of Early Woodland maize. Nevertheless, the record of early squash from Leimbach is secure. Small fragments of rind were recovered from several Early Woodland features in good context.

Another apparently equivocal report of Early Woodland maize is from the Hornung site in the Ohio Valley of northcentral Kentucky. R. I. Ford (personal communication) has indicated that the Early Woodland association is not certain. However, there is some chronological overlap between assemblages referred to as "Early Woodland" and "Middle Woodland." Therefore, it is to be expected that maize would be present in some of the later Early Woodland occupations. Specific, confirmed radiocarbon dates on closely associated materials are needed to demonstrate the early occurrence of cultigens. They are not culture specific as artifacts may be. There is a possibility of maize transfer from "Middle Woodland" peoples to "Early Woodland" peoples late in the first millennium B.C., because there appears to be some overlap in time of these two periods.

The earliest convincingly dated maize in the East was recovered from the Jasper–Newman Hopewellian site in southcentral Illinois. A radiocarbon date of 80 B.C. $\pm$ 140 on associated charcoal is supported by a date of 50 B.C. $\pm$ 140 for the same occupation (Struever and Vickery 1973: 1200). There are several other Hopewellian sites in Missouri, Illinois, and Ohio that have produced small quantities of maize (see Struever and Vickery 1973). Maize also has been recovered from one Adena site: the Daines II mound in southern Ohio, with a radiocarbon date of 280 B.C. $\pm$ 140 (Murphy 1971). A second confirming radiocarbon date would make this date more convincing. These data at least are compatible with the position taken here that maize was introduced from the Southwest across the Plains into the Midwest riverine area at approximately 200 B.C. $\pm$ 100 and that this event roughly coincided with the end of the Late-Archaic–Early-Woodland development of plant husbandry as exemplified by the occupational sequence in the Mammoth Cave area (see Watson 1974). If this was indeed the case, there was a period of 2000 years after squash was introduced to the cultivated plots before maize was added to the crop plant inventory of the East. The length of time probably varied considerably from place to place and may have been reduced to zero in regions where plant husbandry was adopted after maize arrived in the East.

Presumably, the date of cultigen introduction was generally later from west to east and from downstream to upstream east of the Mississippi River. Topography, climate, and subsistence specializations probably were responsible for reducing rates of cultigen transmission.

Judging from the evidence, the common bean (*Phaseolus vulgaris* L.) was the last domesticated food plant to be adopted prehistorically in the East. Beans have been identified more often than they actually have been recovered. Persimmon seeds and honey locust seeds probably are most frequently misidentified as beans. In one case, a botanist identified a carbonized incomplete kernel of Northern Flint maize as a bean.

Wedel (1943: 26) has reported beans from the Renner Hopewellian site in Platte County, Missouri. Unfortunately, they disintegrated in the field, and the report was never verified by an authority on seed identification. Nevertheless, the Renner site may be on or near the route of introduction of beans from the Southwest, if that region were the source.

The earliest verified report of beans in the East is from the early Owasco Roundtop site in Broome County, New York, excavated by W. A. Ritchie. Two beans were in a storage pit sample which he sent me to analyze. The date of A.D. 1070 ± 80 (Y-1534) agrees well with Ritchie's estimate (personal communication). Otherwise, beans in the East have come mainly from other Owasco sites, Iroquoian sites, Fort Ancient sites, Mississippian sites, and relatively late sites in the Prairie region.

Recently, James Adovasio has reported much older beans from a rockshelter near Pittsburgh which are dated at 800 B.C. to 300 B.C. (Page 1974: 6). The age is impressive, but until the identifier and details of context are reported, it is well to reserve judgment. If the report is correct, there is a serious problem because of the absence of bean records between 300 B.C. and A.D. 1070.

At present, I am inclined to suggest that beans entered the East at approximately A.D. 800 ± 100. This would be a millennium after the postulated time of maize introduction and three millennia after the introduction of squash. This would mean that it took these plants 500 to 2000 years to reach the East after they had arrived in the Southwest. Squash and gourd traveled rapidly if they came from the Southwest. Beans may have traveled more slowly; possibly it was because they were less adaptable to different environmental conditions or because they were more difficult to integrate into the plant husbandry systems of the East. The assumption is that beans arrived early in the Southwest and late in the East.

Additional recovery and careful analysis of archaeological plant remains could alter the picture dramatically and probably will change it to some extent. More important, it will reduce the uncertainty of many of the assumptions that now have to be made in order to depict the origins and development of plant husbandry in the East.

14

"Twitching": A Minor Ailment Affecting Human Paleoecological Research

Bruce D. Smith

Introduction

During this century, American anthropology has operated under a succession of different paradigms (Stocking 1968). Each successive paradigm change or theoretical restructuring that has taken place within anthropology has eventually influenced the theoretical framework of the subdiscipline of prehistoric archaeology. The influence has, however, been far from instantaneous.

Prior to the most recent crisis period, which began during the early 1960s, such theoretical debates were, for the most part, thrashed out by social anthropologists, with the results then passed on to archaeology. Archaeologists neither precipitated nor directly participated in the theoretical restructuring in the field but, rather, received the news second-hand from social anthropology. As a result, archaeologists long suffered from a lingering malady that recently has been diagnosed as "paradigm lag" (Leone 1972: 16–17). Because of both the lack of communication between social anthropologists and archaeologists and the difficulty in theoretical retooling within archaeology, the acceptance of a new theoretical framework within social anthropology always has been followed by a lag of a number of years before the necessary theoretical restructuring was accomplished within archaeology. During such lag intervals, archaeology has "acknowledged the theoretical requirements of the current anthropological paradigm but in practice actually has addressed its substantive contributions to the preceding paradigm" (Leone 1972: 16). Archaeology in the past has received its paradigms second-hand and has, during lag intervals, claimed to be operating under the recently established paradigm while actually addressing problems defined under the paradigm recently rejected by social anthropology. Not surprisingly, social anthropologists tended to consider archaeology as a theoretically impure and intellectually stunted sibling.

This situation has, however, changed somewhat during the last 10 years. Both social anthropology and archaeology have been undergoing a period of theoretical and methodological soul-searching, and both are exhibiting the classic symptoms of paradigm crisis (Kuhn 1970). Although the crisis in archaeology is clearly home-grown rather than another hand-me-down from social anthropology, there are a number of similarities in the events taking place in the two subfields, in terms of both emergent theoretical schools and the issues being discussed.

Human ecology, for example, has emerged as a powerful theoretical school in both social anthropology and archaeology. Since the theoretical underpinnings, problem orientation, and research design of the ecological approach are generally the same whether the human population being studied is contemporary or prehistoric, communication and discussion between these separate subfields of social anthropology and archaeology have increased greatly. Once the human ecology subfield of social anthropology recovered from the initial shock of discovering that archaeology, the supposedly retarded sibling, not only was operating with a vocabulary in excess of 500 words but also was capable of participating in discussions of theoretical issues, the traditional barriers between the subfields began to erode. Paradigm lag, at least for those archaeologists employing the ecological approach, no longer exists.

The ecological approach in archaeology still suffers from a number of minor ailments, however, and it is one of these minor ailments that I would like to consider in this chapter. The ailment in question is "twitching" (the derivation of the term will be explained later).

Twitching is a symptom of a paradigm lag that exists within that subfield of archaeology which deals with the identification and analysis of nonhuman skeletal remains from archaeological sites.[1]

Faunal analysis is of obvious relevance to ecologically oriented analyses of prehistoric human populations. In analyzing and interpreting the interrelationships of prehistoric human populations with the nonhuman components of the ecosystem, archaeologists are, in effect, attempting to define accurately the niche of the human component in the ecosystem. Defining the nature of the relationships that existed between the human component and the animal species composing the faunal section of the biotic community is an important aspect of any such attempts at niche analysis of prehistoric human populations. Obviously, animal skeletal remains recovered from archaeological sites represent a primary source of data concerning such prehistoric man–animal relationships and are capable of yielding answers to a series of interrelated and very basic questions about prehistoric human–animal coaction pairs. Unfortunately, much current research that involves analysis of faunal materials does not raise such basic questions, much less seek answers to them. This obvious discrepancy between what the theoretical goals and problem orientation of faunal analysis should be in terms of the ecological approach, and what they, in large measure, actually are, is a result of paradigm lag. The human ecological approach is now well-established within archaeology. It has gained wide-scale acceptance within the field, and ecological-systemic models have been articulated successfully with the archaeological data base. Although faunal analysis is an integral aspect of such human ecological studies, the necessary theoretical restructuring of research within the subfield has, in many cases, not yet been carried out. Many people involved in faunal analysis, while paying lip service to the ecological approach, follow a research design that has remained basically unchanged for 20 years.

There have been some successful attempts, however, to make the necessary changes in the research design of faunal analysis. A number of excellent ecologically oriented studies of prehistoric and historic man–animal relationships have appeared during the 1960s. There exist, then, two distinct theoretical approaches within the subfield of faunal analysis. The first, which can be termed the "ecological approach," is oriented toward analyzing prehistoric human–animal coaction pairs within an ecological framework. The second approach encompasses those individuals still suffering from paradigm lag who

---

[1] Of the numerous descriptive labels that have been used to identify this subfield, including *faunal analysis, ethnozoology, archaeo–zoology, zoo–archaeology,* and *osteo–archaeology,* the term *faunal analysis* carries fewest theoretical overtones and will, therefore, be employed in this article.

have not yet made the necessary changes in the problem orientation of their research. For lack of a better term, this second theoretical school will be called the "twitching" approach.

The "Twitching" Approach

The term "twitching" is borrowed from a current debate taking place within birding (sometimes referred to as "birdwatching"). Those birders primarily interested in adding to their list of sighted species are referred to as "listers" in the United States, whereas in England, they are known as twitchers "for their habit of 'twitching off' to see a bird" (Martin 1974: 90–91). This primary interest in a species list is also characteristic of the twitching approach in faunal analysis. In this case, of course, the list is of animal species represented at an archaeological site. Explaining why such species lists are of primary importance to twitchers involves a brief discussion of the historical development of faunal analysis in the United States.

Until fairly recently, the skeletal elements of animal species recovered from archaeological sites were not considered part of the analytical domain of the archaeologist. They were not eyed with the same interest as, for instance, ceramic or lithic materials. This attitude is not simply a failure to recognize the potential value of faunal remains but involves the more serious error of not considering faunal materials part of the archaeological data base (Daly 1969: 152). This distinction has become distressingly clear in recent years. Although archaeologists now recognize the potential importance of faunal data and are modifying and refining recovery techniques accordingly, many still view faunal samples, once recovered, as something to be analyzed by nonarchaeological specialists, usually zoologists. Olsen (1971: 1–2) recently has described the gallant efforts of such overburdened vertebrate specialists, who in the past have graciously and generously (and usually *gratis*) turned from their own projects to identify the dusty, unsorted fragments of bone brought to them by archaeologists.

Zoologists typically approached archaeological faunal samples with a certain impatience, and with the belief that the only possible worthwhile return from such an undertaking would be the identification of an unusual species, or perhaps the expansion of the geographical range of a known species.[2] As a result, "only the bare minimum of

---

[2] I do not mean to imply that research interests such as expanding the known prehistoric geographical distribution of a species are not inherently interesting projects. The point is that zoologists quite often have a definite set of goals in mind when they analyze archaeological faunal samples and that these goals are clearly zoological in nature.

time is expended, and the result is the 'laundry list' type of report"
(Olsen 1971: 1). Such laundry list faunal reports, which, up until fairly
recently, were the rule rather than the exception, consist of a list of
species represented, including the number of skeletal elements per
species and perhaps minimum number of individual counts and
corresponding projected meat yield values. The brief text that accom-
panies such lists does little more than describe in words what is shown
in the species list. Nonarchaeological specialists in the United States
have been producing such reports for almost 50 years.

The practice of turning over faunal materials to zoologists for
analysis and the type of twitching report that has resulted have had
several unfortunate consequences. Archaeologists have come to view
faunal remains as within the domain of zoology rather than archaeology, and thus have tended to accept such reports as presenting all the
information that could possibly be extracted from such faunal samples.

Many recent attempts by nonarchaeologically trained specialists to
analyze faunal samples from archaeological sites have, however,
progressed well beyond this ("laundry list") level of analysis. The
basic procedural steps that are being followed in these faunal research
projects are shown in flow chart form (Figure 14.1) and briefly
described here. The 15 steps illustrated in Figure 14.1 can be separated
into an identification phase and a description phase. The identification
phase comprises 7 steps.

1. *Modification.* Modification of bone fragments recovered from
archaeological sites can be observed at any point in the identification
phase; it was placed first simply for convenience. Types of modification include decoration, polish, striations, butchering marks, evidence
of burning, and so on. Except for butchering marks and burning, these
various types of modification usually indicate secondary use of
osteological materials as tools, items of personal adornment, food
utensils, gaming devices, and so on.

2. *Identification as to skeletal element.* As each bone fragment is
considered, it is initially separated into one of three categories:

   a. *Unidentifiable.* Many bone fragments recovered from archae-
      ological sites are so small and/or so modified (by fire, for
      example) that it is impossible to identify them other than as to
      type of material (bone).

   b. *Identifiable to class.* Many bone fragments recovered from
      archaeological sites are too small to allow determination of
      what skeletal element they are; yet, because of structural
      characteristics, they can be identified to taxonomic class
      (Pisces, Aves, Mammalia, Mollusca, and so on).

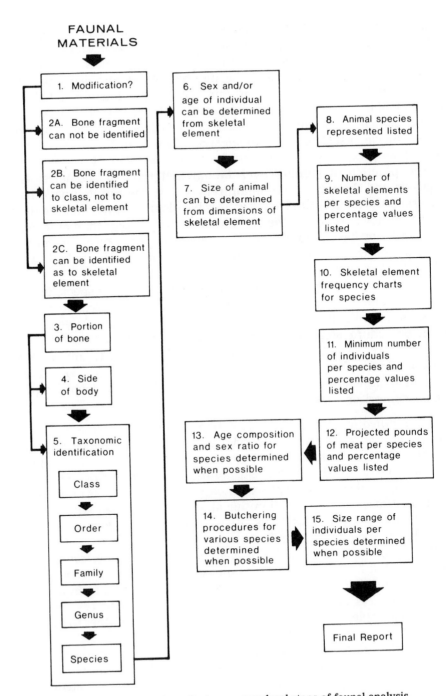

Figure 14.1 The basic preliminary procedural steps of faunal analysis.

c. *Identifiable to skeletal element.* Some bone recovered from any archaeological site can be identified to the specific skeletal element represented (radius, humerus, premaxilla, and so on). It is from this portion of the faunal sample that further steps in the identification process may proceed.

3. *Portion of bone.* Whether the bone fragment represents the proximal, distal, or shaft portion of a long bone (or a more specifically defined portion of the element) is usually, but not always, recorded.

4. *Side of body.* It is usually, but not always, possible to determine whether the skeletal element is from the left or the right side of the animal represented.

5. *Taxonomic identification.* Once the bone fragment has been identified as far as possible in terms of skeletal element, portion of bone, and side, it is identified in terms of the taxonomic group it represents. That a bone fragment can be identified to species or only to the order or family depends upon a number of variables, including: *(a)* the specific skeletal element in question (that is, rib versus mandible), *(b)* the amount of diagnostic surface present, *(c)* the ability of the person who is identifying the specimen, *(d)* the size of the comparative collection being employed, and *(e)* the degree of morphological similarity of species within the taxonomic group.

6. *Determining age or sex.* It is possible in some cases to determine the sex or age of the animal represented from certain skeletal elements. Age or sex determinations are based upon criteria developed from modern studies of the species in question. Because of the increasing research into finding accurate osteological age and sex indicators, the number of species for which such skeletal indicators have been found is increasing significantly.

7. *Determining size.* Using criteria developed from research done on modern animal populations, it is sometimes possible to estimate the size of the animal from the dimensions of specific skeletal elements.

Once these seven steps of the identification phase have been completed and the information obtained has been recorded, the description phase, consisting of eight additional steps, is initiated.

8. *List of species represented.* It was a common practice prior to 1950 to sum up the interaction between the prehistoric human population being studied and the animal species exploited by giving a basic list of animal species exploited. Only Step 5 in the identification phase was necessary to produce such a list.

9. *Adding the number of skeletal elements identified and assigned to each taxonomic group.* This provides slightly more information than a basic list of species represented.

10. *Skeletal element frequency charts.* Such charts rarely are

presented in faunal reports even today, but they are nonetheless a necessary prerequisite for Step 11.

11. *Determining the minimum number of individuals represented per species.* Such a practice was first suggested by Theodore White (1953). Although the minimum number of individuals per species is a much more reliable indicator of the relative importance of various species in the diet of prehistoric human populations than the number of skeletal elements recovered per species, it was neither immediately nor universally adopted by individuals involved in faunal analysis. The minimum number of individuals represented per species in a faunal sample is determined by the most frequently occurring skeletal element by side and portion (for instance, left distal humerus). Criteria of age or size are used quite often to increase minimum number of individual values.

12. Using live weight values and live-weight–edible-meat ratios derived from modern population studies, *projected meat yield values* can be determined for each species. These meat yield values, although in many cases little more than gross estimates, provide the most accurate assessment of the relative importance of the exploited animal species in the diet of the human population being studied.

13. Utilizing the information obtained in Step 6, *age composition charts* of various species sometimes are given. Such age composition charts rarely are included in faunal reports for any species but the white-tailed deer, however.

14. Utilizing the information obtained in Step 1, *butchering procedures* are mentioned quite often, especially for the white-tailed deer.

15. *Determining the size range of individuals* usually is done only for species such as fish and aboriginal dogs.

When the 15 steps briefly described here are completed, the information is integrated into a faunal report, which usually appears as a separate chapter or faunal appendix within a larger archaeological monograph. The faunal report can be expected to include a list of species, including the following information for each species represented: the number of skeletal elements recovered, the estimated minimum number of individuals, and the projected meat yield, as well as unidentified fragment totals. It may be broken down according to provenience units or cultural units or may represent the faunal materials recovered from the entire site. A faunal report may also contain: *(1)* a discussion of deliberately modified osteological specimens, *(2)* an age composition chart for a few species, *(3)* a rough estimate of seasonality of exploitation for a few species, *(4)* a discussion of butchering procedures for a number of species, or *(5)* a brief discussion of the relative importance of a number of species in the diet of the human population being studied. The text of such reports generally only reiterates the data already presented in the lists, tables, and graphs.

I would assert that these more recent reports, although they involve more procedural steps and may, in passing, mention current theoretical concerns, are still basically laundry lists. The theoretical and methodological base employed is still that of the twitching approach.

The primary research goal of faunal analysis under the twitching approach is the identification of each individual skeletal element as to species, body part, side, and so on, and the presentation of this information in the final report. Such reports are almost entirely descriptive in nature. Any attempts at interpretation or explanation of the presented data are brief, to say the least.

Since identification, quantification, and description of skeletal elements is the primary research goal under the twitching approach, it is not surprising that the basic problems confronting the subfield are then thought to be problems involving identification. This attitude is illustrated clearly in the many recent publications on faunal analysis that are devoted to the problems of telling one bone from another. This attitude also is displayed in the continual efforts on the part of twitchers to ridicule erroneous identifications on the part of inexperienced individuals, who, incidentally, usually turn out to be archaeologists. Most people, including myself, invariably laugh with each retelling of the anecdote concerning the unfortunate individual who misidentified a catfish pectoral spine as a woodpecker bill. While such stories reflect the attitude on the part of twitchers that problems of identification are the major problems that exist in faunal analysis, they may also reinforce the feelings on the part of many archaeologists that faunal analysis is best left to nonarchaeological specialists. I would suggest that, although the problems involved in the correct identification of skeletal elements certainly should not be passed over lightly, they do not represent the central problem areas of faunal analysis. Similarly, identification, quantification, and description of skeletal elements should not be viewed as the final goal of faunal analysis. The procedural steps outlined in Figure 14.1 should, rather, be viewed as the first analytical step necessary for an adequate consideration of the prehistoric human–animal interface. Faunal reports produced under the twitching approach invariably stop just where they should begin.

Another major criticism that can be leveled against the twitching approach involves the complete lack of an explicitly scientific methodology. This fact too is an indication of paradigm lag within the subfield. Although now it generally is accepted that archaeological reasoning should employ the full scientific cycle, the twitching approach is still solidly inductive. General research problems, specific hypotheses, and associated test implications are not developed prior to either excavation or laboratory analysis.

Under the twitching approach, each skeletal element is viewed as containing a separate identity, a kernel of truth. The task of the faunal researcher is to extract this kernel of truth, to determine the identity of each bone fragment, and to compile all of these bits of truth into a final report. Once this is done, and the truth is revealed, there is little further that can or should be done.[3]

Practitioners of the ecological approach in faunal analysis, on the other hand, would argue that such final reports represent a preliminary stage of analysis, and there is much more that can and should be done.

The Ecological Approach

Interpretation, rather than identification, should be stressed as the final goal of bone examinations [Olsen 1971: 1].

The primary research goal of the ecological approach in faunal analysis is to explain, in the form of predictive models, the interface that existed between prehistoric human populations and the faunal section of the biotic community. Such models then can be integrated into more general models concerned with the overall subsistence-settlement strategies of prehistoric human populations.

Analysis of this interface area theoretically should encompass every aspect of each complex coaction pair formed between prehistoric human and animal populations, from toleration to exploitation (Lawrence 1971: 598; Smith 1975a). The available data concerning many aspects of such prehistoric man–animal coaction pairs are, however, very limited. As a result, the only aspect of such coaction pairs that can be studied in any detailed manner is the trophic relationship that existed: specifically the nature of the energy-capturing strategy employed by prehistoric human populations. This somewhat narrowed goal of analyzing energy input (in the form of animal meat), energy distribution and storage, as well as the parallel energy output on the part of the human population, can be expressed more specifically in a series of five interrelated questions:

1. What was the relative importance of various species of animals in the diet of prehistoric human populations?

---

[3] Rather than replaying many of the points that have been recently made concerning the need for the full employment of the scientific cycle by archaeologists (see Hill 1972 for a summary), let me simply point out the obvious: An explicitly scientific approach is needed just as much within the subfield of faunal analysis as it is in archaeology in general.

2. Was exploitation of animal populations primarily a seasonal activity, and, if so, during what season of the year was each species hunted?
3. What procurement strategies were employed to obtain exploited species?
4. To what degree was human predation of animal populations selective?
5. What was the overall seasonal pattern and strategy of human exploitation of the faunal section of the biotic community?

Before considering each of these five questions, one must consider first the methodology of the ecological approach. The methodology employed under the ecological approach is explicitly scientific and uses a simple hypothetico–deductive approach. Specific hypotheses and associated test implications relating to the five primary research goals just listed are formulated prior to excavation or laboratory analysis, and care is taken to ensure that excavation and analysis is carried out in a manner that results in the accumulation of as much data as possible that relates to testing of formulated hypotheses. Research under the ecological approach is problem oriented, and basic assumptions, general research goals, and specific hypotheses, as well as their linked test implications, are explicitly and clearly stated. It is, of course, recognized that the strength of all archaeological arguments rests ultimately upon the strength of the bridging arguments employed, which invariably take the form of arguments from analogy (Sabloff, Beale, and Kurland 1973). The extent to which arguments by analogy are employed already in the preliminary stages of faunal analysis can be illustrated by observing that Steps 6, 7, 12, 13, and 15 in Figure 14.1 all involve arguments by analogy drawn from modern wildlife studies. Arguments involving present-day animal study analogs are also an integral part of the methodology employed in seeking answers to the five questions just listed. Let us now look at each of these questions in more detail.

1. What was the relative importance of various species of animals in the diet of prehistoric human populations?

The relative importance of various animal species usually is expressed, or reflected, in projected meat yield values. Arriving at such meat yield values involves a number of implicit assumptions, the validity of which are difficult to determine, as well as a number of procedural steps, each of which has come under recent scrutiny. The first implicit assumption made is that animal skeletal elements brought back to a settlement are representative of the animals actually killed and utilized by the prehistoric human population. The degree to which this assumption is justifiable is difficult to assess, but the possibility that such faunal debris represents a biased sample of the animals actually utilized is, in many situations, a very real and disturbing one. It is not surprising that this assumption is discussed rarely. A second major assumption is that the total sampling universe of skeletal elements with which the archaeologist has to deal is representative of the skeletal elements actually deposited. Do the skeletal elements present at the site just prior to excavation accurately reflect the skeletal elements present during occupation? The obvious sources of bias here include differential destruction of skeletal elements as a result of prehistoric human activities, the activities of scavengers, and the possibility of nonuniform preservation of skeletal elements. Although these sources of bias have been recognized for some time, it is still very difficult if not impossible to accurately quantify the extent to which such sources of bias have affected faunal samples recovered from archaeological sites. A third major concern is that the faunal sample actually recovered through excavations be representative of the total sampling universe. Obviously, excavational sampling procedure and recovery techniques should be designed to ensure a representative sample, and the researcher involved in the analysis of the faunal remains should participate in such planning (Payne 1972).

Once the faunal sample is processed through the identification phase of analysis, the minimum number of individuals per species (MIND) represented in the sample is determined. Although the MIND procedure is not without some shortcomings, especially when small bone samples are involved (Uerpmann 1973), and although it is important to indicate the specific method employed in determining minimum number of individual counts (Clason 1972; Grayson 1973), it is still the most accurate and reliable method of determining the relative importance of different animal species in prehistoric human diets.

Total meat yield values for each species then are projected by multiplying MIND values by an average edible meat weight value per individual for each species. While the use of an estimated average live weight value obtained from modern wildlife research produces accurate meat yield estimates for species of animals that rapidly reach a characteristic maximum adult size, it may introduce considerable bias when applied to species that show variation in live weight among individuals of the same population. The accuracy of such meat yield values can be improved by strengthening the arguments of analogy. This involves understanding how such factors as age and sex influence animal weight in present-day situations, and, at the same time, utilizing more fully the available archaeological data concerning these factors (Smith 1975b). The determination of the relative importance of various species of animals in the diet of prehistoric human populations is only the first step in analysis of the prehistoric man–animal interface.

2–3. Was exploitation of animal populations primarily a seasonal activity, and, if so, during what season of the year was each species hunted, and what procurement strategies were employed to obtain the exploited species?

Data from three separate sources are employed to construct arguments concerning the seasonality of exploitation of prehistoric animal populations and the possible procurement techniques employed by human hunters (Figure 14.2).

a. *Partial niche reconstruction of primary prey species.* The first source of data is detailed wildlife studies done on modern animal populations. Information concerning present-day animal species is employed to partially reconstruct the niches of those animal species and species groups that were of primary importance to the prehistoric human population being studied. Such partial reconstructions are selective in that only those aspects of the niches of the species in question that are directly relevant to their interaction with the human population are considered. Some of the aspects that should be considered in such reconstructions include seasonal variation in habitat preference, foraging patterns, food preference, density, and group size and composition, as well as seasons of mating and birth, biotic potential, recruitment rates, and mortality factors. Many of these attributes are as characteristic of a species as such obvious physical ones as weight, and, thanks to the detailed wildlife studies done over the last 30 years, their range of variation is, in most cases, well enough known to justify application of the data to prehistoric populations of the same species. Such selective niche reconstructions of animal species should not, however, be confused with the thumbnail sketches of animal species that are often inserted in reports. The validity of niche reconstructions depends upon adherence to a number of principles that are analogous to the guidelines followed in employing ethnographic analogs (Ascher 1961).

1. The modern data that are employed should be taken whenever possible from original case studies rather than from secondary sources.
2. The studies that are utilized should have been done on animal populations that were relatively undisturbed by man.
3. The wildlife studies should involve animal populations situated in locations that are geographically close and environmentally similar to the archaeological region under study.

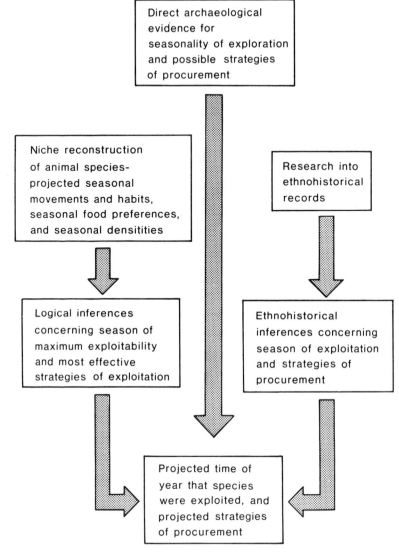

Figure 14.2 The process of employing data from three separate sources to construct arguments by analogy concerning the seasonality of exploitation of prehistoric animal populations and the possible procurement techniques employed by human hunters.

4. All pertinent data extracted from primary sources for use in niche reconstruction should be cross-checked with numerous other references to confirm its general accuracy.

Once such selective niche reconstructions of primary prey species are complete, an attempt can be made to determine if there is any period of time during the yearly cycle that the species could be more easily and more effectively exploited and to determine the possible procurement techniques that could have been employed. In some cases at least (for example, migratory waterfowl), there are obvious seasons of the year when particular species are more vulnerable to human predation. Once logical hypotheses are formulated concerning the most advantageous periods of the year to exploit a certain species and the possible procurement techniques, they can be compared with any pertinent ethnohistorical or present-day information concerning seasonality and strategies of exploitation of the species in question. It is important, of course, to formulate a number of hypotheses at this stage of analysis, rather than limit the range of possibilities (Chamberlain 1965).

b. *Ethnohistorical and present-day information.* Ethnohistorical accounts of Amerindian populations are the primary source of such information. If the direct historical approach cannot be applied, analogs should be drawn from human populations utilizing the same species of animal in a similar environmental situation and having the same level of technological proficiency in hunting as the prehistoric population under study. Such ethnohistorical accounts also should be drawn, if possible, from Indian groups in close geographical proximity to the archaeological study area. The usual care should, of course, be taken in interpreting and utilizing such ethnohistorical information. Historical and even modern-day accounts of strategies of exploitation of animal species also can be useful sometimes, as long as the guidelines given here are followed. Once the test implications of hypotheses formulated on the basis of wildlife studies are compared with available ethnohistoric, historic, and modern information, the validity of such hypotheses can be tested further by seeing how well they are supported by the available archaeological evidence.

c. *Direct archaeological evidence.* Data recovered through archaeological excavation that can be employed to test the validity of hypotheses concerning seasonality and strategies of procurement are of a number of types. In most cases, the strength of such "direct" archaeological evidence rests ultimately on arguments by analogy. Such is the case, for instance, with the most obvious type of archaeological evidence for seasonality of exploitation: osteological indicators of the season of death of animal species. As a result of the continuing research by wildlife ecologists into osteological indicators of not only the season of death of an animal but also its sex, age, and nutritional status, the amount of information that an archaeologist can extract from faunal samples is increasing every year. Application of such osteological markers of age, sex, season of death, and nutritional status of animals to prehistoric faunal samples involves an implicit assumption of uniformity between modern and prehistoric animal populations; it involves an argument by analogy. The sex ratio and age composition of prehistoric harvests of animal species, when compared with information concerning seasonal variation in the size, age, and sex composition of species groupings, also can lend support to hypotheses concerning seasonality of exploitation and strategies of exploitation.

If preserved, fragments of implements employed in procuring animals, such as snares, nets, spears, and fishhooks, can suggest not only methods of procurement but also the season of the year when such methods would have been most successfully employed.

In addition to osteological and artifactual indicators of seasonality and strategy of exploitation, locational information of faunal materials also can be of importance in some cases. Features such as pits, for instance, that were filled with bone refuse over a short seasonal period and then sealed could yield information concerning species exploited during that season, based on any osteological indicators of season of death present in the feature.

Based on this brief discussion, faunal research certainly should be directed along a number of paths of inquiry in determining the seasonality of exploitation and possible techniques of procurement of animal species by prehistoric human populations. More accurate selective niche reconstructions should be undertaken. Ethnohistoric accounts should be analyzed to extract pertinent information. And, finally, excavation should focus on recognizing and recovering important osteological, artifactual, and locational data, while laboratory analysis should focus on careful identification and interpretation of such data against the backdrop of expectation provided by wildlife and ethnographic analogs.

4. To what degree was human predation of animal species selective?

The projected meat yield values for each species represented at an archaeological site usually give a fairly accurate representation of the importance of different animals in the diet of prehistoric human populations. It is not possible, however, to determine accurately from such meat yield values if some animal species were being exploited more intensively than others. The white-tailed deer, for instance, represents a significant percentage of the total meat yield at many archaeological sites in the eastern United States. Is this high representation a function of selective human predation, concentrating on white-tailed deer populations to the relative exclusion of other species? Or is it, on the other hand, simply a function of the high biomass levels and high biotic potential of the white-tailed deer? To measure the extent to which exploitation of animal populations by prehistoric human groups was selective, some idea of the abundance of different species in the faunal portion of the prehistoric biotic community obviously is needed as a reference base. Two such criteria of relative abundance that can be obtained from selective niche reconstructions are the estimated annual productivity of a species and the estimated biomass of a species. Of these two, the estimated biomass level is both more easily obtained and a more appropriate criterion to employ (Smith 1974: 285). The biomass of an animal species is a function of a number of complex factors, and rather than simply obtaining an average biomass or density estimate for a species from a general source, it is better to follow the guidelines suggested earlier for selective niche reconstruction. Although this method of measuring prehistoric human selectivity of exploitation of animal populations by comparing estimated biomass levels with meat yield projections was employed by a number of researchers in the late 1960s, the first published application of the method did not appear until 1971 (Munson, Parmalee, and Yarnell 1971).

Once the pattern of selective exploitation of the faunal section of the biotic community by a prehistoric human population has been quantified, hypotheses concerning why some species are selectively exploited to the relative exclusion of others can be formulated and tested. Factors that have been found to have influenced the selectivity of prehistoric human exploitation of animal species in the eastern United States include biotic potential, amount of edible meat per individual, ease of capture, and seasonal changes in the density levels of prey species (Smith 1974: 288, 1975a).

To quantify more accurately the selective nature of prehistoric human predation, faunal research should be directed toward obtaining more accurate estimates of the relative importance of animal species in prehistoric human diets and toward more accurately estimating the prehistoric seasonal biomass levels of a variety of animal species.

Faunal research should be directed also toward obtaining a wider range of models of both human and nonhuman predation. Our ability to explain such patterns of selective exploitation will be increased as the range and depth of our knowledge concerning possible analogs increase.

5. What was the overall pattern and strategy of human exploitation of the faunal section of the biotic community?

Answering this question involves drawing together all the interrelated lines of evidence obtained from a variety of sources concerning both the pattern of predation and the underlying strategy that produced the pattern. The important dimensions of the pattern of energy capture are the primary prey species exploited, the degree to which predation was seasonal and selective, and the methods employed in the procurement of prey species. The important factors to be identified and explained in terms of the strategy of energy capture are those which determined why certain species were exploited selectively by certain methods during certain seasons of the year. The underlying strategies of predation employed by prehistoric human populations in North America reflect a continual adaptation to, and evolution within, a variety of ecosystem situations over a period of at least 10,000 years. These prehistoric human populations employed some variation of the energy capture strategy that is employed by all predator populations, both human and nonhuman: a seasonal round of selective utilization of prey species that were dependably available at high seasonal densities, that were obtainable with a minimum of energy expenditure, and that could sustain, within limits, continual annual predation.

Once a model is constructed that explains the pattern and underlying strategy of energy capture involving animal species as fully as possible, that model then can be integrated into a more general model of the overall subsistence-settlement strategy of the prehistoric human population being studied. The construction of such general predictive models for prehistoric human populations is one of the basic research goals of the ecological approach in archaeology.

Prognosis

The twitching approach is both a symptom of the paradigm lag that exists in the subfield of faunal analysis and an ailment affecting human paleoecological research. How long this ailment will continue to retard the development of more accurate predictive models of prehistoric strategies of predation depends upon two interrelated factors: first, how quickly archaeologists realize that faunal remains belong solidly within the domain of archaeological analysis, and, secondly, how quickly archaeologists realize that the validity of models concerning prehistoric human predation of animal populations rests ultimately upon the strength of the arguments by analogy employed. The needed analogs, as well as the knowledge necessary to correctly and accurately employ such analogs, will be found largely within the field of wildlife ecology.

15

Prehistoric Hunting of New World Wild Sheep: Implications for the Study of Sheep Domestication*

Gary A. Wright   Susanne J. Miller

Introduction

The paleontological record of the genus *Ovis* extends into the Pliocene in the Old World (Vereshchagin 1959) and into the late Middle Pleistocene glaciation in North America (Péwé and Hopkins 1967). In the Crimea, *Ovis* was hunted before the Acheulian and, in China, by the time of the Mindel glaciation (Korobitsyna, Nadler, Vorontsov, and Hoffman 1974). In eastern Europe and southwestern Asia, the earliest evidence for hunting by humans dates from the Mousterian during the Würm glaciation (Perkins 1964; Radulesco and Samson 1962). The domestication of *Ovis* was an Old World phenomenon, but the time range during which the process took place is imperfectly known. Presumably, it occurred during the end-Würm and/or early post-Pleistocene in a number of localities in southwestern Asia. A major problem has been identification of early domesticates, particularly

* An earlier version of this chapter was presented to the Symposium on Recent Research in Anatolian Prehistory at the 72nd general meeting of the American Anthropological Association on 1 December 1973 in New Orleans.

since there seem to be few if any morphological differences from their wild counterparts.

Five approaches have been proposed by which a newly domesticated species may be differentiated from the wild species. The first involves the identification of the morphological changes incurred during the evolutionary process from the wild to the domesticated state (Hole, Flannery, and Neely 1969: 262–314). The second suggests that the natural habitat zones for the wild species be determined. If a species is found in large numbers outside that zone in archaeological sites, even if there is no morphological evidence of domestication, this still would imply a change in man–animal relationships. For example, sheep constitute about 20% of the fauna at PPNB Munhata in the Jordan Valley. Morphologically, they are "wild" (Ducos 1968), but they must have been introduced from their natural habitat zone, the Zagros–Taurus arc, by man and, hence, should be considered domesticated (Wright 1971: 463–464).

The third approach involves the study of thin sections of bone under polarized light (Drew, Perkins, and Daly 1971). The most characteristic difference between the domesticated and wild forms is the appearance of a "blue rim" outlining the cross section of the articular surfaces of the domesticated animals. This indicates a layer of bone in which the mineral crystallites were oriented strongly (see pp. 310–311, this chapter) compared to the articular surfaces in wild animals.

The fourth approach considers the full faunal complement of a stratified site or a series of stratified sites through time. If a pattern is seen when animals that have never been domesticated (e.g., *Cervus elephus*) begin to be outnumbered by later-domesticated animals (e.g., sheep), the implication is that the process of domestication is underway (Coon 1951; Dyson 1953; Radulesco and Samson 1962).

The final approach focuses on the age structure of the individual species under consideration (for example, sheep). One hypothesis is that hunters predominantly kill mature animals, whereas mainly the young are removed from the domesticated herds. Therefore, the process of domestication should be reflected in archaeological sites by a change in the age structure of the fauna, and the immature animals should replace the mature ones as the major component of the species represented in the archaeological levels through time (Coon 1951; Perkins 1964; Radulesco and Samson 1962). We wish to consider further this final hypothesis.

Our inquiry revolves around several questions. Do herders predominantly kill immature animals? Precisely what is meant by "immature" (or "young")? Do hunters predominantly slaughter mature wild sheep? If so, under what conditions might large numbers of immature wild sheep be killed?—that is, could the age structure of kills in a domesticated population be reproduced by hunters?

To investigate these questions, we have used as our study animal North American wild sheep, concentrating mainly on the Rocky Mountain bighorn (*Ovis canadensis canadensis*). We do this for several reasons. The Rocky Mountain (and desert) bighorns have been well studied and we are able to obtain behavioral data and population statistics from the literature. Second, because these sheep were never domesticated, we do not need to consider problems of identification of domesticates. Third, we have several ethnographic accounts of hunting procedures utilized by Native Americans. Fourth, we have access to several faunal collections for direct comparison of skeletal materials.

Rocky Mountain Wild Sheep

In North America, there are two major species of wild sheep, the bighorn *(O. canadensis)* and the thinhorn *(O. dalli)*.[1] For the bighorn, our study animal, there are eight subspecies, one of which, the badland or Audubon's bighorn, is extinct. These subspecies may be placed into three types: *(1)* the Rocky Mountain bighorn *(O. c. canadensis); (2)* the lava bed or California bighorn *(O. c. californiana);* and *(3)* five subspecies of desert bighorns *(O. c. nelsoni, O. c. mexicana, O. c. texiana, O. c. cremnobates,* and *O. c. weemsi)* (Geist 1971: 9). Unless otherwise noted, we will be dealing with the Rocky Mountain bighorn but will integrate supporting data concerning other subspecies when necessary. There are two questions we wish to examine in detail: annual movements and population composition, both seasonally and overall.

Geist (1971: 62–97) has described the annual movements of bighorn sheep in Banff Park, Alberta, Canada. His studies, and those of other researchers show that wild sheep in North America are mobile, occupying several distinct home ranges. In the fall, they begin to gather in large bands 2 to 5 weeks prior to the rut, after coming down from the high country to lower elevations (the timing will, of course,

---

[1] The question of the number of species of sheep—wild plus the domesticated sheep—is still not settled. Many investigators are concluding that only one single polytypic species of sheep should be recognized, *Ovis ammon*. This species then would include five wild groups, *musimon, orientalis, ammon, nivicola,* and *canadensis,* each made up of numerous morphologically distinct subspecies (see Bradley 1968, and Uloth 1966), plus the domesticated sheep as a distinct group but not as a separate species. For purposes of clarity in this chapter, we will continue to employ the usual specific names for the wild sheep to which we are referring.

vary slightly, depending on elevation and latitude). During the rut, they disperse, either individually or in small groups, to seek ewes and move over considerable distances during the 6- to 10-week rut period. After the rut, they do one of three things: *(1)* return to the pre-rut range; *(2)* remain on the rutting range; or *(3)* inhabit a midwinter range, when they often will be found on the same ranges as the ewe bands but usually separated from them. During the late spring, most rams return to the fall or pre-rut range and are found in large groups. With the beginning of summer, they return to the high country in dispersed groups.

The ewe bands contain ewes, lambs, yearlings, and, occasionally, Class I rams, 26–36 months old (Geist 1971). The ewe groups arrive later and depart earlier from the winter ranges, where they remain from early fall until late winter or early spring. They then move to a spring range, which is usually different from that used by the rams. In the late spring or early summer, the lambing season begins with the females moving to the lambing range. Gravid ewes then may be left behind while the barren females and yearlings proceed to the summer ranges, to be joined later by the new mothers and their lambs.

Geist (1971: 64) notes that "once a ram forms the habit of moving at a specific season to a specific locality he sticks to it. . . . Females usually inherit their home-range pattern from the ewe band in which they were born and raised." Geist's remarks on patterning of movement and fidelity to home ranges apply to both bighorn and thinhorn sheep and have been corroborated by other investigators. This is one reason it is so difficult to transplant bighorn sheep to new areas away from their traditional ranges.

Group size varies considerably within a season. The highest numerical concentration of rams occurs on the pre-rut range and during the concentration just prior to the movement to summer pastures (Geist 1971: Figure 8). The highest concentration of ewes occurs just prior to the movement to the lambing grounds and summer ranges. Even in the winter grounds, the number of sheep does not remain constant (Geist 1971).

The times of the pre-rut congregation of rams and the lambing by the ewes are highly predictable. Other movements are less synchronized. The stimuli for other movements are complex and probably include climatic and forage factors (Geist 1971: 95). Where different seasonal patterns of winter range utilization have been reported, Geist (1971: 94) argues that these may be relict populations "whose traditional movements and home-range patterns have been mutilated by man."

In general, rams will summer on higher, more rugged terrain than will ewes (Woolf, O'Shea, and Gilbert 1970). Sex groups usually will remain separate. Within each individual sex group, however, there may be continual dispersal and reformation of bands during the late spring and summer even though mature individuals of the two sexes rarely will intermingle (Woolf, O'Shea, and Gilbert 1970).

Females generally remain on the home range of the maternal female group. The male will begin the disassociation process from the female band shortly after his second year begins (Geist 1971). The result is the formation of distinct, mature sex group bands. Table 15.1 presents age ratios of bighorn ewes, lambs, and yearlings in female bands from several areas at different seasons of the year.

There are two things of interest in Table 15.1. First, a ewe group may consist of up to 67% of lambs and yearlings. This may be found under two conditions. One is just prior to winter when the major mortality of lambs occurs. The other is during times of population increase when large numbers of lambs have survived the winter and have reached yearling age. Secondly, lamb survival is generally very low, thus resulting in what appears to be a very low yearling–ewe ratio compared to the lamb–ewe ratio for that year. A mortality rate (owing mainly to malnutrition or disease rather than to predation) of 70% or greater for lambs has been recorded. This is characteristic of a stable population (see, for example, Buechner 1960, and Wilson 1968).

If a lamb survives to yearling age, it will have an average life expectancy of an additional $6\frac{1}{2}$ years (Bradley and Baker 1967). After the high rate of lamb mortality, there is generally a low mortality rate until about 8 years of age. Terminal age extends into the midteens. Thus, a stable population contains, overall, a far greater percentage of animals classified as adults (for our purposes, +36 months of age) than subadults. On the average, 80% of the members of the herd may be greater than 36 months of age. A ram band will contain mainly adult males with a few Class I rams (26–36 months); a mixed band, predominantly adults of either sex; and ewe bands, a *minimum* of 33% adult females.

The implications for sampling through hunting are obvious. If ram bands are hunted, more than 90% of the animals will be males of more than 36 months of age. Mixed bands, consisting mainly of adults, can be hunted only during the winter. Large numbers of lambs can be exploited only if ewe bands are hunted just prior to winter or if the population is expanding. The first condition can be demonstrated through seasonality data, the second by the addition of large numbers of yearlings in the sample which would give a yearling–ewe ratio similar to that of an expanding population. Sizes of some average bands are compiled in Table 15.2.

Table 15.1 Observed Age Ratios of Ewe Bands, Ovis canadensis[a]

Location	Date	Lamb–Ewe	Yearling–Ewe	Reference
Tarryall, Colorado	November, 1940	54:100	30:100	Buechner 1960
Tarryall, Colorado	November, 1946	69:100	65:100	Buechner 1960
Tarryall, Colorado	September, 1950	75:100	58:100	Buechner 1960
Rocky Mountain National Park	Summer, 1939	29:100	10:100	Buechner 1960
Southwestern Arizona	Summer, 1951	60:100	28:100	Buechner 1960
Southwestern Arizona	Summer, 1952	43:100	11:100	Buechner 1960
Southwestern Arizona	Summer, 1953	50:100	17:100	Buechner 1960
Sun River, Montana	Winter, 1942–1943	78:100	*	Buechner 1960
Sun River, Montana	December, 1951	56:100	*	Buechner 1960
Sun River, Montana	December, 1954	45:100	*	Buechner 1960
Sun River, Montana	December, 1955	49:100	*	Buechner 1960
Yellowstone Park	March, 1940	27:100	*	Buechner 1960
Yellowstone Park	March, 1941	55:100	*	Buechner 1960
Yellowstone Park	March, 1945	43:100	*	Buechner 1960
Yellowstone Park	March, 1949	20:100	*	Buechner 1960
Yellowstone Park	February, 1955	35:100	*	Buechner 1960
Yellowstone Park	Winter, 1965–1966	47:100	20:100	Oldmeyer, Barnmore, and Gilbert 1971
Yellowstone Park	Summer, 1966	59:100	28:100	Woolf 1968
Yellowstone Park	Summer, 1967	48:100	*	Woolf 1968
San Juan County, Utah	Mid-July, 1965	37:100	41:100	Wilson 1968
San Juan County, Utah	Mid-July, 1966	60:100	20:100	Wilson 1968
Buffalo Peaks, Colorado	1965–1969	Ave. 59:100	Range 11–32:100	Streeter 1969
Desert Game Range	1948–1964	Ave. 50:100	Ave. 15:100	Hansen 1967
Grassy Mountain, Banff	November–December, 1966	50:100	43:100	Geist 1971
Bare Mountain, Banff	November–December, 1966	67:100	27:100	Geist 1971
Palliser Mountain, Banff	November–December, 1966	51:100	26:100	Geist 1971

[a] Asterisks (*) indicate that the count is not given.

Table 15.2 Male and Female Band Sizes, *Ovis canadensis*

Sex	Average band size	Maximum observed	Number of bands	Number of sheep	Location	Season	Reference
M	5.2	20	115	604	Banff	Midwinter	Geist 1971
F	9.5	24	48	458	Banff	Midwinter	Geist 1971
M	8.2	49	159	1302	Banff	Late spring	Geist 1971
F	11.5	41	36	416	Banff	Late spring	Geist 1971
M	5.5	33	138	763	Banff	Early fall	Geist 1971
F	9.0	23	33	296	Banff	Early fall	Geist 1971
M	5.8	24			Yellowstone	Summer	Woolf, O'Shea, and Gilbert 1970

Hunting Techniques and Archaeological Sites

Aboriginal hunting methods for sheep have been reviewed by Miller (1972). The Sheepeater bands and many others relied heavily on dogs to hunt. Sheep were driven by a group of men (three preferred) and dogs toward jumping-off ledges or inclines, or into specially constructed traps. Stone enclosures—corrals of various shapes—were used in sheep drives and are common in the mountain ranges of the western United States: for instance, the Wind River, Teton, Absaroka, and Sierra Nevada Ranges, as well as Death Valley. (Wright is currently studying prehistoric procurement methods for wild sheep in northwestern Wyoming.) Sheep, which often will bunch up when panicked (Geist 1971), were driven into an ambush where several hunters were waiting. This could be staged in a narrow canyon, a mountain pass, or behind a stone blind. The hunters would kill as many as possible by firing arrows or throwing spears which may have been poisoned. Domesticated dogs may have been used in wild sheep hunting in North America for more than 11,000 years, as we will document. Whole bands of sheep would be, and usually were, killed when these techniques were used.

We checked the ethnographic literature for indications of seasonal hunting, either of sheep in general or of rams opposed to ewes. Teit (1930: 243) reports the following of the Salishan Okanagon and Similkameen of the Western Plateau:

> In the winter sheep hunt mostly ewes were killed and the rams were let go. The latter were hunted on their summering grounds when fat by small parties in the late summer or early fall, either by still hunting (the chief object being to catch them in their lairs on hot days), or with dogs.

We have, therefore, evidence of selectivity by sex according to season. The subspecies most likely involved was *O. c. californiana*.

We now may use some of these observations to examine data from Weston Canyon Rockshelter (10 Fr 4), Idaho (Miller 1972). The canyon lies in southeastern Idaho, in Franklin County, 10 miles north of the Idaho–Utah border and bisects the Bannock and Malad Ranges of the Middle Rocky Mountains with a maximum elevation of 5500 feet above sea level. Radiocarbon dates and projectile-point styles indicate that the site was occupied from about 6000 B.C. to about A.D. 1. Mountain sheep was the major game animal found in all 12 culture-bearing levels; lesser quantities of bison, elk, bear, and porcupine were also present.

Table 15.3 presents the preliminary assessment of the age and sex of the mountain sheep for all levels combined. Age calculations based

Table 15.3 **Age and Sex Data for *Ovis* from All Layers at Weston Canyon Rockshelter, Idaho**

Mandibular dentition		Horn cores	
Age	Minimum number of individuals	Age	Minimum number of individuals
0–12 mo.	1	0–12 mo.	2
12–24 mo.	2	12–24 mo.	3
24–30 mo.	2	Male 2–5 yrs.	6
30–36 mo.	34	Adult female	7
+36 mo.	97	Male +6 yrs.	3
Total	*136*	*Total*	*21*

upon mandibular dentition are included. Criteria suggested by Cowan (1940), Deming (1952), and Mosby (1963), such as size and wear on permanent and deciduous dentition, were utilized. The identification of sex is based upon horn cores (see Baker and Bradley 1966).

A total of 136 animals could be aged by dentition. About 70% were over 3 years old (actually over 42 months, based upon their teeth). Horn-core data for 21 animals also indicate that animals over 3 years of age predominate. Our preliminary assessment suggests hunting primarily of mature females; some yearlings of both sexes and "young" males (that is, mostly those found in bachelor herds who were not sexually or socially mature) also were hunted. A few lambs and mature (+6 years) rams were taken also. We believe it was largely a late fall to early spring hunting pattern (with a lesser amount of summer hunting) when animals of all ages and sex classes would have been congregating in close proximity in large groups.

This seasonality of kills can be seen even more clearly in Table 15.4 which isolates Layers 4 and 5 (around 1000 B.C.). Here, the data are broken down into more discrete age categories. The largest number of sheep killed, of those less than 3 years of age, are in the 30–36-month class. Lambing in this area is probably from mid-May to about June

Table 15.4 **Ovis from Layers 4 and 5 at Weston Canyon Rockshelter, Idaho**

	0–6 mo.	6–12 mo.	12–24 mo.	24–30 mo.	30–36 mo.	+36 mo.	Total
Minimum number of individuals	0	1	2	2	21	48	74
Percentage	0	1	3	3	28	65	100%

1—kills of the 30–36-month-old animals would have been made from mid-November to mid-May. Also note that the largest number of kills come from the +36-month-old category.

These data tend to support the concept that hunters take predominantly adults (+36 months). For the Weston Canyon hunters, hunting occurred when the sheep would have been congregating on the restricted winter ranges at lower elevations; thus, both male and female bands would be present. The sex data indicate only a slightly greater tendency to hunt the ewe bands. Secondly, owing to winter kill-offs of lambs during this time of year, the age structure will contain much smaller numbers of lambs and yearlings than of older animals. The theoretical ratio of ewes to rams is 1:1 in the wild herds (Bradley and Baker 1967). Using the population data cited earlier, we would expect that around 70%–80% of the closely spaced sex bands would have been animals over 3 years of age at that time of year. The kill statistics are a good reflection of this seasonality and the population composition.

In many areas of the western United States, mountain sheep were a major game animal. The faunal reports from many widely spaced sites (such as Ventana Cave, Humboldt Cave, and Danger Cave) indicate the importance of this species.

One important site is Jaguar Cave in the Beaverhead Mountains of Idaho (Sadek-Kooros 1966). Two radiocarbon dates, 11,580 ± 250 B.P. and 10,320 ± 350 B.P., have been obtained (Sadek-Kooros 1966). The fauna were largely *Ovis*, the minimum number of which is 268 individuals. Fetal material suggests hunting just prior to lambing. There are no age or sex statistics published. [2] The site also has yielded skeletal remains of domesticated dogs (Lawrence 1967); therefore, the possibility exists that dogs may have been used in hunting wild sheep for over 11,000 years.

A second potentially important site is Mummy Cave in the Absaroka Mountains, northwestern Wyoming (Wedel, Husted, and Moss 1968). The cultural sequence is slightly more than 9000 years in duration. It is our understanding that the main component of the faunal remains is *Ovis* (Wedel, Husted, and Moss 1968: 186). This would give us our longest continual record for the prehistoric hunting

---

[2] Thanks to Barbara Lawrence, Wright was able to study some of the Jaguar Cave faunal material in April, 1973, although he promised not to publish any of his observations. Paleontologically, this sample is also of great importance. Fossil *Ovis* specimens from southern Canada and the mountainous western United States are considerably larger than their modern counterparts. Selection for this size reduction occurred at the close of the Wisconsin glaciation. The critical date appears to be between 11,000 B.P. and 10,000 B.P. (see the discussion by Harris and Mundel 1974). Jaguar Cave falls into this time interval.

of this animal. Further, the local spring lambing range is in view of the rockshelter.

In this discussion, we have outlined some of the directions we are taking in our study of procurement patterns for New World wild sheep. This animal was hunted for at least 11,000 years in the New World, possibly through the employment of many of the same methods that have been described ethnographically. The dog has been an important feature of wild *Ovis* hunting as far back as we can trace sheep kills in North America. The hypothesis that hunters kill adult animals for the most part can be tested, and we have indicated how this may be done. Now we will turn our attention to Old World *Ovis*.

Old World Sheep: Wild Herds and Herders

Obviously, it is necessary to ask: How typical are the behavioral and population characteristics of New World wild sheep? May they be used where data on Old World wild sheep are lacking? There are several studies from the Old World, but none is all-inclusive. Much information comes from "sportsmen," and there are several reports in Russian, which we do not read. Recently, however, a study was conducted on the Urial sheep (*O. a. orientalis*, *O. a. vignei*, or *O. orientalis* of different authors) in the Mohammed Reza Shah Natural Wildlife Park in northeastern Iran (Kowalski 1972). A summary of Kowalski's studies on Urial sheep, including comparisons with Rocky Mountain bighorn sheep is presented in Table 15.5. As can be observed readily, with three unimportant exceptions, the two species are behaviorally comparable.

Kowalski did not give population compositions of separate bands. He did, however, provide data on overall population numbers. The lamb–ewe ratio was estimated at 97:100, which he thinks may be incorrect because it was determined during the lambing season and all ewes had not yet lambed. Further, he feels that some yearling females may have been counted as ewes (Kowalski 1972: 41–42). He supports the latter by pointing out that the yearling–ewe ratio is 19:100. Overall, 54% of the female band is composed of yearlings and lambs. Lamb survival is low, although the population may be increasing somewhat.

Behavioral data on the other Old World wild sheep are more difficult to obtain, particularly that regarding seasonal movements, home ranges, and population compositions. Lydekker (1898) presents some information, but generally does not specify season(s) of observation. In one instance, he notes that the Argali (*O. ammon* with several subspecies?) in the Changchenmo district of Ladek inhabits the lower

Table 15.5 **Comparisons of Urial and *Ovis canadensis* Behavior**[a]

Behavior	Similar	Different
1. Seasonal movements, use of several home ranges	X	
2. Bedgrounds and bedding	X	
3. Lack of routine in daily activity	X	
4. Group compositions and sizes	X	
5. Topographic separation of sex groups during late spring and summer	X	
6. Ram groups largest during pre-rut and early spring	X	
7. Owing to restricted range during winter, separation of sex groups less evident	X	
8. Ram group mean sizes lowest during rut and summer	X	
9. Overall inconsistencies in group sizes	X	
10. Leadership in mixed groups generally matriarchal	X	
11. Alarm posture	X	
12. Escape terrain and escape routes	X	
13. Herding or grouping prior to escape-flight	X	
14. More wary on summer ranges	X	
15. Timing and length of breeding season	X	
16. Pre-rut behavior	X	
17. Ram agression and fighting during rut to establish social dominance	X	
18. Ram mobility during rut	X	
19. Female courtship by rams during rut	X	
20. Failure of rams to maintain harems during rut	X	
21. "Battles royal"	X	
22. Terrain of lambing areas	X	
23. Rare twinning in ewes	X	
24. Reformation of larger ewe bands after lambing	X	
25. Lamb caching by ewes	X	
26. Browsing (more by Urial)		X
27. Tolerance to humans even after prolonged contact (less by Urial)		X
28. Triplets (by Urial)		X

[a] Kowalski 1972.

secluded valleys during the winter, with both types of sex bands on the same range. During the summer, the sex bands separate. Further, the same home ranges are used year after year; the sex bands neglect "other hills which apparently possess similar advantages with regard to pasture and water" (Lydekker 1898: 184; Sjolander 1922: 145). A survey of other Argali populations suggests that these general characteristics are common (see Sjolander 1922). Thus, we believe that there are important similarities between the Old and New World wild sheep and that the same procurement systems may have been employed in both areas.

The proposition that groups keeping domesticated animals (whether nomads or villagers) kill mainly lambs or young animals must be substantiated. Bates (1973: 143–156) found that Turkish Yörük nomads keep two types of herds. The first—*Toklu*—is a herd composed of male yearlings and male lambs that have been removed from the main herd and are raised entirely for cash. Here, then, male lambs (about 6 months old) are culled from the main herd and are killed before reaching reproductive age. The main herd—*Koyun Sürüsü*—contains a few breeding rams, adult ewes, immature ewes, and a few yearling rams, ewe lambs, ram lambs of less than 6 months of age, and a few ram lambs over 6 months of age but less than 1 year. In general, only about 5% of this herd consists of male animals, and the median age of the *Koyun Sürüsü* is about 36 months. Since males and females breed only 4 to 5 years and since 95% of the rams are slaughtered before they finish the yearling stage, a survivorship curve would show that the largest percentage of rams are slaughtered before the age of 36 months.

In the modern Turkish village of Asvan, the ram–ewe ratio is about 1:50–60, and 90% of the rams are killed before reaching the age of 36 months (Payne 1973). There are three kill-off patterns in the modern village, however, depending on whether the animals are kept for meat, milk, or wool. Payne (1973) has developed three separate models to deal with them. For our purposes, the important one is meat, since there is presently no reason to believe that sheep produced significant quantities of milk or wool in the earliest stages of domestication. Payne's model suggests that the kill-off pattern for meat will result in the heaviest culling of males who are 18 to 30 months old (Payne 1973: Fig. 1). About 90% of the males, according to the model, will be slaughtered before 36 months of age.

In using data from modern nomads or villages, one further point must be made. Many animals, particularly young males, are sold to the cities to be consumed during festivals. Thus, their bones will not be found in the refuse middens at the home locations of the herders themselves. For a study of the early stages of domestication, this is not important, since there were no urban areas drawing off the country-side. By the Bronze Age, however, this must be taken into consideration when interpreting village site or nomad encampment faunal remains.

Implications

One major difficulty we face in using the published data (and there are far too few) from archaeological sites in the Old World is the apparent confusion over the terms "mature" and "immature." Several investigators use the word "young" without explicitly stating the age range of which they are speaking: lambs, or lambs plus yearlings, or lambs through 3 years of age (e.g., Higgs, in Rodden 1962; Hilzheimer 1941; Radulesco and Samson 1962). Perkins (1964) and Coon (1951) state that 12 months is their dividing line. We would like to point out that bighorn rams mature sexually between 1.5 and 2.5 years of age but do not reach mature body form until 8 to 9 years of age (Geist 1971). In contrast, ewes attain both sexual and body form maturity by about 2.5 years (Geist 1971).

We will look at two sets of examples, each using different concepts: immature versus mature, and survivorship curves. Table 15.6 contains data from four sites—Belt Cave (Coon 1951), Zawi Chemi Shanidar and Shanidar Cave (Perkins 1964), and Suberde (Perkins and Daly 1968). At the first three, there are dramatic increases in the percentages of lambs (0–12 months) taken through time. The pertinent levels for seeing these increases are the Ceramic Neolithic at Belt Cave, B1 at Shanidar, and the Proto-Neolithic at Zawi Chemi.

The data from Zawi Chemi are particularly impressive because of the larger numbers of individuals involved. Direct comparisons are difficult, however, because of the few published data on sites where hunting, rather than domestication, is suspected. At Yafteh (Hole, Flannery, and Neely 1969) for the Upper Baradostian level, only 3% of the animals were less than 12 months of age (see later and Table 15.7). In Shanidar C, also Upper Baradostian, 16.7% were immature; but the total sample is only 12 individuals.

We are more puzzled by Perkins and Daly's (1968) interpretation of

Table 15.6 **Immature versus Mature Ovis[a]**

Site	Level	I	M	%M	Approximate date B.P.
Belt Cave	Ceramic Neolithic, B, 1–7	10	5	67	7,500
Belt Cave	Neolithic, 8–10	2	18	10	8,000
Belt Cave	Upper Mesolithic, 11–17	0	25	0	
Zawi Chemi	Proto–Neolithic, 0.5–1.0 m	26	22	54	10,870
Zawi Chemi	1.0–1.5 m	78	98	44	
Shanidar Cave	B1	11	8	58	10,600
Shanidar Cave	C (Baradostian)	2	10	17	33,000–28,000
Suberde[b]	All	—	—	35	8,600–8,200
Suberde[c]	All	—	—	28	8,600–8,200

[a] Data based on Coon (1951), Perkins (1964), and Perkins and Daly (1968).
[b] Tooth eruption
[c] Bone fusion

Suberde, where immature (less than 12 months of age) animals account for either 35% or 28%, depending upon which aging criteria are used. Perkins and Daly (1968) believe the sheep were wild and that whole flocks were being killed through cooperative drives. This is, as we noted, a major technique in North America. However, with the data broken down more fully in age groups, we find that "no sheep specimens represented animals younger than three months or older than three years, although the sample was in general evenly distributed between these two extremes" (Perkins and Daly 1968: 102). They use these age statistics and compare them with comments by Adolph Murie (1944) on Dall sheep, where he points out that predators largely kill very young lambs and old adults. Therefore, the authors conclude the Suberde *Ovis* were wild. Murie, however, did not mean to imply either that predators were a major or even an important population check on wild sheep or that no or few +3-year-old animals are present in the wild (that is, that the wild population is composed only of animals between 3 and 36 months of age). Both propositions are false; the latter we have discussed in some detail. Further, Murie's life table is probably incorrect itself (see Bradley and Baker 1967). We shall return to Suberde and suggest that this is precisely the pattern one should find under domestication.

The second approach considers survivorship curves and has been used by a number of authors (e.g., Flannery, in Hole, Flannery, and Neely 1969; Jarman and Jarman 1968; Ducos 1968). We have such data for three wild species of *Ovis*, two hunting sites, several phases or sites where domestication is certain from other criteria, or is suspected, and a modern Turkish village (Table 15.7). We can make several observations.

For the three wild herds, Nelson, Dall, and Urial, most animals do not reach the yearling stage. The largest number die between birth and 12 months. But some, particularly rams, may live well into their teens (Bradley and Baker 1967). This is reflected not only by population statistics but also in archaeological sites, where horn cores of very old rams are often found. Again, +3-year-old animals are statistically the most frequent in the wild herds and are thus most likely to show up in large numbers in the archaeological sites, particularly when herds are sampled by the culling of whole sex bands.

Suberde's sheep population does not fit this model, as *all* specimens are less than 3 years old. We can see this by comparing the Suberde data with Weston Canyon Rockshelter and the Upper Baradostian of Yafteh (Table 15.7). The Upper Baradostian of Yafteh compares favorably with Weston Canyon; 65% of the animals were at least 36 months of age, and the lamb and yearling stages compose only 10% of the animals killed at the former site.

Table 15.7 Survivorship Curves for Percentage of *Ovis* Alive at the End of Each Age Interval[a]

Age in years	Wild			Weston Canyon	Yafteh	Bus Mordeh	Ali Kosh	M. Jaffer	Tepe Sabz	Camp	Knossos		Suberde[b]	Ghassoulien		Bir-es-Safedi	Modern Turkish village
	Nelson	Dall	Urial								ENIa	ENIb		Jabot Road	Metier		
0–1	21	34	20	99	97	68	91	88	90	88	83	81	65/72	66	88	61	45
1–2	21	33	20	95	90	50	67	67	65	36	29	21	33/36	42	66	21	20
2–3	20	32	19	70	65	32	42	42	40	6	1	6	0	21	4	6	10

Archaeological sites or phases

[a] Data from Bradley and Baker (1967), Kowalski (1972), Hole, Flannery, and Neely (1969), Jarman and Jarman (1968), Ducos (1968), and Payne (1973). The modern Turkish village is Asvan; 0–1 year figure is higher because it also includes lambs dying under natural conditions.

[b] Suberde figures based on estimates from Perkins and Payne, who give 35 or 28% for 0–1 year, all less than 3 years, and equally divided in other age classes less than 3 years.

At Suberde, as we noted earlier, 35 or 28% are 3 to 12 months old. In Table 15.7, then, 0–1 year becomes 65 or 72%. Since the remainder of the *Ovis* specimens were no older than 36 months and were almost equally divided in all classes containing animals younger than 36 months, we can estimate the figure for 1–2 years by halving the 0–1-year percentage. We obtain 32.5 or 36%. The resultant curve is unlike that of the hunting sites but is similar to the rest of the sites in Table 15.7 and to Asvan.

Leaving aside the Bus Mordeh phase for the moment, in the remainder of the sites, there is morphological evidence present that we are dealing with domesticated animals. The sites range from the early Neolithic to the Ghassoulian of Palestine at around 3800 to 3000 B.C. (Ducos 1968). Under domestication, according to our ethnographic and archaeological data, the major culling of the herds is done when lambs reach about 10 months of age. Very few animals in many of these sites reached 3 years of age; the highest figure is 42%. The large numbers of individuals in the 12–36-month-old range under domesticated conditions is a total contrast to the hunting sites and to wild populations.

The reason for this, of course, is that the lambs are better protected under domestication. In the wild, most lambs never reach the yearling stage; we noted earlier that usually 70% or more will die before reaching 1 year of age (see Table 15.7; Bradley and Baker 1967). Thus, population numbers for 1–3-year-olds are low (for yearlings, see also Table 15.1). In contrast, in herds of domesticated sheep, 1–3-year-old animals constitute a large proportion of the herd. If as many as 50% of the lambs die, it is considered a bad year. Significant numbers of 1–3-year-old animals are available for slaughter; faunal remains from the sites reflect a herd composition that is very different from that occurring in the wild. Suberde fits the model of domesticated herd composition, not the one of a wild herd.

The only morphological evidence for domestication in the Bus Mordeh phase is the presence of hornless females (Hole, Flannery, and Neely 1969). But it should be noted that hornless ewes do occur in the wild (Kowalski 1972; Schaffer and Reed 1972). However, the survivorship curve more closely fits those for which domestication is certain; it is totally unlike our examples of hunted populations. We also should point out that herders and villagers will kill wild *Ovis* whenever possible. Thus, in areas where wild sheep are found or are nearby, their remains may be intermingled. Perhaps this is why the +3-years-of-age category is still high in the Deh Luran sites. Further, sheep are rare in this phase, a point we shall return to later.

To summarize, our preliminary study indicates that there are two types of survivorship curves. One involves wild sheep for which most kills start at the age of 2.5 years. This is understandable on the basis of population statistics of wild *Ovis*, since lamb mortality is high and yearlings are numerically low in the total population. Many lambs might be killed when ewe bands are hunted, especially during the summer before winter mortality occurs. In this situation, the adult animals killed would be females. For this reason, we need to know the season of the kill and the sex of the adults. Yet, the same kill should show significantly lower numbers of yearlings because few lambs have survived to reach yearling age. The only other possibility for large lamb kills is in an expanding population which will also show large numbers of yearlings. Again, this may be determined by sex and seasonality data.

We can illustrate the first situation by looking at a natural kill. In the desert region of Imperial County, California, bighorns are almost entirely dependent upon natural water tanks *(tinajas)* for water, for springs are rare. In 1968, biologists from the California Department of Fish and Game found one tank that had served as a natural trap. Lying in it were the remains of 21 ewes, 11 lambs, and 2 yearling rams. They had slipped into the tank while attempting to drink and were unable to escape. They represent a sample of one or more ewe groups (Mensch 1968; Weaver and Mensch 1969; Weaver, personal communication). It is perhaps worth emphasizing again that the lamb–yearling ratio in this case was 11:2.

The second survivorship curve occurs under domestication; here, we are interested particularly in the earlier evolutionary stages of the process. Culling begins around 10 months of age and levels off at about 36 months. The important figure, we believe, is not immature versus mature or young versus old, but the age range of 12 to 36 months. This conclusion was reached independently by Payne (1973) and is supported by data from the modern village of Asvan, where the peak of herd culling is during the 18-to-30-months interval.

Thus, for the two types of exploitation by human populations—hunting and herding—survivorship curves are very different. Not only are the patterns of exploitation different, so are the age–sex compositions of wild and domesticated herds. The faunal data from the archaeological sites can be used to reconstruct these herds.

There is one additional point we wish to make. The morphological changes occur after domestication when selective pressures are reduced or removed. We still do not know the rates of change in variation of horn-core structure or other morphological features. We believe the survivorship data clearly indicate that the Suberde sheep were domesticated. We have noted already that Perkins and Daly's (1968) interpretation of Murie's survivorship curve for Dall sheep is incorrect. It also has been suggested that the Suberde sheep were wild, because thin sections of bone under polarized light do not show the blue rim characteristic of domesticated animals (Drew, Perkins, and Daly 1971). This blue line is a result of a morphological difference in the weight-bearing bones of domesticated and wild animals. The weight-bearing bones of a domesticated animal are more fragile than those of the wild animal, with thinner trabeculae and larger marrow cavities (MASCA 1973: 1). It has been suggested

> that the orientation of crystallites noted at the articular surfaces and in the shafts of the long bones developed as a response to stress in the weight-bearing bones of domestic animals which, through lack of exercise, poor nutrition, or genetic deterioration, lacked sufficient material in their bones to form the sturdy bones characteristic of wild animals [MASCA 1973: 1].

Like other morphological changes, this did not occur immediately or even within the first few generations following domestication. If the Suberde sheep were domesticated recently, there is no conflict between the survivorship curve and the lack of a blue rim.

Conclusions

We can summarize briefly by returning to the question of age structures. The age structures we are looking for in *Ovis* are as follows.

1. For hunted populations, we expect animals in the +36-months-of-age category to predominate. Since whole bands were culled regularly by cooperative drives, based on population statistics of wild herds, +3-year-old animals should constitute 65% to 70% of the faunal specimens. If ram bands exclusively were hunted, the figure will be nearly 100% males of +3 years of age, with possibly a few Class I rams included. We see no possibility of reduplicating the domesticated herd statistics through hunting if survivorship curves are employed for analyzing the site data, since no wild herd (or sex band) has a population composition like that of a domesticated herd. Even under an expanding population, if ewe bands are selected for hunting, the resultant curve will show about equal numbers of lambs and yearlings, plus adult ewes and a few Class I rams. No domesticated herd is constructed in this fashion.

2. Under domestication, the survivorship curve should show the highest percentages in the 12–36-month range. Lambs and +36-month categories will be low. In this regard, a curve probably should be constructed for Zawi Chemi Shanidar, where lambs are high. We do understand, however, that this area is not in the natural habitat zone

for wild *Ovis,* lending further support to the hypothesis that they were being herded (H. T. Wright, personal communication).

Obviously, we are advocating a kind of "Shepherd's Pie in the Sky" approach. If it is difficult to separate the sheep from the goats (Hole, Flannery, and Neely 1969), it can be even harder, particularly these days, to tell the boys from the girls. Yet, if this method to distinguish wild from domesticated sheep is to be successful, certain criteria have to be met. It is our feeling that survivorship curves, in conjunction with behavioral and other ecological data, must be employed. Let us also point out that proper survivorship curves for wild herds involve the separation of rams from ewes; their curves are very different (Bradley and Baker 1967). Herders think sex is important. We believe archaeologists and ethnozoologists should too. We hope to examine further one end of the spectrum by investigating more sites involving hunters.

Since it is difficult or impossible to distinguish between sheep and goat bone, these counts often are given as sheep–goat in reports on southwest Asian sites. Comparing wild goats with wild sheep may be entirely wrong. The Bus Mordeh sample is predominantly goats, for example. We do know that they inhabit very different ecological niches and have little information on their behavior. They may have necessitated a hunting pattern other than that necessitated by sheep.

Acknowledgments

We would like to thank Sebastian Payne, Charles Reed, Patty Jo Watson, and Henry T. Wright for commenting on the earlier manuscript of this chapter and Phil Lehner for a copy of Kowalski's thesis.

References for Part IV

Ascher, R.
1961 Analogy in Archaeological Interpretation. *Southwestern Journal of Anthropology* **17**:317–325.

Baker, L. R., and W. G. Bradley
1966 Growth of the Skull in Desert Bighorn Sheep. *Desert Bighorn Council Transactions* **10**:98–109.

Bates, D.
1973 Nomads and Farmers: A Study of the Yörük of Southeastern Turkey. *Museum of Anthropology, University of Michigan, Anthropological Papers,* No. 52.

Bradley, W. G.
1968 Evaluation of Recent Taxonomic Studies of Wild Sheep of the World. *Desert Bighorn Council Transactions* **12**:18–27.

Bradley, W. G., and D. P. Baker
1967 Life Tables for Nelson Bighorn Sheep on the Desert Game Range. *Desert Bighorn Council Transactions* **11**:142–170.

Brewer, A. J.
1973 Analysis of Floral Remains from the Higgs Site (40 Lo 45). In Excavation of the Higgs and Doughty Sites, I-75 Salvage Archaeology, by M. C. R. McCollough and C. H. Faulkner. *Miscellaneous Papers, Tennessee Archaeological Society* No. 12. Pp. 141–144.

Buechner, H. K.
1960 The Bighorn Sheep in the United States: Its Past, Present, and Future. *Wildlife Monographs* No. 4.

Chamberlain, T. C.
1965 The Method of Multiple Working Hypotheses. *Science* **148**:754–759.

Chapman, J., R. B. Stewart, and R. A. Yarnell
1974 Archaeological Evidence for Pre-Columbian Introduction of *Portulaca oleracea* and *Mollugo verticillata* into Eastern North America. *Economic Botany* **28**:411–412.

Clason, A. T.
1972 Some Remarks on the Use and Presentation of Archaeological Data. *Helinium* **12**:129–153.

Coon, C. S.
1951 Cave Explorations in Iran, 1949. *The University Museum, University of Pennsylvania, Museum Monographs.*

Cowan, I. McT.
   1940   Distribution and Variation in the Native Sheep of North America. *American Midland Naturalist* **24**:505–580.
Cutler, H. C., and T. W. Whitaker
   1961   History and Distribution of the Cultivated Cucurbits in the Americas. *American Antiquity* **26**:469–485.
Daly, P.
   1969   Approaches to Faunal Analysis in Archaeology. *American Antiquity* **32**:146–153.
Deming, O. V.
   1952   Tooth Development of the Nelson Bighorn Sheep. *California Fish and Game* **28**:523–529.
Drew, I. M., D. Perkins Jr., and P. Daly
   1971   Prehistoric Domestication of Animals: Effects on Bone Structure. *Science* **171**:280–282.
Ducos, P.
   1968   L'Origine des Animaux Domestiques en Palestine. *Publication de l'Institut de Préhistoire de l'Université de Bordeaux, Mémoire* No. 6.
Dyson, R. H.
   1953   Archaeology and the Domestication of Animals in the Old World. *American Anthropologist* **55**:661–673.
Geist, V.
   1971   *Mountain Sheep: A Study in Behavior and Evolution.* Chicago: University of Chicago Press.
Grayson, D. K.
   1973   On the Methodology of Faunal Analysis. *American Antiquity* **38**:432–439.
Hansen, G. C.
   1967   Bighorn Sheep Populations of the Desert Game Range. *Journal of Wildlife Management* **31**:693–706.
Harris, A. H., and P. Mundel
   1974   Size Reduction in Bighorn Sheep (*Ovis canadensis*) at the Close of the Pleistocene. *Journal of Mammalogy* **55**:678–680.
Hill, J. N.
   1972   The Methodological Debate in Contemporary Archaeology: A Model. In *Models in Archaeology,* edited by David L. Clarke. London: Methuen. Pp. 61–107.
Hilzheimer, M.
   1941   Animal Remains from Tell Asmar. *Studies in Oriental Civilization* No. 20. Chicago; University of Chicago Press.
Hole, F., K. V. Flannery, and J. A. Neely
   1969   Prehistory and Human Ecology on the Deh Luran Plain. *Museum of Anthropology, University of Michigan, Memoir* No. 1.
Irwin-Williams, C.
   1973   The Oshara Tradition: Origins of Anasazi Culture. *Contributions in Anthropology, Eastern New Mexico University* **5**.
Irwin-Williams, C., and S. Tompkins
   1968   Excavations at En Medio Shelter. *Contributions in Anthropology, Eastern New Mexico University* **2**.
Jarman, M. R., and H. N. Jarman
   1968   The Fauna and Economy of Early Neolithic Knossos. *Annual of the British School at Athens* **63**:241–264.
Korobitsyna, K. V., C. F. Nadler, N. N. Vorontsov, and R. S. Hoffman
   1974   Chromosomes of Siberian Snow Sheep, *Ovis nivicola,* and Implications

Concerning the Origin of Amphiberingian Wild Sheep (Subgenus *Pachyceros*). *Quaternary Research* **4**:235–245.

Kowalski, G. R.
1972 Behavior and Ecology of the Urial Sheep. Master's thesis, Colorado State University.

Kuhn, T. S.
1970 *The Structure of Scientific Revolutions.* 2nd ed. Chicago: University of Chicago Press.

Lawrence, B.
1967 Early Domestic Dogs. *Zeitschrift fur Saugetierkunde* **32**:44–59.

Lawrence, D.
1971 The Nature and Structure of Paleoecology. *Journal of Paleoecology* **45**:593–605.

Leone, M. P.
1972 Issues in Anthropological Archaeology. In *Contemporary Archaeology,* edited by Mark P. Leone. Carbondale: Southern Illinois University Press. Pp. 14–27.

Lydekker, R.
1898 *Wild Oxen, Sheep and Goats of All Lands.* London: Rowland Ward.

Mangelsdorf, P. C., H. W. Dick, and J. Camara-Hernandez
1967 Bat Cave Revisited. *Harvard University, Botanical Museum Leaflets* **22**.

Marquardt, W. H.
1974 A Statistical Analysis of Constituents in Human Paleofecal Specimens from Mammoth Cave. In *Archaeology of the Mammoth Cave Area,* edited by Patty Jo Watson. New York: Academic Press. Pp. 193–202.

Martin, W. C.
1974 Game Time in Cloud-Cuckoo-Land. *Harpers* **249**:88–95.

MASCA
1973 Technique for Determining Animal Domestication Based on Study of Thin Sections of Bone under Polarized Light. *MASCA Newsletter* **9**:1–2.

McCollough, C. R., and C. H. Faulkner
1973 Excavation of the Higgs and Doughty Sites, I-75 Salvage Archaeology. *Miscellaneous Papers, Tennessee Archaeological Society* No. 12.

Mensch, J. L.
1969 Desert Bighorn *(Ovis canadensis nelsoni)* Losses in a Natural Trap Tank. *California Fish and Game* **55**:237–238.

Miller, S. J.
1972 Weston Canyon Rockshelter: Big-Game Hunting in Idaho. Master's thesis, Idaho State University.

Mosby, H. S. (Editor)
1963 *Wildlife Investigational Techniques.* New York: Wildlife Society.

Munson, P. J., P. W. Parmalee, and R. A. Yarnell
1971 Subsistence Ecology of Scovill, A Terminal Middle Woodland Village. *American Antiquity* **36**:410–431.

Murie, A.
1944 The Wolves of Mount McKinley. *Fauna of the National Parks Series* **5.** Washington, D.C.: U.S. Government Printing Office.

Murphy, J. L.
1971 Maize from an Adena Mound in Athens County, Ohio. *Science* **171**:897–898.

Oldmeyer, J. J., W. Barnmore, and D. Gilbert.
1971 Winter Ecology of Bighorn Sheep in Yellowstone National Park. *Journal of Wildlife Management* **35**:257–269.

Olsen, S. J.
  1971 *Zooarchaeology: Animal Bones in Archaeology and Their Interpretation.* Chicago: Addison-Wesley.
Page, J. K., Jr.
  1974 Phenomena, Comment and Notes. *Smithsonian* **5:**6–14.
Parker, A. C.
  1910 Iroquois Uses of Maize and Other Food Plants. *New York State Museum, Bulletin* No. 144.
Payne, S.
  1972 On the Interpretation of Bone Samples from Archaeological Sites. In *Papers in Economic Prehistory*, edited by E. S. Higgs. Oxford: Cambridge University Press.
  1973 Kill-Off Patterns in Sheep and Goats: The Mandibles from Aşvan Kale. *Anatolian Studies* **22:**281–303.
Perkins, D. P.
  1964 Prehistoric Fauna from Shanidar, Iraq. *Science* **144:**1565–1566.
Perkins, D. P., and P. Daly
  1968 A Hunter's Village in Neolithic Turkey. *Scientific American* **219:**96–106.
Péwé, T. L., and D. M. Hopkins
  1967 Mammal Remains of Pre-Wisconsin Age in Alaska. In *The Bering Land Bridge*, edited by D. M. Hopkins. Palo Alto, California: Stanford University Press. Pp. 266–270.
Radulesco, C., and P. Samson
  1962 Sur un Centre de Domestication du Mouton dans le Mesolithique de la Grotte "La Adam" en Dobrogea. *Zeitschrift fur Tierzuchtung und Zuchtungs Biologie* **76:**282–320.
Rodden, R. J.
  1962 Excavations at the Early Neolithic Site at New Nikomedia, Greek Macedonia (1961 season). *Proceedings of the Prehistoric Society* **28:**267–288.
Sabloff, J. A., T. W. Beale, and A. M. Kurland
  1973 Recent Developments in Archaeology. *Annals of the American Academy of Political and Social Science* **408:**103–118.
Sadek-Kooros, H.
  1966 Jaguar Cave: An Early Man Site in the Beaverhead Mountains of Idaho. Ph.D. dissertation, Harvard University.
Schaffer, W. M., and C. A. Reed
  1972 The Co-evolution of Social Behavior and Cranial Morphology in Sheep and Goats (Bovidae, Caprini). *Fieldiana: Zoology* **61:**1–88. Field Museum of Natural History, Chicago.
Sjolander, D.
  1922 The Distribution and Habits of the Argali Sheep of Central Asia. *Royal Asiatic Society North China Branch* **53:**131–157.
Smith, B. D.
  1974 Middle Mississippi Exploitation of Animal Populations: A Predictive Model. *American Antiquity* **39:**274–291.
  1975a Middle Mississippi Exploitation of Animal Populations. *Museum of Anthropology, University of Michigan, Anthropology Papers* No. 57.
  1975b Toward a More Accurate Estimation of the Meat Yield of Animal Species at Archaeological Sites. In *Archaeological Studies: The Proceedings of the Groningen Conference*, edited by A. T. Clason. Amsterdam: North Holland Publ.

Smith, C. E., Jr.
1968 The New World Centers of Origin of Cultivated Plants and the Archaeological Evidence. *Economic Botany* **22:**253–266.

Stewart, R. B.
1974 Identification and Quantification of Components in Salts Cave Paleofeces, 1970–1972. In *Archaeology of the Mammoth Cave Area*, edited by Patty Jo Watson. New York: Academic Press. Pp. 41–48.

Stocking, George
1968 *Race, Culture and Evolution.* New York: Free Press.

Streeter, R. G.
1969 Demography of Two Rocky Mountain Bighorn Sheep Populations in Colorado. Ph.D. dissertation, Colorado State University.

Struever, S., and K. D. Vickery
1973 The Beginnings of Cultivation in the Midwest-Riverine Area of the United States. *American Anthropologist* **75:**1197–1220.

Teit, J. A.
1930 The Salishan Tribes of the Western Plateau. *46th Annual Report of the Bureau of American Ethnology,* pp. 25–396.

Uerpmann, H. P.
1973 Animal Bone Finds and Economic Archaeology: A Critical Study of "Osteo-archaeological" Method. *World Archaeology* **4:**307–322.

Uloth, W.
1966 Die Taxonomie der Rezenten Wildschafe im Blickpunkt der Verkreuzung. *Saugetier Kundliche, Mitteilungen* **13:**273–278.

Vereshchagin, N. K.
1959 *The Mammals of the Caucasus.* Moskva-Leningrad: Izdatel'stvo Akademii Nauk SSSR. [Translated into English in 1967 by the Israel Program for Scientific Translations, Jerusalem.]

Watson, P. J. (Editor)
1974 *Archaeology of the Mammoth Cave Area.* New York: Academic Press.

Weaver, R. A., and J. L. Mensch
1969 A Report on Desert Bighorn Sheep in Eastern Imperial County. W-51-R-14, Resources Agency, Department of Fish and Game, California.

Wedel, W. R.
1943 Archaeological Investigations in Platte and Clay Counties, Missouri. *United States National Museum, Bulletin* No. 183.

Wedel, W., W. M. Husted, and J. H. Moss
1968 Mummy Cave: Prehistoric Record from Rocky Mountains of Wyoming. *Science* **160:**184–186.

White, T. E.
1953 A Method of Calculating the Dietary Percentage of Various Food Animals Utilized by Aboriginal Peoples. *American Antiquity* **18:**396.

Wilson, L. O.
1968 Distribution and Ecology of Desert Bighorn Sheep in Southeastern Utah. Publication 68-5, Utah State Department of Natural Resources, Division of Fish and Game.

Woolf, A.
1968 Summer Ecology of Bighorn Sheep in Yellowstone National Park. Master's thesis, Colorado State University.

Woolf, A., T. O'Shea, and D. L. Gilbert
1970 Movements and Behavior of Bighorn Sheep on Summer Ranges in Yellowstone National Park. *Journal of Wildlife Management* **34:**446–450.

Wright, G. A.
  1971 Origins of Food Production in Southwestern Asia: A Survey of Ideas. *Current Anthropology* **12**:447–479.
Wright, H. T.
  1964 A transitional Archaic Campsite at Greenpoint (20 Sa 1). *Michigan Archaeologist* **10**:17–22.
Yarnell, R. A.
  1972 *Iva Annua* Var. *Macrocarpa:* Extinct American Cultigen? *American Anthropologist* **74**:335–341.
  1974 Plant Food and Cultivation of the Salts Cavers. In *Archaeology of the Mammoth Cave Area*, edited by Patty Jo Watson. New York: Academic Press. Pp. 113–122.
  In press Native Plant Husbandry North of Mexico. In *The Origins of Agriculture*, edited by Charles Reed. The Hague: Mouton.

V

Ethnohistory, Historic Archaeology, and Ethnicity

16

Patterns of Acculturation at the Straits of Mackinac

James E. Fitting

Culture change is perhaps the most important aspect of cultural history, one too often neglected as archaeologists deal with sites as static units rather than "frozen" moments within a continuous and dynamic process. This often has been excused by the necessity of making interpretations from single sites within a region; however, archaeologists still must be faulted for not making better use of the comparative data available to them. A particularly noticeable weakness is the failure to integrate ethnohistorical data for archaeological interpretations. Significantly, even 30 years after its publication, James B. Griffin's *Fort Ancient Aspect* (1943) is still possibly the best example of the combination of data from many archaeological sites and ethnohistorical sources for a cultural–historical and anthropological interpretation.

Not only are the research concerns of this chapter a direct outgrowth of the problems and orientations of Griffin's own research, but the area on which the chapter focuses, the Straits of Mackinac, reflects Griffin's interests as well. The bench-mark study on which this research is based is work at the Juntunen site (McPherron 1967), implemented under Griffin's overall direction and financed with funds obtained from the National Science Foundation through his application.

Historians have long recognized that the seventeenth-century fur trade in the Upper Great Lakes disrupted the Native American cultures of the area. Unfortunately, their work (see, for example, Hunt 1940) has focused on European political and geographical concerns rather than internal changes taking place within the cultures themselves. Even a cursory reading of these studies demonstrates that the changes were of considerable magnitude, involving, in some instances, the destruction of entire nations, such as the Huron and Erie.

Although archaeologists have dealt with the phenomenon of acculturation in the seventeenth century as a result of French contact, they usually have emphasized changes in material culture of the peoples involved. Quimby's *Indian Culture and European Trade Goods* (1966), for instance, was faulted by some reviewers for not emphasizing change except in the sphere of material culture. The weaknesses in Quimby's book, however, stimulated those archaeologists working in the Upper Great Lakes to examine further the questions of culture change and acculturation. In 1966, the author (Fitting 1966) in a review of a typological study of American Indian tomahawks, speculated on changes that might be expected from the introduction of iron tools into the Late-Woodland–Early-Historic culture. Brose (1970) asked the key question: Can a brass kettle be considered solely as a utilitarian item or must it be viewed as a status symbol and, therefore, in its broader cultural context? Most recently, Cleland (1971) has considered the problems of the great accumulation of grave goods found in Contact period cemeteries in the area. These questions have been posed by Griffin's students working within the speculative framework he provided for them.

This particular study of acculturation deals with a limited number of sites in a restricted geographical area, Michigan's Straits of Mackinac. Late Woodland village debris from the Juntunen site on Bois Blanc Island will be compared with village debris from the seventeenth-century Tionontate Huron village in St. Ignace; the Juntunen burial practices will be compared with those at the seventeenth-century Lasanen cemetery in St. Ignace.

The Juntunen site is located on the western end of Bois Blanc Island, the largest of the islands within the Straits of Mackinac. Discovered during Robert Braidwood's survey of the area in the 1930s, excavations were conducted at the site under the supervision of Alan McPherron in 1960–1961. Additional testing was done in 1962, and a major monograph was published in 1967 (McPherron 1967). Charles Cleland (1966) also has published an extensive analysis of the faunal remains from the site. The Juntunen site has served as a type site in the generation of a late prehistoric settlement model for the region (Fitting and Cleland 1969).

During the period of occupation (A.D. 800–1400), the subsistence pattern seems to have been constant except for some minor climatic fluctuations. The Juntunen site contains village debris from the entire occupation with a group of burials from the fourteenth-century Juntunen phase. The Early Historic Lasanen and Tionontate sites may be viewed against the prehistoric Juntunen site.

Lasanen, located in St. Ignace, is approximately 7 miles north of the Juntunen site across open water. Field parties from the Mackinac Island State Park Commission and the Michigan State University Museum conducted excavations in 1966–1967 (Cleland 1971). Cleland has interpreted this as an Ottawa burial locality used primarily between A.D. 1690 and 1700.

In 1972, an aboriginal longhouse pattern was discovered while test pits were being opened in the area adjacent to the Marquette Mission site, approximately 1 mile north of the Lasanen site (Fitting, in press). This excavation started as a 5-ft. test square which was directly superimposed on the postmold pattern. Eventually, about 1000 ft.² were cleared to reveal the larger part of a 20-ft. by 40-ft. double post-row structure in the "West Trench" excavation. A number of storage pits and several sheet middens also relating to this component were excavated. From the written accounts of Cadillac and the Jesuits and from the 1688 LaHontan map, this structure was probably part of the Tionontate village located next to the Jesuit Mission. Tionontates have been called "Petun," "Tobacco Huron," or, simply, "Huron." This village, established in 1671, was largely abandoned after the establishment of Fort Pontchartrain in Detroit in 1701.

The report on these excavations and the materials recovered from them, including a report on the faunal material by Elizabeth Cardinal, soon will be forthcoming (Fitting, in press). In 1973, we returned to the site and opened an additional 3300 ft.² containing one more longhouse, over 100 ft. of palisade, and 78 features, primarily hearths, storage pits, and midden concentrations. The area was larger and the cultural deposits were richer. Although the artifact analysis is not completed, the 1973 assemblage seems to be similar to that from 1972. Only data from the 1972 excavations have been used for the analysis presented in this study.

We have then a prehistoric and historic village and burial area within close proximity and in the same general environmental setting. Therefore, differences between the sites could not be caused by differential access to natural resources. While the Juntunen burials probably represent people who were living at the site, there are Ottawa burials and a Tionontate village site at St. Ignace. Prior to A.D.

1650, the Tionontate and Ottawa were known to have had discrete economic and social patterns (Fitting 1972). However, after that date, the Tionontate and some Ottawa groups traveled together and lived in adjacent villages for 40 years before the major period of utilization of the Lasanen site. According to late-seventeenth-century accounts, both their material culture and economic adaptation probably did not differ.

This is the historical background against which we may study acculturation in the Straits region. Our first hypothesis might be that the introduction of European trade goods, particularly axes, kettles, knives, and guns, altered the subsistence patterns of the area to the point that social and ideological orientations changed as well. The effect of European trade items on the subsistence habits can be determined by comparing the faunal remains from the Juntunen site and Tionontate village. The area excavated at the Juntunen site was approximately 6 times greater than that from the 1972 excavations at the Tionontate village. The density of food remains, however, was about the same, since the total bone count from Juntunen was about 5.5 times greater than that from the Tionontate village. The number of bones identified to the species level at the Juntunen site was 2469, whereas 408 were identified to species at the Tionontate village. The 6:1 ratio indicates that differences between the sites are not an artifact of different site functions.

The 10 most prevalent species at Juntunen accounted for 76% of the total bones identified to species. The number of species present in the Tionontate sample was less, but 7 of the 10 most prevalent Juntunen species were found there, and the accounted for 83% of the bone assemblage identified to species. Not only were the assemblages comparable in size (in terms of density) but the same species were paramount in both assemblages.

Differences between the frequency of the major species between the two sites are striking (Table 16.1) and may have an historical explanation. In the prehistoric site, dogs commonly were used for food, and most dog bones were found in the midden debris. Father Marquette, as well as several of the later priests, expressed their revulsion of eating dogs and their outrage at the sacrifice of dogs. If these animals could not be kept for food and sacrifice without incurring the anger of the priests, one may assume that there was little point in keeping them at all; hence, a tenfold decrease in the frequency of dog remains.

A decrease in the number of dogs would have a secondary impact on other bone samples. Dog coprolites from the Schultz site (McClary 1972) indicate a primary diet of fish offal. Without the dogs to clean up part of the debris, an increase in the frequency of fish remains would

Table 16.1 **Most Frequent Species: Number of Bones and Relative Frequency of the Ten Most Common Species at the Juntunen Site with Similar Occurrences at the Tionontate Village**

	Juntunen		*Tionontate*	
	Number	*Percentage*	*Number*	*Percentage*
Sturgeon	888	47	268	79
Whitefish	262	14	28	8
Beaver	245	13	6	2
Dog	196	10	2	1
Loon	75	4	—	—
Walleye	61	3	1	<1
Passenger pigeon	57	3	11	3
Snowshoe hare	37	2	—	—
Lake trout	36	2	22	7
Longnose gar	29	2	—	—
Total	1886		338	
Total all species	2469		408	
Percentage in top 10		76		83

be expected at the Tionontate village, and this is precisely what occurs.

The decrease in beaver, and possibly snowshoe hare as well, might be a result of the fur trade. With intensive specific trapping, the supply of fur-bearing animals in the immediate area of a village site would be rapidly depleted. A major characteristic of the fur trade is the search for new trapping grounds as the older ones become exhausted. If one must travel great distances to obtain furs, the furs rather than the meat are brought back. The meat would have been discarded or consumed on the return journey. Meat brought back to the village probably would have been in a processed form rather than as an entire carcass and, therefore, would not even appear in the faunal record.

The faunal analysis shows an increase in the number of fish bones in the Tionontate assemblage, with a decrease in the number of mammals. Essentially the same pattern can be noted in comparing the meat weight counts represented by the bones from the two sites (Table 16.2). At the Juntunen site, bear, moose, and deer each accounted for less than 1% of the bone refuse count, yet they provided 22% of the meat consumed at the site.

The 10 most important food species in terms of meat weight from the Juntunen site have been compared with the counterpart counts and weights from the Tionontate village (Table 16.2). The average

Table 16.2 Most Important Food Species: Comparison of the Relative Importance of the Ten Major Food Species at the Juntunen and the Tionontate Village Site

| | Juntunen | | | | | Tionontate | | |
	Number of bones	Number of individuals	Bones per individual	X̄ lbs. meat	Percentage of meat	Number of bones	Estimated number of individuals	Percentage of meat
Sturgeon	888	350	2.54	36	58	268	105	89
Moose	10	7	1.43	400	13	—	—	—
Beaver	245	46	5.33	38.5	8	6	1	1
Bear	7	6	1.17	210	8	—	—	—
Whitefish	262	119	2.20	10.4	6	28	13	3
Dog	196	30	6.53	20	3	2	.3	<1
Lake trout	36	36	1.00	14.4	2	22	22	7
Caribou	8	3	2.67	100	1	—	—	—
Deer	4	4	1.00	14.4	2	—	—	—
Porcupine	10	10	1.00	10.5	<1	—	—	—
Loon	75	20	3.75	4.9	<1	—	—	—
Percentage of fish					66			99
Percentage of mammals					34			1

weights are taken from Cleland's (1966) analysis. The number of individuals was not analyzed in the faunal analysis of the Tionontate village but was extrapolated by applying the Juntunen ratio of bones to individuals to the Tionontate bone sample.

In doing this, the trends noted in the bone count analysis became even more evident. Sturgeon accounted for 87% of the meat in the food refuse from the site. Fish account for 99% of the entire food refuse at the Tionontate village, although they account for only 66% of the meat in the refuse from the Juntunen site. Cleland (1966: 209) has characterized the Juntunen site as a warm-season fishing village occupied by a group that was only marginally agricultural or nonagricultural. The trends in species utilization at the Juntunen site, which led Cleland to this conclusion, are amplified at the Tionontate site. The Tionontate village is more like the "ideal" Juntunen site than the Juntunen site is itself. If the introduction of European trade goods had any effect at all on the subsistence base, it was to amplify the trends already present. The quantity of food, as exemplified by the density of food debris, did not seem to have changed. We must reject the hypothesis that European trade goods drastically altered the subsistence base of peoples in the Straits of Mackinac. Therefore, the changes taking place in the acculturation process must have been in areas other than the subsistence base.

Having rejected our first hypothesis on subsistence, we can move to a second hypothesis that European trade goods altered the material culture of native peoples of the area. This may be an oversimplification, since the introduction of something that has not been there before, by definition, alters what is there. A better statement might be that the introduction of European trade goods altered the internal patterning of the material culture by changing the relative importance of different types of items.

Three major artifact categories, food procurement and processing, containers, and ornamentation, are compared in Table 16.3. The percentage of the total assemblages devoted to food procurement and processing does not differ greatly at the two sites. The major differences are in the importance of ceramics at the Juntunen site and the importance of ornamentation at the Tionontate village. The Juntunen assemblage is almost totally related to food procurement, processing, and storage, while only one-quarter of the Tionontate assemblage can be placed in these categories. This is certainly a major shift in societal emphasis on a certain aspect of material culture.

There is also a significant difference in the size of the two artifact assemblages. Even though we still can safely compare percentages of artifact categories, we cannot equate the actual artifact counts from the two sites unless we can weigh the samples in terms of some

Table 16.3 Artifact Comparisons: Numbers and Frequencies of Some of the Major Artifact Categories at the Juntunen and Tionontate Sites[a]

	Juntunen		Tionontate	
	Number	*Percentage of site total*	*Number*	*Percentage of site total*
Food procurement and processing				
Bone tools	120		1	
Chipped stone	17,261		42	
(Stone tools)	(660)		(3)	
Iron tools	0		5	
Copper tools	79		1	
Total	17,460	15	49	20
Containers				
Pot sherds	101,477		10	
(Ceramic vessels)	(1,688)		(1)	
Kettle parts	0		5	
Total	101,477	85	15	6
Ornamentation				
Beads and pendants	27		168	
Tinkling cones	0		5	
Bone, shell, and wampum	0		7	
Total	27	<1	180	74
Site totals	*118,964*		*244*	

[a] Numbers in parentheses are part of preceding category and not included in the totals.

standard value. The excavations were six times more extensive and the total bone counts and identified bone counts were also five to six times more extensive. If we multiply the artifact counts from the Tionontate village by a conservative factor of 5.5, we can compare the sites in terms of a constant, which can be either a constant of area or pounds of meat.

This weighted artifact comparison (Table 16.4) adds little to the information in Table 16.3, although it does document a significant shift from food procurement and storage items to ornamentation, as indicated before. Further, a base is provided for a direct comparison of the technological efficiency of items of European and aboriginal manufacture which can be measured in terms of the subsistence system. A direct comparison of the artifact counts in Table 16.4 is based on a "pounds of meat" constant. Table 16.5 deals with efficiency—as this table demonstrates, one iron tool has the efficiency

Table 16.4 **Weighted Artifact Comparisons: Numbers of Artifacts from the Juntunen and Tionontate Sites with Sample Size Adjusted to a Pounds of Meat Constant**

	Juntunen	*Tionontate*
Food procurement and processing		
Bone tools	120	6
Chipped stone	17,261	231
(Stone tools)	(660)	(17)
Iron tools	0	28
Copper tools	79	6
Total	17,460	271
Containers		
Pot sherds	101,477	55
(Ceramic vessels)	(1,688)	(6)
Kettle parts	0	28
Total	101,477	83
Ornamentation		
Beads and pendants	27	924
Tinkling cones	0	28
Bone, shell, and wampum	0	39
Total	27	991

of 23 stone tools. One copper kettle has the efficiency of 60 ceramic vessels.

However, it has been demonstrated already that this technological efficiency, which would have involved a significant freeing of fabrication time if nothing else, was not channeled into developing a new

Table 16.5 **Relative Efficiency of Aboriginal and European Goods (from the Weighted Sample)**

A. Stone tool efficiency

$$\frac{\text{Juntunen stone tools} - \text{Tionontate stone tools}}{\text{Tionontate iron tools}} = \frac{660-17}{28} = 22.96:1$$

1 iron tool = 23 stone tools

B. Vessel efficiency

$$\frac{\text{Juntunen ceramic vessels} - \text{Tionontate ceramic vessels}}{\text{Tionontate kettles}} = \frac{1688-6}{28} = 60.1:1$$

1 brass kettle = 60 ceramic vessels

subsistence base—or even into an expansion of the existing base.

Leslie White (1958) has suggested the formula $E \times T = C$, where E = the energy utilized by a group, T = the technology of the group, and C = the level of cultural development. The hypothesis that European trade goods altered the internal patterning of the material culture has been accepted. The White formula shows the direction of this change. There is an elaboration of emphasis on ornamentation with major developments in the native crafts (bone and catlinite carving) as well as the accumulation of European-made decorative items. Cultural change may have taken place in the social sphere as well. In fact, the third hypothesis to be tested by the Straits data is that such social and ceremonial changes did take place.

The elaboration of both ornamentation within the material culture and of ritual within the total cultural pattern can be seen in a comparison of the Juntunen and Lasanen sites' burial patterns. The full skeletal analysis from the Juntunen site has never been published but has been summarized by both McPherron (1967) and Wilkinson (1971). Wilkinson has included information on 55 Juntunen phase burials in his study. Clute (1971) has presented information on 76 burials from the Lasanen site.

The mortality rates of the two groups are not directly comparable but seem to be roughly similar. Of the Juntunen burials, 42% are subadult, and 58% are young adult or older. Of the Lasanen population, 46% are subadult and 54% are adult. This would, again, suggest that both groups had a similar life expectancy, which would suggest, in turn, a similar subsistence pattern. The data on sex distribution for the two sites are interesting; female burials are more common at the Lasanen site. However, the low frequency of individual burials that could be sexed, and the different techniques used in the two studies, make these data suspect.

The differences in burial association between the two sites are overwhelming. Among the 55 Juntunen phase burials, only four, representing five individuals, had associated grave offerings. One individual was interred with approximately 50 items in a medicine bundle; a second was buried with 2 miniature ceramic vessels; a group of 75 marginella shells was found between two individuals; and "several" shell beads were associated with one burial. Approximately 130 items were found with five individuals. Less than 10% of the burials had grave goods with an average of 26 items per burial. There is an average of less than 3 items per burial for the entire site. Because about half of the items in the medicine bundle could be considered utilitarian, utilitarian items accounted for approximately 20% of the total burial assemblage.

At the Lasanen site, 22,160 items were found with the 54 burials uncovered during the 1966 field season. This is an average of 410 items per individual, or more than 130 times as many items per burial as the Juntunen site. Approximately 1% of these are purely aboriginal items; the rest are either trade goods or items manufactured with the introduced European technology. Actually, the raw numbers of aboriginal goods recovered from the two sites are roughly comparable: about 130 items at Juntunen and a little over 200 items from Lasanen. The changes in mortuary association were primarily a result of the influx of European goods. Less than 1% of the items from the Lasanen site were related to food procurement or other strictly economic tasks, whereas 20% of the items among the Juntunen burials were so related. Therefore, the trend toward artistic elaboration noted in the comparison of the village sites is amplified in the comparison of the burial sites. Furthermore, the grave goods clearly indicate an elaboration of burial ritual, so we can accept the third hypothesis that changes in the ritual emphasis were brought about by the introduction of European trade goods.

Although we have rejected one and accepted two of the three hypotheses, all seem to point in the same direction. The introduction of trade goods in the seventeenth century had little effect on subsistence, although trends that already were present were amplified. The introduction of trade goods led to major changes in the artifact assemblage, but, for the most part, the same tasks were performed with the new artifacts. That the increasing emphasis on ornamentation was not a new trend but an old one amplified by the new technology could be argued. By the same token, burial ritual with grave offerings did exist in the precontact period but was considerably amplified in the late seventeenth century.

Other native social patterns, such as the feast of the dead, also seem to have gained importance. Perhaps trade relationships were increased as well. In his study of seventeenth-century exchange systems in the Upper Great Lakes, G. A. Wright (1967, 1968), using models developed by Sahlins and Harding, has suggested a balanced reciprocity. Actual bargaining was looked on with disfavor. Instead, diadic alliances were formed between French traders and resident lineages in a specific area. Gifts were given between trade partners according to the ability of each. Thus, the goods were kept flowing in one direction even if nothing was moving against them in a particular year—for instance, a bad year for furs or a year when a shipment of trade goods failed to arrive on time.

In a reciprocal exchange system, status accrues to the person who gives away the most. This may be one reason for the influence of the Jesuits, who gave away things in a society where this was the expected order. Distribution of rings and rosaries are mentioned more frequently in their accounts than are hunting and fishing, yet they rarely starved to death. Their participation in exchange assured them not only food but status as well.

The French traders followed the Jesuit's lead with trade partnerships, and the native trade partners certainly augmented their own status by further distribution of goods. Such reciprocal gift-giving probably has a long history in the region, possibly going back to the Late Archaic, but it, like other aspects of native culture, was amplified by the influx of European goods. The really important people in the Lasanen community were probably not the people who were buried there, but the individuals who presented the grave offerings.

Another consideration is that European trade goods have diminishing utility. One gun can make a person a more efficient hunter—a hundred guns do not make him any more efficient than his one gun. With no change in the subsistence base, the society would have been saturated rapidly with trade items of economic utility. Once this saturation point was reached, the value of these items would become more social than utilitarian.

Brose's question about the brass kettle serving as a part of a woman's work kit or a man's status symbol can be answered on several levels. The first kettle is both functional and a status symbol. This is true until every family has a kettle, all of which have the same functional and social value. When kettles are present in numbers greater than that required for cooking, they have purely a social value. This social value can be realized only by giving them away, since stored wealth is incompatible with seasonal mobility. When the society is saturated with functional trade goods, the surplus of social trade goods ends up in the cemetery.

The pattern in which this happened in the Straits area is related to the local history. When the report first appeared (1971), there was some skepticism about Cleland's suggestion that the Lasanen cemetery was used primarily between 1690 and 1700. More recently, Nern and Cleland (1974) have suggested that the Gros Cap cemetery, which earlier researchers had relegated to the eighteenth century, dated to the same 1690–1700 time period.

A close examination of the historical documentation suggests that Gros Cap may be dated even more closely. The initial 1671 St. Ignace Mission community was not large. There is no direct evidence of a secular French use of the area for trade until 1678, and then only on a sporadic basis. The intensive use of the area as a trading site probably postdates the establishment of Fort Du Buade in 1689. The peak of resident population, over 6000, and, probably, the peak of trading activity took place after Cadillac became commandant in 1694. In 1696, the fur trade was prohibited by royal decree, and, by 1698, Fort

Du Buade was abandoned and Cadillac returned to France. In other words, the high point of the St. Ignace trade was between 1694 and 1696. Relatively little took place before 1689 or after 1698.

The high point in trade history was also the peak of the population curve for the area. The 6000 people mentioned by Cadillac in 1695 had dwindled to 50 by 1703. Since total mortality is related to total population, more people probably died between 1694 and 1696 than in the preceding or following 30-year time period. Therefore, the largest and richest of the burial areas should date to the very period when the saturation of European trade goods caused a shift from utilitarian to social in their primary function.

One of the main reasons the fur trade was prohibited in 1696 was the saturation of the European market with furs which also had a diminishing utility. The mercantile strategy of France, based on Colbert's economic outlook, called for government interference to prevent declining prices. Trade was to be limited to Montreal where the Indians were to bring the furs. Perhaps the Indians, suffering from a social surfeit of no longer utilitarian trade goods, viewed this with as much relief as did the Montreal merchants.

The overall significance of acculturation during the French occupation of the Upper Great Lakes can be understood best by contrasting it with the later British and American occupations. The French occupation was mercantile but not colonial. Local economic and social traditions were supported, and the effect of the French occupation was twofold. First, the aboriginal population became dependent on imported utilitarian goods, and, secondly, these imported goods were utilized to reinforce and augment economic, social, and ideological components of prehistoric origins. The French helped the Indians be better Indians with the introduced trade goods.

British policies were different. An initial complaint about the British, "they did not give gifts," sums up the situation quite well. The British were concerned with exploitation rather than colonization, and their economic attitudes were more capitalistic than mercantilistic. Exchange took place within a market framework, something that was outside the traditional local exchange pattern. The local cultures which had been enriched by their dependence on an imported technology were destroyed as the traditional concepts of gift-giving gave way before their dependence on imported goods.

Initially, the American pursued the fur trade in the area, but this preoccupation soon gave way to colonialist expansion with the actual taking of land, something that had not been attempted seriously by either the French or the British. This destroyed the traditional subsistence base as surely as the British had destroyed the social values and the French had altered the local technology.

The French trade system was a gentle one, marked by either a conscious or unconscious policy at maintaining the integrity of local groups within the Straits of Mackinac. The changes brought about by the French were amplifications of existing cultural elements. These same cultural trends were affected by vacillations in French economic policy and were later destroyed by the British and American pattern of exploitation. The artifacts taken from the ground in the Straits of Mackinac are not only a part of a regional story—they show how a small area was incorporated into a worldwide economic system on the eve of the industrial revolution. More than just a study of regional culture change, the sites in the area have provided a picture of the acculturation process itself.

17

Historic Identification and Lake Winnebago Focus Oneota

Carol I. Mason

The traumatic historic rupture in the evolution of culture in North America has been like an archaeological Grand Canyon, more easily looked across than spanned or jumped. Yet archaeologists have persisted in the attempt to produce a single culture history that convincingly links archaeological information with ethnographic data. In spite of difficulties and discouragements, there have been many successes and many kinds of research strategies aimed at bringing archaeological complexes to life as ethnographically identifiable, sociologically functional communities. One has only to consider Tuck's Onondaga sequence (1971), the work at Hochelaga (Pendergast and Trigger 1972), and the most recent efforts in Puebloan archaeology (Longacre 1974) to be impressed by the techniques and sophistication of scholars in this difficult pursuit. The preliminary matter of ethnographic identification is often one of the hardest nuts to crack, even in areas where historic source material is plentiful and answers seem the most straightforward. Once an ethnographic identification has been made, however, that identification, for better or for worse, becomes part of the intellectual environment within which archaeologists must operate. It becomes a factor in all future archaeological analysis in the same region and an entrenched cultural tradition for archaeologists and any other scholars who work in that area.

Perhaps one of the most influential of these traditions has been the linkage of the Oneota complex, in one of its widest senses, with Chiwere–Siouan speakers—specifically the Ioway, Oto, Missouri, and, in Wisconsin, the Winnebago. The identification of historic Winnebago culture with Oneota, and particularly Lake Winnebago focus Oneota, has become a fixed point of reference in all our discussions of the origins, evolution, ecological adaptations, and final disposition of Oneota in northeastern Wisconsin. This concept was first presented in its present form by W. C. McKern in his "Preliminary Report on the Upper Mississippi Phase in Wisconsin" (1945), which was completed some years prior to its publication. As early as 1931, McKern was speculating in print about Oneota pottery and the Winnebago, but, by 1935, he was quoted as saying quite specifically that " 'the Lake Winnebago does seem to be a focus of the Oneota aspect, and it is rather definitely tied up with the historical Winnebago' " (Mott 1938: 304). In 1939, he affirmed that the Lake Winnebago focus is actually the culture of the Winnebago Indians (McKern 1939: 5). More broadly construed as part of the whole Chiwere–Siouan problem, James B. Griffin elegantly delineated the sequence in several publications, including his paper "A Hypothesis for the Prehistory of the Winnebago" (1960), where he meticulously marshaled all the evidence then available bearing on the origins of Oneota from its presumed Middle Mississippian forebearers. Of the Oneota–Winnebago question, he said, "One of the excellent results of the more recent archaeological work in the Upper Mississippi Valley is the clear recognition of distinctive prehistoric and historic complexes which were Winnebago, Ioway, Missouri, and presumably Oto" (Griffin 1960: 809).

Other scholars working in the Upper Great Lakes have essentially agreed with the Oneota–Winnebago identification. Ritzenthaler felt that "concrete evidence is available to determine that both the Winnebago and Iowa are descendents of Upper Mississippi peoples" (1949: 36). Hall, citing McKern, stated that "bearers of Oneota culture have been recognized in the Ioway and Oto, Winnebago, and Missouri" (1962: 102). He further speculated that the Koshkonong focus itself has some relevance to Winnebago history on the strength of "ethnic identification of the Lake Winnebago Focus with protohistoric Winnebago in the valley of the Fox River of Green Bay" (Hall 1962: 150). Henning, in his 1961 paper on Oneota ceramics, felt that evidence "seems fairly conclusive that the remains [of Lake Winnebago focus Oneota in Wisconsin] can be attributed to the protohistoric Winnebago occupation" (1961: 36). Other writers have had no reason to quarrel with the Lake Winnebago focus identification of the

Winnebago, including Quimby (1966: 37), Mott (1938), Peske (1965: 5; 1966: 188), Hurley (1974: 116), Bullock (1940: 29), Buckstaff (1939: 23), and Bennett (1943: 40).

Yet, some archaeologists always have been uneasy with these conclusions, although unwilling to question very seriously the now embedded and respectable tie of Winnebago culture with the Lake Winnebago focus Oneota or, for that matter, the exclusive identification of Oneota with Chiwere–Siouan speakers. Joan Freeman, for example, was uncomfortable with McKern's identification as early as 1956, citing his evidence as "not conclusive" (1956: 39). Guy Gibbon felt that the correlation was "probably too restrictive" (1972: 179). Other scholars have chafed at the constraints put upon their own conceptualizations by the Chiwere-Siouan–Oneota paradigm in its broadest sense. Fitting expressed the unease of many when he examined the wide distribution of Oneota ceramics up through the Door Peninsula of Wisconsin into Michigan, which he found he could not "interpret . . . as a result of an intrusion of Siouan speakers" (Fitting 1970: 191). Mildred Wedel articulated the problem even more cogently when she found the Chiwere–Siouan designation for Oneota too confining to admit complexes that she felt clearly to be Oneota and just as clearly not Chiwere–Siouan (1963: 120).

The evidence upon which historic Winnebago peoples are linked to the Lake Winnebago focus Oneota is presented in three papers by W. C. McKern (1931, 1942, 1945). Methodologically, he is very explicit and leaves no doubt as to how he arrived at his conclusions. His line of reasoning connects Oneota and the Winnebago Indians through two separate kinds of evidence: ethnographic and ethnohistorical. Ethnographic descriptions of pottery and pottery making, especially those collected by Radin (1923: 119), were used to establish one kind of tie, but even McKern felt that recent statements by modern Winnebago Indians on obsolete techniques were open to the charge of ex post facto rationalization. Many ethnographically obtained details, especially those concerning molding of pots in holes in the ground or the use of glue from sturgeon vertebrae as tempering, clearly will not support the case for identification. Nevertheless, Radin's description of Winnebago pottery making and McKern's use of it have become part of the underpinning for the archaeological intellectual tradition uniting Oneota with the Winnebago (see Lurie 1960: 796 for an example).

McKern's ethnohistorical evidence is the most germane to analyses of the Lake Winnebago focus and the Winnebago Indians. His approach to ethnic identification was straightforward and sensible, beginning with the known fact that Winnebago villages in 1634 existed in northeastern Wisconsin at the time of contact and that many villages later appeared on nineteenth-century land deeds and maps. This part of the state is, in fact, the "heart of known Winnebago territory" (McKern 1945: 125). Several sites listed on maps as historic Winnebago villages also contained Lake Winnebago focus ceramics, often as only one part of many components, and he was extremely careful to locate a pure Lake Winnebago focus village in a place that was "traditionally . . . an old Winnebago habitation site" (1945: 125) before proposing that the archaeological complex known as "Lake Winnebago focus Oneota" was indeed the remains of the people known as "Winnebago."

McKern's methodology is faultless, but his identification founders upon the expanded chronology given the Lake Winnebago focus by radiocarbon dating and upon the temporal gap between that focus and nineteenth-century recollections of Winnebago villages in the same area. The three principal Wisconsin sites (Figure 17.1) that McKern used in his analysis were McCauley, Karow, and Lasley's Point, although he was not directly involved in excavations at the latter site. Lasley's Point has been excavated a number of times (Buckstaff 1939; Bullock 1940; Kannenberg 1938; Peske 1966), and the recent work of G. Richard Peske has provided a series of radiocarbon dates: A.D. 1270 ±80 (Wis-57); A.D. 990 ±70 (Wis-50); A.D. 1170 ±80 (Wis-62; Wis-47); A.D. 1400 ±70 (Wis-161); A.D. 1220 ±65 (Wis-159); and A.D. 1480 ±60 (Wis-158; Wis-164). The contexts of these dates have yet to be published in any detail, but if they accurately reflect Lake Winnebago focus Oneota at Lasley's Point, then, conservatively construed, they may indicate a time range between A.D. 1000 and A.D. 1400 or 1500.

Between these dates and identifiable historic Winnebago occupations in northeastern Wisconsin, there is a temporal hiatus that has not as yet been filled by any body of convincing historic artifacts from the site. The extensive early excavations there produced "nothing . . . which shows that these Indians had ever made contact with the white man in any way" (Bullock 1940: 31). Peske recovered a few nondiagnostic historic materials (Peske 1965), but there is as yet no way to associate them with the Lake Winnebago focus occupation. Whether these materials are seventeenth-, eighteenth-, or even nineteenth-century debris from local farmers, migratory Indians, or whatever is impossible to say. If Lasley's Point represents a continuous occupation from prehistoric Oneota to historic Winnebago, then there should be historic artifacts to testify to the fact, artifacts at least as plentiful as those from the short-term occupation at the Bell site (Wittry 1963) or from the long series of historic villages on Rock Island. Without solid artifactual evidence, there is nothing to link the historic Winnebago to Lasley's Point other than the earlier excavators' unsupported convictions that the site must be prehistoric Winnebago (Buckstaff

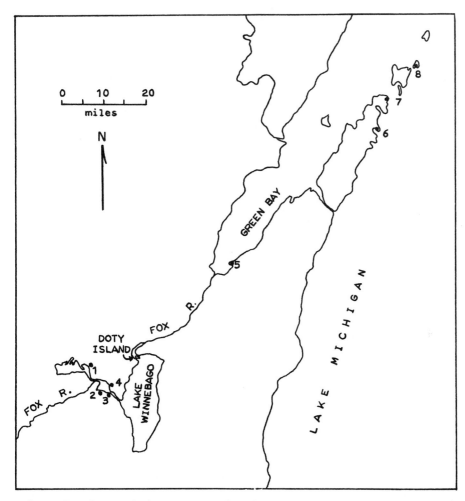

Figure 17.1 Sites and places mentioned in the text: (1) Lasley's Point, (2) Bell, (3) McCauley, (4) Karow, (5) Point Sauble and Beaumier Farm sites, (6) Mero, (7) Porte des Morts, and (8) Rock Island.

1939; Bullock 1940; Kannenberg 1938) and McKern's reading of nineteenth-century maps.

The McCauley site was even more important to McKern's identification since the Milwaukee Public Museum actually excavated there and the materials were, therefore, more accessible. He never described any historic materials in the collections from the site, but Henning more recently discovered some "brass, glass beads, bottle fragments, items, and white vitreous china fragments" (1961: 36) from there in the Milwaukee Public Museum collections. These may belong to the "known historic and traditionally protohistoric camp site of the Winnebago Indians" (McKern 1945: 124), but they indicate nothing about the important issue of demonstrating a linkage between a nineteenth-century Winnebago village and a prehistoric Oneota site in the same area. McKern's use of local tradition and recent maps does not build a convincing picture of an *in situ* evolution of Lake Winnebago focus Oneota into a historic Winnebago culture, nor does it establish even the likelihood of a close relationship between them. The only way such an identification can be adequately supported is through meticulous historical documentation, buttressed by the same kinds of artifactual evidence presented by Mott for the Ioway (1938) or by Wittry (1963) for the Bell site. Local tradition simply is not enough.

The same is true of the Karow village site, which was "locally believed to have been occupied by the Winnebago in the early historic period, and for a long preceding period of time" (McKern 1945: 140). Yet, even the burials from the Karow site (excavated by Peske [1966] as the Furman site) contained no trade goods, which is strange if the village were in fact even partly historic. As far as historic trade artifacts are concerned, there is no direct way to tie the Lake Winnebago focus Oneota, bracketed within the 400- or 500-year time span following A.D. 1000, to nineteenth-century Winnebago villages that were established in the same vicinity.

There is a much stronger argument presented by McKern to support an Oneota origin for the Winnebago, although not necessarily a Lake Winnebago focus origin. This is basically a linguistic syllogism: Ioway and Oto occur as Oneota archaeological manifestations; the Winnebago are linguistic relatives of the Ioway and Oto; therefore, the Winnebago also must appear archaeologically as Oneota sites. This linguistic association was employed by Griffin in an early paper as part of his hypothesis for the Chiwere–Siouan origins of the Oneota tradition from a Middle Mississippian base (1937), although it apparently was suggested first by Keyes (Mott 1938: 228). Between Iowa and Wisconsin, scholars have used each other's identifications in a mutually reinforcing way (McKern 1942: 160; Mott 1938: 228). The Ioway–Oneota equation has the best documentation (Mott 1938), and it seems likely that the Oto must share in it. However, Mildred Mott Wedel has felt that it is quite difficult to tie in even the Oto in spite of the overwhelming reasonableness of the equation unless, as she suggests, Ioway and Oto may have become separate ethnic groups only in the historic period (Wedel 1959). Such admirable restraint in pinning ethnographic labels to archaeological complexes well might be imitated in areas where the documentation is much less secure.

The linguistic syllogism is still the strongest argument rooting the historic Winnebago in an Oneota past; it still seems more than reasonable to look for Oneota ancestors for the Winnebago. Yet, proof that those ancestors are represented by the Lake Winnebago focus Oneota is simply not available at this time. There is also a growing realization that Oneota itself cannot be restricted to the Chiwere–Siouan linguistic pool, which presently is being engulfed in a much larger Oneota ocean. The Oneota tradition as defined by Hall, the Wedels, and others (Hall 1962: 106) is now too broad in space and time to be a simple one-to-one correspondence between Chiwere–Siouan speakers and Oneota ceramics. In 1962, Hall was willing to include parts of Apple River and Silvernale as Oneota; Henning reported Oneota-like material from a site on the Elkhorn River in Nebraska in association with pit houses and trade goods (1961: 39). There are even materials in Kansas (Wedel 1963: 120) that are unquestionably Oneota and, additionally, probably prehistoric Omaha. There are, then, Oneota materials present in Iowa, Wisconsin, Missouri, Nebraska, and Kansas identified with Osage, Kansa, and Omaha, as well as the more familiar Ioway, Oto, Missouri, and Winnebago. Some Oneota-like rimsherds from Wright's Peninsula Woodland along the north shore of Lake Superior could be prehistoric Ojibwa (J. V. Wright 1968: Pl. 13). For the student of Oneota today, there is always the bothersome question of "what else?"

In Wisconsin, McKern's support of a direct tie between Lake Winnebago focus Oneota and the Winnebago Indians has been very influential, but, besides his three sites, there is little archaeological information that ever has been used to support it. Lake Winnebago focus ceramics have appeared on many sites in Door, Winnebago, Brown, and other counties in the northeast, but never in association with trade artifacts in contexts that could be unequivocally linked to the ceramics. The Porte des Morts site at the tip of mainland Door Peninsula, for example, yielded Lake Winnebago focus pottery, but the only trade artifacts were a few beads and fragments of brass kettle scrap in a test pit well away from any major habitation area (C. Mason 1970). The Mero site, north of Bailey's Harbor on the Lake Michigan shore, similarly has produced Lake Winnebago focus ceramics, but no trade goods at all (R. Mason 1966). There are classic Lake Winnebago focus ceramics from the multicomponent site on Rock Island, north of Washington Island in Lake Michigan, but attempts to relate any of them with trade materials have been frustrated. Even without the compelling evidence of the radiocarbon dates from Lasley's Point, archaeologists should have been suspicious of a historic identification that has left so little archaeological evidence behind it.

Perhaps the most detailed use of McKern's Lake Winnebago focus identification with the Winnebago Indians occurred in Hall's Carcajou Point report, but Hall was ultimately unsuccessful in establishing the tie independent of McKern and his three original sites. Carcajou Point, like the McCauley and Karow sites, was a known Winnebago village— White Crow's village—in the nineteenth century (Hall 1962: 8); but, again, there is no train of evidence to link the prehistoric peoples with this late historic occupation. European artifacts at Carcajou Point occurred in no context that could provide conclusive information either on their dates or about what kind of pottery the historic Winnebago might have been making there—if indeed they were making pottery at all at such a late date. In one case, 12 shell-tempered body sherds were in a refuse pit (F 70) with trade artifacts, but these occurred with grit-tempered cord-marked sherds as well. If this pit belonged to White Crow's nineteenth-century village, there is still no reason to believe that any of the sherds in it were actually historic Winnebago, since the pit was dug in an area previously occupied by other, earlier tenants who happened to be making shell-tempered pottery themselves. Hall felt then that "the presence of shell-tempered pottery [in pit F 70] agrees with what is known of the Winnebago as an Upper Mississippian people" (1962: 149). Indeed it may, but the association is a non sequitur.

Assuming that the tie between the Lake Winnebago focus Oneota and the historic Winnebago Indians has not been documented adequately, what then? How can the protohistoric Winnebago be interpreted if they are not identified as Lake Winnebago focus Oneota? What else could represent the Winnebago in the area that was their traditional heartland? They might be dismissed as a non-Wisconsin native group, their traditional history and origin myths to the contrary. Or they might be identified with some of the effigy mound builders with the concurrence of some of their origin myths (Gibbon 1972; Radin 1923), archaeologists to the contrary (Hurley 1974: 115). Or, more consistent with their linguistic affiliations to the Oneota–Ioway, one might look to see what kind of late Oneota sites there are in the "Winnebago heartland" that might be reasonable candidates. In Iowa, the documented Ioway sites are not numerous; they are characterized by small villages with few historic artifacts, and the ceramic complex associated with them is Orr focus Oneota with Allamakee Trailed as the distinctive pottery type. In Wisconsin, documentation for the Winnebago begins with Jean Nicolet's voyage of 1634 and their presence somewhere in the northeastern part of the state. Nicolet's traditional landing place is in the Red Banks area, along the eastern shore of Green Bay, north of the modern city of Green Bay. This traditional history is as yet unsupported by any evidence, and the choice of a landing place is open to the charge of having been picked solely because Nicolet must have landed somewhere in the vicinity and because there is a large aboriginal site located at nearby Point Sauble.

Point Sauble (Freeman 1956) is a multicomponent site disfigured by years of cottage construction along the Green Bay shore. It is known archaeologically only from surface collections, test-pitting by many individuals and institutions, and the brief University of Wisconsin excavations there in 1950. Since it is a large Oneota site in the general vicinity of historic Winnebago villages, it is critically important to understanding Oneota development in northeastern Wisconsin and perhaps to bringing the Winnebago into a known archaeological framework. Joan Freeman originally thought that the Oneota component at Point Sauble resembled the Orr focus in many of its attributes, and Griffin agreed when he examined the pottery from the site (Freeman 1956: 19). However, in her report, she tentatively assigned it to the Lake Winnebago focus, albeit a very unusual and probably early variant. Her original diagnosis of Orr focus affiliations probably will stand as the correct one for, as Robert Hall observed some time later, there are no known examples of Lake Winnebago Trailed at Point Sauble or at the nearby Beaumier Farm site, which is probably part of the Point Sauble complex (Hall 1962: 131–132). Allamakee Trailed, the diagnostic Orr focus ceramic type, does occur there. Allamakee Trailed has an as yet unknown distribution in northeastern Wisconsin, and a concentrated search in local museum and private collections is needed before its full geographic range is known. It occurs as far north as Rock Island, where it is probably of historic age, and as far around Green Bay as the mouth of the Fox River (Hall 1962: 132). The range of its distribution along the Fox River toward Lake Winnebago remains unknown. The Orr focus, of course, already is known to be of historic age elsewhere in the Middle West. In discussing the Allamakee Trailed pottery from the site near the mouth of the Fox River, Hall suggested that it might be the remains of Ioway Indians wintering among the Winnebago, but it certainly seems a useful working hypothesis that Allamakee Trailed and at least part of the Orr focus in Wisconsin represent the Winnebago themselves and not their Ioway guests.

It is one thing to propose that the historic Winnebago are archaeologically Orr focus rather than Lake Winnebago focus and another thing to document it with historic source materials and with historic artifacts. The radiocarbon dates in Wisconsin are certainly compatible with a very late prehistoric to early historic placement: A.D. 1420 $\pm$ 70 and 1630 $\pm$ 60 for the Midway site all the way across the state on the Mississippi River (Gibbon 1970: 83). But the necessary trade artifacts have not yet been found, and one cannot take much comfort from the fact that not all proposed Ioway sites themselves contained trade artifacts (Wedel 1959: 40). Freeman lists a copper tinkler and copper beads attached to buckskin as probable "trade" copper (1956: 32) at Point Sauble, but there is no context for these artifacts, and they might just as well be aboriginal. A few glass beads (Freeman 1956: 33) were recovered from the site, but Indians were not the only people who wore beads, and extensive nineteenth-century remains occur there as well (a Peter Dorni pipe, a USA pipe, Staffordshire china, bone-handled knives and forks). As Freeman remarked, "trade goods were not found in any direct association with evidence of a prehistoric occupation by the Indians. They were all found on the surface of the ground or else in areas disturbed by bulldozing" (1956: 33). Some surface finds, though, belong to the proper time period: Jesuit rings (Brown 1943: 7) and a seventeenth-century bronze compass. However, Point Sauble is an extensive site and relatively little of it actually has been excavated. That there were at least *some* historic materials in the ground with some aboriginal remains is attested to by a multiple burial removed from the site in 1940 (Hall 1962: 49). It contained several heavy brass bracelets as well as a whole pot. The bracelets are in the collections of the Neville Public Museum, Green Bay, but that critically important pot is "lost" and of an unknown vintage. If ever found and identified, it could contribute materially to an understanding of the role Point Sauble plays in Winnebago history.

The conspicuous absence of known historic Oneota sites in northeastern Wisconsin, the "heartland" of the Winnebago, is a burdensome problem not easily resolved, given the present state of Winnebago ethnohistory. It has been useful to those supporting a Lake Winnebago focus origin for the Winnebago, since it could be argued that the great population reduction of the mid-seventeenth century simply reduced the people to a point at which sites with trade goods need not really be expected. However, beginning with the viewpoint that the Winnebago may belong to the historic Orr focus instead, some resolution of the paucity of sites should be attempted. The problems in such an attempt are multitudinous and include such issues as: *(1)* How populous were the Winnebago? *(2)* How many Winnebago villages were there at the time of contact? *(3)* Where were the villages located? *(4)* How large were Winnebago settlement clusters? and *(5)* Did the Winnebago have any recognizable trade artifacts before their famous population reduction?

Previous efforts at unscrambling the events surrounding Nicolet's contact with the Winnebago have been handicapped seriously by McKern's identification of them with the Lake Winnebago focus Oneota. For example, Nancy Lurie's (1960) evidence for an incredibly rapid change in lifeway for the Winnebago between 1620 and 1670 rests, in large part, upon the image of late prehistoric and early historic Winnebago villages on the order of Lasley's Point. She felt that archaeologists had proved that the prehistoric Winnebago "lived in large villages which were occupied over relatively long periods of time" (1960: 790), thus finding it extremely difficult to explain why the ethnographic Winnebago were a "people differing in only minor details of culture from surrounding Algonkian speaking tribes" (1960: 791). The culture change of those 50 years between 1620 and 1670 could be described by Lurie only as "revolutionary" (1960: 791), as indeed it would have had to have been to accomplish so radical an alteration.

The primary problem to be considered when dealing with the problems of the contact Winnebago is that of population estimates. On this question hinges archaeological expectations of sites, and it is, therefore, an exceedingly important issue. Nicolet is the single source for the actual numbers of Winnebago Indians in the period before the great population reduction, and he unfortunately left no direct account of his voyage. Our knowledge of what he found has been preserved in the *Jesuit Relations*, where his findings were mentioned by Le Jeune in the *Relations* of 1640 (Thwaites 1898) and where Barthelemy Vimont, 10 years after the event, recorded some of the details. "Very numerous" is the attribute Le Jeune applied to the Winnebago, apparently on Nicolet's testimony (Thwaites 1898: 233), but he recorded no exact numbers. At one point, however, Vimont cited Nicolet as observing 4000 or 5000 men assembled in his honor. The famous history of Bacqueville de la Potherie contains a great many more details about the Winnebago of Nicolet's time and afterwards, and he also mentions a population of 4000 or 5000 men (Blair 1911: 293). La Potherie was removed even farther from the event than Le Jeune or Vimont, since his history was not written until nearly 1702. Both Vimont's and La Potherie's figure seems to indicate a very large Winnebago population, since 4000 or 5000 men might mean 16,000 or 20,000 people if there were, additionally, 4 or 5 women and children per man.

The curious collusion in the population figure cited by these two accounts may mean that both derived it from a common source (Nicolet?) or that La Potherie himself took it from the *Jesuit Relations*. Much of La Potherie's information was derived from the inestimable Nicolas Perrot, but he apparently consulted other sources as well. The figure of 4000 or 5000 men, and perhaps 16,000 or 20,000 people, is very difficult to reconcile with the absence of many scattered village sites unless, of course, all 16,000 Winnebago were living together on a site now under the modern cities of Green Bay or Neenah–Menasha. Gibbon's model of Oneota factionalization from A.D. 1300 to 1650 (Gibbon 1972: 176) suggests, on the contrary, that we should expect small communities dispersed over a broader hinterland with seasonally occupied larger settlements where certain resources were plentiful (as at Point Sauble?).

The figure of 4000 or 5000 men rests solely on the testimony of Nicolet, recorded second-hand through the Jesuits or conceivably third-hand through Perrot to La Potherie. Yet, one wonders how he arrived at that figure or indeed if it was his figure in the first place. His visit was brief, unrepeated, and isolated as an event. His impressions were not recorded on the spot or even in the near temporal neighborhood. His activities during his stay included feasting and celebration, not census taking or even examining the limits of Winnebago territory. Nancy Lurie felt his account, as surviving in the *Jesuit Relations*, confusing enough to question whether or not he visited any Winnebago villages at all (1960: 800). She has pointed out that it is also impossible to tell if some of the people he met were Menominees as well as Winnebago (1960: 801). Given his exuberance and euphoria at having made successful contact with the people of Green Bay, Nicolet may not be a reliable source for absolute numbers of Indians.

The very high population estimate derived from Nicolet is the major reason there is so much emphasis on the romanticized population reduction after Nicolet's 1634 voyage and before 1670. By that date and with a greater familiarity with the Winnebago, French sources no longer speak of them in terms of thousands, only of small villages with hundreds of warriors, compatible not only with the Gibbon model but also with the kinds of villages cited for the Ioway (Wedel 1959: 34–41). There is no reason to doubt that the Winnebago suffered as much as other native peoples from wars, diseases, and other disasters in the historic period, but the fantastic death rate of 15,000 to 20,000 in less than 40 years seems almost incredible. A more modest population estimate for the Winnebago in the first place would require less of a holocaust among them in the years immediately following Nicolet's visit.

La Potherie provides a remarkable set of figures covering those population losses: at least 2500 men lost to disease (Blair 1911: 293), 500 warriors drowned in a storm (pp. 294–295), and the remainder killed or captured by the Illinois (p. 300). What survived at the end of these disasters was a group of 150 warriors, the figure cited by Perrot more than 30 years after the Nicolet voyage. How La Potherie arrived at any of his figures is unclear. Even with Perrot as a possible source, the very specificity of the numbers is suspicious. La Potherie may have had the Nicolet figure of 4000 or 5000 men and the Perrot figure of 150 men and was filling in estimates of population losses to reconcile his two sources. It is difficult to question La Potherie's accounts or Nicolet's figures since both have had the weight of favorable historic opinion behind them for many years, but the present lack of sites to substantiate the size of the Winnebago population certainly opens them to more careful scrutiny.

Where to look for pre- and post-Nicolet villages belonging to the Winnebago and how to adequately document them is doubly difficult, because of the scarcity of historic source materials. Before Nicolet, there are very few records, and, even in the post-Perrot period, there are very few documented villages. One of the most important of these is the early-eighteenth-century village site on Doty Island, located in the channel of the Fox River where it flows out of Lake Winnebago through the city of Neenah (Brown 1905: 421; Thwaites 1906: 23). Because of heavy modern occupation by homes and industry, Doty Island has yet to provide a clue to the Winnebago artifact inventory of the early eighteenth century, and because it remained a Winnebago village until 1837, expecting early material may be too optimistic. Excavations there in 1973 by Lawrence University and the University of Wisconsin, Fox Valley Center, of a burial in a house construction site produced no trade goods and no ceramics of any kind.

Early accounts of archaeological sites in Winnebago County and the surrounding areas (see Lawson 1903, in particular) mention historic materials of many kinds, but these are most often associated with isolated burials or surface finds. Documented sites are the exception. The Bell site (Wittry 1963) is potentially important in identifying the Winnebago archaeologically, since historic records indicate that a small group of Winnebago was present at the Bell site at a time when aboriginal pottery was still being made. The shell-tempered, possibly Winnebago ceramics from the Bell site were, unfortunately, only undecorated body sherds.

The presence of trade goods will be a critical factor both in identifying early Winnebago villages and in documenting whether or not trade reached them before Nicolet. Sagard is the source for the information that the Winnebago were trading with the Ottawa as early as 1623 (Lurie 1960: 791). The kinds of objects flowing to the Winnebago through this trade is unknown; Sagard (Lurie 1960: 792) cited the content of the trade going from the Winnebago to the Ottawa as " 'furs, pigments, wampum, and other rubbish'," but what was given to them in return was not recorded. It would be surprising if the enterprising Ottawa did not carry on a brisk trade in European goods long before the first Europeans arrived to carry it on for themselves. La Potherie (Blair 1911: 293) describes the Winnebago as having only "stone knives and hatchets," but in the same breath he mentions "knives, bodkins, and many other useful articles" (Blair 1911: 293) brought to the Winnebago by some of the Ottawa traders. Trade and access to it seems to have been at the root of internal problems among the Winnebago and external problems with their Ottawa trading partners; these problems culminated in the Nicolet voyage, which gave the French their first direct contact with the fur-rich country beyond Lake Michigan.

Tentatively, archaeologists seeking early Winnebago sites should anticipate trade goods from Quimby's Early period (1966: 102–116)—perhaps not many but enough to testify to an active Ottawa presence there. At least some of the diagnostic bead types should occur: star chevrons, large monochromatic black beads, and perhaps tubular redwood beads with blue-on-white stripes. Seed beads should be infrequent, and when they occur, they should be black, white, or aqua. Other trade artifacts might include hawk-billed trade knives or those with sword points, awls with a square cross-section, and ornaments made from brass kettles. If the population figures so casually included in the Nicolet account are accurate and the villages generally small, then Winnebago archaeological sites of this earliest historic period should outnumber those of the latter part of the seventeenth century by a figure of 36:1. If the Nicolet estimate was more impressionistic than exact, then the Wisconsin countryside cannot be expected to yield a much greater number of early sites than of later ones.

Much work must be accomplished before Winnebago archaeology is anchored to the historic sequence as securely as the Ioway. For many years, the traditional identification of the Winnebago Indians with the Lake Winnebago focus Oneota has been an immutable part of the intellectual landscape, and archaeologists have not given Winnebago archaeology more than a passing glance. Yet, the actual evidence upon which this identification originally was made is so slim as to be almost nonexistent. If the Winnebago are disengaged from an archaeological identification that has not been proved and if the whole question of where in the Oneota tradition the Winnebago belong is thrown open to discussion, then much more than just the protohistory of the Winnebago is at stake. The Lake Winnebago focus then can be examined without requiring it to metamorphose into historic Winnebago and without requiring it to be eternally present when that metamorphosis occurred. The archaeological tradition that gave us the Winnebago–Lake Winnebago focus Oneota identification need not constrain or direct future conceptualizations until such time as a convincing body of evidence is marshaled to confirm it.

18

Ethnicity and Archaeology in the Upper Great Lakes

Ronald J. Mason

At least in the abstract, it would seem a relatively modest task for the archaeologist working with historic period sites to identify them according to the ethnic names familiar to ethnologists and historians. Experienced at the recovery of scraps of cultural behavior over time slopes of thousands of years, and at home with the analytical techniques for defining, dating, and reconstructing long-extinct cultures, the archaeologist studying historic sites certainly has advantages denied the student of prehistory. For one thing, the temporal recency of historic period materials should, in theory, produce fewer problems and more tractable ones in isolating and identifying cultural units. Moreover, working within the time for which there are relevant written sources has the additional advantage of the observations recorded in those sources—an independent fount forever denied the prehistoric archaeologist. The recency of his material and its augmentation by means of the written record—sometimes compiled over several centuries—has the further advantage of making more immediately relevant to the archaeologist the descriptions and analyses of ethnographers and social anthropologists working in the full complexities of living communities. This is not to deny the relevance of such mainly synchronic studies to prehistoric archaeology, but to point out the proportionately greater and more varied data resources of the historical archaeologist and the greater immediacy of common interests with ethnology and social anthropology.

Some archaeologists have argued that a range of sociocultural activities of past societies much fuller than that traditionally realized is recorded in the archaeological record if we possess the wit to ask questions of that record in the proper way (for example, Binford and Binford 1968). Regardless of the degree to which this view may be subscribed, many historic period sites must be acknowledged as first among equals as site sources of information about the widest spectra of past human behavior. Historic period sites are the Pleistocene epoch of archaeology. Just as recency and freshness of preservation tied to still common processes of the geosphere (large-scale glaciation, for example) make the Pleistocene the most finely delineated of the epochs of Cenozoic time, so the same considerations apply with approximately equal consequences to archaeology.

Another factor makes ethnographic and historical studies of more obvious and immediate utility to the historical archaeologist than to his colleague in prehistory. In most of the world, the beginning of the historical period meant the arrival of Europeans. In the Americas, Oceania, Africa, and parts of Asia, the appearance of European man was dramatically underlined by the initiation of cultural changes the results of which are still not understood fully by anthropologists. The magnitude of these alterations in demography, epidemiology, technology, ideology, and in whole fabrics of social relations and economic arrangements were certainly unprecedented in most of these areas. Indeed, significant and ramifying shifts in aboriginal institutions were more often than not already under way when the earliest written accounts were compiled. This being the case, the archaeologist of prehistory especially must guard against a conceptualization of the past uncritically influenced by ethnohistorical or ethnographic information that is the product of highly atypical conditions in the "life histories" of the peoples whose remains he studies. Elman Service's impressive but incompletely successful attempts to project into prehistory sociocultural models based on ethnographic data provide fascinating exemplification of some of the problems to be met (Service 1962, 1971). Unless we are willing to suspend adherence to the uniformitarian principle in paleoanthropology and are willing to seriously entertain the possibility that prehistoric men behaved in ways qualitatively different from modern, historical men—in which case ethnology and social anthropology cease to be of relevance to archaeology—it is apparent that historic archaeology is especially situated among the anthropological disciplines to benefit from the kinds of data that only eye-witness accounts in one form or another can provide.

The problem of ethnicity, or the determination of social divisions in such a way as to approximate the distinctions made by the members of now extinct social systems, would seem to be a problem more amenable to the historical than the prehistoric archaeologist. Ideally, the historical archaeologist excavates a (hopefully) single-component site which has been located rigorously in time and space by unambiguous historical sources and which yields appropriate native and/or European artifacts. If the group of people who lived at the site are named clearly in the documentary sources, that name may reasonably be attached to the material remains found at the site. The latter, in turn, may be employed (cautiously) to help identify other sites unaccounted for in the historical record. This kind of societal, tribal, or ethnic labeling of an archaeological site or component may be called *site-unit ethnicity.*

Site-unit ethnicity is dependent on the existence of one or more historical documents that can be related to a specific site or component of a site, which in turn yields corroborating evidence such as dated coins, clay pipes with cast makers' names or reliable statistics on stem diameters, or properly seriating glass trade beads. Although there are numerous examples of site-unit ethnicity in Iroquoia (for instance, Tuck 1971), they are conspicuously rare in the Upper Great Lakes. A good specimen in the latter region is the Bell site in Winnebago County, Wisconsin—an early eighteenth-century Fox village (Wittry 1963). Another example is Rock Island Site II in Door County, Wisconsin, where late-seventeenth- and early-eighteenth-century Potawatomi remains (among others) have been recovered (Mason 1974). That the ideal prerequisites for claiming site-unit ethnicity usually are approximated, and rarely attained fully, in the real world of disturbed sites and fragmentary documents must be stressed. This is undoubtedly true in the foregoing examples. Furthermore, there may be more (or less, for that matter) in a name than the student of ethnic groups may have bargained for. Reification of names has not been a sin peculiar to anthropologists.

Another category of ethnicity, which is based on grounds somewhat different from those just described, should be delineated. *Territorial ethnicity* may be thought of as the attribution of the name of a group to archaeological sites or components because of a suggestive correspondence in the areal distribution of the latter and part or all of the territory historically known to have been occupied by members of the named group. Even with great care and the necessary control of time depth in hand through stratigraphy, cross-dating, radiocarbon dating, or other methods, the utilization of territorial ethnicity in identifying archaeological materials and as an aid to understanding the past is probably a less reliable procedure than the use, if feasible, of site-unit ethnicity. In the time spans represented by his sites, the historical archaeologist may confuse contemporary ethnic divisions or fail to discern small-scale sequences because the margins of error intrinsic to his tools of measurement are insufficiently calibrated to the magnitude of the chronology. More fundamentally, territorial ethnicity suffers from the same weaknesses of site-unit ethnicity and additionally lacks the time–space specificity the latter provides. Notwithstanding these shortcomings, the method is a useful one and the archaeologist is obliged to employ it where less equivocal means are lacking. Some Upper Great Lakes examples of territorial ethnicity are available in W. C. McKern's (1945) identification of Winnebago sites in eastern Wisconsin and in J. V. Wright's (1965) proposed Ojibwa components in western Ontario. Inasmuch as the problem of the archaeological identity of the Winnebago is dealt with in another chapter in this volume by Carol Mason (Chapter 17), a brief look at Ojibwa archaeology will be more useful in the explication of the difficulties in dealing not only with territorial ethnicity but with ethnic archaeology in the Upper Great Lakes in general.

Excavations at the Shebishikong, Michipicoten, and Pic River sites (the first on Georgian Bay, the latter two on the north shore of Lake Superior) provided Wright with most of his data on aboriginal materials sometimes associated with European trade goods of the late-seventeenth and first half of the eighteenth century. These data were augmented by more procured from a series of small Late Woodland components distributed from Lake Simcoe to Lake of the Woods (J. V. Wright 1965).

According to J. V. Wright, the problem of ethnic identifications in the Upper Great Lakes is complicated by two factors: the culture of the peoples involved and the paucity of historic period sites. Regarding the former, he (J. V. Wright 1965: 190) observes that:

> The broad mosaic of politically independent bands, loosely related at the specific level through clan and/or marriage and, at a more general level, through language and way of life, limits, in part, the reality of discrete tribal designations to taxonomic units of anthropological convenience. Within the major tribal units of Ojibwa, Cree, Algonkin, Montagnais, and Naskapi (Jenness 1955: 266) the degree of geographically influenced blending defies the establishment of clear cultural boundaries.

In his search for an ethnicity worth specifying—that is, one broad enough to be susceptible of archaeological identification in a vast country noted for its thin and mobile population, and yet narrow enough to exclude Iroquoian and Siouan groups (if not also non-

Ojibwa Algonquian ones)—Wright indicates some of the confusions in names, places, dates, and spellings with regard to Upper Great Lakes Algonquian speakers. He refers to many of the names in the historical literature as synonyms or, variously, as the designations of clans, bands, or simply geographical regions. He then subsumes, under the designation Ojibwa, the Ottawa, Missisauga, Potawatomi, Sauteur, Amikwa, Nipissing, Ondataouauoat or Cheveux-Relevés, Kishkakon, Mousonee, Nassauaketon, Nikikouek, Sinago, and Gens de Terre. These *nomina dubia* become in subsequent discussion "sub-groupings of the Ojibwa" (J. V. Wright 1965: 190). Hoping that refinements would be possible in the future, Wright had to admit that his was a "broadly inclusive" archaeological and ethnological conception of the Ojibwa (J. V. Wright 1965: 216). It was also a pioneering attempt to tie together, however tenuously, a few of the threads of the rent fabric of Indian culture history in western Ontario.

The problem of defining ethnic units is an anthropological one in the pursuit of which the archaeological specialist, notwithstanding his peculiar needs, forfeits benefit of live informants. Unfortunately, ethnologists and social anthropologists have paid little detailed attention to the material attributes that might be expected to survive the demise of such culture-binding aggregates and, accordingly, would be of particular interest to archaeologists. This is not surprising, given the difficulties they have had with their contemporary objects of study in reaching consensus on the meaning and use of such terms as "society," "ethnic," "tribe," and so on (for example, Helm 1968; Southall 1970; Service 1971). They have provided some formulations, however, that the archaeologist may find useful in thinking about his material in sociological terms.

Citing Raoul Narroll's 1964 essay "On Ethnic Unit Classification" as a summary example, Fredrik Barth has outlined what the term "ethnic group" generally has been intended to mean in social anthropology. In this exposition (Barth 1969: 10–11), an ethnic group is a population that:

1. is largely biologically self-perpetuating
2. shares fundamental cultural values, realized in overt unity in cultural forms
3. makes up a field of communication and interaction
4. has a membership which identifies itself, and is identified by others, as constituting a category distinguishable from other categories of the same order.

While showing why and how his approach to the study of ethnicity differs from this formulation and "ideal type definition," Barth (1969: 11) does observe that "it is close enough to many empirical ethnographic situations, at least as they appear and have been reported, so that this meaning continues to serve the purposes of most anthropologists." In diachronic perspective, perhaps Barth's most pertinent dissent from this attribute list is his suggestion that the sharing of a common culture—"generally given central importance"—is less a definitional characteristic of ethnic groups than a result of their existence.

As pointed out by Narroll (1964), anthropologists have cited a variety of features said to be diagnostic of ethnicity. Not infrequently, ethnic group or unit has been equated with tribe (for example, Helm 1968).

Referring to the work of social anthropologists ranging from Berndt to Whiting, Narroll (1964: 291) lists six of the possible criteria for defining basic societal (or, evidently, ethnic) units:

> (1) language (which nearly everyone thinks is important), (2) political organization, (3) territorial contiguity [you don't have to cross another unit's territory], (4) distribution of particular traits being studied, (5) ecological adjustment, and (6) local community structure.

He opts for the first three criteria in establishing "cultunits" for the purposes of comparative studies. It would not violate Narroll's list or the larger one from which it is drawn if the archaeologist chose to consider instances of attribute 4 dependent variables, identifying them ethnically by as many of the other criteria as possible. In fact, unless historical accounts yield access to such other information, the archaeologist in practice usually has to rely on attributes 3 and 4 in combination (sometimes making a stab at 5), and runs the risk of circular reasoning.

Another important attempt at resolving the implications of ethnic identities with the understanding of archaeological features is in James E. Fitting's synthesis of Michigan and Upper Great Lakes archaeology (1970). Like Wright, Fitting cogently argues against the view "every name a different society." In somewhat greater detail than is developed in Wright's paper, he explores a number of problems besetting the direct historical approach in the Upper Great Lakes region. For example, he cites McKern's (1945) identification of the Winnebago with the Oneota Lake Winnebago focus and Griffin's (1937) suggestions of connection between Oneota archaeological materials and Chiwere Siouan-speaking peoples, and points out the incongruities that more recent archaeological research has brought to light—particularly in the distribution of Oneota ceramics far beyond the known territories of Winnebagoes or other Chiwere Siouan-speakers (Fitting 1970: 190–191). Questioning MacNeish's (1958) incorporation of Blackduck pottery in Assiniboine material culture, supporting the Fox identity of the Bell site (Wittry 1963), and maintaining that Huron ceramics in Ontario are most likely Ottawa or Chippewa ceramics when found in Michigan, Fitting demonstrates the confused and confusing nature of archaeological ethnic correlations. At least up to A.D. 1600, he argues, the Sauk, Kickapoo, Potawatomi, Mascouten, and (probably) Fox cannot be distinguished as separate entities and should be referred to only collectively as the "Fire People" (1970: 191). However, Fitting thinks that sites in the Chicago area, which others have suggested may represent Siouan groups, are Miami; certain other sites in northeastern Wisconsin and adjacent Michigan may be Miami also, or Chippewa or Potawatomi. These are interesting and disturbing alternatives.

Fitting embraces as Chippewa (Ojibwa) such groups as the Noquet, Marameg, Nopeming, Mississagi, and also, perhaps, the Nipissing and Amikwa. Exempted from this conscription are the Ottawa, Potawatomi, Nassauaketon, and, maybe, the Kiskakon (Kishkakon)—all groups considered as Ojibwa by J. V. Wright—as well as other entities similarly not included on Wright's list (1965: 192–199). The Ottawa are elevated by Fitting to a level of taxonomic abstraction, if not consistent inclusiveness, paralleling the Chippewa (Ojibwa). A third grouping, the "People of the Fire," are similarly defined. Other one-time Michigan tribes having separate status are the Miami and the Huron. Notwithstanding sites that, with implications of equal plausibility, he allows might be identified as Miami or Chippewa or Potawatomi (presumably postdating A.D. 1600), Fitting believes these groups, together with the Ottawa and Huron, basically represent different kinds of ecological adaptations to the resources of the western Great Lakes.

Most anthropologists probably would not object if terms such as "pseudosociety" and "quasiethnic" were used in reference to some of the named groups of people reported by Europeans in their explorations of North America. These terms would apply wherever there were mistaken equations of seasonal, regional, kinship, or activity-related temporary aggregates of people with whole, viable societies. The trouble, of course, is in distinguishing the spurious from the real. Fitting, for instance, maintains that archaeologists must use broadly encompassing ethnic labels in the Upper Great Lakes at least for periods before approximately A.D. 1600. Presumably, this is the most prudent course because finer discriminations will be confounded by the myriad names and frequently brief appearances of pseudo- and barely glimpsed real societies that fill the pages of early documentary sources. Finer perceptions, he allows, might be possible in later historical times (1970: 191). Most anthropologists, however, have argued the reverse, pointing to the displacements, extinctions, amal-

gamations, and the leveling of ethnic distinctions with the rise of
pan-tribal culture which proceeded with the expanding fur trade (see,
for instance, Keesing 1939; Quimby 1960, 1966; Hickerson 1970; Stone
and Canouts 1971).

Even readily admitting the usefulness—indeed, even indispensabil-
ity in some cases—of multigroup-inclusive nomenclature like Chippewa and "People of the Fire," it may be insisted that something vital
(a "structure" that *is* there) has been missed when it is concluded that
Ottawa simply means trader or that "to be an Ottawa was to
participate in the Ottawa system, which centered more about trade
than most other groups in the area" (Fitting 1970: 195). This statement
is not wrong, it is insufficient.

In the *Jesuit Relations* for 1666–1667, Father Claude Allouez
remarked that "the Outaouacs claim that the great river belongs to
them, and that no nation can launch a boat on it without their consent.
Therefore all who go to trade with the French, although of widely
different nations, bear the general name of Outaouacs, under whose
auspices they make the journey" (Thwaites 1896–1901, 51:21). It
would appear from this that there were Ottawas and Ottawas, and
that some were more Ottawa than others.

The foregoing passage may be taken, as it often has, to indicate that
the name Ottawa was conferred on more than one group ("nation")
engaged in the French trade. And there is other ample evidence to
support such a contention. So taken, however, the statement is not
emptied of all its contents. One still must ask: Who *were* the Ottawas
who claimed the river and under whose auspices did others go in trade
to the French? For some, being Ottawa involved more than taking furs
to Montreal or Quebec. That Fitting himself thinks so is indicated in
the model he uses of the "Ottawa subsistence pattern" which he
contrasts with the Potawatomi, Chippewa, and other patterns earlier
referred to. Such ecologically oriented use of these names, however,
was not intended to describe as valid in all places and at all times the
subsistence practices of particular ethnic groups, but as designations
for at least broadly contrasting patterns exemplified at some point by
the peoples whose names they bear. But the employment of such
ethnic labels in this connection does suggest that anthropologists
know more than they do about the peoples so named.

As an ethnohistorian, Harold Hickerson (for example, 1970) has
dealt with many of the challenges encountered in using the names
Europeans attributed to the Indian groups they met or of whom they
received reports from their Indian allies. His cautions are essentially of
the same order, although of different emphasis, as those of archaeologists Wright and Fitting. Of particular value are the suggestions by
both Hickerson and Fitting that names must be correlated carefully

with the dates of their employment as well as with place and circumstance of their attribution. This is especially critical, of course, in attempts to recognize pseudosocieties when they appear and in following the careers of known or thought to be bona fide named groups subsequently absorbed by others. Hickerson's (1962, 1970) reconstructions of the incorporation of earlier, small, territorial, autonomous societies into the historical Chippewa tribe provide examples of the worth of such a perspective. The disappearance of genuine named and located societies is a complex phenomenon and one not confined to just the earlier portions of the historical record. The Yellowknives of the Mackenzie District, for example, were a group not only extinguished as recently as the early years of the present century, but also expunged in the memories and oral histories of their Dogrib and Chipewyan relatives and neighbors (Gillespie 1970).

Certain ethnicities cannot be identified archaeologically before a particular period because they had not yet emerged as isolable sociological aggregates (for example, Chippewa or Ojibwa, Wyandot) or they left no remains after a given time because of societal extinction (such as Noquet, Nipissing, Yellowknife). Thus, designations like Wright's early historic Ojibwa for the Shebishikong, Michipicoten, and Pic River components in Ontario reflect a different societal reality than, say, James A. Tuck's (1971) specification of Onondaga identities for the Barnes, Sheldon, and Indian Hill sites in New York. Unfortunately, the terminology is inadequate to the distinction. Given the nature of the case, the former's employment of Ojibwa, as he points out, was as the name of a very broad ethnicity or "culture" whose constituent societies an ethnologist or social anthropologist certainly would want to segregate. It is analogous in kind, if not magnitude, to the Mississippian "culture" in which, it has been suggested, the Potawatomi marginally participated, or the Fort Ancient "culture," a part of which may have been Shawnee (Griffin 1952: 364). The people from Tuck's Onondaga sites, on the other hand, probably would have viewed themselves as a more distinct people than would Wright's. They undoubtedly would have exhibited that greater solidarity and sense of societal identity implicit in relatively sedentary agriculturalists having pan-tribal sodalities and greater formalization of leadership roles. Different kinds of societies are represented in these comparisons ("bands," "band segments," "localized clan communities," "segmentary tribes," or whatever), and the taxonomist has yet to appear who can sort them all out. And determining ethnic affiliations of archaeological sites is further complicated by the failure of the inhabitants to behave in ways compatible with ease of classification. It is at our risk that we establish by definition that which we seek to discover (Barth 1969: 9–38).

That commingling of Indian populations and large-scale tribal intermarriages were an accompaniment of growing European hegemony is a familiar truth. In the western Great Lakes, examples abound (for example, Allouez [Thwaites 1896–1901, 54:205]; Perrot [Blair 1911: 270]; La Potherie [Blair 1911: 277, 319; and Thwaites 1902: 3]). As pointed out by James A. Clifton (1974: 31), Perrot used his knowledge of this phenomenon in a hypothetical rebuke of his country's Indian allies to draw attention to the fact that half of the Potawatomi tribe (at least sometime before 1714) consisted of Sauks, that the Sauk in turn were part Fox, and that both the Sauk and the Fox had an abundance of in-laws who were Potawatomi. Indeed, at least two (and perhaps three) of the highest Potawatomi war leaders were Sauk (Perrot, in Blair 1911: 270).

Referring to a slightly earlier time, Charles E. Cleland cites an example of what he calls "the cosmopolitan quality" of many Indian settlements in the Upper Great Lakes (1971: 93). The *Documents Relative to the Colonial History of the State of New York* (O'Callaghan 1855) contain a record of a meeting in Montreal in 1682 between Frontenac and western Indians seeking protection. The Indians expressed fear of Iroquois retaliation because an Illinois had murdered a Seneca in a village of Miamis and Kiskakon, Sinago, and Sable Ottawas! Such abundant information on ethnic mixing and role interdigitation among relatives of different tribes must be considered by historical archaeologists dealing with ethnic affinities of sites and assemblages. Michilimackinac, the Sault, Green Bay, Keweenaw, and Chequamegon, and all of the intervening posts and missions together with their supporting hinterlands, were new habitats in the fur-trade period. Here, sometimes briefly, new societies coalesced out of the elements of the old in novel combinations with European ideas and technology. This makes for difficult but exciting archaeology. Further enhancing the challenge is the fact that the ethnohistorical data were supplied by many scores of men, each one an individual, some cross-culturally perceptive and others impervious to values foreign to their upbringing, and some with causes to be served which transcended naive observation.

Making due allowance for Francophobia, the reminiscences of the English explorer Jonathan Carver concerning his 1766 voyage from Michilimackinac to Green Bay raise the question of deliberate obfuscation of the names of peoples and places by some early writers. Indicating that he thought Frenchmen capable of duplicity for diplomatic and economic ends, Carver believed that they sometimes called "the different nations of the Indians by nicknames they had given them, and not by those really appertaining to them" (1798: 21–22). He wrote that one of the reasons the French used nicknames (besides wanting to confuse the British) was to be able to converse among themselves in the presence of Indians who, if hearing themselves identified, might become suspicious of French intentions. "The only bad consequence arising from the practice is, that English and French geographers, in their plans of the interior parts of America, gave different names to the same people" (Carver 1798: 37–38). Except for the "nickname" of Green Bay, he does not give examples of the objects of his complaint. One also wonders in this connection at the significance of many of the "names" proffered by the Indians themselves, particularly with regard to their enemies or potential trading competitors, and to what extent and how these have been incorporated in the writing of "history."

Within historical time in the Upper Great Lakes, ethnic groups well may have existed for which no names survive; conversely, some names survive for groups now extinct. Some groups of people were given different names at different times and places. Some group names evidently embraced multiple ethnicities, and some *sometimes* embraced multiple ethnicities. Pseudoethnicities haunt the pages of history because they at one time were given names and, having names, took on a reality they had never had. Dissimilar kinds of societies were coetaneous in almost any segment of the historic period, though they lost to pan-tribalism in the end. These ranged at the times of first accounts from such noncorporate collectivities as the Cree with their acephalous, fluid, hunting-and-gathering bands on one hand, to such sedentary agriculturalists as the highly integrated and confederated Huron tribes on the other. As J. V. Wright (1965) has argued so ably, ceramic or other artifact variability must mean somewhat different things in such divergent sociocultural systems. That it must reflect, however remotely, the respective societies' "sense of themselves" binds the common concerns of archaeologist and ethnologist.

What does it mean to assert that a given archaeological component is Fox, or Potawatomi, or Ojibwa? In most cases, we can never be completely sure. In others, we may know in one instance but not another. But if a name is used in historical sources in reference to the occupants of a known, identified locality, the archaeologist is obligated to take due note of it. It then becomes a piece of information to be manipulated with others in the reconstruction of culture history and the study of the processes of adaptation and change.

As previously reviewed, the complexity and scale of social and cultural transformations in the Upper Great Lakes in the historical period militate against *simplistic* one-to-one correlations of particular artifacts or assemblages and specific ethnic identification wherever

those artifacts or assemblages occur. What were complex relationships can only be obscured by group identifications that are taken to
mean more (or less) than can be substantiated through detailed
ethnohistorical and archaeological research which check on themselves through each other. That in some sense unique cultures are a
product of the existence and viability of ethnic groups is a view held
by most social anthropologists (Barth 1969: 9–38; Honigmann 1959:
873; Narroll 1964). This provides a means of testing the meaning of
ethnicity in archaeological terms through indirect evidence bearing on
the kinds of social anthropological criteria earlier reviewed; thus,
group self-identification through artifact styles clustering among sites
of a region, assumption for further testing of linguistic correlation
with artifact style "dialects," and degree of a population's biological
self-sufficiency (presumably breaking down toward later historic
times) through measurements of genetic dental anomalies of skeletal
populations sampled by independent criteria (see methodological
strategies in Binford 1972; Binford and Binford 1968; Caldwell 1966;
Deetz 1965). Spurious ethnicities should not have assemblages recur-
ring at multiple sites. Within clustered cultural groupings known or
believed to have shared a generally similar way of life (for example,
Ojibwa), the shared archaeological attributes necessarily will be fewer
and more attenuated than in intersite comparisons of one of the
precursor constituent societies (say, Amikwa). Enormously complicat-
ing such tests, of course, are differences not only of site preservation
and sampling, but in the comparability of the original communities.
Winter hunting camps cannot be expected to look like summer fishing
stations in artifacts and features; pre- and postdiaspora Huron will
look different archaeologically, not just geographically.

The relative rarity of historically fixed sites, migrations and faction-
ing populations, the origin and sociological reference of group names,
pseudosocieties, and emergent ethnicities following from the commingling and disappearance of earlier ones are not just traps for the
unwary (they are certainly that) but are multifaceted research opportunities focusing on an epoch of regionally unprecedented upheaval
and change. Ethnic identifications are an important part of such
studies.

The two major—and complementary—approaches to ethnic affiliation of archaeological materials have been referred to as "site-unit"
and "territorial" ethnicities. The strength of the former, by definition,
is its highly specific localization in space and time of the remains of a
named group. It provides a restricted ethnic locus. Its weakness
resides in the rarity, at least in the Upper Great Lakes, of unambig-
uously located sites with ethnic affinities unequivocally supported by
primary historical documents. Also, the remains of a single commu-

nity at a particular point in time cannot be taken to represent the totality of the society of which it was a part. Care must be taken not to assume that because, say, the Bell site has been identified as Fox, then all Fox sites, or even just contemporaneous ones, must yield the same artifacts, culinary features, or settlement patterns. Conversely, the establishment of a particular assemblage as one thing at one site does not preclude completely the possibility of a similar assemblage being something else at another site.

Territorial ethnicity offers the advantage of not requiring tight historical documentation on specific localities, but simply on a district or area. This makes it feasible to at least approach the identification of archaeologically represented ethnicities, as in the Ojibwa case, even where discrete localities mentioned in the historical literature have not been found. Its drawback is this same vagueness as to time and place; it may result in ethnic identifications that, by their inclusiveness, depart more from the constitution of original, real societies than is the case with site-unit ethnicity. Territorial ethnicity is a dubious strategy in areas of migration and for times of heavy acculturation. As has been stressed, both site-unit and territorial ethnicities are hostage to the historical vagaries of naming.

Archaeologists have long been interested in the "direct historical approach" and other methods for assessing the ethnicity of sites and assemblages. Such interests are even more timely today with the growing emphasis on archaeological contributions to the study of the processes by which societies adapt to their circumstances and cultures evolve along new lines. As this chapter has attempted to show, the problems are many. Easy answers to the questions of how archaeological ethnicity is to be determined in particular cases and what a name alleged to socially align a given assemblage really means are frustrated by ambiguities in both historical documents and anthropological terminology, the continuing destruction of sites, and the persistent difficulties in trying to bridge that barely plumbed chasm between prehistory and the societies of the ethnohistorical and ethnographic records.

But to recognize the problems, to show examples of limited successes, and to argue for the most rigorous standards of verification (which must necessarily vary with the individual case) is to stress the high potential such concerns as archaeological ethnicity have for the mutual benefit of the students of man past and man present. These ethnicities must be as multidimensional as possible, not only for the indispensable purposes of opportunities for convergent verification, but to approach the study of the whole societies represented by the cultural fragments called "sites."

References for Part V

Barth, F. (Editor)
    1969   *Ethnic Groups and Boundaries.* Boston: Little, Brown.
Bennett, J.
    1943   A History of the Mississippi Cultures. *Wisconsin Archeologist* **24**:33–42.
Binford, L. R.
    1972   *An Archaeological Perspective.* New York: Seminar Press.
Binford, S. R., and L. R. Binford (Editors)
    1968   *New Perspectives in Archeology.* Chicago: Aldine.
Blair, E. H. (Editor)
    1911– *The Indian Tribes of the Upper Mississippi Valley and Regions of the Great*
    1912   *Lakes, as Described by Nicolas Perrot, French Commandant in the Northwest;*
          Bacqueville de la Potherie, French Royal Commissioner to Canada; Morrell
          Marston, American Army Officer; and Thomas Forsyth, United States Agent
          at Fort Armstrong. Vol. 1, 1911; Vol. 2, 1912. Cleveland: Arthur H. Clark
          Company.
Brose, D. S.
    1970   Summer Island III: An Early Historic Site in the Upper Great Lakes. *Historical*
          Archaeology **4**:3–33.
Brown, C. E.
    1905   A Record of Wisconsin Antiquities. *Wisconsin Archeologist* **5**:3–4.
    1943   Indian Trade Finger Rings. *Wisconsin Archeologist* **24**:7–9.
Buckstaff, R.
    1939   Serrated Shells of the Winnebago. *Wisconsin Archeologist* **20**:23–28.
Bullock, H. R.
    1940   Lasley Point Mounds. *Wisconsin Archeologist* **21**:28–33.
Caldwell, J. R. (Editor)
    1966   *New Roads to Yesterday.* New York: Basic Books.
Carver, J.
    1798   *Three Years Travels through the Interior Parts of North America.* Edinburgh:
          James Key.
Cleland, C. E.
    1966   The Prehistoric Animal Ecology and Ethnozoology of the Upper Great Lakes
          Region. *Anthropological Papers, Museum of Anthropology, University of*
          Michigan No. 29.
    1971   The Lasanen Site: An Historic Burial Locality in Mackinac County, Michigan,

edited by C. E. Cleland. *Publications of The Museum, Michigan State University, Anthropological Series* Vol. 1.

Clifton, J. A.
1974   Potawatomi Leadership Roles: On Okama and Other Influential Personages. In *Proceedings of the 1974 Algonquin Conference.* Ottawa: National Museum of Man, Mercury Series. Pp. 1–58.

Clute, R. D.
1971   The Physical Anthropology of the Lasanen Site. In The Lasanen Site: An Historic Burial Locality in Mackinac County, Michigan, edited by C. E. Cleland. *Publications of The Museum, Michigan State University, Anthropological Series* Vol. 1.

Deetz, J.
1965   *The Dynamics of Stylistic Change in Arikara Ceramics.* Urbana: University of Illinois Press.

Fitting, J. E.
1966   Review of "American Indian Tomahawks" by Harold L. Peterson. *Michigan History* **50**:274–276.
1970   *The Archaeology of Michigan.* Garden City, New York: Natural History Press.
1972   The Huron As an Ecotype: The Limits of Maximization in a Western Great Lakes Society. *Anthropologica* **14**:3–18.
In press   Archaeological Excavations at the Marquette Mission Site in 1972. Mackinac Studies in History and Archaeology.

Fitting, J. E., and C. E. Cleland
1969   Late Prehistoric Settlement Systems in the Upper Great Lakes. *Ethnohistory* **16**:284–302.

Freeman, J. E.
1956   An Analysis of the Point Sauble and Beaumier Farm Sites. Master's thesis, University of Wisconsin, Madison.

Gibbon, G.
1970   The Midway Village Site: An Orr Phase Oneota Site in the Upper Mississippi River Valley. *Wisconsin Archeologist* **51**:79–162.
1972   Cultural Dynamics and the Development of the Oneota Lifeway in Wisconsin. *American Antiquity* **37**:166–185.

Gillespie, B. C.
1970   Yellowknives: *Quo Iverunt?* In Migration and Anthropology, edited by Robert F. Spencer. *Proceedings of the 1970 Annual Spring Meeting of the American Ethnological Society.* Seattle: University of Washington Press. Pp. 61–71.

Griffin, J. B.
1937   The Archaeological Remains of the Chiwere Sioux. *American Antiquity* **2**:180–181.
1943   *The Fort Ancient Aspect.* Ann Arbor: University of Michigan Press.
1952   Culture Periods in Eastern United States Archeology. In *Archeology of Eastern United States,* edited by J. B. Griffin. Chicago: University of Chicago Press. Pp. 352–364.
1960   A Hypothesis for the Prehistory of the Winnebago. In *Culture in History: Essays in Honor of Paul Radin,* edited by Stanley Diamond. New York: Columbia University Press. Pp. 809–865.

Hall, R. L.
1962   *The Archeology of Carcajou Point.* Madison: University of Wisconsin Press.

Helm, J. (Editor)
1968   Essays on the Problem of Tribe. *Proceedings of the 1967 Annual Spring Meeting of the American Ethnological Society.* Seattle: University of Washington Press.

Henning, D. R.
1961 Oneota Ceramics in Iowa. *Journal of the Iowa Archaeological Society* **11**:3–47.
Hickerson, H.
1962 The Southwestern Chippewa: An Ethnohistorical Study. *American Anthropological Association Memoir* **92**. (*American Anthropologist* **64**.)
1970 *The Chippewa and Their Neighbors: A Study in Ethnohistory*. New York: Holt.
Honigmann, J. J.
1959 *The World of Man*. New York: Harper.
Hunt, G. T.
1940 *The Wars of the Iroquois*. Madison: University of Wisconsin Press.
Hurley, W. M.
1974 Culture Contact: Effigy Mound and Oneota. In Aspects of Upper Great Lakes Anthropology: Papers in Honor of Lloyd A. Wilford, edited by Elden Johnson. *Minnesota Historical Society, Prehistoric Archaeology Series* No. 11:115–128.
Jenness, D.
1955 Indians of Canada. *National Museum of Canada, Bulletin* **65**. (*Anthropological Series* No. 15.) Ottawa.
Kannenberg, A. P.
1938 Spoons and Dippers, Prehistoric Winnebago Culture Pottery. *Wisconsin Archeologist* **19**:21–24.
Keesing, F. M.
1939 The Menomini Indians of Wisconsin. *Memoirs of the American Philosophical Society* No. 10.
Lawson, P. V.
1903 Summary of the Archeology of Winnebago County, Wisconsin. *Wisconsin Archeologist* **2**:40–85.
Longacre, W. A. (Editor)
1974 *Reconstructing Prehistoric Pueblo Societies*. Albuquerque: University of New Mexico Press.
Lurie, N. O.
1960 Winnebago Protohistory. In *Culture in History: Essays in Honor of Paul Radin*, edited by Stanely Diamond. New York: Columbia University Press. Pp. 790–808.
Mason, C.
1970 The Oneota Component at the Porte des Morts Site, Door County, Wisconsin. *Wisconsin Archeologist* **51**:191–227.
Mason, R. J.
1966 Two Stratified Sites on the Door Peninsula of Wisconsin. *Anthropological Papers, Museum of Anthropology, University of Michigan* No. 26.
1974 Huron Island and the Island of the Poutouatamis. In Aspects of Upper Great Lakes Anthropology: Papers in Honor of Lloyd A. Wilford, edited by Elden Johnson. *Minnesota Historical Society, Minnesota Prehistoric Archaeology Series* No. 11:149–156.
MacNeish, R. S.
1958 An Introduction to the Archaeology of Southeast Manitoba. *National Museum of Canada, Bulletin* **157**.
McClary, A.
1972 Notes on Some Late Middle Woodland Coprolites. *Memoirs of the Museum of Anthropology, University of Michigan* No. 4:131–136.
McKern, W. C.
1931 Wisconsin Pottery. *American Anthropologist* **33**:383–389.
1939 Wisconsin Archeology in the Light of Recent Finds in Other Areas. *Wisconsin Archeologist* **20**:1–5.

1942   First Settlers of Wisconsin. *Wisconsin Magazine of History* **26:**153–169.

1945   Preliminary Report on the Upper Mississippi Phase in Wisconsin. *Milwaukee Public Museum Bulletin* **16:**109–285.

McPherron, A.

1967   The Juntunen Site and the Late Woodland Prehistory of the Upper Great Lakes Region. *Anthropological Papers, Museum of Anthropology, University of Michigan* No. 30.

Mott, M.

1938   The Relation of Historic Indian Tribes to Archaeological Manifestations in Iowa. *Iowa Journal of History and Politics* **36:**227–314.

Narroll, R.

1964   On Ethnic Unit Classification. *Current Anthropology* **5:**283–312.

Nern, C. F., and C. E. Cleland

1974   The Gros Cap Cemetery Site, St. Ignace, Michigan: A Reconsideration of the Greenless Collection. *Michigan Archaeologist* **20:**1–58.

O'Callaghan, E. B. (Editor)

1855   *Documents Relative to the Colonial History of the State of New York.* Vol. 9. Albany.

Pendergast, J. F., and B. G. Trigger

1972   *Cartier's Hochelaga and the Dawson Site.* Montreal: McGill–Queen's University Press.

Peske, G. R.

1965   A Discussion of the Lacustrine–Riverine Environment and Other Environmental Factors of Two Upper Mississippian Sites in Wisconsin. Manuscript on file at the Department of Anthropology, University of Wisconsin, Madison.

1966   Oneota Settlement Patterns and Agricultural Patterns in Winnebago County. *Wisconsin Archeolgist* **47:**188–195.

Quimby, G. I.

1960   *Indian Life in the Upper Great Lakes.* Chicago: University of Chicago Press.

1966   *Indian Culture and European Trade Goods.* Madison: University of Wisconsin Press.

Radin, P.

1923   The Winnebago Tribe. *Bureau of American Ethnology Annual Report* No. 37:47–560. Washington, D. C.: U. S. Government Printing Office.

Ritzenthaler, R. E.

1949   Tie-ups between Prehistoric Cultures and Historic Indian Tribes in Wisconsin. *Wisconsin Archeologist* **30:**36–38.

Service, E. R.

1962   *Primitive Social Organization: An Evolutionary Perspective.* New York: Random House.

1971   *Cultural Evolutionism: Theory in Practice.* New York: Holt.

Southall, A. W.

1970   The Illusion of Tribe. *Journal of Asian and African Studies* **5:**28–50.

Stone, L. M., and V. Canouts

1971   Introductory Remarks. In The Lasanen Site: An Historic Burial Locality in Mackinac County, Michigan, edited by C. E. Cleland. *Publications of The Museum, Michigan State University, Anthropological Series* **1**(1):1–5.

Thwaites, R. G. (Editor)

1896–   *The Jesuit Relations and Allied Documents: Travels and Explorations of*
1901   *the Jesuit Missionaries in New France, 1610–1791.* 73 vols. Cleveland: Burrows Brothers.

1902 The French Regime in Wisconsin, I: 1634–1727. In *Collections of the State Historical Society of Wisconsin*. Vol. 16. Madison: Wisconsin State Historical Society.

1906 The French Regime in Wisconsin, II. *Collections of the State Historical Society of Wisconsin*. Vol. 17. Madison: State Historical Society.

Tuck, J. A.
1971 *Onondaga Iroquois Prehistory: A Study in Settlement Archaeology*. Syracuse, New York: Syracuse University Press.

Wedel, M. M.
1959 Oneota Sites on the Upper Iowa River. *Missouri Archaeologist* **21**:1–181.
1963 A Note on Oneota Classification. *Wisconsin Archeologist* **44**:118–122.

White, L.
1958 *The Science of Culture*. New York: Grove Press.

Wilkinson, R. G.
1971 Prehistoric Biological Relationships in the Great Lakes Region. *Anthropological Papers, Museum of Anthropology, University of Michigan* No. 43.

Wittry, W. L.
1963 The Bell Site, Wn 9, an Early Historic Fox Village. *Wisconsin Archeologist* **44**:1–57.

Wright, G. A.
1967 Some Aspects of Early and Mid-Seventeenth Century Exchange Networks in the Western Great Lakes. *Michigan Archaeologist* **13**:181–197.
1968 A Further Note on Trade Friendship and Gift Giving in the Western Great Lakes. *Michigan Archaeologist* **13**:165–166.

Wright, J. V.
1965 A Regional Examination of Ojibwa Culture History. *Anthropologica* **7**:189–227.
1968 The Michipicoten Site, Ontario. *National Museums of Canada, Bulletin* **224,** *Contributions to Anthropology VI: Archeology*. Ottawa.

Subject Index

A

Abri Pataud (France), 47
Absaroka Mountains, 150
Activity areas
  correlation, problem of
    attenuation, 43, 46
    behavioral patterning and, 50–57
    pooling, role, 46–48
    Q-mode analysis, 57
    random error, 43–45
    reliability, 43–46
    R-mode analysis, 57
    sampling error, 43
    systematic error, 43
    when data are expressed as percent-
      ages, 48–49
  spatial distribution
    agglomerated activity areas, 51
    agglomerated disposal areas, 51–52
  tool kits
    correlation, problems of
      data expressed as raw frequency
        counts, 36–48
      zero–zero cells, 38–40

Acculturation
  Straits of Mackinac, 322–334
    European trade goods, effect of, 324
    longhouses, excavation of, 323
  Tionontate site, 324–327
  European trade goods, effect on
    material culture, internal pattern,
      327–330
    social value and, 332
    subsistence pattern, 324–327
  Juntunen site, 322–323
    burial pattern at, 330–331
    faunal remains at, 324–327
    trade relationships, 331–332
  Lasanen site, 323
    burial pattern at, 330–331
    trade relationships, 331–332
Agate Basin, 171–172
Agave, 178
Agglomerated activity areas, 51
Agglomerated disposal areas, 51–52
Agglomerated storage areas, 52
Alaskan needlecases, 188
Allamakee Trailed pottery, 343
Altithermal period, 169–171

A
B
C
D
E
F
G
H
I
J